Investing in

CORPORATE SOCIAL RESPONSIBILITY

A Guide to Best Practice, Business Planning & the UK's Leading Companies

Consultant editor
JOHN HANCOCK

KOGAN PAGE

London & Sterling, VA

Dedicated to Crena and Camilla for their love and support

Publisher's note

Every possible effort has been made to ensure that the information contained in this book is accurate at the time of going to press, and the publishers and authors cannot accept responsibility for any errors or omissions, however caused. No responsibility for loss or damage occasioned to any person acting, or refraining from action, as a result of the material in this publication can be accepted by the editor, the publisher or any of the authors.

First published in Great Britain and the United States in 2004 by Kogan Page Limited.

120 Pentonville Road
London N1 9JN
United Kingdom
www.kogan-page.co.uk

22883 Quicksilver Drive
Sterling VA 20166-2012
USA

© John Hancock, 2005

ISBN 0 7494 4147 X

British Library Cataloguing-in-Publication Data

A CIP record for this book is available from the British Library.

Library of Congress Cataloging-in-Publication Data

Investing in corporate social responsibility: a guide to best practice, business planning and the UK's leading companies / John Hancock.
    p. cm.
  Includes index.
  ISBN 0-7494-4147-X
  1. Social responsibility of business. I. Hancock, John, journalist.
HD60.5.G7I58 2005
658.4′08 — dc22

                    2004021167

Typeset by Datamatics Technologies Ltd, Mumbai, India
Printed and bound in Great Britain by Cambrian Printers Ltd, Aberystwyth, Wales

Contents

Foreword

Nigel Griffiths MP
Parliamentary Under Secretary of State for Construction,
Small Business and Enterprise

CSR, or corporate responsibility as I call it, is about the way businesses take account of their economic, social and environmental impacts in the way they operate – maximizing the benefits and minimizing the downsides. Not surprisingly there are many different views about the proper role of business and how businesses should contribute to improving all our lives and the world we live in. But we all agree that business has a vital role to play in our national and global wealth and well-being. We need businesses to succeed because they create the wealth that will secure the best future for all our citizens, families and communities.

The lead on CSR within government is with the DTI because we believe CSR is fundamentally about good business. There need not be a conflict between the interests of the wider social and environmental goals of the community at large and of those of successful businesses. Taking a wider view of their stakeholders and the factors which can affect their business can help companies to build long-term sustainable success. Improving our national competitiveness and raising productivity are central to our aims at DTI.

We see the drivers of prosperity as investment, innovation, skills, enterprise and competition. Corporate responsibility and sustainable business practices can make a contribution to each of these: they can help recruit the brightest and best people, motivate and develop the skills of the workforce, raise the skills and employability of those not currently in the labour market, build trust and confidence among customers, manage risks and opportunities better for the long term, enhance reputation and license to operate as well as enabling businesses to identify the potential for new markets, processes and products. So I don't encourage companies to make CSR part of the way they do business out of altruism but because it is good for their businesses as well as good for the world we live in.

If CSR is about what business does, what is the role for government? I see our role as helping to provide the right conditions and policy framework to maximize that business contribution. And I remain convinced that the best approach should continue to be a voluntary one. CSR must of course start with compliance with the law, and in the UK we have a strong record of regulation on the range of issues relating to corporate activity including health and safety, employment terms and conditions, environmental protection and more recently bribery and corruption. And as standards and expectations change, we need to keep the regulatory framework under review. But the regulatory framework represents the baseline for company behaviour while CSR is what companies do voluntarily to raise their performance beyond minimum legal standards. Our approach is therefore to set decent minimum standards while stimulating companies to raise performance beyond those levels.

CSR embraces a wide range of important but often complex and sometimes controversial issues including health and safety, labour rights, climate change, supply chain management and so on. And for companies some of these issues will be more critical than others depending on their size, the nature of the business and where they operate in the world. There is no 'one-size-fits-all' guide for all companies on what CSR should mean for them and what they should be doing. One of the things that I find most encouraging and exciting about CSR is its dynamism and creativity. It is very important to see that energy principally applied to practical action, learning from and sharing best practice. And where regulation is the answer, it should be well designed and focused.

That is the approach the government is taking with our proposals for a statutory Operating and Financial Review (OFR). Fundamental to the OFR is the recognition that companies should be run in the collective best interests of the shareholders. And, in acting in the collective best interests of the members, companies should recognize the need for good relationships with employees, customers and suppliers and the need to maintain their reputation and to consider their impact on the community and the environment. But each business is different and the factors that affect it will vary. The OFR is about providing a balanced and comprehensive analysis of the individual business.

For CSR to fulfil its potential and have a long-lasting impact, it needs to be mainstreamed into business decision making, which is why I launched the CSR Academy in July this year. I hope this will act as a catalyst for the integration of socially responsible practice into day to day business practice by spreading the understanding, experience and skills for CSR widely across business.

The dynamism and wide variety of the CSR agenda are reflected in this guide to best practice. I welcome its contribution to the debate.

Introduction: Why this subject? Why this book?

John Hancock

Corporate social responsibility: the very term falls on some ears with the dull and ominous thud of another burden on business, another book of forms to be completed, yet more boxes to tick. Visions spring to mind of non-productive, time-wasting and costly exercises to comply with the whims of some ivory-tower-bound regulator or to satisfy the extreme demands of people with little or no experience of the real world. There may even be a sense that those demands can never be met because, like some trade union negotiators or single-issue zealots, 'these people' will simply treat every concession to their modus operandi as the base line for the next campaign and because their demands are incompatible with the very conduct of capitalist commerce.

To be honest, there are campaigners who fit the above descriptions but they are a minority. What is significant about corporate social responsibility (CSR) is not that it attracts campaigners but that the largest and most powerful global corporations now embrace it as a core business principle. These are the kinds of businesses that usually thrive by, among other things, being able to assess what are going to be the future directions for successful business practice. So, far from a burden, CSR is an opportunity to re-energize the business and is certainly an idea worth exploring further and worth considering for inclusion in your own business plans.

The idea of businesses including social responsibility in their operating system is not new and it is not that radical. In the 19th century, those who built the Cadbury, Rowntree and Lever Brothers businesses as well as the Great Western Railway and many other enlightened employers ran their businesses as large families, providing decent housing, community facilities and libraries. It has since been slightly disparagingly referred to as 'paternalism' but was really no more than people who believed that they knew how to make their workers' lives better and were prepared to invest in the structures to put those beliefs into practice. At the same time these business owners often held strong religious convictions that guided them to conduct the whole of their business in what, for the time, was an honest and decent manner. In fact, it can best be summed up in the titles of four consecutive addresses from that great preacher and speaker, John Wesley:

Gain all you can
But not at the expense of your conscience
Not at the expense of our neighbour's wealth
Not at the expense of our neighbour's health.

I often use these lines, which were first brought to my attention by Charles Jacob, founder of the first ethical investment fund, and which so elegantly express the concept that is CSR. The words should also put to rest those concerns highlighted above. There is no problem in profit – indeed, if the success right up to the present day of some of the businesses mentioned above is anything to go by, profit is a fair and just reward for enterprise and industry (today, we might also call it 'added value'), as long as they are the sources of that profit. But profit should not be falsely boosted by actions that cannot be squared with your conscience, by accounting, pricing or buying practices that unfairly reduce the profits earned by others or by practices that damage the health of those involved. In short, corporate social responsibility is little more than acting in a decent, honest and considerate manner as a good citizen should but on a corporate scale. And, because it requires some initial structuring of the business and some long-term planning and monitoring for the business, in the longer term that turns out to be a means of achieving predictable and stable levels of profitability.

So now that we have established what CSR is, why produce a book about it? CSR is fast becoming one of the principles on which modern business is built. At this stage in the game, most businesses will be able to consider their performance against the standards already established for acceptable corporate behaviour, identify areas where improvements could be made, select possible strategies to address CSR issues in the business and incorporate those strategies along with appropriate actions in future business plans. To start to address CSR now will ensure that it remains something wholly within the control of the business; to ignore it is not really an option, unless you relish the idea of having the business's plans and policies dictated by outside forces not under your control.

One thing that has become apparent from my dealings with a range of businesses as a journalist is that, while large corporations have by and large realized this reality and acted on it with directors, individuals and departments in the business focusing on nothing else, most medium and small companies have yet to even face up to this great change in the business conduct landscape. This is not, I believe, because these businesses have any less inclination to act responsibly but rather because they fear the diversion of resources that they believe would be necessary from the moment they start down the CSR road. There is some logic in this view.

Whereas the establishment of a CSR department of, say, five full-time people led by a manager and reporting to a director may be only a drop in the human resources ocean of a large and/or global corporation, it may appear as a significant diversion of resources away from productive activities to a smaller business. However, that way of seeing the matter is dangerous and wrong. Dangerous because, as already stated above, businesses that do not soon address their CSR requirement will find themselves marching to the beat of somebody else's drum, a beat that may not best suit the priorities of the business. Wrong because, far from adding a non-productive burden to the business, a strong CSR policy can add commercial advantage to the business's activities.

While it is well and good a journalist telling you what he feels is an important development that you should address with some urgency, I do not have to run your business or face your board and shareholders at the end of the year. So rather than write a book of theories or even second-hand experiences and the truths that they seem to reveal, the content of this book has been largely contributed by people who are leading lights in the development of CSR as a business system and people who have to live and work with the subject every day, who have to implement CSR in working businesses with responsibility to generate profits for investors and who, like the reader, do have to face the board and shareholders of the business to explain their actions and the outcomes that have flowed from those actions.

This book will not attempt to prescribe what the reader's business should do but will endeavour to show, through the experiences of others, how CSR can impact on a business and what ways there are to include this forward-looking operating philosophy in a business. To achieve this we have enlisted the efforts of a number of people and organizations who are currently either developing or implementing CSR policy in their businesses. While they might eschew the mantle of 'experts', they are involved in the topic more than most and have had to face and deal with most of the issues (opportunities and challenges) that arise when dealing with CSR. Sometimes they have contributed general truths, sometimes real examples from the commercial experience of their business that illustrate a point more clearly than a thousand words might describe it. It would be surprising if their experiences exactly replicated the circumstances of any particular reader but readers will be able to discern threads of familiarity in their contributions, elements that are sufficiently similar to their own experience to be able to transfer some of the ideas to their own businesses.

Although we have designated these contributions as chapters and appendices for ease of indexing and navigation, each one is more of an essay on CSR seen from different perspectives so that, through the directing of different lights from a variety of directions, the subject may be wholly illuminated and its details clearly revealed to the reader. Thus, we may be able to save readers the cost in people, resources and money of getting through the first stage of a CSR policy, ie understanding what CSR is and how it can be understood in any business plus some guides as to how the next stage of establishing CSR in the business might proceed.

Do not simply take the book and try to apply the ideas and policies unaltered to your own situation. Use this book to gain an all-round understanding of CSR, its values and its requirements of the business. Then combine this with your already strong understanding of your own business to start developing a CSR policy. If it is not possible or, in a smaller business, necessary to allocate a full-time member of staff to this aspect of the business, build it into the job description of an appropriate current staff member. This may sound like the opposite of socially responsible behaviour but what you will find is that CSR is more like a way of doing the things that are already done in the business than a whole new set of tasks. So, after the initial establishment of a CSR dimension, it should not add another task to the work of the business but should rather inform the current work.

I hope that none of the above sounds too pompous. I really do not see myself as a CSR guru but rather as an editor and writer who, by assembling a bank of knowledge that already exists in the people who have so kindly contributed to this book, has tried to create a new resource to help businesses (especially, but not exclusively, smaller and medium enterprises) in an area that will continue to grow in importance for the foreseeable future.

And just before you embark on the book proper, I would like to express my thanks to all of those people who helped to make it happen, the authors of the chapters who have given so much of their own and their businesses' time, expertise and real experiences to share with readers in a true act of corporate social responsibility – sharing successful ideas to light the way for others down a similarly successful path.

1

Corporate social responsibility – bottom-line issue or public relations exercise?[1]

Lord Tim Clement-Jones CBE, Chairman, DLA Upstream

The idea of corporate social responsibility would have drawn a round of blank looks just a few years ago. But things are changing. Whether sparked by headline-grabbing protests against globalisation and compounded by the attacks on America on September 11, we are waking up and wanting to know more about the major influence on our world. It's no longer just the radicals who are questioning the impact that business has on society.

Financial Times, 18 February 2002

THE BACKGROUND TO CORPORATE SOCIAL RESPONSIBILITY

The principles of the concept have long been a part of enlightened business strategy. Elements of corporate social responsibility (CSR) are not a new phenomenon nor indeed are the business practices associated with it. Traditions of corporate philanthropy date back to the Victorian era with the activities of Quaker families such as the Cadburys, Rowntrees and Hersheys who sought to improve their employees' standard of living as well as enhancing the communities in which they lived.

In the United States, foundations such as those set up by Rockefeller and Carnegie established a new level in corporate charitable behaviour. During the depression comprehensive public building projects were commissioned in order to provide jobs for those finding themselves newly unemployed. The Rockefeller Foundation went beyond simple charitable giving in establishing research programmes and educational establishments all over the world.

CSR has rapidly grown in the last 20 years, moving up the boardroom agenda of even our most hard-headed companies. At its most passive, there is the 'hands-off' approach, with charitable giving and patronage of charities decided by the chairman or a board committee. Even where there is a more business-based approach a great deal of what passes as CSR at top companies has been described as merely 'passive box ticking driven by external pressures rather than a genuine desire to do business in an ethical way' (Martin Waller, *The Times*, 8 July 2003). These initiatives are not to be disparaged, as anyone who has worked for charities seeking corporate sponsorship will attest. But increasingly there is support for more active CSR involving a range of stakeholders.

Even with flexible working, many people are working longer hours. With consequent restrictions on social time and family life, people want to be reassured that the job to which they devote their energies has wider benefits and status. Staff want to feel aligned with the aims, objectives and behaviour of their employer. Active citizens as well as active companies are those who make more than a solely economic contribution to the community. Active companies can in turn motivate employees to become active in their communities and provide a framework and focus for their efforts.

Many companies now back and organize specific schemes, often in conjunction with the not-for-profit sector, with the belief that this will contribute to both the medium- and long-term success of their business.

Early in the 1980s a wide network of major businesses came together to establish Business in the Community (or BITC), which is a respected and influential force within the business community. The business case for CSR provides an important incentive to companies to consider adopting socially and environmentally responsive policies. Research published by the UK's Institute of Business Ethics, comparing companies in the FTSE 250, provides strong evidence that 'those clearly committed to ethical behaviour perform better financially over the long term than those lacking such a commitment' (Alison Maitland, *Financial Times*, 3 April 2003). It is argued that CSR strategy can help manage the effects of globalization, cut environmental cost, raise productivity and improve staff recruitment and retention rates.

In recent times pressure groups with widespread popular support have successfully targeted companies that have broken no laws but rather have offended modern norms and standards, particularly with regard to human rights and employment practices, for instance the use of sweatshop labour by Nike and Gap in Indonesia and Cambodia, the campaign against Nestlé's marketing of powdered milk in developing countries and criticism of Shell's disposal of the Brent Spar oil platform and conduct in Nigeria. These campaigns marked a sharp increase in expectation about the role of the company in society and declining faith in the power of national governments to tackle social and economic problems that spread across geopolitical borders. The perceived power and reach of multinationals make them appear a better target for pressure group campaigners than domestic politicians.

Furthermore, following the Enron, Andersen and WorldCom scandals, there is a greater recognition by businesses that CSR can help to restore public trust in the corporate world.

There is also a shift in investor attitudes taking place. A survey by Business in the Environment published in May 2001 ('Investing in the future: City attitudes to environmental and social issues') found that over half of analysts and two-thirds of investors believed a company that emphasizes its environmental and social performance is attractive to investors.

Naturally there are critics who question the business case for CSR and who doubt its effectiveness in tackling social and environmental problems. Some even claim it to be nothing more than a management fad designed to ward off the threat of new legislation and a 'jargon-laden industry all of its own, with no relationship to the real business' (Patience Wheatcroft, *The Times*, June 2003). One economic commentator has written: 'Businesses which pursue CSR goals risk losing sight of the profit motive, at the cost of the long term health of the corporate sector and, by extension, the economy as a whole.' The biggest challenge that exists is the ability to reconcile the profit motive with fulfilling social obligation.

WHAT IS CSR TODAY?

Given the number of household names with comprehensive CSR programmes such as Ford, BP, IBM and GlaxoSmithKline, it is perhaps not surprising that the CSR that exists now has many different definitions. There exist, in terms with which it is easiest to extract and label them, a sceptic view, a utopian view and a realist view.

Sceptic view

The sceptic remains highly critical of CSR. Milton Friedman best defines the approach: 'Few trends would so thoroughly undermine the very foundations of free society as the acceptance by corporate officials of a social responsibility other than to make as much money for their stockholders as they possibly can.' Accordingly, the notion of CSR is inimical to democracy and freedom, frustrating business focus on its purpose of wealth creation and the benefits this has brought to millions of people.

Utopian view

The utopian view of CSR reflects the idea that companies have a prior duty to anyone touched by their activity, their stakeholders rather than their shareholders, and especially the vulnerable, who may be exploited by the company's operation. Some holding this set of views go on to state that certain companies, such as those manufacturing weapons or growing tobacco, can never be considered responsible by virtue of the harmful effects of their products. NGOs like Amnesty International suggest that 'the business community also had a wider responsibility – moral and legal – to use its influence to promote respect for human rights... Violations of human rights may contribute to civil instability and to uncertainty in the investment climate, but even where this is not the case, companies should not be silent witnesses.'

Realist view

While I have some sympathy with the utopian view, the view that gathers the greatest following is the realist view. The UK government's Department of Trade and Industry-sponsored Corporate Responsibility Group defined CSR as:

> the management of an organisation's total impact upon both its immediate stakeholders and upon the society within which it operates. CSR is not simply about whatever funds and expertise companies choose to invest in communities to help resolve social problems... it is about the integrity with which a company governs itself, fulfils its mission, lives by its values, engages with its stakeholders, measures its impacts and reports on its activities.

THE CURRENT CLIMATE

The current climate is positive for CSR. A global CEO survey undertaken by PricewaterhouseCoopers/World Economic Forum found that 70 per cent of chief executives globally agree that CSR is vital to profitability (fifth global CEO survey). In Western Europe, 68 per cent of large companies report what has been coined the triple bottom-line performance (economic, social and environmental factors) in addition to financial performance, compared with 41 per cent in the United States (PricewaterhouseCoopers/BSI Global Research Inc, 2002).

In the US, 80 per cent of bosses feel that the CEO's reputation is a major influence on corporate reputation, though interestingly this figure is just 56 per cent in the UK. According to Business in the Community, more than 70 per cent of business leaders believe that integrating responsible business practices makes companies more competitive and profitable.

According to a Harris survey of 800 CEOs in Europe and North America, three out of four international corporations have a corporate reputation measuring system in place.

FUTURE DEVELOPMENTS IN CSR REPORTING

In recent years there have been strong suggestions that compulsory CSR reporting might come into force.

There is a fear from business that a regulatory approach to CSR reporting will reduce it to a defensive compliance issue that involves simply ticking boxes. To date, it has been left to companies, on an ad hoc basis, to show how important CSR policies are to them. The Operating and Financial Review (OFR) is an opportunity for companies to push the boundaries of what is considered material (and therefore must be included in the report). Companies could include areas, policies and issues that competitors may not, such as employee relations, environmental actions, trade policies and ethical sourcing. This, it is argued, can deliver real competitive advantage and place competitors on the back foot, forcing them to act reactively to changes as they occur.

Developments are happening at pace. The Association of Chartered Certified Accountants has called for high-level disclosures of corporate, social and environmental performance and policies by companies in the new OFR. It would take only one company in a sector to widen its interpretation of materiality by providing more details in an OFR than is expected for that to become the benchmark for others to follow.

If one company can demonstrate materiality then others will find it difficult to prove otherwise, effectively forcing competitors into greater disclosure. In the long term this will mean convergence of the information contained in OFRs and a 'best practice' standard emerging.

A quick scan of the CSR reports of just a few PLCs reveals that, at present, companies are reporting non-financial information in a myriad of ways. Information in such reports ranges from the strategic level of CSR management principles and policies and company attitudes to specific areas of the business, such as human rights and health and safety. They also often include outlines of particular governance measures, such as internal review panels, through to anecdotal accounts of CSR activity. CSR reporting can also include the communications strategy for the CSR programme, as well as ranking in public benchmarking surveys.

This is of course a danger with CSR reporting. Companies can overemphasize their achievements, overhyping what they have really done and discrediting their good work. John Monks, former General Secretary of the Trade Union Congress, stated, 'all too often we find companies parading their CSR credentials despite a poor record on relationships, thus reducing CSR to a PR exercise with little substance'.

That there will in time be legislation requiring the compulsory reporting of CSR is doubtful. There exists the will neither from business nor from government. However, such an Act may not be necessary. The current government has not been shy of using enabling pre-existing legislative levers to expand the business case for CSR. For example, the 1999 amendment to the 1995 Pensions Act requires trustees of pension funds to declare their positions on ethical, social and environmentally responsible investment in their statement of investment principles.

Following the recent spate of corporate scandals in the US it is highly likely that rules will be tightened there to ensure better corporate behaviour. The corporate governance disasters of 2001 saw a shift away from the philanthropic tradition CSR had in the US towards a greater alignment of CSR to business strategy and the greater realization of the potential impact of NGOs. The emphasis is now shifting decidedly towards corporate governance. Integrated CSR is now seen as an important antidote to corporate greed and rebuilding trust among stakeholders.

Nevertheless, domestic policies for CSR reporting may be driven from abroad. Five European countries have introduced mandatory reporting requirements: Denmark, the Netherlands, Norway, Sweden and France. The EU has produced a Green Paper on CSR (2001), and in 2004 the European Multi-Stakeholder Forum will report to the European Commission on the merits of voluntary and regulatory approaches.

THE KEY DRIVERS OF CSR

Bottom-line effect

There are many drivers of CSR programmes. By far the most relevant to business is the bottom-line effect of incorporating a socially responsible element into corporate practice. Frankly, this can be surprising but more evidence of this is being gathered.

Lower equity risk premium

Besides the immediately obvious issue of the danger reputational damage can do to customer base and share price, a comprehensive CSR programme, as argued by some ratings agencies, will lower a company's equity risk premium. As this lowers, share price rises concomitantly.

In a survey by CSR Europe and Euronext, 51 per cent of fund managers and 37 per cent of financial analysts said they would put a premium on socially responsible companies.

Investors will pay premiums of between 12 and 14 per cent in North America and Western Europe for companies with high corporate governance standards, according to a McKinsey Global Investor Opinion Survey.

Moreover, research conducted by BITC and Research International in 2003 found that 86 per cent of consumers agree that, when price and quality are equal, they are more likely to buy a product associated with a 'cause'; 61 per cent agree that they would change retail outlets for the same reason; and 86 per cent of consumers agree that they have a more positive image of a company if they see that it is doing something to make the world a better place.

Further investment case

Furthermore, a strong investment case exists for the avoidance of expensive class action suits and the ability to attract, motivate and retain a talented workforce. In terms of a proactive strategy, CSR may give the opportunity for business to inform shareholders of potential risks and issues. Any dialogue engaged in allows companies to understand their stakeholders, including shareholders, better.

Reputation management

A model designed by the global public relations company Bell Pottinger illustrates a direct correlation between reputation and financial outcome measures – share price and credit rating. Intangible assets, or 'soft' values, can be directly equated to hard cash, according to Bell Pottinger. The model was based on the *Fortune/Management Today* 'Most Admired' survey of 500 US and 250 UK companies. It shows that reputation, on average, accounts for 27 per cent of a FTSE 250 company's market capitalization.

A MORI survey among corporate communications directors in October 2002 showed that 93 per cent believe the publishing of non-financial information enhances a company's reputation and makes for better management decisions.

Activists are now playing an important role in how a company's CSR strategy develops. The recent case of *Nike* v *Kasky* and the publicity surrounding it greatly affected Nike. In this case, Kasky, a California-based activist, took Nike all the way to the Californian Supreme Court over issues of dishonesty in its non-financial reporting, alleging that it had exaggerated its report on a CSR programme in the developing world. This has further raised the stakes for companies in their non-financial reporting.

Recent union disputes in South America have seen Coca-Cola accused of employing local militia to suppress employee demonstrations – all of course reported extensively in the Western media.

Similarly, Shell had been a widely trusted household name for many years, yet when the controversy over the sinking of the Brent Spar oil platform developed, the business was left with pickets outside its filling stations, a devastated reputation and a slowly falling share price. Perhaps the worst aspect of the Brent Spar dispute was how Greenpeace came eventually to admit it had overstated the damage the sinking of the oil platform would cause – an admission that, of course, came too late for Shell.

And Starbucks has also become a target for activists, in the United States and elsewhere, 'partly because its socially responsible image makes it an easy target' (*Financial Times*, 11 March 2002, USA).

Personnel

CSR programmes have evolved depending on the groups within an organization responsible for their development and implementation. Initial philanthropic schemes were often run by staff with experience in charitable organizations or human resources departments. With legal obligations, developing a CSR programme is more likely to be overseen by a board member such as the company secretary or HR director. These board members will only add value to the programme and make an attractive proposal to the board if they can prove there is a bottom-line effect.

Interestingly, with the cult of the CEO on the decline as a key source of reputation, there will be the need and opportunity to replace it with something more stable and intrinsically more able to support recruitment and retention strategies for mid-level staff as well as senior managers. CSR is a strong candidate for this role, but its potential needs to be researched and evaluated in the particular context of each organization to determine what will work best. Furthermore, as companies begin to struggle and budgets tighten in less prosperous times, CSR programmes will only survive if they can be proven to add to a company's bottom line.

Influence of the corporate disasters

The corporate scandals affecting Enron, WorldCom and the like have undoubtedly increased the perception of greed among senior business officials in the corporate world. CSR is important in counteracting allegations of corporate greed. As a result, in the US as in the UK there has been a shift away from philanthropy in approaches to CSR and a movement towards the greater alignment of CSR to business strategy and corporate governance.

As Debra Dunn, Vice-President, Strategy and Corporate Operations, Hewlett-Packard, USA, explains it:

> I think [CSR] has evolved significantly over the last year, particularly since Enron. In the US there used to be a big focus on philanthropy and social investment as the manifestation of social responsibility, but I think appropriately the focus is now shifting to more central issues like how you run your business, so ethics and governance have gone up the priority list.

Customer loyalty

Finally and most importantly, a CSR programme can build loyalty with customers and offer a competitive advantage in a marketplace where consumers demand goods and services ethically delivered or produced.

CONCLUSION

CSR is more than a PR exercise. It has a bottom-line relevance, and the way it is communicated and reported is important.

CSR has many drivers. The drivers becoming less influential are charitable behaviour and philanthropy. The need for better corporate governance is set to drive companies towards more ethical behaviour from one direction while stakeholders and customers drive more ethical behaviour from another.

Note

[1] This chapter is adapted from a speech given to the College of Business at Florida State University on 26 January 2004.

2

Corporate citizenship as part of the business model

Geoffrey Bush, Director of Corporate Citizenship, Diageo

> If businessmen do have a social responsibility other than making maximum profits for stockholders, how are they to know what it is. Few trends could so thoroughly undermine the very foundations of our free society as the acceptance by corporate officials of a social responsibility other than to make as much money for their stakeholders as possible.
>
> Milton Friedman, economist, 1970

> We are the drivers of the prosperity that is the only long-term answer to social problems.
>
> David Varney, Chairman, Business in the Community, 2003

It is safe to assume that Milton Friedman would be bemused by the world's current obsession with corporate social responsibility – and not just because it is another piece of cumbersome business jargon. Writing 33 years ago, when anti-globalization protests would have been as bizarre a thought as ethical investment, he reflected the commonplace view that the state was still the most effective force when it came to social change.

But over time, as the state's role has changed and the number of multinationals grew rapidly, so philanthropic efforts by companies in small communities developed into programmes much broader in scope. What was once ad hoc is now established as an integral part of doing business.

For the answers to why such a transformation took place you have to go back to the 1980s and the time of the Thatcher government. Set against a backdrop of enormously high levels of unemployment and urban rioting, there was a sense of unease, not only in the streets but also in the boardroom. There was a strong feeling that companies had a responsibility to the community as a whole, but were not showing it. And the demand for action came from the community itself.

But a concept as broad as corporate responsibility may more easily be understood if explained through the experience of one organization, starting with the first awareness of a need to think beyond the company's walls and the development through a series of initiatives and programmes of CSR as an integral part of the business's character. The examples and ideas that follow have grown from several sources but I have largely drawn on the experience and approach of the company whose records are closest to hand for this writer. Nevertheless, the story has been repeated over the past two or more decades in most of the large businesses (FTSE 100 stocks) that make up corporate Britain.

WHERE IT ALL STARTED

A group of directors at Grand Metropolitan (which, with Guinness and Seagram, subsequently became Diageo) identified chronic unemployment as the root cause of much inner-city unrest. The brewing industry was undergoing consolidation at the time, and was about to make the unemployment situation worse and not better. The response, led by Grand Met, was to help overcome the problem by providing jobseekers with the skills and qualifications that local employers needed. The modest charitable enterprise that they started has become Tomorrow's People Trust, a vital link in a national network of employers, government initiatives and community support groups, working together to help people defeat long-term unemployment.

At the same time, as trouble continued on the streets from Brixton to Toxteth, Business in the Community (BITC) was established. Its aim was to promote corporate community involvement and become a genuine partnership between business, government, local authorities and trade unions.

Those involved felt that, although large companies in Britain were beginning to play a key role in sponsoring major sporting and cultural events, they were nowhere near as involved with their local communities as companies in the United States.

Twenty years on, David Varney, Chairman of BITC, can reflect on the huge strides the organization has made. And he believes that progress has not been made through compulsion, but rather through 'creative partnerships between the private sector and organizations, both in the public and voluntary sector'.

Back at the start, Varney says, companies engaged with the issues in a philanthropic way, but 'now the focus is on examining their total impact on society, through the process of measuring and reporting activities across the business'.

This has progressed to such an extent that this year BITC published its first Corporate Responsibility Index, intended to benchmark the performance of one company against another. The index states that responsible business practice means 'that a company is striving to continually improve its impact on society and the environment through mainstream business practices – through its operations, products and services and through interaction with key stakeholders such as employees, customers, investors, communities and suppliers'.

BUSINESSES AND VISIONS CHANGE AND GROW

In 2005 Tomorrow's People celebrates its 20th anniversary. The charity, which has helped over 350,000 people find employment in that time, laid the foundations for the corporate citizenship programme at Diageo.

Those foundations were built upon when Grand Metropolitan acquired Pillsbury. It was a hostile bid. Pillsbury had an exemplary record of corporate citizenship, yet little was known about Grand Met other than that it was predator. Grand Met's response on the issue of community was that its chairman was a leader of Business in the Community. It had reviewed Pillsbury's community commitments with the same care as it had applied to the company's other business strategies, and had publicly committed to maintaining its community involvement if the bid succeeded. As a company statement said at the time: 'Corporate citizenship could be seen as evidence of managerial and cultural compatibility and part of the company's "software".'

The programme took on a further dimension when Grand Met merged with Guinness and became Diageo. The stakes were raised and the big questions had to be asked: did the company need corporate community involvement at all, was it worth the money and did it fit with the new culture? The decisions were taken at a senior level as discussion centred on what Diageo's values should be. It soon became clear that social responsibility naturally flowed from the company's strategy and values. What was becoming clear was that philanthropy could not be divorced from mainstream business activity.

The political culture had changed. The forces of economic globalization meant that corporations had increased scope to shape and affect the societies in which they operated. As David Logan emphasized in a Lecture to the Royal Society for the encouragement of Arts, Manufactures and Commerce (RSA) in 1998: 'Since the mid-1980s, governments' share of gross domestic product around the world has remained static or declined.' This was in direct contrast to the wealth of the burgeoning number of multinational companies.

Their growth can be seen in the fact that Diageo now operates in 180 countries. Its economic impact on markets (especially those in the developing world) cannot be underestimated. Nick Rose, Diageo's CFO, says: 'Our business can have a significant impact on small economies where our brands are well established. In Seychelles, for example, 13 per cent of the government's tax revenue is currently derived from the Diageo brewing business in the islands.'

Guinness Nigeria was one of the first companies to be quoted on the Nigerian stock exchange, and today provides returns for more than 60,000 local shareholders, employs 1,500 people and helps support around 50,000 jobs through more than 1,000 suppliers. Over half of the company's cash value added goes to the government in excise duty and tax.

The corporate citizenship programme that started at Grand Met reached a new stage with the formation of the Diageo Foundation in 1998. Incorporation under UK charity law makes it independent and ensures its funds do not support the commercial interests of the business whose name it bears. The foundation was established to support the company's businesses around the world in their community involvement through start funding and expertise, providing charitable donations, matching employee fundraising and funding longer-term social investment.

It focuses on three specific areas:

● Alcohol Education (involvement in community-based alcohol education projects, as well as educating and informing consumers);
● Water of Life (humanitarian and environmental programme linked to supply business, promoting biodiversity and sustainability); and
● Local Citizens (encouraging and engaging the company's employees and businesses in their community).

Diageo benchmarked internationally to see what financial contribution it should make through its community involvement – it agreed on 1 per cent of pre-tax profits, a visible sign of its commitment as a new company.

WHY CHARITY IS NOT ENOUGH

It was vital at that stage, as it is now, that everyone across a business understood that corporate citizenship is not just about charitable giving; rather it is the whole way in which a company, its products and services interact with society. For that reason,

Diageo has created a corporate citizenship committee, including representatives from operations, global supply, procurement, marketing, HR and investor relations, who all bring different expertise, knowledge and opinions.

When analysing this interaction with society, many companies have made extensive use of the London Benchmarking Group's (LBG) model. It identifies three basic motives for company involvement in the community:

- social responsibility;
- long-term corporate interest;
- direct commercial interest.

The LBG was formed in September 1994. It comprises senior community affairs managers from leading companies, headquartered in the UK. It was established to meet the need for accurate and comparable information about how different companies define, fund and manage their community involvement activities. In 1997, the London Benchmarking Group Model was devised and then tested by a group of 18 companies across different industry sectors. The model puts a realistic conservative value on a company's contributions and measures the benefits of community investments.

This was another significant change in the approach to corporate citizenship. As a new, values-led discipline, it became part of the mainstream business, and its impact needed to be measured like any other area of a business. In Diageo's case, this meant it affected everything from its marketing code through to its communication with consumers.

Historically, since its beginning, the Seagram spirits and wine business has undertaken a commitment to do more than produce quality products and has advocated responsible consumption through its advertising and education programmes. Many of these efforts began in the United States and were expanded throughout the world as Seagram's business expanded. Through an advertising campaign that ran for more than 65 years Seagram promoted a point of view instead of a product, with a series of frank and direct messages. The first of these advertisements, released in October 1934, led with 'We who make whiskey say: "Drink moderately".' Other ads in the 1930s included such serious topics as 'We don't want bread money' and 'Drinking and driving do not mix'. These special advertisements reflected the belief that the interests of a drinks company, the alcohol beverage industry, the consumer and society as a whole are best served by understanding the need for responsible consumption of beverage alcohol.

When it was formed in 1998, Diageo implemented a marketing code. Three years later the company appointed an independent auditor to report on its compliance with the code. The auditor examined the promotion of 27 brands in 47 countries, reviewing about 1,000 advertisements, and found a high level of compliance with the code. The code was revised in October 2002 based on many of the suggestions made at the time.

The first motive under the LBG model is social responsibility. Increasingly, this is becoming a feature across responsible corporate advertising messages. In the US, 20 per cent of Diageo's broadcast advertising budget is dedicated to branded responsibility advertisements. Smirnoff Ice, Smirnoff, Johnnie Walker Black, Baileys, Captain Morgan and Crown Royal have all developed commercials with a responsibility message. Complaints are also taken seriously as when, in Britain, one advert was withdrawn out of 187 separate advertising campaigns run across 15 brands.

These sorts of decisions are taken in the belief that the business will be more successful in the long term – and consequently provide greater returns for investors – if it trades in prosperous communities in which there is trust between the business and society, and in which social issues are addressed. With this perspective, the imperative is clear.

MULTIPLE RELATIONSHIPS

To create these conditions, a company needs to be in tune with the societies and communities in which it makes its living. This means developing a range of relationships with shareholders, employees, consumers, governments, public health authorities, the environment and community and interest groups. Unlike in the past, the community might not be the most important or influential stakeholder in every case. In a number of cases, it is consumers. Back in 1994, Lord Sheppard, the Chairman of Grand Metropolitan, said: 'Customers are looking through the front door of the companies they buy from. If they do not like what they see in terms of social responsibility, community involvement and equality of opportunity, they won't go in.'

Nearly a decade on, those thoughts were recently echoed by David Varney, Chairman of BITC and mmO2: 'Today, our customers expect us not only to deliver a good service at the right price – whatever business we are in – but increasingly they are interested in how we do that.'

There has to be an element of realism here, of course. If there is a better-value product it is unreasonable to think consumers will ignore it. You have to presume that ethical issues count for more only if you start off on a like-for-like basis. Yet as far back as 1993, research conducted by MORI showed that 73 per cent of UK consumers preferred to buy environmentally and socially friendly goods supplied by companies with the same attributes and with whose values they could identify.

And so such considerations have become equally important to investors. A proliferation of ethical stock indexes in Europe and the US demonstrates ethical investors' interest in companies' behaviour. As Varney adds: 'Businesses that can prove that they are in tune with the spirit of greater openness and greater responsibility will enjoy the competitive advantages that a superior knowledge of their customers and markets can bring. In the long term that means greater value creation for owners or shareholders.'

But corporate social responsibility is as important within a company as it is outside. In competitive times, every business has an interest in becoming an employer of choice, and increasingly people are choosing which company to work for on the basis of how a company demonstrates its social responsibility. Recent research by BITC among 1,000 employers across Britain showed that they see a clear connection between responsible business practice and impact on the bottom line. It found that responsible practice could help attract, motivate and retain a talented and diverse workforce.

'The marketplace is changing,' said Val Gooding, Chief Executive of BUPA. 'If all other things are equal, we have to ask what differentiates our organization, both to our customers and to potential employees. This research shows the close connection between responsible organizations, engaged, motivated and inspired employees and business success.'

Consultation with other stakeholders is equally important. With major corporations just as answerable to NGOs and non-profit organizations as they are to the state they need to put interested parties at the centre of policy development. It is for this reason that, two years ago, Diageo formed a task group to deal with its commitment to human rights. The group reviewed external human rights codes, including the Universal Declaration of Human Rights. Once adapted to Diageo's way of working, it resulted in a draft policy on which the group consulted widely among advocacy groups such as Amnesty International and interest groups in local markets.

But just as brands depend on consumer insight, all stakeholder relationships rely on an understanding of where partners are coming from and what they are trying to achieve. It is the company's job to come up with shared solutions. Sometimes there are necessary trade-offs.

When Diageo decided to close the Strathleven packaging plant at Dumbarton in 1999, the company considered the effect on employees, their families and the local community, as well as consumer reaction. A range of measures was put in place, including enhanced redundancy terms, early retirement packages and counselling services to help people look for new roles.

It is in the area of manufacturing that Diageo has a real impact on the environment. So effort is concentrated in the areas of biggest impact: use of energy, water management, materials and recycling – in many markets return-and-refill bottles are used. In Africa, for example, all of the company's beer is packaged in this way and nearly

90 per cent of bottles are returned. But there is room for improvement. The Corporate Citizenship Company, which recently audited Diageo's first corporate citizenship report, says it is an area where reporting has to be enhanced. Reflecting its approach to CSR as a whole, Diageo intends to take a wider view of its environmental impact, particularly of packaging. As the pressure on resources increases, so programmes must become broader in scope.

But to be most effective in corporate citizenship, a business cannot lose sight of where it has the greatest impact – and where its efforts can have greatest benefit. That, in the case of a company whose core products are alcoholic beverages, will be in the place of alcohol in society, and working closely with independent bodies to promote responsible drinking. This is the single biggest issue on which such a business can give leadership.

Alcohol is Diageo's main product and the company strives to tackle the causes of irresponsible consumption. For example, the TIPS – training for intervention procedures – programme teaches Spanish-speaking bartenders to look for clues that their customers may be drinking excessively. In addition to covering US markets with large Hispanic populations, the goal is to provide similar schemes in Latin America and the Caribbean.

On an industry-wide level, the Dublin principles set out principles of cooperation within the beverage alcohol industry, governments, scientific researchers and the public health community. As a member of the Alcohol Task Force of International Life Sciences Institute Europe, Diageo has co-funded a range of peer-reviewed research overviews and publications.

INDUSTRY LEADERSHIP

As the biggest company of its type, a company like Diageo has a leadership responsibility to its industry. When it enters emerging markets, it is carrying not only its own reputation but also that of its peers. The company has called on all its experience in corporate citizenship, especially what has been learnt from the UK and US, to trade successfully across the globe.

In the early days of the Diageo Foundation, the company got a chance to put its experience to practice in India. It was vital for the business to prove itself as a good corporate citizen if it was to trade successfully. There was ambivalence towards multinationals: alcohol can be a contentious issue and the company was starting from scratch. It had to prove it was respecting social norms and advertising codes, and that it was prepared to invest in the local communities. Corporate citizenship has an important role to play in such emerging markets, because it shows regulators and governments that the company is not in it for short-term gains, that it is not going to take all its profits home and that it is interested in creating employment and supporting communities.

As companies take on a global dimension, so does their corporate citizenship. All multinationals have to make sure that their behaviour is consistent in every market, not just in the home country. Understanding of local markets should inform all of a global business's community projects. Diageo's approach focuses on a few programme areas that are most appropriate to the business, and adopts them as best-practice toolkits for markets around the world. The local markets ultimately own the initiatives and the toolkit is adjusted to take account of the culture and trading climate.

Recently, it has set up a bar skills training programme with its trade partners, which helps disadvantaged young people from the favelas in Sao Paulo. Lessons from the UK and the server training programme from the US were used, but it is very much unique to Brazil. It has since evolved and the template has been adapted for the Seychelles, India and other markets – a semi-blueprint for local cultures.

But there are risks associated with any suggestion of parachuting in a solution; companies cannot be seen to come up with the answer for an individual country. Companies can offer up solutions, but ultimately the local market has to decide what is best for them.

The Diageo Foundation acts as a catalyst and empowerer of Diageo businesses around the world by sharing best practice and project evaluation. Projects have to be locally managed because a crucial part of corporate citizenship is considering all the different stakeholders: investors, consumers and the government. And that dialogue is best served by local expertise.

There are sometimes delicate issues surrounding global and local standards. Contributing to the prosperity of communities, sustaining jobs, serving consumers and working with suppliers are issues with considerable local significance. For example, some of the more detailed human rights policies have to be set down at country level because a policy that is appropriate in the US may have to be very different to work in India.

To that end Diageo has now published four separate reports on its corporate citizenship programmes in different markets (Australia, Nigeria, Poland and Scotland) in order to inform discussion with decision makers and stakeholders.

LOCAL SUPPORT

Business has an important contribution to make because it is an efficient user of resources and influencer of supply lines, but businesses have to remember that companies are not democratically elected. It is governments that have control over public policy. The argument from anti-globalization protesters is that strengthening of large companies comes at the expense of governments and local communities. But true corporate social responsibility is about local, not arm's length, support.

And just as communication with stakeholders is vital, so is external and internal communication with other groups. Part of the criteria for any Diageo Foundation funding is that the project has to be a fully worked-through proposition that sets out not only the business and community benefits but also how it will be communicated.

As crucial as local, as opposed to arm's length, support is the role of the CEO and senior management. Corporate citizenship can only work where the CEO backs it and it can only have credibility if employees believe in it. There is always likely to be a challenge when a new board member comes in: why are we doing this, and are we spending the right amount of money? As David Logan said during his RSA lecture: 'Whether values led or pragmatic or both, most companies should now know that they cannot wait to be hit by a crisis. However, few have the vision to commit management resources. Companies need significant internal capacity to monitor and understand the global relationship with stakeholders.'

Actions such as endorsement of the UN Global Compact in 2002, a public commitment to leadership in social, environmental and economic aspects of sustainability – the so-called 'triple bottom line' – shows this commitment starts at the top and extends to all parts of the company. Businesses must also strive for consistency in areas of the industry where there is not competitive advantage. Diageo has done a lot of work setting up pan-industry social groups, such as the Portman Group in the UK, to look at the effects of alcohol in society, to help the industry self-regulate how it advertises and to combat drink-driving. The company has also sponsored the production of education materials by the UK's Teachers Advisory Council on Alcohol and Drugs Education, including the World of Alcohol for primary school teachers.

There are other external codes that define corporate citizenship principles and standards of conduct. These include the Business Charter for Sustainable Development. It includes 16 principles of environmental management that influenced the approach Diageo took in drawing up the company's first environmental policy.

But, however well intentioned a business, it is never going to free itself from criticism. The problem is that people either over- or under-define corporate social responsibility. That is why it is important that a company states what corporate citizenship means to its business, so it can be challenged. And that is why there is a need to be explicit and transparent about what its purpose is, so people know what a business feels it can achieve. This is something that is clear in the LBG model under what it calls 'commercially led activities'. These are activities led by commercial departments, including the promotion of brands and other social aspects of policies, in partnership with charities and community organizations.

An example is the Tanqueray AIDS rides, where the brand sponsored 20,000 cycle riders in races across the country. Over $180 million was raised over four years for HIV/AIDS causes. From a social point of view the benefits are clear, but the races also have significant business benefits. The company has done it as a commercial proposition to increase sales of Tanqueray and grow consumer loyalty, and has been completely open and transparent about it. That would not be possible unless other elements of corporate citizenship were securely in place.

As Richard Lambert recently noted: 'Competition has commoditized products, and an increasing number of big companies are now in the business of selling the ideas, emotions and beliefs that they want their brands to convey.'

THE NEED FOR INTEGRITY

But what about those who say social responsibility is a cover for commercial motives? Diageo makes no secret that its governing objective is to create value for its shareholders. This ambition it believes is best served by investing in relationships with all its stakeholders.

And that is why from the outset a corporate citizenship programme must have integrity. Scepticism may come internally, most often from middle management, where they have tough business targets and not much time. It is a case of the long-term versus the short-term agenda. Usually the situation with employees is different. Under the company's involvement with environmental charity Earthwatch, 15 Diageo employees can apply to join conservational field trips around the world, and are then tasked to become local environmental champions on their return.

As we have seen, good corporate citizenship is vital on a global scale, but it has to be viewed alongside government and society as a whole. This is why the debate has only really started.

Diageo is a business, with a turnover of nearly £10 billion, so the way it purchases, how it employs its staff, the way it markets its products should be the focus of attention. That is why there will be far more social reporting, and increasing interest will be paid to the effect of its goods, products and services. The aim is consistency – which is not easy when a business operates in 180 markets. The same standards need to be agreed vertically through the supply chain. And there is a need to find out where the boundaries are for employees – how can it all be made tangible for them? There is a need for more data, for more consistent measures, so a business can identify trends year on year.

Like all businesses it must strive to understand the effect and impact it has, both socially and environmentally, while never losing sight of its commercial principles.

A company, once committed to corporate citizenship, must publish regularly on its current performance in that area in order to get a better understanding of that performance and to set improvement targets. And this is what good corporate citizenship is all about – not undermining the very foundations of society, but continuously adapting and extending policies and practices to be in tune with it.

DIAGEO AT A GLANCE

- 24,500 people employed;
- 180 markets around the world;
- £4 billion on goods and services from suppliers;
- £300 million investment in plant and buildings;
- £2.3 billion in the form of taxes and duties in public spending.

3

Legislation, litigation, activism and threats

Stuart Thomson, Public Affairs and Communications Consultant, DLA Upstream, and Honorary Research Fellow, University of Aberdeen

Companies, governments and activists are facing a growing challenge in how to respond to the development of corporate social responsibility (CSR). CSR has grown rapidly, and relatively smoothly, over the last 20 years as increasing numbers of companies take up the banner of CSR in attempts to make their operations more ethical. Governments clearly value the role that these businesses can play in the development of society, while the activist community can point to the growing importance of CSR as a clear victory for the pressure they have exerted on the activities of companies.

Put simplistically, companies introduced CSR programmes and reports in order to counter the damage inflicted on them – on both their sales and reputation – by attacks from activist groups who placed a spotlight on the behaviour of these firms. Aided by the rise of the 24-hour news media, activists have been able to create an environment in which corporate wrongdoing has been given a high profile. Such stories make for compelling news but, very often, good-news CSR stories of companies performing valuable roles in society are not given such prominence as they do not make such exciting news. It is now no longer appropriate for companies merely to make a profit; the way in which the profit is generated is under scrutiny as activists drill down into a business's market behaviour, trade policies, employment relations, sourcing of raw materials, human rights and, for many the most important, a company's environmental credentials. If a company was being exploitative in any of these areas then the activists would place pressure on them, through the media and other activities, making the issue public in order to force a change in behaviour. This analysis pays no attention to the very good work that businesses have done in the past and their contributions to society. One only has to look at the activity of Joseph Rowntree and others and the way in which they developed their workforces, as examples of these earlier contributions. Much of this, however, did not necessarily relate to the core business of the company but was instead a charitable or paternalistic 'giving back' to society.

It was in the 1980s that a network of companies came together to establish Business in the Community (BITC) and later launched the Per Cent Club whose members donate 1 per cent of pre-tax profits to the community. BITC is a very widely respected and influential force within business and in the whole area of CSR.

However, a major problem remains with what corporate social responsibility actually means. The Corporate Responsibility Group defined it as 'the management of an organisation's total impact upon its immediate stakeholders and upon the society within which it operates... it is about the integrity with which a company governs itself, fulfils its mission, lives by its values, engages with its stakeholders, measures its impacts and reports on its activities'. BITC provides a system of benchmarking and a full checklist of items that companies need to fulfil in order to be corporately socially responsible. However, there are many other measures, some local, some national, and others international and even global. Some countries have introduced legislation forcing companies to fulfil certain criteria whereas others are taking a more laissez-faire approach. Many companies issue CSR reports detailing their good work. Again, the form that these reports take varies enormously – from simple statements of intent through to full-colour glossy brochures roughly approaching the size of *War and Peace*.

Much of this confusion has, in turn, led to a huge suspicion among the general public about CSR, its role and what it really means. In essence, the public does not believe that the companies do what they say they do and much CSR is deemed to be driven by the PR needs of the business. The activists have the upper hand; they can attack companies and people believe their attacks. Companies can respond but people do not believe their responses. The dilemma for companies is that if they do not produce clear CSR statements then the activists will attack. However, if they do produce CSR reports then the activists can attack these also. A CSR report will benchmark a company's position so it must keep improving on this. If it does not then it is open to attack. If a company says that it behaves in a certain way then it *must* act in this way. If it does not, then it will be attacked. A further problem for companies is that very often they have tried to cover too much in their CSR activity reports – spreading themselves too thinly.

Companies are, therefore, increasingly wary about CSR – they realize that it can be good for the business, its sales, employee morale and reputation but have to balance this against damage to its reputation from activist attacks, confusion over the form of CSR and little clarity over what it really should entail. Governments wish to be seen to encourage CSR activity but many do not wish to introduce legislation and have no clear idea about what form this legislation would take. Activists wishing to ensure that companies adhere to the highest standards are in danger of turning companies off any CSR activity altogether if they continue to attack too vociferously. All three are, therefore, facing a challenge.

THE CHALLENGES FOR BUSINESS

Companies know that CSR activity can be beneficial. Increasingly, CSR activity has been seen to have a beneficial effect on the company's bottom line. Some of this evidence has only more recently come to light but it is gathering momentum:

- Reputation protection – protecting the company's reputation will protect sales, share price and profits.
- An Institute of Business Ethics report has suggested that companies with ethical commitments have 18 per cent higher profits on average than their competitors.
- In a survey by CSR Europe and Euronext, 51 per cent of fund managers and 37 per cent of financial analysts said they would put a premium on socially responsible companies.
- A Henley Centre report claimed that 60 per cent of institutional investors say that non-financial factors account for between 20 per cent and 50 per cent of their investment decisions.
- According to a McKinsey Global Investor Opinion Survey, investors claimed that they will pay premiums of between 12 per cent and 14 per cent in North America and Western Europe for companies with high corporate governance standards.

Together with these 'bottom-line' issues can be taken:

- Research from the Chartered Institute of Personnel and Development (CIPD) and the Future Work Institute, 'Responsibility: driving innovation, inspiring employees', showed a clear connection between responsible business practice and a positive impact on the bottom line because it helps to attract, motivate and retain a talented and diverse workforce. It also found that the employees believe that this type of workforce is more creative and innovative and this in turn enhances competitiveness and profitability.

- Companies can avoid the expense of class action suits.
- Seventy per cent of chief executives globally agree that CSR is vital to profitability (fifth global CEO survey, PricewaterhouseCoopers/World Economic Forum).
- In Western Europe, 68 per cent of large companies report on what is being called the triple bottom line performance (economic, social and environmental factors) in addition to financial performance, compared with 41 per cent in the US (PricewaterhouseCoopers/BSI Global Research Inc, 2002).
- According to BITC, more than 70 per cent of business leaders believe that integrating responsible business practices makes companies more competitive and profitable.

Reputation management is an increasingly important element of business activity. Many firms have established risk management committees. Barclays has recently established a 'brand and reputation' committee that puts reputation issues on a parallel with financial and operational risks. This is an explicit recognition that companies need to manage risks to their reputation more effectively. A MORI survey among corporate communications directors of FTSE 100 companies in October 2002 showed that 93 per cent believed that publishing non-financial information enhanced a company's reputation and made for better management decisions. A model based on the *Fortune/Management Today* 'Most Admired' survey of 500 US and 250 UK companies showed a direct correlation between reputation and financial outcomes – share price and credit rating. It suggested that reputation, on average, accounted for 27 per cent of the FTSE 250 companies' market capitalization. According to a survey of US business leaders, financial analysts and journalists published in February 2004, a damaged reputation can take up to four years to be restored. According to a Harris survey of 800 CEOs in Europe and North America, three out of four international corporations have a corporate reputation measuring system in place, with the boards of 62 per cent of UK companies monitoring reputation.

It is becoming increasingly clear that companies, for very good business reasons, need to take CSR seriously. Yet this has to be balanced against reports that show that there is a clear scepticism of the way in which companies conduct their CSR activities:

- In a report by Tomorrow's Company, 'Redefining CSR', it is suggested that many companies see CSR as merely a box-ticking exercise driven by external pressures rather than by a genuine desire to conduct business in an ethical manner.
- A survey of 56 leading lobby groups by Burson-Marsteller found that few believed CSR statements produced by companies.
- Research published by the Salvation Army, 'The responsibility gap – individualism, community and responsibility in Britain today', demonstrated that 8 out of 10 Britons believed that companies should contribute to the society in which they

operate but there was a serious concern about the emergence of a 'responsibility gap' that threatened the elderly, children, carers and other vulnerable people in society.

● Christian Aid's report, 'Behind the mask: the real face of corporate social responsibility', suggested that businesses are using CSR as a front behind which they campaign against environmental and human rights regulations.

Companies worldwide are having to face up to these conflicting issues.

THE CHALLENGES FOR ACTIVISTS

During the early part of the 20th century, activism was generally geared around participation in political parties. Since the late 1960s, however, there has been a shift away from this form of participation and a distinct move to campaigns and activity based on single issues. Initially, this revolved around environmental concerns but increasingly this has diversified and in recent years the emphasis has been placed on the negative impact that globalization plays on society both in developing and developed countries. Globalization has been portrayed as a way for big business to make more profit at the expense of citizens.

Companies are increasingly finding themselves liable to attack from activists. These attacks can take a wide variety of forms but the implications for companies are enormous. Activists are now increasingly looking not only to target the core business, the aim of their attack, but also to attack the network of financiers, insurers and suppliers on which the company relies. The focus of activists may not just be on the primary target but also move on to secondary and even tertiary targets and methods of campaigning all with the same aim in mind. Many companies believe that they are immune from attacks from activist organizations. While the most high-profile attacks are made on companies engaged in what may be deemed to be 'controversial' activities and industries – animal testing, tobacco, extraction industries and so on – these are not the only companies that may be at risk. In a recent example, the customers of UK Huntingdon Life Sciences, a research company that tests on animals, went to the High Court to gain injunctions, under anti-harassment legislation, against animals rights extremists who were targeting their employees. These extremists are now targeting the judges who allowed the injunctions.

Increasingly, groups can spring up to campaign against companies that provide services and products that may not ordinarily be deemed controversial. Companies may unwittingly become involved and become targets as the activists shift their focus to secondary and tertiary targets. There is a huge variety of ways in which companies may be attacked:

- Many large organizations have memberships who can be persuaded to letter-write, boycott products and so on. In December 2002, Nestlé decided to call in a £3.7 million debt from Ethiopia. The company has, for many years, been the target of activist attacks primarily because of its marketing of powdered milk to developing countries. Calls from across the world for Nestlé's products to be boycotted forced a reversal of the decision to call in the debt.
- Many activist groups and pressure groups will use existing political structures to try and exert pressure on government to take action against companies, eg by increasing regulatory or environmental sustainability requirements, etc. Such lobbying is not just the preserve of corporations. The UK Breast Cancer Coalition has been at the forefront of using patients as advocates in lobbying government.
- Shareholder activism has placed pressure internally within companies as shareholders vote down motions at AGMs and also introduce their own, often controversial, motions. According to a survey by Watson Wyatt, one in two chairmen of FTSE 350 companies said that shareholder activism had made them look again at their remuneration packages. The TUC launched a campaign at the start of 2003 to increase shareholder activism by pension funds, and even the Association of British Insurers (ABI) believes that its members should play an active role on company resolutions.
- Many pressure groups are using legal recourse to attack companies. This is especially the case in the United States where there has been an even greater reliance on such class actions. In the UK, Greenpeace launched a High Court case against the loans made to British Energy.
- The spread of electronic communications such as e-mail and the internet has meant that the power of activists is often in their homes. Companies can find their websites bombarded with e-mails, phones can be barraged with calls, and networks of activists are becoming increasingly powerful as they communicate more easily, enabling quick and successful action often across countries and even continents.
- The use of people power through demonstrations and activities such as occupations often causes maximum disruption to companies. Such action is enhanced still further if the people do something shocking. A group of around 600 Nigerian mothers and grandmothers protested against Chevron Texaco and forced them to promise jobs, electricity and other improvements to villages in their areas simply by threatening to take their clothes off.
- Many pressure groups are extremely adept at using press, marketing and advertisements to increase the prominence of their cause and will often use these against companies. Viral marketing campaigns, International Buy Nothing Day and the work by Ad Busters are all useful weapons for activity. Ad Busters produce provocative, clever and often humorous perversions of corporate advertisements to make their points.

● Increasingly, companies have found that direct action has led to violent attacks. Activists understand their legal requirements and are often careful to work within, as well as outside, the law. Companies are looking to continue to exert pressure on government to tighten up laws still further to protect their staff.

The reasons for activism and attacks are extremely varied but in essence many people have lost their faith in traditional political institutions and are looking for new ways to voice their concerns. Add to this that companies have an increasingly high profile, which when combined with the phenomenon of 'brand' has encouraged activism while, in several senses, making attacks easier. Activists can rightly point to their success in ensuring that many companies have implemented CSR programmes. They have also made companies much more aware of the issues they need to consider as part of being involved in the wider society. However, sometimes the activists feel that they need to take it a stage further.

Such an instance is demonstrated by the *Nike* v *Kasky* legal proceedings in the US. Kasky, a California-based activist, took Nike all the way to the Californian Supreme Court. His lawsuit claimed that Nike misled the public about working conditions for Vietnamese, Chinese and Indonesian labourers and that its statements amounted to false advertising. Nike denied this and claimed that its statements were protected under the First Amendment of the American Constitution, that of free speech. The California Supreme Court ruled that Nike's corporate statements could be regulated as commercial speech and allowed the lawsuit to go to trial. Before this happened, both sides came to a settlement (September 2003). As part of the settlement, Nike agreed to make additional workplace-related investments of $1.5 million to the Fair Labor Association (FLA).

In its press statement Nike also clearly stated that: 'Nike will continue to advocate for corporate transparency and both parties agreed that the portion of the settlement should explore supporting a multi-sector collaboration on the future evolution of a common global reporting standard and universally applied process for corporate accountability.'

At no point did Nike admit liability in this matter. The settlement means that no court has yet looked at whether Nike's statements were true or false and it also means that there is no clear definition of what commercially can be allowed under free speech. This has obvious implications for companies and now means that companies will be extremely wary before entering debate or publishing any materials for fear of being litigated against. This means that voluntary social reporting could be at risk.

There is also increasing unease about the way in which activist groups can advocate CSR and corporate governance positions without necessarily following the same high standards that they demand. Many commentators have raised the issue of the funding of activist organizations as many are not transparent on this matter. Many activist organizations do not publish their own CSR reports and do not have clear corporate governance structures. Activists are faced with the start of a possible backlash from the public against their lack of transparency and from businesses increasingly wary about publishing CSR reports or statements for fear of even harsher attacks.

THE CHALLENGES FOR GOVERNMENT

Governments across the world have encouraged CSR activity by companies. This can be understood, as activists apply the pressure that governments would sometimes like to put on companies but are otherwise concerned about frightening them away from investing in the country, and all the associated implications for jobs and regional policy that this would have. As developments have progressed, governments are now faced with a situation where some serious decisions about the future have to be made in this area.

The lack of one clear agreed statement on what CSR is and how it can be measured is one of the reasons why governments have been reluctant to introduce legislation. Companies believe that they are best left to police this area and that any new government legislation would increase the level of regulation and, therefore, costs on them. The activists, for their part, are now starting to push for legislation to force compliance on businesses. A brief examination of the current settings around the world begins to show there is a clear momentum towards legislation:

- In the UK, the Department for Trade and Industry (DTI) has begun the process of introducing operating and financial reviews (OFRs) as part of the annual report of large companies. This would contain information on a company's relationship with its stakeholders, its environmental and community impact, corporate governance and risk management. This move to include non-financial elements marks a significant change from traditional financial reporting. The government has also suggested that guidance requirements for the OFR would be provided by a newly created Standards Board. The DTI established an OFR working group on materiality to provide guidance for directors on how to prepare and organize their company so that they are ready to provide OFRs. It will be up to the boards to decide what constitutes materiality and, therefore, merits inclusion in the report. OFRs can be viewed as the first stage towards the institution of formal CSR reporting. Some companies already produce voluntary OFRs, and the Accounting Standards Board in 2003 revised its 1993 statement describing it as 'a formulation and development of best practice, intended to have persuasive effect'.

- Five European countries have introduced mandatory reporting requirements – Denmark, the Netherlands, Norway, Sweden and France.
- Again in the UK, a 1999 amendment to the 1995 Pensions Act requires trustees of pension funds to declare their positions on ethical, social and environmentally responsible investment in their statement of investment principles.
- Following a spate of corporate scandals in the US, it is likely that further legislation will be forthcoming and there is already the powerful Sarbanes-Oxley Act in place.
- The European Union is taking CSR issues very seriously. Initially, the European Council meeting in Lisbon in March 2000 made a special appeal to companies' sense of social responsibility. Then in July 2001, the European Commission launched a Green Paper on CSR, which was followed by public consultation. A follow-up communication in July 2002 saw the establishment of the European Multi-Stakeholder Forum on CSR, which brings together trade unions, employers' organizations, civil society organizations and business networks to discuss the way forward for CSR. The forum is currently holding meetings and is due to submit its conclusions to the commission by mid-2004. This will include discussion of the merits of voluntary and regulatory approaches to CSR. The commission is also keen to explore, in more detail, the relationship between CSR and corporate governance. While they are in essence different, in the broad public sense the behaviour of a firm both internally and externally can be viewed together.

An examination of parliamentary activity in the UK has also seen two high-profile attempts to introduce legislation by Linda Perham MP (Labour, Ilford North) and Andy King (Labour, Rugby and Kenilworth). Perham and King have also introduced motions into Parliament to raise the profile of their calls to force companies to publish reports on the ecological and social impact of their businesses. Over 100 organizations, including charities, faith-based groups and trade unions, have come together to back these calls under the banner of CORE and have asked for laws to be introduced requiring companies to report on their social and environmental performance as well as creating a 'duty of care' for company directors similar to current health and safety requirements. CORE includes Amnesty International, Christian Aid, Friends of the Earth, the New Economics Foundation, Save the Children, Traidcraft and the Unity Trust Bank.

A momentum behind formal rules and legislation appears to be growing.

THE WAY FORWARD

Instead of spreading themselves too thinly, companies need to focus on their core activities and concentrate their CSR activities on these core activities. Instead of trying to do 10 to 15 areas of CSR well, the company should concentrate on the two or three that are fundamental to the business. Companies should also concentrate on financial considerations and financial audiences in their CSR activity to make it fundamental to the very operation of the company. The financial community needs risk to be minimized and this includes CSR-type risks. Companies need to identify their risks, prioritize them, address them (where possible) and then communicate them.[1] Companies need to demonstrate clearly that they are systematically dealing with their risks. Finance and CSR need to be reconnected.

The studies cited above together with even the most cursory examination of shareholder activism show that companies are having to take the financial aspects of CSR and risk seriously. Some companies are even having to rethink remuneration issues and their appointment decisions as a result of shareholder activism. Vodafone, in early 2004, withdrew from a US bidding war with Cingular about AT&T Wireless. More pleasing for shareholder activists was Sir Ian Prosser quitting his chairman elect position at J Sainsbury; this was effectively forced by investor anger at the choice of Prosser and the manner of his appointment.

Businesses are trying to find a way forward, but confusion over what CSR measures to use, how to communicate with stakeholders, especially in the financial community, and problems with participation in league tables are all issues that need to be addressed. If a company's position in a league table falls, it can be open to criticism and attack. Instead of crying out against legislation, companies should embrace the possibility of rules and regulations that would minimize their risks especially in reputational terms. There is already heavy legislation in the corporate governance area, so it would appear that legislation in CSR is a natural extension. A survey from the World Bank Group, 'Race to the top: attracting and enabling global sustainable business', of executives in multinational enterprises found that 61 per cent of respondents were seeking strong laws on CSR when seeking partners, and that these had to be rigorously enforced to create a level playing field and discourage corruption. The survey also found that there were differences in which external standard was favoured in different regions of the world – in developing countries the International Labour Organization (ILO) standards were favoured whereas in the US, Canada and Australia the UN Global Compact was favoured. Again, businesses face confusion and therefore increased risk. This cannot be allowed to continue.

Legislation would enforce certain standards upon all companies, not merely those that choose to engage in CSR. In the UK, an often cited statistic is that three-quarters of the top 350 companies in the UK ignored a challenge set by the Prime Minister, Tony Blair, to file environmental reports by the end of 2001. It could be argued that enforced standards would also prevent 'greenwash' where the real problems are left unresolved and the company's PR department develops the image of good corporate citizenship. The more that companies are seen to act in an unethical way (whether this be environmentally or whether it is a huge corporate scandal similar to recent ones in the US and Europe) the more public sympathy and justification activists will have for calling for legislation. Activists could continue to argue for higher standards over and above those required by legislation and this would involve them in engaging in a debate on best practice and also being able to demonstrate clearly that companies differentiating themselves on social and environmental measures can assist the development of brand and the 'bottom line'. Activists will, however, need to examine seriously their own CSR and corporate governance structures.

Governments can justify legislation on some of the grounds outlined above. Currently many are still failing to grasp the full implications of CSR and are unsure what, if any, their role should be in this area. The development of legislation can provide that role.

CONCLUSION

Corporate social responsibility has now developed to such an extent that the challenges that this has laid down have to be addressed. CSR is beginning to grow up and the easy choices of its early years are now giving way to fundamental decisions that will affect its direction and form going forward – maybe even its very existence. Companies need to refocus their attention on their core risks and ensure that they fully address their financial audience, as otherwise they will continue to flounder. Activists need to put their own houses in order and also argue for coherent international and global legislation. Governments have to realize that they can clear a path through the myriad of different systems, standards and general confusion for all concerned. If corporate social responsibility is to continue to have a beneficial role in societies then governments have to move the agenda forward with legislation as a matter of priority.

Note

[1] See the work of Dr Tauni Brooker of ORM2 (www.orm2.com) for more detail on the non-financial issues that companies need to consider when dealing with the financial community.

FURTHER READING

Business in the Community (BITC) (2002) *Business in the Community*, www.csreurope.org
Connor, T (2002) We are not machines, *Oxfam Community Aid Abroad*, www.clean-clothes.org

Corporate Social Responsibility Europe (CSR Europe) (2002) *About Us*, www. csreurope.org

Deegan, D (2001) Managing Activism, IPR, London

Denny, C (2003) Doubts over corporate consciences, *Guardian*, 14 November

Grefe, E (1995) *The New Corporate Activism: Harnessing the power of grass roots tactics for your organization*, McGraw-Hill, New York

Hertz, N (2001) *The Silent Takeover: Global capitalism and the death of democracy*, Heinemann, London

John, S and Thomson, S (eds) (2003) *New Activism and the Corporate Response*, Palgrave, Basingstoke

Jordan, G (2001) *Shell, Greenpeace and Brent Spar*, Palgrave, Basingstoke

Klein, N (2000) *No Logo*, Flamingo, London

Kripps, K (2003) End of suit good for Nike, but bad for business, *Advertising Age*, 29 September

Liptak, A (2003) Nike move ends case over firm's free speech, *New York Times*, 13 September

Monbiot, G (2000) *The Captive State: The corporate takeover of Britain*, Pan, London

Thomson, S and Hinton-Smith, S (2003) UK takes step towards CSR reporting, *Insurance Day*, 23 July

Tucker, S (2004) Corporate governance has finally grown up, *Financial Times*, 18 February

www.andyking.org

www.foe.co.uk/campaigns/corporates/core/

www.lindaperham.labour.co.uk

www.nike.com/nikebiz/news/pressrelease_print.jhtml?year=2003&month=09&letter

4

Measuring corporate social responsibility[1]

Will Oulton and John Hancock

Over the last three or four years, there have been a number of new entrants to the business of attempting to measure companies' performance quantitatively and qualitatively in terms of their corporate social responsibility activities. This growth has been fuelled by an increasing interest from the investment community in being able to measure these so called 'non-financial' risks. The main spur to this in the UK was the introduction of the Pensions Act in 2000, which introduced the concept of the 'Statement of Investment Principles' or SIP, which has to be published by pension funds. The SIP should state the objectives of the fund and whether or not the fund takes into account ethical or socially responsible considerations as part of its investment strategy.

The majority of UK pension funds today delegate the implementation of their SIP to their agents, the fund managers who manage the funds' assets on their behalf. To do this effectively, those fund managers require social, environmental and ethical performance information on the companies within the pension funds portfolio. In the UK, over 95 per cent of pension funds use the companies in the FTSE All Share Index as their company investment universe. This universe consists of, on average, some 700 of the UK's large, mid and small cap companies (ie the sum of the FTSE 100, FTSE 250 and FTSE SmallCap).

Increasingly, mainstream investors are addressing the issues of non-financial risk measurement and are seeking more sophisticated tools to help them do this. The problem, however, is that there are few suppliers of such information and little if any consistency in what aspects of corporate social responsibility to measure. For example, some investors, particularly in the insurance sector, are becoming increasingly concerned with issues such as asbestosis and climate change that pose real and significant potential liability risks for those companies in the future. Other investors, eg trade union and public pension funds, are particularly concerned with issues such as labour standards, health and safety, human rights and environmental impact risk.

As with any aspect of a business's performance, corporate responsibility needs to be measured if it is to be understood and managed. However, unlike the more traditional performance criteria such as growth, return on capital, profitability, revenue generation, growth of customer base, etc, corporate responsibility cannot be so easily quantified. Indeed, it has been the lack of absolute measurements that has made more difficult the task of bringing responsibility issues and performance to the attention of both the businesses whose behaviour is being considered and the general public whose awareness of this dimension to business performance is essential for any long-term change in attitudes to take effect. So, a key requirement for the incorporation of corporate social responsibility (CSR) considerations into the plans and strategies of businesses has been providing a yardstick and terminology by which performance can be measured and improvements projected.

A very important part of this development has been the growth of research facilities to support socially responsible investors and investment managers. Socially responsible investment (SRI) considers the same criteria of business growth (share value), performance (return on capital) and prospects (future plans and the probability that they will be achieved) but includes a further dimension of responsibility or impact of the business in ethical and environmental areas as well as sustainability and the governance of the business. Of course, there is a moral dimension to this but, increasingly, investment analysts and fund managers are regarding a business with a strong performance in and strategy for activities in these responsibility criteria as having a premium value. That is because such a business is more likely to be thinking about long-term profitability based on the business's own ability to add value in the services and/or products that it sells rather than maximizing this year's bottom line based on its ability to milk a particular short-term situation with little or no regard for future consequences that may flow from that action.

Because of the need for SRI funds, in particular, to be able to explain clearly to investors all of the criteria by which they select or reject investments and then, as part of their own investment management process, to be able to judge the businesses in which they have invested, a process of screening and analysing potential and actual investments has been developed by a number of organizations. Some investment houses do this themselves but many others are increasingly using the services of professional ethical and corporate responsibility analysts who are facing the challenges of how to quantify and evaluate concepts such as responsibility and more recently corporate governance.

SRI RESEARCH AT A CROSSROADS

A recent report from SustainAbility and Mistra, 'Values for money: reviewing the quality of SRI research' (www.sustainability.com, 2004) found that:

> Specialised SRI research houses are clearly at a crossroads in their development. Never before have the opportunities for independent SRI research been so great. The erosion in the perceived quality and independence of mainstream analysts, pressure on financial institutions to outsource their research capabilities, and the decision by large institutional investors to rely more on independent sources of research have all given a considerable boost to specialised research houses. These trends, combined with the gradual but persistent integration of social and environmental issues into mainstream investor analysis, should also significantly benefit independent SRI research houses.

DEVELOPING CSR INTENTIONS REQUIRE BETTER DEVELOPED MEANS TO MEASURE ACTIVITIES AND RESULTS

As more businesses and investors have adopted sustainable development (SD) and corporate social responsibility (CSR) agendas, investors have focused on a number of so-called 'linked concepts', eg reputation risks, corporate governance, management quality. SRI research based on older analytical models has been found to be not sufficiently sensitive or sophisticated to incorporate these multiple or linked concepts into the evaluation of investment value that can, in turn, be reflected as criteria that businesses may use to guide their plans, priorities and behaviour. As the SustainAbility and Mistra report suggests:

> SRI analysts themselves acknowledge that the opportunity to leverage social and environmental issues into mainstream investment decision making lies in crafting 'second generation' tools and methodologies that respond to this growing appetite [for a set of generally accepted and quantified criteria to support the incorporation of non-financial or responsibility issues into corporate performance and planning] in the [corporate and investment] mainstream.

The existence of the SRI market for large pension, insurance and other collective funds has provided a significant impetus to the development of corporate responsibility criteria, which, in turn, has provided the structure for CSR to develop as a core business value. It is clear that socially responsible investment is increasing. In the UK for example it is estimated that there is some £4.2 billion invested into ethical products; in France this number is estimated at €4 billion.

Again, SustainAbility and Mistra provide evidence:

This process [the identifying and analysis of non-financial or responsibility criteria in corporate performance] was described in a recent survey of mainstream European fund managers and analysts by CSR Europe, Deloitte and Euronext. Seventy nine per cent of respondents supported the view that social and environmental risk management has a positive impact on a company's long term market value. Fifty two per cent of respondents believe that social and environmental considerations will become a significant aspect of mainstream investment decisions in the next two years.

The gradual integration of specific elements of the SRI concept – such as reputational risks, corporate governance (including environmental and social issues) and management quality – into the investment decision processes of mainstream financial institutions can already be observed today. Seventy six per cent of fund managers and analysts interviewed by CSR Europe see a clear link between non-financial risks and shareholder value and systematically take into account issues such as the ability to innovate (65%), corporate governance and risk management (54%) and the management of customer relations (49%).

Environmental impact, i.e. the effect that a company's activities have on the biosphere, the physical world in which it operates, and supply chain management, i.e. what happens at various stages in the process used by a company to deliver its goods and/or services, whether or not the company directly controls those stages, are considered to be the most relevant non financial areas of risk for certain sectors and companies.

This is a crucial time, but also a time of potentially huge opportunities for specialized SRI research houses. There is currently a vacancy for a group of institutions whose consistent approach to CSR elements in a business will make the incorporation of such elements into investment decisions more practical and, through that, make the adoption of non-financial criteria as much part of a corporate operation as the application of the more traditional financial and performance criteria. Pressure on financial institutions to outsource some of their research capabilities has increased, and the decision by large institutional investors to rely more on independent sources of research has given a great boost to specialized research houses. SRI research institutions should also benefit from this trend.

MATERIALITY

In 2002 SustainAbility and UNEP published a benchmark report of corporate sustainability reporting. That report drew attention to a growing problem in corporate reporting that the authors called 'carpet bombing'. As was discussed in that report: 'Many reporting companies seem to have resorted to inundating readers with information, presumably in the hope that readers will be able to find what they are looking for.' This as much reflects the uncertainty of businesses about what they will be judged on in matters of non-financial performance as any intention to try and blind the reader with a blizzard of statistics and facts.

And, as much as they are uncertain about what they will be judged on, companies are often uncertain about what is likely to be material to the activities of their business and how they can prioritize their intentions, plans and activities affecting these responsibility matters. So any reporting may lack that sense of purpose or focus that would help a reader to evaluate the information in the context of the business he or she is looking at and the activities in which there is an interest. This context and focus can be summed up in the term 'materiality'. In the SustainAbility and Mistra report, it is explained in this way: 'The concept of materiality was originally derived from the field of financial auditing, and relates to: *Impacts that would cause an informed person to reach a different conclusion or make a different decision about representations shown in financial statements.*' The exclusive financial basis for this definition is, however, now being questioned. Several CSR organizations have argued that materiality ought to be 'redefined' to include a broader set of stakeholders. In particular, the materiality principle that underpins Accountability's AA 1000 Assurance Standard states that: 'The reporting organisation has included in the public report adequate information about its sustainable performance for its stakeholders to be able to make informed judgements, decisions and actions.' In other words, materiality should no longer be limited to issues that would cause an informed person to change his or her mind about financial statements, but should embrace all those issues that would enable stakeholders to make informed decisions, including social, environmental and economic issues.

The UK government has also used the term 'materiality' as a key part of its consultation on reforming company law in the OFR (operating and financial review). Here the government is assessing opinions on what factors would be considered significant or material to a business and specific to that business as determined by the directors of that enterprise. The upshot is that the OFR is expected to come into force in 2006 and will require the UK's top 1,000 companies to report on their social, environmental and ethical business risks.

The SustainAbility and Mistra report also states:

> There is of course a link between the two definitions of materiality. Issues that are 'material' to key stakeholder groups can very quickly become financially material to a company. There are plenty of examples of how bad corporate practice with regard to consumers, the environment or human rights have impacted company financial performance. The relationship between key sustainability issues and investment value drivers is clearly vital for SRI and mainstream investors interested in the financial performance of their investments. Identifying these sustainability issues and understanding how they link with investment value drivers in many ways represents the 'holy grail' [for people and organizations seeking to define and quantify criteria by which CSR performance can be judged and plans laid]...

There are now a number of specialized SRI research organizations in Asia, Australasia, North America and Europe. This list of research organizations (taken from the SustainAbility and Mistra report) contains only SRI and corporate governance research organizations with core businesses focused on the provision of company research, indices and ratings:

- **European organizations:**
    - Centre Info, Switzerland;[SR]
    - CoreRatings, UK;
    - Covalence, Switzerland;
    - Deminor Ratings (France);[CG]
    - Dutch Sustainability Research (DSR), Netherlands;
    - EIRiS, UK;
    - Ethibel/Stock at Stake, Belgium;[SR]
    - Oekom Research AG, Germany;
    - SAM Research, Switzerland;
    - SERM, UK;
    - Vigeo, France.

- **North American organizations:**
    - Investor Responsibility Research Center (IRRC), USA;
    - KLD, USA;[SR]
    - Michael Jantzi Research Associates, Canada.[SR]

[SR]Denotes members of the SiRi Group (now known as SiRi Company).
[CG]Denotes focus on corporate governance only.

Of course, no element of business performance can be considered in isolation from the others. In particular, there is no point in an investment that loses money and, no matter how good a company's record on CSR, if it does not make money and grow it will not attract investors or be able to pay its way. In those circumstances, CSR will be subordinated to business failure and there is nothing responsible to any stakeholder in that. The foundation upon which any business (responsible or otherwise) is and will continue to be built is the development of value in share price and profit. Linking sustainability issues to value drivers is still relatively unusual in SRI research but this is likely to change to reflect the realities of investment pressures as social and environmental issues move further into mainstream business analysis. With funds such as pension funds and other collective investment vehicles having an obligation to seek the best likely return for their investors, the consideration of non-financial values and criteria without regard to their impact on profit and value would simply not be realistic.

So, the need to develop non-financial criteria and indicators that are relevant and measurable by companies is a key consideration in trying to gain an effective insight into the company's operations and impacts that can stand alongside the more traditional financial and performance criteria and indicators. The growing use of standardized indicators significantly simplifies the task facing companies and research organizations, and emerging standards such as the Global Reporting Initiative (GRI) reporting guidelines are proving useful, particularly with regard to performance indicators. The GRI is essentially a multi-stakeholder agreement on what companies should report on. It provides companies with a framework for social responsibility reporting and has a target of attaining use by 500 companies globally by the end of 2004 and 600 by the end of 2006.

IN A DEVELOPING DISCIPLINE, THE YARDSTICKS MUST BE REGULARLY REVIEWED

In other parts of this book, the reader will be able to find a number of ways in which businesses similar to the one in which he or she is working can measure their non-financial performance and can define responsibility in terms relevant to where and how they work. However, because CSR is one of the newest business disciplines, it is still developing at a pace and so any criteria that will serve today may well be out of date tomorrow. New ways will be found to judge a business's non-financial performance and better ways of measuring that performance in order to judge it and to inform future planning will continue to emerge.

As the responsibility agenda continues to expand, diversity of experience among those charged with the business's CSR achievement becomes crucial in understanding the increasing range of issues. The SustainAbility and Mistra report again:

As more research organisations attempt to introduce mainstream elements into their methodologies by including financial business models and assessing issues and impacts against investment value drivers (coupled with increasing engagement with clients' financial analysts), a greater understanding of financial concepts and techniques will be required. Currently the proportion of analysts with financial experience within research teams is very low. As research organisations continue to focus on sector specific issues and risks, the need for more in depth understanding of how business operates in different sectors will be crucial. Analysts with experience in large cap companies will be of particular importance. One of the key issues companies have raised with SRI analysis is the lack of understanding of their unique business issues and impacts. Currently the proportion of analysts with business experience within research teams is also low.

Exactly the same criticisms and requirements will be true of companies' own teams charged with responsibility for delivering CSR objectives. There is no corporate social responsibility in losing money.

THE VOLUNTARY QUALITY STANDARD FOR CORPORATE SUSTAINABILITY AND RESPONSIBILITY RESEARCH

November 2003 saw the release of the pilot version of the Voluntary Quality Standard for Corporate Sustainability and Responsibility Research (EVQS). Drawn up by a number of specialist SRI research organizations, the standard is intended to help improve the quality of management systems, transparency and assurance processes and hence form a basis for further verification procedures of the research processes used by investment analysts seeking sustainability and non-financial performance, in addition to the traditional criteria applied by investors. The standard sets out a number of principles, which address several key criteria and to which signatories commit, and, while it is currently European focused, efforts to achieve full internationalization are expected once it has been developed further. (For more information see www.csrr-qs.org.)

Although readers will not be applying such criteria as investors, it will be these investment analysis criteria that will define CSR and provide the framework and quantifiable definitions of what CSR means in the future. For any company seeking to raise capital in the future, an ability to report on activities in terms used by the investment community will be as important for non-financial matters as it has always been (and will always be) for financial and performance matters.

Some of the key issues that are being monitored by investors, NGOs, unions, governments and other stakeholders include:

- climate change and companies' reductions of CO_2 emissions;
- access to drugs for HIV/AIDS;
- food labelling;
- food and drink marketing practices linked to obesity;
- alcohol use by minors, and marketing practices;
- labour standards in supply chains;
- biodiversity;
- child labour in the consumer goods and commodities industry;
- bribery and corruption – particularly for companies operating in high-risk, politically unstable developing countries;
- lending practices for the retail sector and for infrastructure projects;
- corporate governance practices – particularly compensation related;
- health and safety in high-risk industries;
- environmental impacts in terms of, for example, energy consumption, waste, emissions and toxic release and management;
- tobacco advertising practices and smuggling;
- use of renewable energy sources.

For companies the challenge is the meeting of the expectations of civil society in general while proving to their shareholders that they are taking all possible and reasonable steps to manage their business risks related to their activities and business relationships in these areas.

One way that companies can do this is by stating publicly their policies, management processes and systems of reporting against these issues where they are material and specific to that company or industry. The key elements are therefore transparency and disclosure of performance with a willingness to enter into constructive dialogue with the key shareholders and other stakeholders in that business.

There are many codes of best practice available for companies to refer to, adopt and implement from organizations such as the UN, ILO, OECD, and for more specific issues such as the Ethical Trading Initiative and Transparency International.

The UK government is keen to see companies doing more in the areas of corporate social responsibility and corporate governance and, while companies progress, little regulation will abound. However, if companies fail to take up the challenge, red tape and more binding regulation will undoubtedly be thrust upon what some consider to be overly burdened companies today.

Note

1 With material from the report, 'Values for money: reviewing the quality of SRI research', by Mistra and SustainAbility.

5

What makes a multinational company a global citizen? Sustainable development challenges for companies operating internationally

Robert Barrington, Director of Governance and Socially Responsible Investment, ISIS Asset Management, and Coralie Abbott, Corporate Programmes Manager, Earthwatch Institute (Europe)

THE ROLE OF MULTINATIONAL COMPANIES IN SUSTAINABLE DEVELOPMENT

Anti-globalization protests at Seattle, Davos and Cancun convey a familiar message: that multinational companies (MNCs) are fundamentally antithetical to sustainable development – accused by detractors of causing social and environmental damage in their search for economic advantage. This familiar claim from the anti-globalization lobby is starting to ring hollow. From an economic perspective alone, it is increasingly apparent that investment by MNCs can bring great benefits to deprived areas, whether in the industrialized or non-industrialized world. In the social and environmental arena, there is a growing body of evidence that MNCs can carry out their businesses in a way that is compatible with sustainable development.

Indeed, MNCs are often well placed to address and manage sustainable development issues, having the resources, experience, capacity and project management competencies to define the problem, to develop pragmatic and workable solutions, and to implement them. For example, a mining company seeking to operate in rural Madagascar will bring with it a wealth of sustainable development experience, in addition to its financial wealth and the economic value that it can unlock through mining and processing minerals.

The question facing those opposing such a mining company and those who are not opponents but who wish to ensure a positive outcome for sustainable development is, how this potential can be unlocked. There should be no doubt that MNCs are sometimes able to support and contribute to sustainable development in the course of carrying out their normal business. They should often be able to operate in a way that is compatible with sustainable development.

However, companies are fundamentally created to make a profit and create value for their shareholders. Why should they pursue such a 'sustainable development approach'?

Given a straight choice between profit making, and losing profit but contributing to sustainable development, most companies choose – indeed, they may be required by fiduciary law – to make a profit. But such decisions are rarely black and white. It is certainly possible to argue that sustainable development is in the interests of companies. Business in the Community lists six basic reasons as the 'business case for corporate responsibility',[1] while a recent report from brokerage Goldman Sachs has concluded that 'environmental and social issues will become increasingly important for oil and gas companies seeking to access the new legacy assets, which we view as the key driver of future performance and valuation'.[2] This is important to note, because companies often feel that their investors are not interested in long-term value and therefore that they do not value sustainable development.

To follow the case of a mining company in Madagascar, the case for sustainable development might include: reducing the time taken to gain a permit; building 'social equity' that will help gain faster approval for future licences elsewhere in the world; avoiding future liabilities or litigation; and gaining support from the community that will host the company's operations for the next 40 years, the lack of which could severely impair the mining operations through, for example, civil unrest.

The purpose of this chapter is to explore the challenges faced by companies in evaluating whether and how to take a sustainable development approach, the options that are available to companies and the factors that may influence a company in its decision making. It is notable that many examples and case studies relate to the extractive industries (oil, gas and mining). There are straightforward reasons for this. Extractive companies have the capacity to do great social and environmental damage, and have often done so in the past. Many continue to do so. In the era of globalization, they have become the most global of industries, and encounter almost every sustainable development problem – among them human rights, corruption, health, biodiversity, climate change and pollution. At the same time, they are among the largest and most profitable companies in the world. The sustainable development challenges faced by extractive companies, and their responses, represent in microcosm the fundamental challenge faced by multinational companies: whether, and how, to carry out their business in a manner that is compatible with sustainable development.

CHALLENGES FOR MNCS IN CARRYING OUT THEIR BUSINESSES IN A WAY THAT IS COMPATIBLE WITH SUSTAINABLE DEVELOPMENT

Global and local problems facing MNCs

There is no doubt that MNCs are exposed to a complex range of sustainable development challenges. They are operating in many different countries, each of which has different laws, norms and expectations both with regard to MNCs and with regard to sustainable development. This means that all global operations are to some extent local. There are three distinct challenges that face MNCs in this global/local context.

At a global level, by operating throughout the world, companies are exposed to global problems, such as climate change. One of the most difficult challenges in determining a response is the question of ownership or responsibility. It is unclear what role an MNC should take in solving an issue that is global in scale, but is not addressed by an equivalent global legislation or governance structure, such as the decline of fish stocks or climate change (see box, 'The paradox of global responsibility: where there's a will there's a way', page 63). Moreover, companies sometimes contribute only indirectly to such global problems; sometimes they are unwilling participants; sometimes they turn a blind eye; and sometimes they are actively and knowingly inflicting damage. They may be significant contributors to such problems on a global scale, although each individual operation contributes no more than its local competitors.

Likewise, at a local level, MNCs can at times be responsible for the problems, and at times simply be held responsible for solving them. The challenge at local level is made more complex because the company needs both to understand the local sustainable development priorities and to produce an appropriate response. A sustainable development solution that is appropriate in one country may simply not work in another. For example, employee diversity targets may be inappropriate in countries where working women are not a cultural norm. Similarly, different markets will have vastly differing sustainable development priorities. For example, obesity, ie too much food, may be an important issue for society in one market, while land tenure and failed harvests, ie not enough food, are the priority in another market.

Priorities for sustainable development in one country may thus be very different to those in another, and the appropriate approach to solving an identical issue may be different in different countries. The company needs to be able to encompass this local variety, while answering other pressures, often from government, consumers or civil society in its domestic market, for globally consistent standards.

An additional layer of complexity for an MNC is created by issues that are recurrent in several of its local operating companies, and so become a global priority for that company. For example, if a company operates in countries with high HIV/AIDS infection rates, this is likely to be a far higher priority than for a company operating in markets with low rates of infection.

Strategic responses from MNCs

The overall challenge faced by MNCs that choose to follow a sustainable development approach is to find a strategy that can accommodate responses to global, local and company-specific issues, while meeting the needs of many stakeholders.

At the global level, it may be appropriate to set and attempt to operate by international best practice, such as forbidding employees to make small bribes or 'facilitation payments'. At local level, sustainable development can be a great deal more complicated. For example, a company may have a global anti-corruption policy, and yet find it needs to make facilitation payments in order to carry out its normal business. It may be argued that the sustainable development good practice would be to stop making such payments, even if that meant withdrawing from the country in question. But what if the company's African operations had made a commitment to the local government to build a hospital as part of contract negotiations – and it later transpired that this could only be done if facilitation payments were made to the local police for providing 'security'? The company has to decide between its global standard, breaking a government contract and not building a badly needed hospital. Multiplying this dilemma by 20 different markets, each with its own regulations, cultural norms and languages, makes the challenge of implementing global standards even harder.

Increasingly, MNCs have contact with both local and international stakeholders, who may have very different expectations and demands of the company. The example of protected areas in the box, 'Extractive companies, biodiversity and protected areas: sustainable development means different things to different stakeholders', page 62, illustrates how local development needs, governed by local laws, may at times conflict with global conservation needs, governed by non-binding and sometimes vague international conventions, which are policed by powerful NGOs. Indeed, the emergence of genuinely global NGOs is a phenomenon that is a great challenge to MNCs. In some areas, global NGOs have filled the vacuum left by a lack of global regulation, and yet it can be extremely difficult for companies to enter a constructive dialogue with them, which may be unwilling to enter discussions with an MNC – particularly in certain high-impact sectors.

Faced with both local and global pressures, which may at times seem inconsistent, MNCs need a three-tier strategy for:

- assessing their global responsibilities and managing their global impact;
- ensuring that there is global consistency to their local approaches;
- ensuring their local approaches are appropriate.

Different business models require different sustainable development strategies

Companies are likely to follow a different approach to sustainable development depending on the sector and the business model they are pursuing. For example:

- Extractive companies may wish to implement global standards in areas such as health and safety because they are fundamentally sound business practice.
- Infrastructure development companies operating on a project-by-project basis may find that projects have common international characteristics because they are often designed according to internationally accepted and proven processes.
- The business model of a beverage company may demand global consistency in brand and quality; the product has identical ingredients in all markets and has the same branding and packaging, creating cost synergies and economies of scale. This might equip the company well for dealing with global issues, but makes it less good at adapting to local sustainable development challenges.
- A confectionery manufacturer may wish to penetrate a local market through providing a product that caters to that specific market; this company may be very good at adapting to local sustainable development challenges, but may find it hard to assess and manage its global sustainable development impacts.

In other words, there are several different types of MNC, and different sectors encounter different sustainable development challenges, even when operating in the same markets. A business that needs the support of the local community to operate – because it sells to the community, or because it is not safe to operate during periods of civil unrest – may be governed more by local sustainable development drivers than a business that is simply sourcing supplies from local companies and therefore may be driven more by attitudes of stakeholders in its end markets.

Similarly, the business model may dictate precisely how the company pursues a sustainable development approach. For example, some companies are highly centralized, a model that often lends itself to consistent global standards and addressing global sustainable development issues. Other companies are very decentralized, which can make them well adapted to understand and meet local challenges – but equally can cause local units to miss opportunities to learn of better practices from elsewhere in the group.

Which standards to follow?

An additional challenge for MNCs which decide to operate to a consistent standard is whose standard it should be. For example, when operating in ecologically sensitive areas (see box, 'Extractive companies, biodiversity and protected areas: sustainable development means different things to different stakeholders', page 62), a company could follow an industry standard, its home government standard, the IUCN and NGO standard or create its own standard based on the Convention on Biological Diversity.

In any individual market, there is a different set of standards problems. The company may operate in different governmental jurisdictions, each of which has different requirements – accounting, reporting, regulatory and so on. There may be cultural and societal norms, which may conflict with those of HQ. For example, a no-smoking office might be expected in the United States but controversial in Italy. Should the company impose a global corporate standard? Sometimes it probably should, such as in health and safety. At other times, it may be very unclear which standard to apply and whose rules to play by: local or headquarters, national or international, government standard or international best practice.

The challenge from unsustainable competitors

Importantly, companies will have competitors that take a very different approach to such issues. First, there may be local companies that operate to far lower standards, or appear to have different, usually more lax, regulations imposed by the local government. For example, labour standards may be considerably lower in a locally owned factory. The MNC needs to decide whether it should play by the local rules or potentially add cost by opting for a higher standard.

Second, there may be other MNC competitors that are domiciled in countries with very different standards. An example is the fact that US companies are governed by the very strict Foreign and Corrupt Practices Act (FCPA), while companies from many other countries do not suffer such restrictions when offering bribes. A second example is Chinese oil companies that have far lower health and safety standards, and a lower cost base, than Western majors.[3]

Key challenges

The sustainable development challenge faced by an MNC may be summarized in three fundamental questions:

- Is it in the interests of the business to follow a sustainable development approach?
- What does this mean in practice?
- How can this be implemented?

To some extent, these are only questions that companies need to face up to if they have decided that they want to carry out their businesses in a manner that is compatible with sustainable development. The key challenges for implementation are then fourfold:

- integrating global and local responsibilities and interpretations in a consistent and coherent process;
- establishing which standards to follow;
- facing competitors that operate to different standards;
- continuing to make a profit and generate value for shareholders.

It is easy to imagine that many companies are put off from following a sustainable development approach. The reasons why they may or may not choose to do so, as opposed to falling back on legal compliance or case-by-case sustainable development activities, are examined below.

HOW AND WHY DO COMPANIES RESPOND TO THESE CHALLENGES?

Three ways to address sustainable development

The ways in which companies respond to these challenges can be grouped into some basic approaches, of which managing risks and acting as a global citizen may be described as following a 'sustainable development approach':

- **Do not engage:** the company refuses or fails to engage with the sustainable development agenda, beyond operating to minimum legal requirements. This in itself may lead to sustainable development benefits, as a company may still, through legal or other compliance, operate to higher standards than would be the local norm. For example, EIA and EMS may be required to ensure compliance with regulatory standards and requirements of major customers. Alternatively, a company subject to US law may find that its contract negotiations are covered by the FCPA. Finally, there may be a financial incentive, ie reduced energy costs, to reduce GHG emissions.
- **Manage risks:** the company identifies specific social, environmental and ethical (SEE) risks that it faces, at either global or local levels, and develops responses in order to manage these specific risks. Activities and initiatives to address these specific risks may also help to address an underlying sustainable development issue. For example, a company operating in an area of high HIV/AIDS infection rates may design a programme to protect its employees and their families.
- **Act as a global citizen:** the company seeks to identify the role it can play in addressing broader sustainable development issues that are related to its business, as well as the specific SEE risks that have a clear business relevance, and then designs its business and risk management activities in line with this role. The company does not require each action to be directly linked to a specific business case, but takes the view that there is a broader business case that will benefit the company in the long term. Examples of issues in which this approach might be taken are:
  - Anti-corruption: an extractive company would support the EITI principles (see box, 'Payments transparency in the extractive sectors: same problem, different approaches', page 60) and proactively support the further development and implementation of this initiative through the company's influence on host governments and operating partners.
  - Climate change: a company would withdraw from anti-climate-change lobbies and realign lobbying efforts behind the support of the Kyoto Protocol and alternative technologies; it would support the development and implementation of carbon trading mechanisms and publish details of its own GHG reduction strategies and targets; it might invest significantly in renewable energy technologies.

What factors influence the approach a company takes?

At times, a company lacks the structure that enables it to evaluate, participate in and take advantage of sustainable development opportunities. Characteristically:

- a company may not realize that such an approach would be advantageous; or
- individuals may see the advantages but not be able to steer the company in that direction; or
- the company itself, ie senior managers and the board, may see the advantages, but not be able to interpret or implement their intentions.

Just as important as the structure is the company's personality or corporate culture. A company's mode of behaviour in any circumstance or on any project is likely to be conditioned by a number of factors including its history, its place of domicile, the nationality of its employees, the style of its leadership, and the sector within which it operates. For example, some companies are more aggressive, and some are more transparent, than others, and this may characterize a company's behaviour throughout its activities.

In the context of sustainable development, this means that a company's corporate culture or personality may determine its ability to identify where a sustainable development approach is necessary, or make the company unwilling to take that path even when other companies would consider it good business sense. An example of the different judgements that can be made based on the same set of facts is the EITI (see box, 'Payments transparency in the extractive sectors: same problem, different approaches', page 60).

What are the barriers to taking a sustainable development approach?

In addition to these intrinsic factors, which are largely within the company's power to change, there will be other barriers to following a sustainable development approach, even when a company has decided it wishes to do so. These may include:

- **Management:** barriers may be lack of management vision, or capacity, and management incentives that make it difficult for local managers who are driven by a bonus for completing a job on time to think of the long-term interests of the company in a global context.
- **Financial:** such as additional costs, the perception that there is no added shareholder value from any individual action, fear of competitive disadvantage, and the lack of obvious financial payback.
- **Complexity:** sustainable development is complex and at times it is difficult for companies to see where their self-interest lies or to identify where their interests overlap with sustainable development objectives. The examples of fisheries, climate change and protected areas demonstrate this (see boxes, 'Extractive

companies, biodiversity and protected areas: sustainable development means different things to different stakeholders' and 'The paradox of global responsibility: where there's a will there's a way', page 62).

- **Opposition:** some individuals and groups will try to block the company's sustainable development approach; this may be because they wish to block every aspect of a project they oppose, because they believe the approach is wrong, or because they mistrust the motives of any MNC seeking to be involved in sustainable development initiatives.

Which approach is most advantageous for an MNC?

The difficulty of managing both the intrinsic factors, such as personality, and external barriers may suggest that it is easier for a company to fall back on the minimum requirements for legal compliance rather than seek to take a broader sustainable development approach. This would limit a company's role strictly to that of economic actor, deliberately seeking to distance itself from the role of other players such as national and local government and civil society. In certain circumstances, this might work. The challenge for companies is to assess how likely it is that this approach will work. Companies also need to evaluate the benefits of taking a sustainable development approach, which may be long term and may accrue to the global company rather than any individual local operating company.

If a company fails to make the correct judgement, it can fail spectacularly, effectively becoming excluded from a given market. An example of this is Monsanto, which greatly scaled back its activities in the European market in 2003 after failing to anticipate the reaction of stakeholders to the issue of genetically modified crops.[4]

WHAT WOULD MOVE THE GOALPOSTS?

Some companies all the time, and other companies some of the time, will conclude that sustainable development objectives do not fit with their business interests. However, if a company has decided not to favour the sustainable development outcome, other stakeholders have the option to try and move the goalposts. The issue of access to medicines in developing countries (see box, 'Access to medicines – the benefits of predicting when goalposts will move', page 64) shows how the goalposts can be moved, sometimes substantially, unexpectedly and within a short time-frame.

Companies are only likely to change their strategies if there is self-interest. What, therefore, would move the goalposts so that a sustainable development approach is in companies' self-interest? Some potential routes to this are:

- **Regulation/government action:** for example, the action by the South African government over the 'access to medicines' issue cited above, and the UK government's Extractive Industries Transparency Initiative (see box, 'Payments transparency in the extractive sectors: same problem, different approaches', page 62).
- **Access to capital:** for example, the adoption of the Equator Principles for project finance, establishing environmental and social due diligence as a condition of lending.
- **Sectoral initiatives:** sometimes, sectors perceive long-term threats if they do not self-regulate and voluntarily change the criteria by which they operate. An example is the mining sector, whose MMSD project[5] has resulted in the creation of an industry body[6] that is 'dedicated to economic progress, environmental protection and social responsibility'.
- **Fiscal incentives:** fiscal subsidies, incentives and penalties are traditional means of altering behaviour, and can easily be applied to sustainable development. Two examples are the incentives that the UK government is offering to wind farm operators, and the cap on GHG emissions agreed under the Kyoto Protocol, which has led to emissions quotas and trading.
- **External pressure from other stakeholders:** for example, the decision by IUCN to declare protected area categories I–IV as no-go areas for extractive companies (see box, 'Extractive companies, biodiversity and protected areas: sustainable development means different things to different stakeholders', page 62) has strongly shaped the debate.

Although there are several potential early warning signs about how the goalposts may be about to move, such as research from fund managers specializing in socially responsible investment, speeches by government ministers and NGO campaigns, companies need a system to judge the likelihood and accuracy of these 'predictions'.

CONCLUSION

MNCs can play a legitimate role in sustainable development. This is best done when they carry out their normal business in a manner that is compatible with sustainable development objectives – the 'sustainable development approach'.

At first sight, there may appear to be many challenges, and even barriers, to following a sustainable development approach, although pressure is increasing for MNCs to do so. Companies that are able to identify the overlap between sustainable development objectives and their business interests, and adapt their strategies accordingly, may find that they are better able to anticipate, and to respond to, the constantly changing sustainable development agenda at both global and local level.

In the absence of global rules, global companies need to make up the rules as they go along. It may be hard for a company to judge when, and how, long-term or intangible benefits are sufficient to outweigh the lack of an immediate or short-term business case. MNCs may be tempted to do the minimum. However, it is evident that an increasing number of multinational companies are taking a broader, more far-sighted, global citizenship approach. This is not because they are corporate philanthropists. Rather, they have reached the conclusion that global citizenship represents the most effective means of long-term risk management.

PAYMENTS TRANSPARENCY IN THE EXTRACTIVE SECTORS: SAME PROBLEM, DIFFERENT APPROACHES

Oil, gas and mining companies increasingly find themselves operating in developing countries. They extract mineral resources worth many billions of pounds each year. However, many of the countries within which they operate do not benefit from the billions of pounds generated by their economies. Conversely, the mineral wealth often fuels corruption and civil unrest. Revenues are misappropriated by a small group of officials and government insiders, who then have a great interest in maintaining power, often by suppression and violence.

This well-documented phenomenon is known by economists as the 'resource curse'. The companies involved are often accused of complicity in corruption, promoting poor governance, and failing to invest in the host economy. Moreover, where the oil wealth contributes to civil wars, the operating conditions become less stable and more expensive.

However, companies rightly argue that they are making a contribution to the host nation. They are not on the whole paying bribes, but making legitimate payments in the form of taxes, royalties and signature bonuses, often worth hundreds of millions of dollars per year.

In other words, there is extensive investment that produces significant extractive wealth. But it is not matched by the social or environmental benefits.

Recently, there has been extensive external pressure on companies to resolve this issue. A coalition of NGOs, called Publish What You Pay (PWYP), has called on companies to make the size of their payments to governments a matter of public record. Meanwhile, a UK government-led initiative, the Extractive Industries Transparency Initiative (EITI), has been set up to encourage both companies and governments to sign up to transparency agreements. And over 50 global investors, representing US$6.9 trillion, have announced their support for the principle of payments transparency.

As a result of these pressures, 19 of the world's largest extractive companies have agreed to support the principles of payments transparency. However, they have done so with varying degrees of enthusiasm, taking one of five broad approaches:

- **Leaders:** companies that have tended to take a leadership approach to sustainable development. The leading companies in the initiative were all based in the UK – the leading government in the EITI process – and most had been subject to NGO campaigns on various issues over the past decade.
- **Acquiescers:** the majority of companies, which were content to give quiet support to the initiative, but did not wish to be leaders; they were often the medium-sized companies or those with a lesser track record in sustainable development initiatives. Some companies in this group changed from being opponents of the EITI to being supporters as the initiative gained ground and drew investor support.
- **Passive resisters:** companies that felt that their self-interest was not served by upsetting the status quo; they tended to argue that relationships with developing country governments over contracts are so sensitive that it is not sensible to challenge the rules set by host governments; but if any individual host government decided to require transparency over payments, of course the company would cooperate. These companies argued that they secure contracts and pay taxes legitimately and what governments do with the money is the concern of governments not companies. These companies' own home country governments were not giving strong support to the EITI.
- **Non-participants:** certain companies have simply refused to engage in the process. Typically, these are Chinese and Russian oil companies, and others from emerging markets, reflecting their home country governments' attitudes to payments transparency, and the fact that they are aggressive newcomers to the international arena wishing to secure contracts in competition with well-established developed country MNCs. They often have a poor track record on sustainable development in their own countries.
- **Opponents:** a small number of companies actively opposed the process, and seemed to attend meetings in order to water down proposals to the point where they would become innocuous. Some companies have moved from being opponents to passive resisters or acquiescers.

The EITI has been instructive in revealing the different attitudes and approaches taken by companies to a sustainable development objective, which would benefit all companies. In other words, the business case is broadly similar for all companies, but different companies perceive and approach the solution in different ways. Clear determinant factors have been company culture or personality, home government attitudes and NGO campaigns. It also highlights the fact that emerging markets MNCs, playing by different rules and with little respect for sustainable development, might drive standards lower across the sector.

EXTRACTIVE COMPANIES, BIODIVERSITY AND PROTECTED AREAS: SUSTAINABLE DEVELOPMENT MEANS DIFFERENT THINGS TO DIFFERENT STAKEHOLDERS

Multinational extractive companies often find that areas in which they wish to operate are in or near areas that have been designated for the protection of biodiversity. The great importance attached to these areas by the world community, combined with the economic, political and social importance of such projects to host countries and communities, exposes MNCs to a multitude of conflicting expectations and demands from stakeholders.

Stakeholders with conflicting demands include:

- National host government, local government and communities – possibly pitting a host government's international commitments to biodiversity against the need for national and regional economic development.
- Home government and international agencies – some home governments expect MNCs to follow international guidelines and conventions in order to receive financial backing such as export credits for projects – but the governments of competitor companies may not set such standards.
- International and local conservation NGOs – some NGOs accept careful development in protected areas in return for investment in biodiversity improvements elsewhere, while others reject such compromise. The World Conservation Union (IUCN) has passed a resolution calling for a ban on extractive companies operating in the protected areas designated as IUCN categories I–IV.

MNCs have responded differently to these conflicting demands. For example:

- ICMM members (large mining companies) have made a voluntary commitment not to operate in World Heritage Sites and are discussing their approach to other types of protected area.

- In the oil industry, one company has matched ICMM's stance, some are judging their projects case by case and others are leaving governments to decide.
- Few companies based in developing countries are addressing the issue at all.[7]

Although the debate about protected areas is itself complex, biodiversity issues also often attract international attention to projects taking place outside protected areas, calling into question the relative roles of government and MNCs in managing development and its secondary environmental and social impacts.

THE PARADOX OF GLOBAL RESPONSIBILITY: WHERE THERE'S A WILL THERE'S A WAY

The collapse of fish stocks and rapid climate change are two global problems to which MNCs contribute. MNCs can also contribute to solving the problems, and there can be a business case for some companies to do so because, if these problems are not solved, their businesses will suffer.

For example, a large fish processing company is likely to be contributing to the unsustainable depletion of fish stocks. It could purchase smaller quantities or lobby governments to have fish quotas reduced. It might do so because its long-term interest is that there should be abundant fish stocks in the future.

However, it is difficult for any individual company to contribute to solving the problem because:

- The problem falls outside the jurisdiction of any individual government so there is no clear framework for action.
- The technical solutions are difficult to find.
- If a single company seeks to reduce its contribution to the problem it finds itself at a competitive disadvantage – the classic 'tragedy of the commons', because it will bear the full cost of restraint but get none of the benefits.
- There is a 'weakest link effect' – a responsible company in an industry that is part of the problem may still bear the costs of poor performance by others.

Likewise, climate change is a global problem to which many companies are contributing. They are likely to be negatively affected by climate change in the future. Yet it is not in the short-term interests of any individual company to act unilaterally. For example, no major oil company has plans to transform itself into a renewable energy business.

The paradox of these issues is that, while the sustainable development outcome may be in the long-term interests of a company, legitimate short-term considerations make early or unilateral action self-destructive. However, there are some notable exceptions to this rule. For example:

- BP helped to kick-start the 1997 Kyoto discussions on climate change by becoming the first major oil company to acknowledge publicly that human-induced global warming exists and needs to be tackled.
- Unilever has made the commitment to buy all of its fish from sustainable sources by 2005.[8]

ACCESS TO MEDICINES – THE BENEFITS OF PREDICTING WHEN GOALPOSTS WILL MOVE

Until 2001, most pharmaceutical companies made the assessment that it was not in their business interests to sell their drugs to poor countries at a substantially lower price than in rich countries, or to offer voluntary licences to generic producers to manufacture cheap copies.

For the pharmaceutical companies, the business logic was impeccable. In order to invest in the next generation of drugs, on which their business relies, pharmaceutical companies need to charge prices sufficient to recoup the substantial costs of research and development involved in getting drugs to market. Differential pricing and voluntary licensing can lead to smuggling, which could undermine profits in home markets. Although there had been occasional cases of differential pricing, companies were also concerned that offering discount prices in the developing world would fuel already intense pressure for price cuts in home markets. And, after all, they were merely operating within the framework of international patent regulations, an unimpeachable global reference system.

From a sustainable development perspective, the decision by the pharmaceutical companies had negative consequences: people in developing countries were denied access to certain life-saving medicine, even though several companies had started up a donations programme.

Pressure on the pharmaceutical companies to change came from three directions. First, there was intensive lobbying by NGOs both in Europe and in developing countries. Second, investors – led by ISIS Asset Management and the Universities Superannuation Scheme – issued a joint statement to express their concerns, one of the earliest examples of a joint investor initiative on SEE issues. Third, developing country governments, and in particular South Africa, threatened to break the patent regulations and manufacture or import generic copies of the companies' drugs. This would have severely undermined the international patent system, the foundation on which the major pharmaceutical businesses are built.

Faced with a dramatically altered business environment, some companies have changed strategy and are taking steps to enhance access, through a combination of differential pricing, voluntary licensing and donations programmes. This will allow certain drugs to be made widely available in certain markets before patents would usually expire.

The change has required creative thinking to identify where the business interests overlap with the sustainable development imperatives, where previously there had appeared to be a watertight business case against such compromises. If some of the companies involved had identified earlier how a broader citizenship approach to the matter could be in their interests, they might have reached the same conclusion without the negative press and campaigns, while strengthening relationships with governments, health services and NGOs. In other words, through a broader analysis of the business case, companies could have set the agenda rather than reacting to the agenda of others.

Notes

1 Business in the Community and AD Little (2003) The business case for corporate responsibility, December.
2 Goldman Sachs (2004) Introducing the Goldman Sachs Energy, Environmental and Social Index, February.
3 Goldman Sachs (2004) Introducing the Goldman Sachs Energy, Environmental and Social Index, February.
4 Crops giant retreats from Europe ahead of GM report, *Independent*, 16 October 2003.
5 Breaking new ground: mining, minerals and sustainable development, Earthscan, 2002.
6 The International Council on Mining and Metals (ICMM), www.icmm.com.
7 Are extractive companies compatible with biodiversity?, ISIS Asset Management, February 2004.
8 www.unilever.com/Images/3_11034.pdf.

6

Corporate social responsibility – the investor's perspective

Dr Matthew J Kiernan, Chief Executive, Innovest Strategic Value Advisors

For the most part, the preceding chapters of this book have examined CSR from the corporate perspective; in this one we will shift gears and examine the phenomenon from the investor's vantage point.

Much has been written about the presence or absence of a robust, positive relationship between companies' environmental, social and ethical (ie CSR) performance on the one hand and their financial performance on the other.[1] I will argue in this chapter that the balance of available evidence strongly suggests that such a relationship does indeed exist. Even more important, there are compelling reasons to believe that this relationship will become even stronger over the next three or four years.

Historically, however, mainstream institutional investors have accepted unquestioningly the conventional industry 'wisdom' that excellent environmental and social performance could be achieved only at the cost of lower financial returns for both companies and investors. An important corollary of this argument held that, since environmental and social factors are at best irrelevant to the financial risk/return equation and, at worst, actually injurious to it, prudent fiduciaries are actually precluded from considering them. It turns out that both the conventional wisdom and its corollary are, quite simply, mistaken.

There is now incontrovertible evidence that superior environmental and social performance does in fact have direct impacts on the risk levels, profitability and share price performance of publicly traded companies.[2] Recent pension fund law reform in the UK, Continental Europe and Australia has implicitly recognized that fact; in those countries, fiduciaries are now obliged to report on their plans for incorporating environmental and social risk assessments into their investment strategies. The 'prudent fiduciary' equation is slowly but surely being turned on its head; increasingly, fiduciaries are being seen as derelict in their responsibilities if they do not ensure that environmental and social risks are addressed. This is starting to occur even in the United States, where mainstream institutional investors have heretofore remained largely hostile or indifferent to CSR/SRI. Baker & McKenzie, a prestigious US-headquartered law firm (which also happens to be the world's largest), has gone so far as to publish a report opining that US fiduciaries may be obligated to address CSR issues and risks.[3]

A LEGITIMATION CRISIS FOR TRADITIONAL INVESTMENT APPROACHES

The recent spate of high-profile corporate governance scandals has clearly been a major factor in propelling CSR issues to a more prominent place on the agenda for international investors. The sudden and spectacular implosions of Enron, WorldCom, Tyco, Parmalat and others have seriously – and quite possibly irrevocably – shaken investor confidence in the financial numbers generated by companies in the first place. Subsequent revelations about seriously conflicted (if not outright fraudulent) Wall Street research only exacerbated the problem by calling into question the quality and objectivity of what the analysts actually do with those numbers after they get them. Throw in the mutual fund late-trading scandals of 2003–04, and one has an environment positively ripe for the emergence of alternative, 'non-traditional' investment approaches.

In my own view, this widespread disenchantment is by no means an entirely bad thing; if nothing else, it has provided a powerful impetus for examining new, alternative approaches. It is at least arguable that, up to now, the biggest conceptual breakthrough in investment analysis occurred in the 15th century, with the invention of double-entry bookkeeping by the Italian monks. A bit of a rethink 500 years later would, I think, hardly be premature!

FOUNDATIONS MADE OF SAND

Let us face it: accounting-based numbers are the raw feedstock of virtually all investment analysis. The limitations of these traditional approaches, while little noticed until relatively recently, are both legion and extremely serious. One obvious flaw is that accounting numbers provide, at best, a static, retrospective, 'rear-view mirror' view of companies' finances and competitive positioning. A second failing is their extreme sensitivity to what might be politely termed some rather malleable accounting assumptions. Allow me to illustrate with an example. With a single changed assumption, the combined earnings of Intel, Cisco and Dell, for example, would have changed in an instant from a $4.4 billion profit to a loss of $1.4 billion for the first three quarters of 2002. The accounting assumption in question, which underpins the positive number, is that stock options should not be treated as a company expense. However, most accounting academics and even accounting standards boards now recommend that this practice be reversed. If one makes that one change, presto: the $1.4 billion loss figure becomes the 'real' one most relevant to investors. (This is not simply an academic point; such corporate stalwarts as Coca-Cola and General Motors have already made this particular accounting change.)

Another accounting device – the increasingly popular use of 'pro forma' accounting techniques – allowed the top 100 companies in the US NASDAQ stock exchange to show their investors a combined profit of $82 billion in 2001. Had the more conservative US GAAP (Generally Accepted Accounting Principles) been used instead, the companies would have shown a combined loss of $20 billion! If this level of precision is the best that the accountants and financial analysts can offer after five centuries of refining their craft, I would venture to say there is ample room to try new and different approaches!

But I have saved the most devastating critique for last. As recently as the mid-1980s, financial statements were capable of capturing 75–80 per cent of the true market value of major corporations. According to New York University accounting guru and business professor Baruch Lev, however, by the early 21st century that figure had dropped to less than 20 per cent on average.[4] This tectonic shift reflects the inexorable transformation of developed economies to the point where wealth is now created primarily by knowledge and other intangible assets, rather than by land, factories, physical labour or even finance capital. Intellectual capital has become the most important factor in creating wealth; ergo, identifying and managing it has become the single most important driver of competitive advantage and sustainable value creation. Yet accounting statements have almost no light to shed on these intangible value – and investment risk – drivers.

This leaves institutional investors and fiduciaries with a profound – and growing – information and analysis deficit. So what are strategic, forward-looking investors to do?

THE 'ICEBERG BALANCE SHEET' OF INTANGIBLE VALUE

As we move deeper and deeper into the era of knowledge value and intangibles, conventional balance sheets and profit and loss statements are capturing and reflecting

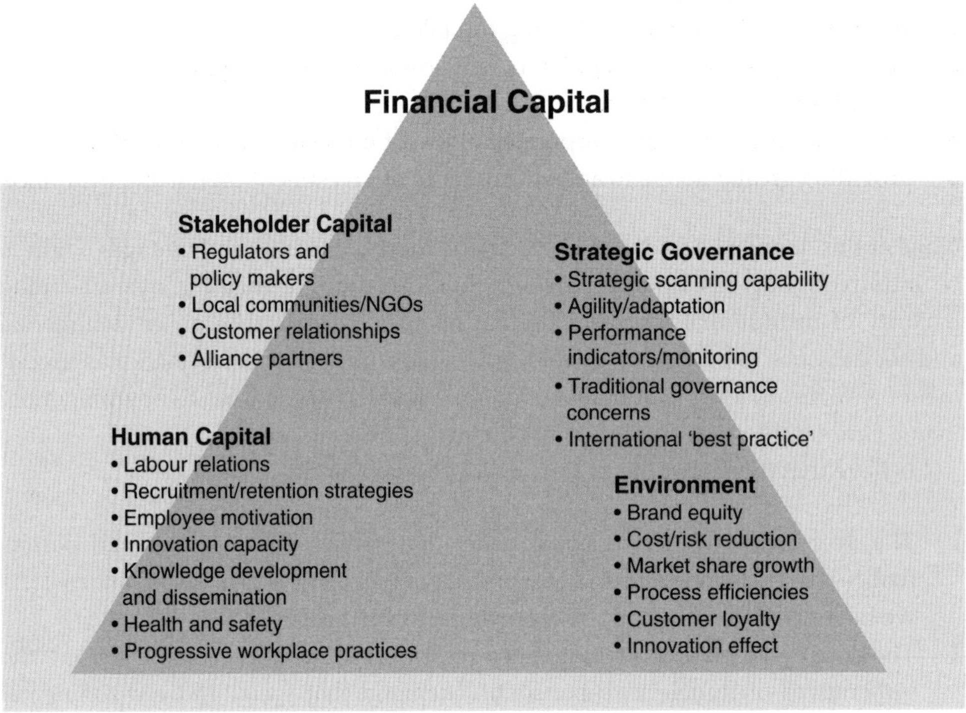

Financial Capital

Stakeholder Capital
• Regulators and
  policy makers
• Local communities/NGOs
• Customer relationships
• Alliance partners

Strategic Governance
• Strategic scanning capability
• Agility/adaptation
• Performance
  indicators/monitoring
• Traditional governance
  concerns
• International 'best practice'

Human Capital
• Labour relations
• Recruitment/retention strategies
• Employee motivation
• Innovation capacity
• Knowledge development
  and dissemination
• Health and safety
• Progressive workplace practices

Environment
• Brand equity
• Cost/risk reduction
• Market share growth
• Process efficiencies
• Customer loyalty
• Innovation effect

Figure 6.1 Key pillars of CSR

less and less of a company's true value, investment risk and competitive potential. What is needed instead is a new, more dynamic, 'iceberg balance sheet' approach, one that focuses investor and senior management attention where it properly belongs, on the roughly 80 per cent of companies' true value that cannot be explained by traditional, accounting-driven securities analysis: in short, one that provides a focus on leading indicators of performance, not trailing ones.

Increasingly, it is the unseen part of the value iceberg, that much larger portion below the surface, that contains the primary drivers of the company's future value creation capabilities and unique comparative advantages. Among the most potent of these intangible value drivers are four of the key pillars of CSR, shown in Figure 6.1.

From the companies' standpoint, managing these CSR drivers effectively can create competitive advantage, reinforce 'brand equity' and boost both profits and shareholder value by:

● generating top-line revenue growth through new products, services and communities and other key stakeholders;
● increasing customer – and investor – loyalty;
● reducing operating expenses, through measures such as improved energy efficiency and waste minimization;

- reducing the risk of legal liabilities and fines;
- attracting, retaining and motivating top talent;
- improving relations with regulators, governments, local suppliers, local communities and other key stakeholders;
- improving the company's corporate culture of innovation and adaptation;
- providing greater access to and affordability of investment capital and insurance.

None of this, it must be said, is rocket science; these competitive advantages ought to be intuitively obvious to a 10-year-old child. Yet despite this, the overwhelming majority of institutional investors find companies' performance on environmental and social issues to be virtually irrelevant to the companies' performance as investments. As a result, few major mainstream investors have seen them as anything more than a curious sideshow to the serious business of investment.

I believe that there are at least four major reasons for this:

1. The deep-seated (but erroneous) belief that social and environmental performance is at best irrelevant and at worst actually injurious to financial returns. (As we have seen, quite the opposite has in fact been proven true.)
2. The equally baseless view that, since returns are 'inevitably' compromised, the imperatives of fiduciary responsibility demand that social and environmental factors be set to one side when investment decisions are made.
3. The silent conspiracy of passive resistance by most pension fund consultants, key gatekeepers who are virtually unanimous in their indifference or even hostility to socially responsible investment (SRI). Unfortunately, few if any of SRI's critics have taken the trouble to test the veracity of their assertions, either through their own original research or by consulting the growing financial literature in this area.
4. The extraordinary deference of pension fund trustees themselves, who tend to be intimidated by their professional advisors, and to forget that the advisors and money managers work for them and not the other way around.

This situation is slowly beginning to change, however, at least in Europe.

Figure 6.2, taken from an authoritative study of European fund managers, analysts and investor relations officers in 2003, captures the growing awareness of intangible assets in Europe.

CSR: MAKING THE INVESTMENT CASE

As we have noted, there is a growing body of evidence in academic finance supporting the investment case for CSR.[5] These results are (to me, at least) entirely to be

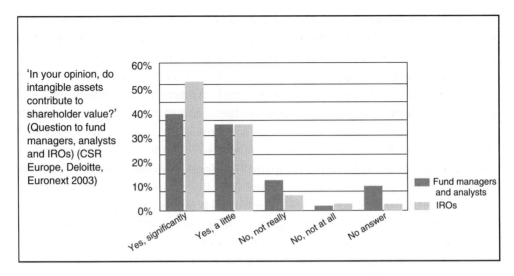

'In your opinion, do intangible assets contribute to shareholder value?' (Question to fund managers, analysts and IROs) (CSR Europe, Deloitte, Euronext 2003)

Figure 6.2 Intangible assets and shareholder value

expected; I would argue that companies' ability to manage the complex, ever-changing kaleidoscope of CSR issues provides an increasingly robust – but hereto-fore neglected – proxy for its management quality, period. And, as any City or Wall Street analyst will confirm, management quality is already viewed as the single most important determinant of companies' ultimate competitiveness and financial performance.

The case for using CSR performance as a proxy for management quality has been nicely summarized by Bill Parrett, CEO of the global accounting and management consulting giant Deloitte Touche Tohmatsu: 'In general, good performance in CSR is considered a key indicator to quality management. A strong reputation for CSR is seen as a binding agent for the intangible assets that deliver shareholder value such as people management skills, management quality, brands trust, product quality and emotional appeal, among other assets.'[6]

A recent report by the Association of British Insurers stresses CSR's potential contribution to yet another dimension of managerial competence – risk management:

> Risk aspects of corporate responsibility are as important as bottom line impacts. Companies need to incorporate these matters into strategic risk management, because they can have important implications for drivers such as brand value, market acceptability, human capital and new technology. Many companies are not yet managing these systematic risks adequately, posing threats to shareholder value, which investors need to take into account.[7]

Despite all this, however, mainstream institutional investors remain for the most part sceptical and unimpressed by the recent academic evidence linking CSR and financial out-performance. What they need to see is concrete investment results.

It must be acknowledged at the outset that any attempts to provide performance comparisons between 'socially responsible' and 'mainstream' investment funds are fraught with inherent methodological difficulties. Most of them stem from the multiplicity of different definitions of just what constitutes 'social responsibility'. Despite this, reasonably close 'apples-to-apples' comparisons can be made from examining data provided by the fund rating company Morningstar. Morningstar generates risk-adjusted performance comparisons among literally thousands of funds, grouped according to investment styles, capitalization levels and geographic focus. The most recent evidence suggests that, contrary to widespread belief, SRI funds are actually over-represented in the top risk-adjusted Morningstar performance categories.[8]

One interesting experiment currently under way in California takes these aggregated findings down to a much more granular, company-specific level. In early 2002, the Contra Costa County pension fund near San Francisco decided to conduct an experiment to see how CSR issues might affect the financial performance of their $2 billion investment portfolio. To do this, they first allocated approximately $150 million to a new, specially designed 'eco-enhanced' index fund created by Innovest Strategic Value Advisors. The fund tracks the Standard & Poor's 500 index fairly closely, but modestly overweights the top 'sustainability' or CSR performers and underweights the laggards. After its first year, the fund had out-performed its benchmark by 150 basis points (1.5 per cent), a strong result for a conservative, risk-controlled 'enhanced index' strategy.

At the same time, the Contra Costa County pension fund also launched what was perhaps an even more innovative initiative: it commissioned a live simulation study to test what would happen if a similar environmental and social tilt were added to their other six portfolios as well. So phantom portfolios were built on top of each of the six actual ones. Interestingly, and despite considerable variations in investment style, geographic focus and portfolio company size, the environmentally and socially enhanced simulation portfolios out-performed the underlying real portfolios in five out of six cases. The country's pensioners would have generated an extra $9 million for their retirement savings plans had these screens been used.[9] (In the case of the sixth portfolio, the strategy's high turnover would have made a sustainability investment strategy inappropriate in the first place.) Figure 6.3 summarizes the results of the study's first year. The bar on the far right-hand side represents the actual, CSR-enhanced portfolio, with an annualized out-performance of 1.5 per cent. Each of the other real portfolios received three levels of simulated tilt towards CSR factors – 0.5 per cent, 1 per cent and 2 per cent. Significantly, the greater the CSR tilt, the greater the financial out-performance margin.

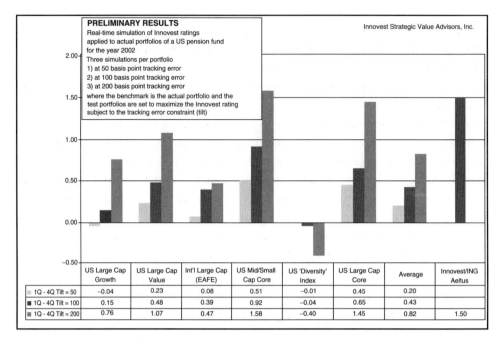

PRELIMINARY RESULTS
Real-time simulation of Innovest ratings
applied to actual portfolios of a US pension fund
for the year 2002
Three simulations per portfolio
1) at 50 basis point tracking error
2) at 100 basis point tracking error
3) at 200 basis point tracking error
where the benchmark is the actual portfolio and the
test portfolios are set to maximize the Innovest rating
subject to the tracking error constraint (tilt)

Innovest Strategic Value Advisors, Inc.

	US Large Cap Growth	US Large Cap Value	Int'l Large Cap (EAFE)	US Mid/Small Cap Core	US 'Diversity' Index	US Large Cap Core	Average	Innovest/ING Aeltus
1Q - 4Q Tilt = 50	−0.04	0.23	0.08	0.51	−0.01	0.45	0.20	
1Q - 4Q Tilt = 100	0.15	0.48	0.39	0.92	−0.04	0.65	0.43	
1Q - 4Q Tilt = 200	0.76	1.07	0.47	1.58	−0.40	1.45	0.82	1.50

Figure 6.3 Contra Costa County pension fund study: first year

As this book is being written, the Contra Costa live simulation is still continuing, and so is the financial out-performance. Buttressed by the out-performance of the real CSR-enhanced index portfolio, the simulation results are impressive, and have begun to attract interest from other public funds in the United States.

What makes the Contra Costa results particularly compelling is that they eviscerate one of the standard rebuttal arguments of the CSR investment sceptics in the mainstream investor community. Typically, any favourable financial results are dismissed as having nothing intrinsically to do with environmental or social performance issues. Instead, any out-performance margin is typically dismissed by investment professionals as attributable to the CSR portfolio's 'bets' on particular industry sectors, investment styles, company size, price/earnings ratios and so on.

In this case, however, those arguments are simply not germane. Why not? Because the simulation portfolios are identical in company composition to the underlying real portfolios. Not a single company has been added or subtracted; only the relative weightings of the companies have been changed – overweighting the top CSR performers and underweighting the laggards. If precisely the same companies are in both the real and the simulation portfolios, it becomes impossible to argue that differences in industry sector, size or traditional financial characteristics can explain the significant performance differentials.

Similar conclusions were reached in a sophisticated quantitative study conducted in 2003 by Dr Rob Bauer, head of research for ABP, the second-largest pension fund in the world.[10] As in the case of the Contra Costa study, Bauer's research took great pains to eliminate the impacts of each of the major investment factors that are traditionally used to explain out-performance. Taken together, these two studies provide perhaps the most compelling evidence to date that adding CSR performance factors can indeed generate investment out-performance.[11] Having said this, however, care must be taken not to over-generalize from these results. Just as there are far too many styles of equity investing to permit a sweeping conclusion that equity investing does or does not out-perform, there are too many flavours of CSR/SRI investing to draw any firm, generalized conclusions about that style either. The most that can be concluded from the Bauer and Contra Costa research – or indeed any other – is that the particular CSR definitions and algorithms used in those cases did indeed out-perform.

THE RISE OF 'FIDUCIARY CAPITALISM'

Social and environmental issues and corporate governance concerns have historically been viewed as entirely separate, and historically have had entirely different political constituencies. Today, the two agendas are converging rapidly. One of the principal drivers of that convergence has been the mounting empirical evidence that CSR issues are indeed financial ones and therefore entirely legitimate concerns for advocates of fiduciary responsibility and good corporate governance.

Institutional investors collectively now own over 60 per cent of the total outstanding equity of the world's largest 1,000 corporations. Their shareholdings have become so broad and diverse that they essentially represent a broad cross-section of the entire economy. As corporate governance pioneers Robert Monks and Nell Minnow have put it, big institutional investors have now become 'universal owners';[12] their concerns transcend the fates of individual companies and now include generic, economy-wide issues such as a well-educated workforce, environmental quality, strong social support programmes, improved company disclosure requirements and the like.

As a direct result of their status as universal owners, institutional investors have a fiduciary duty to minimize the potential adverse financial impacts of these cross-cutting CSR issues on their beneficiaries. Moreover, major institutional investors such as pension funds tend to have relatively long investment horizons; their pay-out obligations extend many years into the future. Moreover, their large size typically precludes them from selling significant holdings without disrupting the market, and a large portion of their assets are indexed to broad stock market indices in any case. Since as a practical matter they rarely sell their holdings, their increasingly preferred option for improving the financial performance of their portfolio companies is to express their views forcefully to company executives and directors as activist shareholders. In short, the large institutional investors have become 'fiduciary capitalists'.[13]

Increasingly, fiduciary capitalism is pursued collectively by institutional investors, which only amplifies their power and impact. One good example is the International Corporate Governance Network (ICGN), which brings together over 300 institutional investors, with combined assets of over $10 trillion. Among other activities, the ICGN is currently helping reformulate the OECD's corporate governance principles, which should be published in 2004.[14]

Another contemporary international illustration of fiduciary capitalism's impact on CSR issues is provided by an unprecedented collaboration among institutional investors called the Carbon Disclosure Project (CDP). Few major issues have been more effective in bridging the historic CSR/corporate governance divide than climate change, described by the leaders at the prestigious World Economic Forum in Davos as the most critical challenge confronting humanity at the beginning of the 21st century. Initiated in May 2002, the CDP currently brings together over 80 major institutional investors, with combined assets of over $9 trillion. For the second consecutive year, the CDP members have written formally to the chairman of the 500 largest publicly traded companies in the world, requesting investment-related information on the companies' risk exposure to climate change and their strategies for dealing with it. The responses – or lack thereof – promise to be illuminating.[15]

In some respects an even more remarkable development was the creation in late 2003 of the Investors Network on Climate Risk (INCR) in the United States. While smaller and less global in its membership than the CDP, the INCR is remarkable simply because it has emerged in the United States, long a bastion of mainstream institutional scepticism about CSR issues in general and climate change in particular. The INCR was launched at an unprecedented 'summit' held at the UN headquarters in New York City in late November 2003. Featuring UN Secretary-General Kofi Annan, former US Vice-President Al Gore and a bevy of both scientific and investment experts, the INCR may well represent a major sea-change in US institutional investor attitudes. Significantly, the summit also included over a dozen US state treasurers, fiduciaries of over $1 trillion in public pension assets.[16]

THE WAY FORWARD

As we have seen, there is now compelling evidence from a wide variety of sources that superior CSR performance is already helping generate financial out-performance for both companies and investors. What is in fact even more important is that both the risks and the rewards of companies' CSR performance and positioning are about to get even larger. At least eight powerful global megatrends are already at work to increase the 'CSR premium' (or risk) even further:

1. Growing empirical evidence of the nexus between companies' performance on environmental, social and governance issues and their competitiveness, profitability and share price performance.
2. Tightening national, regional and global regulatory requirements for stronger company performance and disclosure of non-traditional business and investment risks.
3. Changing demographics for both consumers and investors, substantially increasing the saliency and financial stakes of companies' environmental, social and governance performance.
4. The globalization and intensification of both industrial competition and institutional investment, particularly into emerging markets. This exponentially increases the level of risk both for major corporations and for investors from these new, non-traditional factors.
5. Growing pressures from international non-governmental organizations (NGOs), armed with unprecedented resources, credibility, access to company data and global communications capabilities.
6. A substantial broadening of the purview of what is considered to be legitimate fiduciary responsibility to include companies' performance in these areas.
7. The emergence of fiduciary capitalism: the growing inclination – and capability – among major institutional investors for shareholder activism in the governance of their portfolio companies on these issues. Climate change, for example, has now become the fastest-growing category of shareholder resolutions in the United States.
8. As a direct result of the foregoing seven megatrends, a growing appreciation by senior corporate executives of the competitive and financial risks and benefits of CSR factors.

Each of these megatrends is powerful enough to expand the CSR premium all by itself. Taken together, they form a virtually irresistible force that seems certain to shape the investment landscape for at least the next decade. The arguments for corporate social responsibility thus begin to move well beyond the roughly 1–2 per cent of the global capital markets currently driven explicitly by socially responsible considerations. Companies' environmental and social performance is gaining more and more traction with the other 98–99 per cent – the mainstream institutional investor. What we are currently witnessing, therefore, is the beginnings of a tectonic shift – the transmutation of CSR considerations from a marginal, vertical niche position to a much broader, horizontal analytical overlay brought to bear across the full spectrum of the mainstream capital markets.

Now we can finally begin to talk seriously about the capital markets playing a significant role in accelerating corporate behaviour and strategy towards a more progressive and responsible trajectory. And it will not be before time.

Notes

1. For an excellent synthesis of this academic – and practitioner – debate, see Peter Camejo (ed) (2002) *The SRI Advantage*, New Society Publishers.
2. See, for example, Roger Cowe (2004) *Risk, Returns, and Responsibility*, Association of British Insurers; Rob Bauer *et al* (2003) *The Eco-Efficiency Premium in the U.S. Equity Market*; (2002) *International Evidence on Ethical Mutual Fund Performance and Investment Style*; West LB Panmure (2002) *More Gain than Pain: SRI sustainability pays off*; Forum for the Future (2002) *Sustainability Pays*; UBS Warburg (2001) *Sustainability Investment: The merits of socially responsible investing*; Bank Sarasin (1999) *Sustainable Investments*; (1998) *Environmental Shareholder Value*; European Federation of Financial Analysts (1996) *Sustainability and Financial Analysis*.
3. Valerie Gibson *et al* (2000) *Overview of Social Investments and Fiduciary Responsibility*, Baker & McKenzie.
4. Baruch Lev (2001) *Intangibles: Management, measurement and reporting*, Brookings Institution, Washington, DC.
5. See note 2.
6. Quoted in World Economic Forum (2004) *Values and Value: Communicating the strategic importance of corporate citizenship to investors*, p 23.
7. Roger Cowe (2004) *Risk, Returns, and Responsibility*, Association of British Insurers.
8. See former Morningstar analyst Jon Hale (2002) Seeing stars: socially responsible mutual fund performance, in *The SRI Advantage*, ed Peter Camejo, New Society Publishers.
9. It is perhaps no coincidence that, shortly thereafter, California State Treasurer Phil Angelides began musing publicly about the merits of using environmental screening on the investment portfolios of two of the largest pension funds in the country, on whose boards he sits. Their combined assets are over $250 billion. See *Wall Street Journal*, 25 November 2003.
10. Rob Bauer *et al* (2003) *The Eco-Efficiency Premium in the U.S. Equity Market*.
11. In both studies, the authors used CSR algorithms developed by Innovest Strategic Value Advisors, a specialized international investment research firm.
12. Robert Monks and Nell Minnow (eds) (2001) *Corporate Governance*, Blackwell, Oxford.
13. James Hawley and Andres Williams (2000) *Fiduciary Capitalism*, University of Pennsylvania Press.
14. See www.icgn.org.
15. See www.cdproject.net.
16. See www.incr.com.

7

Managing the interests of stakeholders – an investor relations challenge: socially responsible investors – the new stakeholder challenge

Robert Barrington, Director of Governance and Socially Responsible Investment, ISIS Asset Management

ETHICALLY SCREENED FUNDS AND SEE ENGAGEMENT

Historically, socially responsible investment has been associated with ethically screened funds. These funds, such as the Friends Provident Stewardship range managed by ISIS Asset Management – the oldest retail ethical funds in the UK – construct portfolios that exclude companies based on ethical criteria such as tobacco and defence. In terms of investment return, the best of these ethical funds have performed surprisingly well, given that their risk profile tends to be higher due to the exclusions. They have grown to represent £4.2 billion of investment.[1]

However, from the perspective of being an active shareholder, the ethically screened funds are less of a success as, if investors do not hold shares in a company, they cannot influence it. On the other hand, investors who do hold shares in a company can have a very great influence. Indeed, such influence is apparently on the increase. The past year has seen a significant rise in the intervention of investors over governance issues such as the structure of the board and directors' remuneration.

Just as ethically screened funds grew during the 1980s and 1990s, the new millennium has seen a new investment philosophy enter the arena of socially responsible investment (SRI). This is variously described as 'engagement' and 'SEE risk management'. The principles behind this are threefold:

1. As a company's shareholder, the investor has both a right and a duty to engage the company in active dialogue about its management strategy and performance. This has been reinforced by the Combined Code, recently supplemented by the Higgs Report.[2]
2. A legitimate area of such engagement is risk management. This was the premise of the Turnbull Report.[3]
3. Such risks include both financial and non-financial factors, the latter including social, environmental or ethical (SEE) risks. This has been given a strong impetus by the ABI Guidelines.[4]

The combination of these codes and regulations means that, in the new millennium, shareholders engage in active dialogue with the management of companies over their management of SEE risks.

WHAT ARE SEE RISKS?

This, of course, raises the important issue of what constitute SEE risks. While it is often very clear what social, environmental and ethical issues are current in the press and wider society, it is not always the case that those issues represent risks to a business. Moreover, some issues will present risks to some companies but not others. For example, human rights are likely to be of less relevance to companies operating solely within Europe, where states possess and implement extensive legislation on human rights, than to companies operating in Burma.

Investors need to analyse SEE issues in the light of 'materiality' – that is, the extent to which the management or mismanagement of an issue may have a financial impact on the companies in which they are shareholders. The debate about risks and materiality is extremely lively within the investment community. The picture is made more complicated by the fact that a risk may only become material over the long term. Climate change, for example, has been identified for several years by SRI analysts as a potentially material risk, but it is only recently, with the introduction of the EU's Emissions Trading Scheme following the Kyoto Protocol, that climate change has started to affect companies' bottom lines directly.

Faced with this discussion over long-term materiality, SRI analysts often make the case that companies that move first to understand and address such risks are better placed to respond when they do become material. It is likely that the discussion over what constitutes materiality will become much clearer when the UK government publishes its guidelines for the operating and financial review (OFR) during 2004. The OFR is likely to suggest that companies should report annually on the material risks faced by the business and that the concept of materiality should be widely drawn.

WHO ARE THE PRACTITIONERS?

Another debate prevalent in the SRI community is whether the purpose of analysing companies' SEE risks is to decide which companies to invest in, or to protect the value of an existing investment by ensuring that SEE risks are well managed. In general, the trend seems to be that it is rare for SEE issues to be so material that they single-handedly inform a buy–sell decision on a particular stock. An example where this is the case might be an oil company with extremely poor management of health and safety systems. On the other hand, there are many examples in which the potential materiality is long term, and shareholders view it as in their interests to engage the companies in which they are invested, in order to make sure the risks are addressed.

This means that some investment houses have formed specialist 'engagement' teams, which have expertise both in the issues concerned and in developing the kind of dialogue necessary with companies to achieve change. The largest of these teams in the City is the 12-person GSRI (governance and socially responsible investment) team at ISIS Asset Management. There are seven such teams in investment houses in the UK, with several other houses having 'lone practitioners'. However, all large investment houses have one or more individuals who specialize in corporate governance and, increasingly, these governance experts are broadening their remit to include SRI issues. The Responsible Investors' Network is a forum for SRI discussion and debate within the City, which meets every two months and has around 30 regular attendees representing the governance and SRI communities.

ELEMENTS OF A SUCCESSFUL ENGAGEMENT?

Even when there appears to be a good business case for a company to manage an SEE risk differently or just better, the company does not always respond positively. One thing that experience has taught the GSRI professional is that helping to facilitate change at the corporate level is a 'slow burn' process.

It can take several years to build the dialogue with a company, develop a business case and effect change. Two key elements that are common to successful engagement are that the approach should be constructive and that it should be based on sound research and analysis. If SRI engagement is working well, it should be because the interests of shareholders and management are identical – that the company should be financially successful. The investor may need to develop or demonstrate the materiality or business case to the company, and this must be based on good understanding of the issues. Because there is a common interest, the constructive approach is usually the most effective. The most successful engagement is not carried out through the pages of the media or publicly naming and shaming companies that are not operating to good SEE standards, although such methods can be a last resort, as can filing shareholding resolutions or voting against management.

There are three broad types of approach, illustrated by the case studies below. First, a group of investors might lend their combined influence to a specific proposal or objective. Examples here include the Equator Principles and the Extractive Industries Transparency Initiative.

THE EQUATOR PRINCIPLES

The Equator Principles was an ambitious new project finance initiative announced at the start of 2003 by international banks Citigroup, Barclays Bank, ABN AMRO and West LB. It was aimed at raising the standard of social and environmental risk assessment in project finance. Reportedly, the banks provided financing for $14.5 billion of projects including oil pipelines, dams and power stations in 2002, accounting for around 30 per cent of all such projects globally.

The 'Equator Principles', which relied heavily upon the International Finance Corporation and World Bank Standards, would require signatories to carry out more stringent due diligence based upon the level of social and environmental project risk, putting such principles at the heart of the funding process by integrating them into loan covenants.

ISIS, along with other dialogue partners, was invited to provide early feedback on a draft version of the principles in a detailed meeting with representatives from Citigroup. Although 6 European banks were already close to signing the principles, ISIS went on to write to a further 11 major European banks to invite their participation in the consultation process. This succeeded in bringing both the HVB Group and Credit Suisse Group to the table in time to be among the 10 initial signatories when the scheme was eventually launched in June 2003.

On 4 June 2003, the *Wall Street Journal* reported:

The banks 'believe this will lead to more secure investments on the part of our customers and safer loans on the part of the banks,' said Chris Beale, head of Citigroup's global project-finance business. 'Because if you finance something that's dirty or something that harms people, there's a likelihood that the host government or local people will interfere with it or even take it away from you.'

THE INVESTORS' STATEMENT ON TRANSPARENCY IN THE EXTRACTIVES SECTOR

On this occasion, ISIS enlisted the support of 58 other investors worldwide, representing $6.9 trillion, to endorse a joint statement supporting the Extractive Industries Transparency Initiative (EITI). The Investors' Statement calls on global extractive companies to play an active role in the EITI, which seeks to bring companies and governments together to make payments from companies to governments public knowledge.

The investors are concerned that legitimate payments by companies to governments – such as taxes, royalties and signature bonuses – can, through their large size and confidential nature, be open to misuse. This can fuel corruption, poverty and conflict in developing countries, which in turn create unstable and high-cost operating environments for multinational companies. The statement notes: 'This is a significant business risk, making companies vulnerable to accusations of complicity in corrupt behaviour, impairing their local and global "licence to operate", rendering them vulnerable to local conflict and insecurity, and possibly compromising their long-term commercial prospects in these markets.'

While significant companies such as Anglo-American, BHP-Billiton, BP, Rio Tinto and Shell were already on record as supporting the principle of payments transparency, the EITI process, in conjunction with the Investors' Statement and continued engagement from ISIS, has now encouraged a total of 19 major extractive companies to declare their support. Importantly, this has been followed by the Nigerian government's decision to implement the EITI's principles in active partnership with Shell, ChevronTexaco, Total and other companies supporting the EITI.

Second, a single investor may identify a trend or SEE risk that affects one or more sectors, and engage with a selection of the companies within that sector, usually selected by the size of shareholding (ie the risk exposure to the shareholder). A good example of this is the ISIS palm oil study.

BIODIVERSITY AND THE PALM OIL INDUSTRY

In 2003, ISIS published the results of its survey of palm oil use and supply chain management in its report, 'New risks in old supply chains: where does your palm oil come from?'

Background: Palm oil production has doubled in the last 10 years and is expected to do so again within the next 20 years. However, palm oil plantations have been blamed for the destruction of rainforests and for the increasing pressure placed upon indigenous communities – especially in the likes of Malaysia and Indonesia where the majority of world supplies are ultimately sourced. Palm oil derivatives are widely used in products such as margarine, mayonnaise, crisps and pastry as well as cosmetics, soaps and detergents.

Initial action: ISIS engaged with 27 investee companies considered likely to be significant users of palm oil. The results of a survey that was included in the process revealed that many companies did not know where their palm oil comes from, how it is grown or even how much they use.

Subsequent activity: ISIS's research highlighted the potential risk of investing in companies that were ignorant of their supply chains in an area subject to increasing public scrutiny. It therefore issued the following four recommendations to investee companies:

1. Companies should ensure that practices in relation to palm oil sourcing meet their published quality, supply chain or sustainable development policies.
2. Companies should undertake an adequate assessment of the volumes of palm oil or palm oil derivatives they use to see if these are significant.
3. Significant users, or those in sectors likely to face consumer pressure, should ensure they have adequate supply chain monitoring systems in place.
4. All user companies should influence quality and production standards by participating in collaborative industry initiatives on the topic.

Results to date: ISIS has played an important role in highlighting this issue to companies. Accordingly, 21 per cent of companies contacted by ISIS now report they are developing supply chain policies specifically relating to palm oil.

Third, a single investor may identify a specific risk within a specific company and engage the company on that issue. Wal-Mart is an example here.

WAL-MART AND NON-DISCRIMINATION

With its two-year dialogue with US retailing Goliath Wal-Mart, ISIS Asset Management demonstrated how persistence can turn an apparent impasse into a breakthrough. Although the company had previously considered ISIS's requests to enhance its non-discrimination policies, the move had been rejected.

However, following continued engagement by ISIS, in 2003 the company announced it planned immediate action to prohibit discrimination in hiring, firing and promotion based upon sexual orientation. As a result, the company now includes sexual orientation in its equal opportunities policy.

The timeline for the engagement illustrates the kind of concerted effort required to change the practices of such enormous enterprises:

- January 2001 – ISIS writes to Wal-Mart raising concerns as to competitive disadvantage from weak non-discrimination policy. ISIS encourages the company to meet with investors while other investors submit a joint letter.
- September 2001 – ISIS meets with Wal-Mart at Bentonville, Arkansas headquarters along with Trillium Asset Management, Walden Asset Management and the Pride Foundation to make presentations on emerging business standards and the need for enhanced protection of homosexual employees.
- Autumn 2001 – The follow-up includes additional investor information.
- January 2002 – Investors meet with Wal-Mart to discuss the issue internally.
- March 2002 – Wal-Mart executive committee rejects changes to employment policies, believing that the existing culture of 'respect for the individual' was sufficient.
- April 2002 – Strongly worded objection letter from investors.
- May 2002 – Continued investor pressure for disclosure on related areas.
- August 2002 – Wal-Mart provides parts of the information requested.
- August 2002 – Investors opt against a shareholder resolution for the 2003 season.
- March 2003 – Investors send Wal-Mart new studies showing the extent of take-up by similar companies and rising shareholder votes in favour of such policies. Investors threaten to file a shareholder resolution for 2004 if no progress is achieved.
- June 2003 – Letter from Wal-Mart to shareholders stating its intention to amend its non-discrimination and harassment policies.

An inevitable question about successful engagements is how success is measured. Initially, SRI teams have focused on process measurements, such as the numbers of companies the investment team has met. However, both clients and the management committees of investment houses are beginning to look for harder evidence.

If an investor starts an engagement dialogue with very clear and specific objectives, success becomes easier to prove at one level: it is that the company does what the investor has asked. However, at a deeper level, the question is then whether this has genuinely affected the value of the company or share price, either in the short or long term. In these terms, success is extremely difficult to measure – just as, from the mirror perspective, it is often difficult for companies to demonstrate the shareholder value in corporate social responsibility (CSR) programmes.

HOW DO COMPANIES RESPOND?

Companies respond to engagement from the SRI community in different ways. The responses usually echo a company's corporate culture and reflect a similar approach to transparency and dialogue as that characterized by its communication with financial analysts.

Among the FTSE 100, investor relations departments are very used to requests from investment houses with SRI departments to meet and discuss SEE issues. A small number of companies refuse such meetings and seem to suspect that SRI analysts are seeking information that may encourage fund managers to 're-rate' the company or sell the stock. This represents a failure of communication from the SRI community – or a failure in understanding by investor relations professionals. The message from the SRI community should be: there is nothing to fear, and indeed there is a common interest in company and investor seeking to ensure that SEE risks are fully identified and well managed.

Some of the larger companies, such as BP, have appointed individuals within the corporate communications function who are specifically designated as a 'clearing house' for SRI dialogue. BP is an unusually open and transparent company, and channelling SRI interest through this mechanism does not close off debate. BP and other companies that have made a feature of transparency are willing to introduce SRI analysts to their project staff and discuss issues in detail, usually in the presence of a representative from the investor relations department. There is also an increasing number of FTSE 350 companies that no longer include their investor relations departments in this dialogue, or do so for an initial meeting but not thereafter.

The most negative response from companies is therefore to refuse to engage. Companies are more likely to take this approach if the shareholder involved has only a small stake in the company. It is perhaps no coincidence that the increasing receptiveness of companies has gone hand in hand with several large mainstream investors, such as ISIS Asset Management and Morley Fund Management, extending SEE analysis and engagement over their full equity portfolios. However, most companies respond positively, albeit cautiously at times when they are not sure in what direction the debate is heading.

The most enthusiastic responses are found when a company has already identified an issue, is starting to tackle it and wishes to benchmark its performance against others. SRI analysts are extremely well placed to help companies do this, as they are able to build up an in-depth knowledge of many companies over a wide range of sectors.

The response that SRI analysts are seeking is that companies that manage SEE risks badly or not at all should improve their practices. Investment houses differ as to whether they are encouraging 'best practice' or 'good practice'. The argument in favour of promoting good practice is that not all companies need to be perfect, but they need to be good enough to mitigate their SEE risks. In other words, the SRI challenge from a risk management perspective is to make the poor good, not the good better. In assessing whether this has been achieved, and to communicate clearly to companies what the expectations are, it is important to have very clear objectives.

The current detailed objectives used by ISIS Asset Management are listed in the box below.

MANAGING PRIORITIES

Engagement priorities for ISIS Asset Management

ISIS is one of the City's top 10 active asset managers with £63.5 billion of funds under management as at 31 December 2003. It applies its responsible engagement overlay (reo) approach to all the companies in which it invests. Each theme identified for engagement is backed by detailed research to set engagement objectives, examine the issue of materiality and lay out an appropriate business case.

The areas in which ISIS operates engagement, and the specific objectives set for each engagement activity, are set out below.

Governance objectives

- **Corporate governance**:
  Ensure high standards of corporate governance in line with ISIS Corporate Governance Guidelines with a focus on:
  – board structure and composition;
  – remuneration.
  Aim to issue voting instructions on 100 per cent of shares held.

- **Bribery and corruption**:
  Ensure effective anti-bribery and corruption policies and systems are in place with a specific focus on:
  - payments transparency – encourage extractive companies to support the EITI and other initiatives;
  - whistle-blowing – ensure effective and appropriate whistle-blowing procedures are in place;
  - UN Global Compact – encourage adoption of the 10th principle of the UN Global Compact.

- **Transparency and performance:**
  Encourage adherence to ISIS corporate social responsibility governance (CSRG) policies with a focus on:
  - board responsibility and effective structures to exercise this responsibility;
  - formal policies on all significant CSR issues;
  - management and monitoring systems for implementation of CSR policies;
  - public reporting and disclosure.

Environmental objectives

- **Biodiversity management:**
  Encourage all companies to adopt a policy and define and implement a process for managing biodiversity impacts.
- **Sustainable forestry:**
  Encourage legal and sustainable timber sourcing to include target setting for independently certified timber.
- **Palm oil:**
  Encourage relevant companies to adopt ISIS recommendations on sustainable palm oil sourcing.
- **Environmental management:**
  Ensure key environmental risks are identified and incorporated into an environmental management system.
- **Climate change:**
  Encourage public reporting of GHG emissions and for high-impact companies to publish their climate change strategies.

Social objectives

- **Labour standards:**
  Encourage good practice in the workplace including non-discrimination codes and the disclosure of diversity data.

Encourage a code of conduct on labour standards and working conditions (based on ILO Core Conventions).

Develop a formal management system to ensure compliance with the code and undertake audits of compliance.

- **Human rights:**

Encourage implementation of policy based on Universal Declaration of Human Rights (UDHR).

Encourage HIV/AIDS management strategy and undertake assessment of global impact on business.

Ensure Burma-based companies recognize and manage the risks to their business from operating there.

Encourage extractive companies to adopt human rights risk management.

Encourage companies to improve performance on access to medicines in line with the ISIS best practice framework.

Specific sector objectives

- **Financial sector:**

Encourage integration of social and environmental credit risk assessments in lending decisions with a specific focus on:

– adoption and implementation of Equator Principles for project finance;

– adoption of ISIS good practice recommendations on ECRA.

- **Information, communication and technology sector:**

Encourage practice in line with ISIS guidelines on labour standards in the supply chain and waste management.

It is also worth noting that many companies still seem confused as to the difference between ethically screened funds and the broader role of SRI 'engagement' analysts. Such confusion is natural. Within the world of ethically screened funds, a company's transparency and performance can genuinely mean the difference between a buy and sell decision. By contrast, SRI engagement analysts, as outlined above, at present seldom directly influence the investment process, as it is neither their role nor objective to do so. Notwithstanding this, some companies specifically seek eligibility for screened funds. This can act as an external endorsement for a company's CSR performance. For companies in certain sectors, this can sometimes result in additional access to capital.

HOW EFFECTIVE IS IT? CASE STUDIES OF SUCCESSFUL ENGAGEMENT BY INVESTORS

GLAXOSMITHKLINE AND DIRECTORS' REMUNERATION

In the autumn of 2002, GlaxoSmithKline (GSK) widened its consultation on proposals to raise the remuneration of Chief Executive JP Garnier. However, investor concerns as to board structure and wider remuneration issues meant that the proposal was hardly welcomed by investors.

Prior to GSK's annual general meeting, ISIS had met with GSK Chairman Sir Christopher Hogg to discuss a wide range of issues. While useful, the discussions came too late to allow agreement to be reached and ISIS, along with the majority of shareholders, voted against the directors' remuneration proposals.

While the structure of the board and the make-up of the remuneration committee had initially attracted stakeholder ire, other concerns such as the length of executive directors' contracts, the differences between the structure of GSK's long-term incentive packages and industry best practice and the fact that targets were seen as too soft also attracted shareholder censure as did the pensionable bonus and ex gratia payments made to a former executive. At the time, the company gave an undertaking to consult with investors and incorporate their views into the new remuneration policy.

There followed meetings with both Sir Christopher Hogg and John McArthur, the chairman of GSK's remuneration committee, where all such investor concerns were properly aired. Later, prior to the amended remuneration policy going before the board, ISIS was invited along with a small number of other institutions to discuss the changes made. Once board approval had been given, the company announced the change of policy in December 2002.

GSK has now started to restructure its board and remuneration committee. Directors' contracts have been reduced to 12 months without compensation while ex gratia payments are no longer made without prior shareholder approval. The company has also equalized the pension position across the company.

Exceptional rewards are still attainable through the company's incentive scheme but now are linked directly to exceptional performance. Such performance targets are now reviewed annually and take account of industry expectations for profit growth.

Even so, concerns remain over flexibility and the possible outcome of the model chosen to inform target pay levels, meaning that ISIS will continue to consult with the company until such issues have been resolved and investor confidence in the company's internal structures has once more been restored.

CONCERNED INVESTORS REJECT ITV'S 'GREEN' POLICY

An exceptional example of shareholder venom was witnessed in the early stages of 2003's planned merger between the Carlton and Granada television networks. ITV plc, the company formed by the deal, singularly ignored the concerns of shareholders and put forward the existing principal directors from the two companies as CEO and chairman respectively.

Such blatant 'high-handedness' on the part of the company attracted unprecedented shareholder outrage. ISIS, like several other major investors in the two groups, joined the largest single investor – in this case Fidelity – to invite the company seriously to rethink its approach or face the imminent defeat of any such proposals.

An overnight – and very public – reversal of the board's support for Carlton CEO Michael Green saw him quickly depart from the stage with Sir Brian Pitman now taking up the role in accordance with shareholder wishes.

CORPORATE GOVERNANCE: THE MOST VISIBLE SIGN OF SHAREHOLDER ACTIVISM

Good corporate governance centres on encouraging 'joined-up thinking' by corporate boards. This ensures that they are accountable for the delivery of management structures that include all significant business risks, whether from their finance functions, their corporate social responsibility programmes or their statutory environmental exposures. Effective engagement with companies to encourage best practice in governance and CSR issues requires a great deal of informal contact, not just the exercise of company votes.

Still, as a global investor, ISIS votes in line with its policy on a worldwide basis. Where matters of particular concern might arise, every attempt is made to contact the management involved and discuss the particulars. On occasions where such talks prove fruitless, ISIS may then exercise the influence of its voting rights by choosing to abstain from a given company vote or even, on occasion, voting against the resolutions in question.

In the same way that ISIS publishes the details of all of its corporate engagement activities across the globe in its quarterly Responsible Engagement Overlay (reo®) report, the company also publishes the results of all of its voting activity online at www.isisam.com.

The scale of this activity demonstrates what it means to be an active shareholder. In 2003, for example, ISIS voted on 15,253 resolutions. In 11 per cent of cases, ISIS voted against the company's management – and in each case wrote to the company concerned explaining the rationale for voting in this way. In other words, solely exercising 100 per cent of voting rights for a major shareholder is a significant exercise in itself.

Above and beyond this is the dialogue and engagement that takes place to persuade a company to change or modify its position. As with engagement on SEE issues, this tends to be more fruitful than simply voting against management, as it is seldom that shareholder resolutions gain enough support to force a company's management to act. Indeed, in the USA, shareholder resolutions are advisory and not binding. However, investors in the USA have a tradition of filing resolutions as company management has a tradition of not entering into dialogue unless a resolution has been filed. Consequently, dialogue-focused engagement strategies are far less developed than those employed by their European peers and instead tend to be more confrontational in nature.

The net result of this activity is that shareholders can have a very significant influence on a company's corporate governance, as is demonstrated by the case studies in this chapter. Increasingly, this extends to engagement and voting on SEE issues, as governance teams interpret their role to include the governance and management of all non-financial risks.

In addition to this rationale, and perhaps equally significant, is that governance specialists within investment houses are used to constructive dialogue with management about improving performance on non-financial issues. It is this experience as much as logic that places governance engagement in the same team as SEE risk or SRI engagement.

LIKELY DEVELOPMENTS

With such a weight of activity now under way in the sector and the accelerating rate of cultural change within industry itself, there are likely to be major headlines generated in every field in the coming years. The issue of corruption, for example, has grown enormously in recent times and is likely to catch the eye of more than a few editors in the year ahead. Once absent from the typical SRI 'roster', anti-corruption practices, especially in areas of investment, lending and finance, are becoming crucial.

Until recently the prevailing attitude among many shareholders was that local bribes and inducements, while not encouraged, generally served company interests. The recent implosion of Italian dairy giant Parmalat in a paper trail that could run to almost €14 billion exposes the danger of such thinking.[5]

It was the recognition of the reputational risks associated with corruption that lay behind Procter & Gamble's recent closure of a manufacturing plant in the developing world for four months. The refusal by P&G to pay a $5,000 bribe to a local customs official obviously cost it far more in terms of lost business, but it protected the integrity of a company that operates nearly 300 global brands.[6]

A similar 'crossover' issue due for increased attention is 'whistle-blower protection'. The corporate culture of the past too frequently allowed the 'shooting of messengers', meaning that fraud or other wrongdoing was perpetuated until the lonely whistle-blower inevitably sought outside agencies such as the press, authorities or even the police – usually inflicting the maximum share price damage in the process.

We can also expect biodiversity to emerge strongly as an issue in the year ahead. Even now, this is still regarded as a somewhat esoteric field but recent corporate experience has thrust it to the top of the agenda as companies begin to realize the reputational, liability and regulatory risks at stake.

The findings of the latest ISIS research into the information, communication and technology (ICT) sectors is also likely to become required industry reading. The image of such 'high-tech' industries as relatively benign in environmental terms is about to change, as greater exposure of supply and disposal chains focuses on the low-tech conditions that prevail in many third world production sites, the hazardous wastes that are produced and the health and safety issues arising. As a result, you can expect to read a lot more about 'upstream' and 'downstream' management and the rising dangers posed by 'electroscrap', as companies are persuaded to take greater responsibility for where their materials are sourced and how their waste products are disposed of. Of course, one of the emerging strengths of today's governance and SRI industry is that few protagonists struggle with an issue on their own for long. This is certainly the case with supply chain management.

In early 2004, FTSE announced that companies without clearly defined policies on labour standards in their supply chains could soon be excluded from the FTSE4Good family of indices. Its proposed new criteria would, it said, see companies in the retail, household goods, textiles and food sectors banned from the indices unless they could demonstrate system-backed public policies on the issue. It was intended that the requirement – based on International Labour Organization (ILO) standards – be rolled out later to include all 2,450 FTSE4Good index constituents. At the time, the final criteria, and a timetable for their introduction, was planned to be introduced early in 2004.

Tragically, the AIDS pandemic will also be a key focus of activity for investors. Where once the virus was 'simply' a public health issue, in a little over a decade it has become a major corporate concern. The sub-Saharan region is now blighted by the virus, threatening resource production for companies around the globe and making it more cost effective for extractive companies to issue free AIDS drugs to employees and their families, rather than face the cost of continued workforce attrition and ballooning pensions costs. Worryingly, the rates of HIV infection in emerging economies such as Russia, China, Indonesia and Thailand now match those of South Africa a decade ago while the same culture of denial is also pervasive.

One of the great issues is likely to remain global climate change. While UK investors have long since recognized the potential exposure here, not least by forming an influential body of institutional investors to address the issue (the Institutional Investors' Group on Climate Change, or IIGCC), take-up in the USA has always been muted. The scientist behind the latest examination of climate change figures was not exaggerating when he said, 'Climate change is the most severe problem we are facing today – more serious even than the threat of terrorism.'[7]

November 2003 saw promising signs of progress here, though, as the United Nations played host to a US summit of investor interest groups. As more and more individual US states take up their own positions on the issue, often in opposition to that of the White House, we can expect some new developments here as US pension funds and trade unions begin to lend their enormous influence to the issue.

THE END OF THE BEGINNING

In case you missed it, 2003 was by far the most high-profile year so far for governance and SRI activity but the years ahead are likely to be still more prominent.

According to a leading consultancy, 2003 saw mainstream press coverage of governance- and SRI-related issues reach an all-time high.[8] This certainly rings true, as even those with a passing interest in the topic cannot help but have noticed the flood of front pages devoted to issues as diverse as board remuneration, off balance sheet activities, corporate fraud, threats to biodiversity or the AIDS pandemic in the last year. Each instance does nothing but reinforce the need for companies to take a long, hard look at the kinds of business risks their practices are creating.

After years of struggle, it seems, we have now been catapulted into a situation where companies can simply no longer shrug off governance and corporate responsibility issues – the risks to their businesses and those that own them are just too great.

With the wind now at their backs, governance and SRI practitioners have never been in a better position to deliver their key objective, namely ensuring that shareholders properly fulfil their role as watchdogs of a company's management. It is this focus on the oversight of management – rather than just selectively choosing to follow a single-issue banner, as too many still do – that makes it so important for the agendas of governance and SRI to merge. This enables a leveraging of resources, rather than isolating protagonists – something that is crucial in today's business environment where issues arising from both tend to intertwine.

As for the GSRI industry itself, 2004 will inevitably be a year of growing pains as activity constantly mounts. The successful practitioner teams will be those able to draw the strings together to create dynamic units capable of responding to the multifarious demands of today's market – anything else is likely to ultimately weaken their engagement potential.

With the UK as the centre and clear leader of European SRI activity, it is now time for governance and SRI professionals to focus on finding a unified and informed voice. As it stands, the industry must vigilantly guard against shouting loud on those occasions when it has little of worth actually to say.

Notes

1   According to the Ethical Investment Research Service's (EIRIS) latest figures, the estimated size of pooled ethically screened funds in the UK stood at £4.2 billion by the end of February 2004.
2   In April 2002 the Secretary of State, Patricia Hewitt, and the Chancellor, Gordon Brown, appointed Derek Higgs to lead a short independent review into the role of non-executive directors. Higgs, who served as chairman of Partnerships UK plc and a non-executive director of Egg plc, the British Land Company plc, Allied Irish Banks plc and Jones Lang La Salle Inc, published his findings in his 'Review of the role and effectiveness of non-executive directors' on 20 January 2003.
3   The report, 'Internal control: guidance for directors on the Combined Code' (The Turnbull Report), was produced by the chairman of the Institute of Chartered Accountants in England and Wales (ICAEW), Nigel Turnbull, and its findings made available to the investing public in September 1999.
4   While the government considered legislation requiring institutions to intervene in investee companies, the ABI, along with other leading bodies, argued that a voluntary approach would produce a more effective outcome. This led in October 2002 to the publication of a statement of best practice on the responsibilities of institutional shareholders. After publication, the government said it would defer legislation for two years while it examined the extent of behavioural change.
5   According to the *Daily Telegraph* of 24 February 2004, 'Parmalat began its precipitous slide just before Christmas [2003], when a €4billion credit which it claimed to be holding was unmasked as bogus. The hole in its accounts has since deepened to €13.6 billion.'
6   According to P&G chairman Alan G Lafley in the company's 2003 Sustainability Report, 'A customs official in a developing country once blocked the entry of our $250,000 raw material shipment until a payment of $5,000 was made. P&G's regional president did not hesitate to refuse the blatant extortion demand... The plant remained closed for four months, until our appeal reached the country's President, who arranged for the shipment to be released.'
7   In February 2004, speaking at a global conference in Seattle, the UK government's chief scientist, Sir David King, challenged the Bush administration to take climate change more seriously. Writing in *Science Magazine* earlier, he argued: 'Climate

change is the most severe problem we are facing today – more serious even than the threat of terrorism.'

8   At the start of 2004, international reputation consultancy Echo Research reported on the findings of its analysis of 5,324 press articles on CSR topics published since January 2000. It concluded that mainstream press coverage of corporate social responsibility issues had increased significantly around the world during the previous three years and that most of it was still largely favourable. Overall, the number of articles on CSR rose 52 per cent between 2000 and 2001 and 407 per cent between 2001 and 2002.

8

Mutual benefit and responsible business practice

Dr CP (Kit) Burdess, Policy and Corporate Affairs, Accenture

Good, responsible business practice is about taking a positive approach in relationships with key stakeholders in a way that generates value not only for your own company but for others around you. In the bigger picture this will mean that the good corporate citizen is contributing towards making a better operating environment, which will in turn help towards its own success in the future.

But this approach of enlightened self-interest (see the other aspects of this discussed in the box, 'Mutual benefit and the business case for corporate citizenship', page 105) may well seem rather remote, too much of a big picture, for the factory manager whose focus is naturally on getting product out of the door, or other managers with their own particular problems, concerns and deadlines. What does it mean for them and where can they start?

The practical step forward on this is to look for mutual benefit, a solution that gives benefit to both the company and the other stakeholders. When, at Accenture, we first started looking at this issue, with a number of major multinational companies operating in Poland, we found some interesting reactions. Companies could see this as a way of solving some problems that had been intractable. At the same time, the first reaction of those who were advocating more corporate community involvement was to feel that they had not been looking for something that would benefit the companies. There was still a feeling that corporate citizenship/corporate social responsibility (CSR) was like old-fashioned medicine – it could not possibly be doing any good unless it hurt the companies. Indeed a number of community advocates would only consider companies' community initiatives to be valid if they were not connected with the operations of the company.

Since then CSR supporters have increasingly recognized that responsible companies can make a greater contribution to the community if they work to increase value for society as they go about their core activities, and if they make good use of their assets, skills and other resources when they are consciously working on their corporate community involvement.

For the companies the great advantage of mutual benefit is that it is not all one way – it benefits the company too. In many cases the benefit to the company will be direct and achieved quickly enough to meet the needs of operational managers. And there is a lot to be said for starting off with the clearest wins for the company, the 'low-hanging fruit', to get managers into the mutual benefit way of thinking. After all, for many of them it will be something of a change, albeit hopefully a satisfying one, to go from their being used to finding some problems to be intractable, beyond their purview or apparently needing a huge effort chivvying people to do things they did not really want to do, and moving to an approach where they are looking for where they can benefit from a common interest in achieving a common goal.

If all that sounds a bit like falling off a log or finding the Holy Grail perhaps I should mention that in practice working for mutual benefit has its own challenges, particularly in needing to mesh what can be considerable differences in ways of working, especially between companies and 'third sector' organizations. Fortunately, some very useful work has been done on how to partner with other organizations for mutual benefit, and companies can now take advantage of that experience.

What is the secret, then, of mutual benefit? Well, in one area at least, successful companies are already in a good position to recognize mutual benefit. They are producing goods and services that their customers want. The companies explore just what it is that the customers need and look at how they can provide it. They are also used to reconciling the wants and needs of consumers with what the company can reasonably achieve. Increasingly, companies take that one step further in customer relationship management. For example, they may want to ensure that their products have a reputation for reliability. They do what they can to build reliability into the product, but how do consumers see it?

Part of the answer to that is in what happens if consumers' own cars or whatever go wrong. Do they get a friendly and efficient rectification at the dealership, and get left with the impression that faults are rare and rectified promptly, and the company cheerfully stands by its warranty? If they do, the chances are that the consumers will buy that brand again and, perhaps at least as important, recommend it to friends. If, on the other hand, unlucky consumers get a lot of hassle and expense, then the company stands to lose out on future sales. There is a clear mutual benefit between consumers' needs and the company's needs for marketing and future sales. At the same time the company needs to follow through the implications of its approach – it may mean some costs in warranty work, and a bit less income for the dealerships, to be reconciled against the reputation of the company and its impact on future sales.

So where else can we find mutual benefit? The answer to that is: wherever you have key stakeholders. The opportunities may be more obvious in some circumstances than in others. For example, in transition and emerging economies it is often clear where the opportunities are to work with suppliers, contractors, distributors and retailers in a way that improves their ability to work with you and deliver what you need. Indeed, it is often clear in such circumstances that, if you do not work with them in that way, the quality will not be there and you will need to import it from elsewhere, with all the higher costs that involves, or even that you simply will not be able to operate. In more developed economies you can expect to find similar opportunities, but they may be less obvious, and less obviously essential. Nevertheless they will be worth looking at. For those who want to explore this general context of working with others in the 'value chain' further, see the box, 'Co-opetition', page 106.

SUPPLIERS AND CONTRACTORS

When VW bought the Czech company Škoda shortly after the collapse of the centrally planned economies in Central and Eastern Europe, they recognized that the quality of both the cars and the company's service had to increase dramatically to comply with VW's international standards. Set a tough challenge, Škoda responded well: the company's quality ratings improved to a level considered excellent even by VW Group standards. Working with suppliers was an important element in this turnaround, and the work with Škoda had a huge impact on the development of the supplier base in the Czech Republic. VW convinced foreign suppliers to partner with Czech supplier firms or to establish greenfield operations in the Czech Republic. Over half of the new joint ventures were with Czech firms and during the subsequent few years their quality improved immensely, and they also delivered components to other automotive companies, both inside and outside the VW group. They took on parts of the assembly process, delivering whole sub-assemblies, such as the dashboard and doors. The overall result was a clear win–win for both Škoda/VW and the suppliers.

In South Africa we have seen a range of initiatives for bringing up the quality of suppliers and contractors to levels where they can satisfy the needs of major companies. In one mining company, for example, much heavy equipment was discarded when it broke down because there was no local capability in making sound repairs.

Expensive replacements had to be imported and delivery times were often a serious problem for the company. But by working with a local small engineering workshop the mining company was able to help build local capacity in the skills needed to make the sound repairs that were needed. The result was a cheaper and quicker solution for the mining company, and good business for the engineering workshop. Another mining company worked with a small catering firm to help them improve what they could offer – and then took them on to run the canteen for the company.

But it is not just in transition and emerging markets that initiatives of this kind can bring startling results. One of the oil majors had a small oilfield off Scotland, which looked too small and expensive to be worth developing. So it experimented with a new approach to working with contractors. Instead of the usual industry arrangements it offered to work with contractors in such a way that both oil company and contractor would work together to minimize costs, while not, of course, jeopardizing safety. The idea was that a field that would not otherwise be developed could be developed in this way, and the benefits of savings would be shared between the oil company and the contractor. As a result, ways were found of bringing down the cost of development to a point at which it was viable. Moreover, continuing the spirit of cooperation during the construction phase not only saved more – bringing the project in considerably under even the revised budget – but it brought the oilfield on stream some nine months early, with further benefits for the company's cash flow. The experience of that project was that it was by no means easy to get people into a new way of thinking and working, but when they did the advantages were immense.

DISTRIBUTORS AND RETAILERS

There was the story about a man who went into a small store and found the shelves almost entirely stocked with packets of salt. Surprised at this, he asked the shopkeeper whether he was able to sell a lot of salt in the area. The shopkeeper replied 'No, it's dreadful. I can't sell any salt at all. But the man who sells me salt – can he sell salt!' For any company wanting to get its production out of the factory and down the distribution chain to the consumer, there can be a great temptation to press retailers and stockists to stock up. This can work, up to a point, but especially for some products, more perishable than salt, it can bring problems for the company as well as the distributors. The mutual benefit approach, following that in Co-opetition, is to find a practical solution that will benefit both the company and the distributor. For example, a straightforward stock management system can help ensure that the distributor or retailer is not overstocked on some items, while being out of stock on others. And good stock control will make the distributor have a stronger, more effective business, more likely to prosper and sell more product in the longer term. The benefits to the manufacturer of helping a stockist with a stock management system can be not only to ensure that the stockist has appropriate stock of all items – and so does not run out of stock on some items – but that it turns over its stock in good time, reducing the risk of returns of out-of-date stock. It can also mean that the manufacturer has a healthy business partner. The costs for the manufacturer can be very modest – more a question of time spent in thinking out the strategy and, perhaps, persuading its own salespeople that shifting product is not all that is needed.

EMPLOYEES

For many companies, and especially for a professional services firm like Accenture, employees are a key consideration in the corporate citizenship of the company. It helps to look at two aspects of this: 1) the way that the overall corporate citizenship approach of the company interrelates with employees, particularly over recruitment and retention; and 2) mutual benefit at the individual level.

Groucho Marx is quoted as saying, 'I don't want to belong to any club that will accept me as a member.' By contrast, companies want to attract the best talent, and increasingly those prospective employees are keen to ensure that the company they are joining has an approach and values that mesh well with their own. Increasingly they are looking at the character of the company, and that shows in its approach to corporate citizenship. As a result, companies themselves project to prospective employees what they are doing in company community involvement and in other areas. They also recognize that their commitment to such values has to be deep rooted and genuine; it will soon be found out if it is just 'PR spin'. When it comes to mutual benefit, it is very important that the values of the company and those of its employees are closely aligned. It will not only help to ensure that employees are well motivated. It will help the quality of action and decision making in the company. If the approach and values of employees are well aligned with those of the company, then the employees will be making decisions directly from their own basis of values, not trying to second-guess what the company would want. And in a more extreme case, if employees do not respect the company for its approach and values they may not respect its assets much either and do less to protect them, or even be tempted to sequester them. Overall, then, the values and approach of a company can have a real impact on its ability to attract and retain good, talented employees, and keep them well motivated.

On the individual level, there are several aspects where mutual benefit is an important factor. The employees will ask themselves, perhaps only subconsciously, whether this is a company that really meets their needs. Does it have an approach to training and personal development that will allow them to grow within the company, or will it just be a place to get some experience before moving on elsewhere to get to the next level? Does it have enough flexibility in approach to allow for other possible options while still offering the context of a career in the firm? Does it provide opportunities in volunteering, etc, that will enable employees to 'give something back' on a personal level?

In Accenture we found that many of our employees were keen to 'give something back' in this way, including taking a short career break to carry out voluntary work overseas. Along with Shell, we were the founding members of the VSO (Voluntary Service Overseas) Business Partnerships Scheme to develop arrangements in which our staff could use their business skills and experience in assignments overseas. They could go on volunteer assignments of about six months or so while still retaining their link with the firm and, indeed, getting some help from the firm towards meeting their continuing expenses at home while they did so. This scheme has been very much welcomed by staff, and very successful in delivering suitable business skills to the overseas non-profit organizations, etc, involved, and it is now being extended to Accenture offices in other countries. There is also a benefit back to the participants and the company, in terms of developing additional skills such as adaptability, resourcefulness, innovation, etc, which they can make good use of when they return. This very successful initiative also led us to work on other possible arrangements to deliver consulting skills for the benefit of international development, and we now have a non-profit organization within Accenture – Accenture Development Partnerships. In this, employees work on short-term overseas development projects. They themselves contribute, through accepting a reduced rate of pay, and the company makes no margin, in order to deliver high-quality consulting skills at rates that can be met in the development sector.

There is also an emphasis on flexible working, especially to enable people to combine a job with their carer commitments. At first sight, many employers will see this as all benefit for the employee and little benefit for the company. But a flexible approach can actually have some surprising benefits, and not just in keeping on staff who might otherwise not be available. For example, some years ago, at a time when job sharing was less common, my secretary decided that, with her carer commitments, she could no longer work full time and wanted to go to half-time. I will admit that I thought it likely that that would result in the job being much more difficult to manage (if indeed it could be done satisfactorily at all). But she and the other sharer were left to work out their arrangements together. What was to me a very pleasant surprise was that they actually delivered the job remarkably well and, moreover, with less management on my part than for one full-time employee. The underlying reason for this was the combination of mutual benefit – they were keen to deliver well under arrangements that suited them, and they also responded to being given the opportunity to work those out for themselves. They came up with the idea of working alternate Thursday to Wednesday weeks, which fitted best in with the need to look after the family. This just shows that it is surprising what people will come up with when they are well motivated.

CUSTOMERS, COMMUNITY AND OTHER COMPLEMENTORS

The examples given above all relate to areas of business that will be familiar to the company, but you may be wondering how these ideas relate to the 'community' and other interests that are more usually covered in discussions on corporate social responsibility. The same approach works there too.

When BOC Gases established themselves in Poland they decided on an initiative that not only leveraged their own knowledge, skills and other assets for the benefit of the community but also brought some substantial benefits to themselves. They were producing gases for welding that related to new welding techniques for which there were few experts in Poland at the time. They decided to set up a training school in which people who were then unemployed would learn the new techniques and then be able to get jobs in that expanding craft. The initiative was remarkably successful. Not only did it help the individuals – and get some welcome publicity for the company – but it was providing a pool of people who were real 'complementors' for BOC Gases, trained in the new techniques and naturally having a positive impression of the company.

Companies that rely heavily on access to highly trained scientists and technologists have an interest in increasing the pool of available talent. Many such companies have recognized that they and others in the relevant industries can help encourage that pool of talent by supporting initiatives in schools to get children to think about a career in science and technology. A modest investment in such initiatives – supporting science competitions or producing useful display materials like the periodic table, etc – can help. Some of the positive impressions from such initiatives will accrue to the individual firm, some just towards increasing the overall pool of talent available.

There are particular issues for companies operating in areas where, in effect, the 'licence to operate' is limited by public concerns. Taking a positive approach to such a challenge, a number of companies producing alcoholic drinks work together in the Portman Group to try to promote an approach of responsible drinking and to find solutions that will minimize problem drinking and therefore help maintain a 'licence to operate' that the public – and they – will find appropriate. There is now a similar challenge arising over increasing obesity levels, and some of the food and soft drinks companies are working on positive strategies to deal with that issue. These are only a few examples of how an approach of mutual benefit can help to solve problems for companies as much as for others in society.

It is perhaps also worth mentioning that the mutual benefit approach provides two further advantages when it comes to deciding which corporate community involvement or 'corporate philanthropy' projects and initiatives are the right ones for the company. First, the company is looking at issues and concerns it knows about and thus it is in a better position to make informed decisions – and to avoid unwittingly getting involved in charity issues that are controversial. And second, it gives a reasonable basis for deciding among the different requests for help – the company can support those that give mutual benefit, confident that this will in fact leverage the benefit for the community.

HOLISTICALLY SPEAKING

Most of the above examples involved only one of the functions of management in a company, such as operations, human relations or marketing. But one of the characteristics of corporate citizenship that makes it at the same time both rewarding and challenging is that it spans the 'silos of management' and concerns the whole of the functioning of the firm. For that reason, it is often most easily appreciated by the CEO and the senior management group and can find difficulties in reaching through all the different functions at middle management level.

There have, however, been some remarkable initiatives that have reached across different functions and proved to be a strategy that has satisfied a number of objectives. See the box, 'BPTT – a Caribbean collaboration', page 108.

FINALLY

In summary, then, mutual benefit is a useful approach and tool for responsible companies both for achieving more in core business activities and as a means of leveraging assets for corporate community involvement. The upside is that you are no longer pushing water uphill. The downside is that you are now herding cats. Fortunately there is some good advice on cat herding, from the International Business Leaders Forum[1] and other sources.

MUTUAL BENEFIT AND THE BUSINESS CASE
FOR CORPORATE CITIZENSHIP

We are concentrating here on mutual benefit as an approach to securing value for the company – and for others in society – in corporate citizenship or corporate social responsibility. This is, indirectly, a large part of the answer to the question of the business case for corporate citizenship, but it is still worth looking at the question more generally.

Different organizations tend to use different definitions of corporate citizenship, depending largely on their focus and interests, but typically they include the following elements.

Good corporate citizenship is about pursuing normal business in a way that ensures companies develop positive, sustainable relationships with key stakeholders, eg suppliers and contractors, employees, customers, shareholders, community, throughout companies' operations, in a way that supports the attainment of their business objectives and makes a positive contribution to the wider community in which they operate. Good corporate citizenship is about responsible engagement by companies with the world around them – both in the way they conduct their business and in proactive initiatives that make a positive contribution to the wider community in which they operate.

One way of answering 'What is the business case?' is an all-encompassing comment that good corporate citizenship is good business. Positive, sustainable relationships with the stakeholders contribute to the success of the company, making it more robust and more prosperous. By being in tune with the interests of key stakeholders there is less risk of something going seriously wrong for the company – in that there will be more chance of identifying problems and issues when they arise and dealing with them before they cause a crisis. There is also more chance of the company identifying opportunities. On this basis corporate citizenship is just an extension of what each and every company should be doing in getting its operations right and managing its risks. It will be putting more management effort into these, but the benefits will quite clearly outweigh the costs.

However, behind the question 'What is the business case?' there is frequently the assumption that corporate citizenship/corporate social responsibility inevitably includes significant resources spent on activities of little benefit to the company, such as large corporate philanthropy programmes. Looked at another way, this is also a reflection of an assumption, especially by lobby groups, that, unless corporate citizenship activities cost the company a significant part of their profits, they cannot be doing any good. This attitude was reflected in an approach by some companies, which wanted to demonstrate that they were devoting a certain percentage of profits to community involvement projects. This is an expression of community benefit in terms of inputs – what they cost – rather than outputs – their significance and impact. This is increasingly seen as being out of place, and measurement of corporate community involvement programmes is increasingly emphasizing outputs rather than cost.

All this can perhaps best be illustrated by the difference between 'clean technology' and 'clean-up technology'. Consider two companies. One has never really thought about environmental impact until it was forced by regulation to clean up its discharges by expensive add-ons at the end of the plant, taking out serious pollutants and then disposing of them. Another had taken a different approach, anticipated the tightening of environmental regulation and had gone for 'clean technology', designing the plant to generate less waste and handle any residual waste more effectively. In doing this it found that the attention to clean technology paid off in an unexpected way – by generating less waste the plant was actually more efficient, so the company actually saved by a clean technology approach. If the two companies were challenged on what they have spent on the protection of the environment, it would be ironic if the less responsible 'clean-up' company were regarded as making the greater contribution!

This all makes it important to look at outputs as measures of effective corporate citizenship, and to avoid having the costs paraded as if they were a virtue. The assessment then of the business case for any particular initiatives can be made on a more rational basis.

And this brings us back to mutual benefit. Companies can decide what they can sensibly do on the basis of the benefit it brings to them and on the corresponding benefit for the community – which may well be bringing the company benefits in terms of enhanced reputation or improved access to resources. Through using a mutual benefit approach, the company can both decide on and justify which initiatives to take part in and, when it comes to the sort of projects that are intended largely to benefit community organizations, ensure that it is leveraging the company contribution by efficiently using other resources in addition to any financial contribution. This can also be seen as enlightened self-interest.

CO-OPETITION

In their book, *Co-opetition*,[2] Barry Nalebuff and Adam Brandenburger look at how to create value and to capture value in business – where it pays to cooperate in business and where competition is the name of the game. Essentially, it can pay to cooperate with what they call 'complementors' – the suppliers, contractors, distributors and others in the value chain who are helping you create the item of value you are delivering to your customers. Those other people in the value chain are helping you to make the cake, and you can best cooperate with them in doing so, even if at the same time you need to decide how to divide the cake between you. They also point out that there are other complementors – sometimes even your business competitors can be complementary in some respects.

What Nalebuff and Brandenburger are doing is applying Game Theory to business. Do not be misled by the natural reaction to think that something called Game Theory cannot be seriously useful. It really is. We are very used to thinking of the sort of games played on the school playing field. One team wins, the other loses. Those are the 'zero sum games' of most sports. But in the real world of business your interactions are rarely zero sum games – they are more complex than that.

Interactions can be 'win–win', that is to say positive sum games, in which both players benefit. This is what we are aiming at with the mutual benefit approach. The analogy is with individual good citizens who will usually try to do things in a way that helps the community while at the same time making a good life for themselves. You will recognize that this takes a positive mindset, the ability to see that helping others does not necessarily bring a disadvantage to you – indeed it can help you, too.

In zero sum games we start to see the more negative aspects coming in. In some individual sports the outcome relies only on how well the individual does compared with the others who are competing. There is little or no opportunity to win by making the opponent do less well. But we are all familiar with team games in which one side could win by ensuring that the other side performs badly and, despite attempts to make rules against fouls, etc, it can be a feature of the sport.

Negative sum games are even worse, where the interaction loses value for both. Perhaps one of the clearest examples is the price war in which one company thinks it has enough strength to outlast its competitor in a price war. Maybe it has, but at the end of the fight, with the other company on its knees, can the stronger company really get back to more than the original prices and recoup the margin lost in the meantime, or does it find that the customers have got used to the lower prices and are reluctant to buy when the prices go up again? In another field, politicians often seem to be playing a negative sum game. In their own context it seems that commenting negatively on the other party makes them shine in comparison. But how does it look to the average voter? Listening to the two parties emphasizing the faults of each other, they are more likely to get the impression that all politicians are untrustworthy, sleazy or whatever, and politicians generally get low ratings for trustworthiness etc. As the little old lady said, 'I never vote – it only encourages them.' The voter does have another choice – not to participate in the game – and that is not good for democracy.

Co–opetition is, then, a different way of looking at business interactions. One of the important features of it is that, instead of regarding the structure of markets as being fixed (as in a zero sum game), it regards it as dynamic and evolving. Thus, people in business – especially larger companies, or business interest groups working together – have the ability to change the game. If they do this in a positive way, working in tune with others in society, they can build a better working environment for themselves and for the rest of society. And if, of course, they try to do so just for their own benefit, at the expense of others in society, they are likely to find their game blocked in some way or other by those adversely affected. Better to look for mutual benefit, for the positive sum game.

BPTT – A CARIBBEAN COLLABORATION

All over the world, countries that depend on oil, gas and other natural resources are demanding that more of the wealth generated by production be spent locally. In a highly innovative programme that could set a global trend, BP Trinidad and Tobago (BPTT) decided that, rather than find itself reacting to government regulations, it would establish a new kind of collaboration with the local community. The project has the potential to produce tangible benefits for all involved, with the company achieving lower costs, better-skilled employees and more flexible, locally attuned suppliers, while the community will gain more and better job opportunities for local people, as part of a growth in entrepreneurial activity.

The energy sector already accounts for a significant proportion of the Trinidad and Tobago economy, but BPTT, the biggest player in the sector, has traditionally relied on global suppliers for exploration equipment such as rigs and well services, with only an estimated 10 to 15 per cent of BPTT's suppliers coming from Trinidad and Tobago. The Trinidad and Tobago government wants to extract more value from the country's natural gas reserves – and to ensure economic success even after the oil and gas runs out.

Speaking at a recent conference with industry executives, Tony Paul – a Trinidadian who is head of the BPTT Sustainable Developments team – said, 'The real issue is that Trinidad thinks of itself primarily as a raw materials producer, and doesn't add enough value to its own products. With this project, and all the consequences that flow from it, we're helping to change that.'

BP's first step was to move its main base for operations in Trinidad from Houston, Texas, to a considerably enlarged, locally run office in Trinidad. Then the company rethought the way it procured services. Historically, BPTT had tended to sign short-term contracts with big suppliers for which small-scale local firms were ill equipped to compete. Longer-term contracts, together with joint ventures and alliances, are now being encouraged to promote local participation and capability development. Furthermore, BPTT expects its global suppliers who bid for contracts to incorporate a local dimension. Robert Riley, CEO and Chairman of BPTT, stated that:

> In evaluating all proposals for the procurement of goods and services we look at a number of dimensions that bring value to BPTT: cost/commercial, technical, HSE and sustainable development. We also look at the company's plans to further deepen local participation. We establish how aligned the contractor's strategy is with our own as we would prefer to contract with companies that share our aspirations.

For instance, Damus, a local firm, has been engaged to design and build sections of a platform for a major offshore gas field – with the aim of improving local capabilities to such an extent that new platforms can be manufactured and tailored to local conditions in the islands themselves.

BP has been instrumental in setting up a bond scheme that improves capital markets on the islands. Other initiatives include giving Trinidadians much greater opportunities to own their businesses, running training schemes and sponsoring geology degree programmes at the university. These initiatives are vital for providing a ready supply of highly trained staff and contractors who understand local conditions and the quality requirements of the energy industry, as well as creating a bank of skills that will allow the islands to become globally competitive and diversified in the future.

The company will save a significant amount of money by using local firms, and by improving relations with the business community it has achieved all sorts of ancillary benefits. This is an outstanding example of sustainable development, with a business model that is geared to improving the quality and speed of supplies as well as supplier relationships, both globally and locally, while integrating BP even more closely with the islands' future.

BP has demonstrated a clear commitment towards innovative ways of working – within its own organization, among its business partners and in the country in which it operates. The BPTT model of sustainable development is seen by BP as having great potential for use in other resource-rich developing countries, where it will create, as Tony Paul comments, 'a whole different way of thinking, encouraging others to become the innovators themselves'.

Notes

1 The Partnering Toolbook (February 2004) and The Learning Curve (December 2003), available from the website of the International Business Leaders Forum at http://www.iblf.org.
2 Barry J Nalebuff and Adam M Brandenburger (1997) *Co–opetition*, HarperCollins Business, London.

9

Corporate governance, best practice

Gareth Llewellyn, Group Corporate Responsibility Director,
National Grid Transco plc

WHAT IS CORPORATE RESPONSIBILITY?

The difficulties in defining precisely what corporate responsibility covers is in part reflective of the way in which this topic has developed. For some, it has grown out of community investment or corporate philanthropy with a clear emphasis on social improvements. For others, corporate responsibility has a much broader definition and is closely related to, if not a surrogate for, the sustainable development agenda launched at the UN's Earth Summit in Rio de Janeiro in 1992.

Ultimately, however, corporate responsibility is simply the application of values and principles in the way in which a company undertakes its business. Nevertheless, the confusion in terminology can affect the integration of such issues within a sensible approach to corporate governance and so a few definitions are necessary:

- **sustainability** – a goal for society as a whole where economic development, environmental impact and quality of life are balanced;
- **sustainable development** – the activities across society aimed at achieving sustainability;
- **corporate responsibility** – the contribution a company can make through responsible business practices to sustainable development;
- **corporate governance** – the implementation of policies, procedures and reporting arrangements to ensure a company understands and manages its risks effectively;

- **corporate social responsibility** – those elements of a company's responsible business practice that enhance the quality of life of society and the working environment of its employees;
- **corporate community investment** – the support, financial or otherwise, provided by companies to projects aimed at improving the quality of life of sections of society.

This section looks at the way in which corporate responsibility and a company's framework for corporate governance interact.

CORPORATE RESPONSIBILITY THEMES

The board of a company is primarily concerned with ensuring that the company delivers value to its shareholders. Profitability is a key component of this, but to some, such as those involved in the anti-globalization protests, it is seen as indicative of the irresponsibility of business. Nothing could be further from the truth. Profitability is in fact the cornerstone of an effective corporate governance strategy. Without profits it is less likely a company will make significant capital investments, which by its nature has consequences for employment in supply companies. It may also be tempted to cut corners on environmental management in order to reach profitability, or put employees under pressure to take short cuts as regards safety. Profitability is an essential feature of corporate responsibility.

The role companies play in underpinning the economy is also a central feature of corporate responsibility. For some companies this contribution takes the form of essential services, such as secure supplies of electricity. For others it takes the form of increased employment due to the ability to export goods and services. Whatever the form this takes, a responsible business will play a key role in economic development.

Companies sometimes have a reputation for damaging the environment whether it be through pollution, profligate use of natural resources or the unsustainable generation of waste. However, another theme of corporate responsibility is the effort to which responsible companies go to reduce emissions, beyond those permitted by the regulator, and to find alternative sources of raw materials. The governance of environmental performance, whether it be through ISO14001 or through systems put in place by the board, is important in the context of corporate responsibility.

Finally, as indicated by the definitions above, there is a strong social element to corporate responsibility. These social aspects include the well-being of employees, the training provided to develop their skills, the rewards and recognition provided as part of their packages, and workplace practices such as equal opportunities. There are also broader societal aspects at play. Issues such as human rights and the interaction with minority groups, investment in deprived communities, and the respect shown to stakeholders are relevant here.

Corporate responsibility covers a wider range of facets, many of which vary from company to company. While some companies such as National Grid Transco have sought to identify those that are most relevant to their business, others have adopted models such as 'Winning with Integrity', developed by Business in the Community. The identification of the themes is an important step in defining a suitable approach to corporate governance.

FORMAL ASPECTS OF GOVERNANCE

Corporate responsibility is seen by some as an 'add-on' to the day-to-day business of a company. Again nothing could be further from the truth. In recent years there have been a number of developments that have formalized the need for corporate responsibility to provide a wider context for a company's approach to governance.

The Turnbull Report

The publication of the Turnbull Report in 1999 brought with it an increased focus on the extent to which non-financial risks can affect shareholder value. The report, subsequently implemented through the Combined Code, clearly set out the need for non-executive and executive directors alike to give due consideration to issues such as health and safety, environment, reputation, business probity and diversity. These are issues we now take to be at the core of any company's approach to corporate responsibility.

The report also commented on the provision of assurance to the board, and the review of the effectiveness of management controls. While corporate governance had until this point been primarily concerned with financial risks, the report recommended extending these activities to non-financial risks.

Since 1999, therefore, there has been a clear formal requirement for company boards to integrate corporate responsibility and corporate governance.

The Higgs Report

The Higgs Report into corporate governance, published in 2003, also made a number of observations as regards the role of non-executive directors. In particular, it looked at the independent oversight role of non-executive directors and the knowledge and skills they require in order to discharge their responsibilities. There is a clear expectation that the provision of independent oversight extends into the non-financial risk matters in the way originally envisaged in the earlier Turnbull Report.

The Higgs Report is therefore a natural extension of Turnbull. The need to address non-financial risks identified in the latter report was not at that stage accompanied by a recommendation that boards should have the necessary expertise or training to undertake the review of management controls. Most non-executive directors have considerable experience in financial management and control. This is not, however, always true of areas such as environmental management or evaluating business ethics.

It is essential therefore that company boards either contain non-executive directors with experience in some areas of non-financial risk management, or have access to suitably experienced external experts. As we will see later, the review of management controls and the evaluation of assurance provided by internal experts will be greatly aided by such skills.

Legislation and compliance

Any sound approach to corporate governance is built on an understanding that a company will be compliant with all relevant laws and legislation in the jurisdictions in which it operates. Interestingly, much of this legislation focuses on non-financial matters and aims to ensure that businesses meet *de minimis* standards and do not pose undue risks in areas such as the environment, human rights and safety.

Corporate responsibility therefore includes a strong element of governance to ensure a company remains compliant with legislation. Indeed, non-compliance is a key obstacle to a company's corporate responsibility approach, and an indication that governance needs to be strengthened.

It is also important that the board and non-executive directors in particular have access to high-quality advice on both existing and forthcoming legislation in areas such as health and safety, employment, disability, environmental protection and human rights. This will help the board determine the robustness of existing management controls and the progress being made to minimize the impact of future legislation on company profitability.

Risk management

Risk management is a key tool within the corporate governance framework. As recommended in the Turnbull Report, identifying the material risks facing a business and being able to evaluate the robustness of management controls aimed at minimizing the risks or mitigating their effects are central to good governance.

The assessment of financial risks, that is those risks inherent in the way in which a company is financially managed, is well established. Indeed, both the internal audit function present in many companies and external auditing and verification of accounts contribute to this.

Corporate responsibility, however, widens the field of risks that may be considered to be material, and therefore has a bearing on the overall governance approach. This at first may appear to be rather onerous, but many of the approaches to risk management adopted in the financial field are just as relevant. The principal difference is the extent to which most non-financial issues impact on the reputation of a company.

The measurement of reputation is an ongoing issue for most companies where the views and preferences of consumers are business-critical issues. However, few companies regularly assess how their reputation is affected by their management of issues across the corporate responsibility spectrum. The key here of course is to focus on those non-financial risks that may have a material affect on the company. This may relate to restricting future growth, increased legislative control or reluctance of shareholders to increase their holding.

An example may be useful here. With the expansion of companies into the developing world comes a responsibility to address human rights in a more formal way than might otherwise be expected. Initially, it is a company's reputation that is principally at risk (as opposed to the bottom line) if concerns about the human rights record of a company are identified. Eventually, this could adversely affect the share price if a company's profitability is affected by the cost of addressing public concern, or if the company is no longer seen as an attractive investment.

The process of risk management as regards non-financial risks as set out in the Turnbull Report is now a key component of a corporate governance framework designed to address corporate responsibility matters.

The strong link between corporate responsibility and corporate governance will require companies to examine more closely reputation impact as opposed to just financial impact in their risk management process.

Providing competitive edge

Corporate responsibility clearly has a formal side to it, which provides a strong link into a company's approach to corporate governance. Across the companies within the FTSE 250 there are some that limit their corporate responsibility activities to those required by the formal factors identified in the previous section.

However, there are increasing numbers of companies that have taken corporate responsibility a stage further, principally to underpin the long-term security of the business. In doing so, the approach to corporate governance has also required some modification.

Context for the business

The recent anti-globalization campaigns and demonstrations have highlighted the risk companies face from a lack of public understanding of their wider role in society.

Companies by their very nature contribute far more to society than simply making profits. In the case of the energy industry, the provision of secure supplies of energy is a prerequisite for economic development and quality of life for society as a whole. Through paying taxes due in the jurisdictions in which they operate, companies support the social infrastructure of those countries. Other examples include the provision of employment, investment in infrastructure and services leading to secondary employment, investment in environmental technology leading to environmental enhancements, and investment in community projects.

It should not be forgotten that generating profits is the cornerstone of any successful approach to corporate responsibility. The additional benefits brought by companies to the wider society are greatly hampered if profitability is in question.

The traditional approach to corporate governance has been to focus on financial performance and control with assurance provided by the audit committee. It is not surprising therefore that the integration of corporate responsibility within the governance process has required some modification of the governance framework, as is discussed below. However, it has resulted in a much more rounded and balanced view of a company's role in society.

Licence to operate

Effective corporate governance is designed to ensure the long-term viability or licence to operate of a company. Against this background, therefore, factors that may bring such viability into question will be subject to close scrutiny by the board.

In the case of Enron and WorldCom there were clear issues of corporate ethics that went beyond matters of financial control and accounting. In the UK, the removal of Railtrack's licence to operate was in part related to a loss of public confidence in the ability of the company to manage the rail network safely. Many high-profile corporate failures involved non-financial mismanagement as well as financial irregularities such as accounting malpractice or fraud. A company's licence to operate is as much at risk from the public's perception of irresponsible business practice as it is from such business practices themselves.

It is clear from these examples that an effective approach to corporate governance needs to encompass all aspects of corporate responsibility if it is to ensure the long-term viability of the company.

Adding value to the business

Corporate responsibility can add significant value to a company beyond just the protection of reputation and maintaining licence to operate.

Securing growth that is sustainable in the long term is a key objective for many companies. Companies that demonstrate responsible business practices are better positioned to secure future growth. Consumers increasingly distinguish between responsible companies and those that are irresponsible, and governments and regulators are more likely to grant concessions or sell off utilities to companies that are able to demonstrate an exemplary record of corporate responsibility.

It is important in this regard that the elements of corporate responsibility are translated through the governance framework into guiding principles for the business development process. In doing so, a company is better able to secure long-term growth on the back of responsible business practices.

CORPORATE RESPONSIBILITY AND THE BOARD

Scrutiny from the board

The principal role of the board, as mentioned above, is to ensure the company delivers value to the company's shareholders. There are those who argue that the board has a responsibility to the wider stakeholder community affected by or interested in the company's activities. Maintaining the support of the wider stakeholder community is essential in delivering value to shareholders. Indeed, few shareholders would be supportive of a company that is at odds with its stakeholders, and the share price would soon be affected if shareholders were of the view that the board was failing in this regard.

The value delivered to shareholders is therefore dependent upon a wider range of issues than simply profitability of the company. Although many companies experience a wide range of stakeholder interests, the principal issues of concern are usually non-financial in origin. The Environment Agency's 'Spotlight on business performance' highlights those companies with poor environmental records, which has in the past led to adverse publicity for those contained within the report. Equally, Amnesty International has highlighted companies operating in countries with questionable human rights practices. These examples illustrate the breadth of stakeholder issues that can affect shareholder value.

The market capitalization of many companies includes a significant component of intangible assets, of which reputation for most companies is the most valuable. The board's role in enhancing this reputation is just one example of how relevant corporate responsibility is at the top level within a company.

So it is clear that integral to delivering shareholder value is the board's primary role of ensuring the company operates in a responsible manner.

Of course, the board also has a less formal role in delivering a company's approach to corporate responsibility. As described below, the most productive approaches to corporate responsibility are built on a suite of values that apply to all employees throughout the company. In this regard, the board has a key role in setting an example by living these values through its actions. This type of leadership is the only way in which progress on behavioural issues such as safety, environmental stewardship, business ethics and transparency can be made.

It is also true to say that few board directors would wish to be seen as instrumental in managing an irresponsible company.

Appropriate levels of review

The ever-increasing expectations of company boards are such that it is unlikely a board would have sufficient time to review in any depth the robustness of management controls aimed at reducing risks in the areas covered by corporate responsibility.

As with issues such as audit, remuneration and nominations, the board is likely to wish to delegate such activities to a subcommittee. A number of companies have established committees of the board to address issues such as safety, sustainability or, in the case of National Grid Transco, risk and responsibility. These committees report back to the board on a periodic basis, and in conjunction with the audit committee will take a view on the overall state of corporate governance within the company.

Such a committee, focused on non-financial risks (as opposed to the audit committee's role of dealing principally with financial risks), allows for significantly more review of corporate responsibility matters than might otherwise be possible at the board. Indeed, this additional review will not only lead to a greater level of confidence in the governance of a company, but also improve the effectiveness of the board in managing these important risk areas.

Issues covered by National Grid Transco's risk and responsibility committee are:

- employee health;
- occupational and public safety;
- environment;
- business ethics;
- human rights;
- security;
- the company's role in society.

Non-executive directors

In the UK, non-executive directors play an important role in reassuring shareholders that the activities of executive directors are clearly focused on delivering shareholder value. As mentioned above, shareholder value is much wider than profits and dividends. Operating in a way that has the support of the company's stakeholders and that secures the long-term future of the company also has an important bearing on shareholder value.

So non-executive directors also play a key role in monitoring the business practices of a company to ensure they are in line with shareholder expectations and existing best practice.

It is likely therefore that corporate responsibility delivered through an effective governance approach will be influenced to a great extent by the non-executive directors. Indeed many of the board committees, including National Grid Transco's own risk and responsibility committee, are chaired and staffed entirely by non-executive directors.

The importance of non-executive directors in leading corporate responsibility is a feature of both the Turnbull and Higgs reports.

Executive directors

The Turnbull and Higgs reports have principally focused on the role of non-executive directors. However, executive directors have an equally important role in delivering effective corporate governance through responsible business practices.

Delivering shareholder value, meeting the aspirations of the company's varied stakeholder community and ensuring the company is a long-term business are all factors implicit in every decision taken by executive directors. It is also rare for such decisions to be one-dimensional in nature. For example, a decision to downsize a company has financial aspects, alongside issues such as employee welfare, industrial relations, future skills requirements and loss of intellectual capital. As such, executive directors are faced with decisions involving all aspects of corporate responsibility on a daily basis.

Of course, their ability to make such decisions in a balanced manner, weighing up financial and non-financial aspects, is a key component of their role. However, having a framework through which such business-critical decisions can be evaluated is helpful in providing a sound approach to corporate governance.

THE CONTEXT FOR CORPORATE GOVERNANCE

A framework for responsible business

Most of the focus to this point has been on the importance of a sound governance structure in enabling the board to deliver value to shareholders as well as the wider benefits of corporate responsibility.

However, a clearly defined strategy or framework within which accepted business practices are set out is essential for the governance of a company. It should be remembered that the implementation of the strategy or framework will, on a routine basis, principally be in the hands of the employees. In this regard there are clear benefits from involving employees and for that matter other stakeholders in the drafting of such a strategy or framework.

A number of companies have established and publicized business principles. These have served not only to convey the overall ethos of the board's approach to managing the company, but also to provide a framework within which company policies become more meaningful.

In the case of National Grid Transco, the business principles have been set in terms of a 'framework for responsible business'. This framework not only provides the context for the company's approach to corporate governance, but is based on three business goals:

- sustainable growth;
- profits with responsibility;
- investing in the future.

The framework is built around a series of values through which every employee can contribute not only to the success of the company, but also to the positive impact the company can have on the economy, the environment and society at large. In this

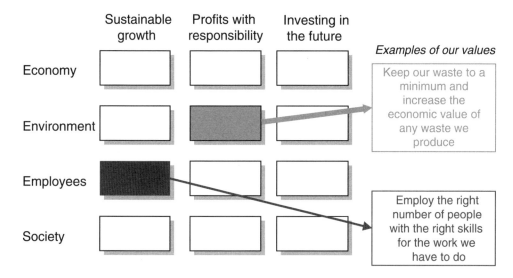

Figure 9.1 National Grid Transco's 'Framework for responsible business'

regard there is a close linkage between the business principles and the three 'pillars' of sustainable development.

Company policies

As stated above, the framework provides a useful context for those policies of most relevance to the company. An example that illustrates this coherence lies in the company's approach to safety. National Grid Transco believes that making profits at the expense of the well-being of employees is irresponsible business practice. Equally, having employees at work making the fullest contribution to the business will certainly make the company more profitable. Investment in safe ways of working is therefore a justifiable use of financial resources that might otherwise be returned to shareholders. Supporting this value is a policy on safety and occupational health that defines in more detail the responsible approach to the management of these issues.

By linking the overall approach to corporate responsibility to the long-term aims of the company, the underpinning policies have significantly more relevance and context.

BOARD REVIEW OF CORPORATE RESPONSIBILITY

Setting a framework for responsible business supported by relevant company-wide policies is an important part of corporate governance. These are effectively the board's reference points through which it is able to determine whether the company is indeed delivering shareholder value in its widest sense. The provision of assurance to the board is a key step in the approach to corporate governance.

The assurance provider

The process by which the board comes to a view on the robustness of management controls is heavily dependent on the provision of assurance by specialists within the company (or external specialists where in-house staff are not available). In the financial world, this is delivered by the internal audit function established by many companies. The head of the internal audit function will often have a direct line through to the chair of the board's audit committee (a non-executive board member) as well as a day-to-day line management line to an executive director. This dual line provides for independence of advice to the board on the performance of management.

This structure for the assurance provider in the financial field is well established. Some companies have mirrored these arrangements for non-financial issues such as health and safety or environmental management. This is particularly true where a board committee has been established in parallel with the audit committee to look at the company's management of non-financial risks. The assurance provider in such cases will generally be an environmental, safety, human resources or business ethics professional.

Providing assurance

Providing assurance on non-financial matters is a somewhat more difficult task than that involved in traditional financial audits. Non-financial risks may indeed have financial consequences, but they always involve significant reputational aspects, where the assessment of materiality to the business is less straightforward. Equally, the measure of risk itself is more complicated in the non-financial field. For example, the point at which employee diversity becomes a possible risk for a company is a complex one to define. It may be related closely to the economic sector in which a company may sit, the future strategic direction of the company and the pool of potential employees from which a company may be recruiting.

The key areas in which non-financial assurance is generally provided to the board include:

- **health and safety** – including facets such as behavioural safety, procedural safety such as ISO18001, and process safety;

- **environmental management** – often in line with ISO14001 certifications where they have been implemented and focusing on compliance with existing and future legislation;
- **diversity** – using initiatives such as Opportunity Now;
- **business ethics** – including the investigation of whistle-blowing incidents;
- **security** – particularly where the assets or processes are of material importance;
- **human rights** – processes for providing such assurance will be developed by the Business Leader's Initiative on Human Rights.

Providing assurance to the board on the management controls put in place to minimize the risks to the business is an integral part of an effective approach to corporate governance. Alongside the traditional financial audits, company boards are increasingly reliant on non-financial audits to provide a complete picture of the governance of their company.

SUMMARY

Corporate social responsibility, which for some companies has had its roots in community investment, is seen as peripheral to the issue of corporate governance. However, the wider field of corporate responsibility is not only significantly more relevant, but is in fact the driver for corporate governance in most forward-thinking companies.

The contribution made by companies is significantly wider than financial profitability. Economic development, environmental management and improvements to the quality of life are key themes of corporate responsibility, to which most companies make significant contributions through their day-to-day activities. The boards of forward-thinking companies have identified corporate responsibility as justifying scrutiny to the same level as financial performance and have established board committees to achieve this. In doing so, corporate responsibility has become an important driver for effective corporate governance.

10

Human rights in the global marketplace

Peter Frankental, Economic Relations Director,
Amnesty International

WHY ARE COMPANIES AT RISK?

Since the fall of the Berlin Wall companies have faced unprecedented opportunity and unprecedented threat. The growing dependence of states on international investment has been accompanied by a growth in conflict within states, a vacuum in governance and a lack of effective rule of law in many parts of the world. In consequence, companies with global operations are increasingly likely to find themselves caught up in human rights violations. At the same time, the increasing pervasiveness of the internet and of a well-informed international human rights community has exposed companies to greater external scrutiny. In recent years, a number of corporations have been embarrassed by human rights controversies that they were inadequately equipped to address.

The human rights community, including Amnesty International, has identified a number of areas where companies are most vulnerable to the costs and reputational damage associated with human rights violations. While that is not to say or even to imply that companies operating in those areas are complicit in human rights violations, there is a risk that people will conclude that they are contributing to such abuses, given the locations and industries in which they operate. The most effective way to combat this is to have appropriate human rights assurance mechanisms and practices in place that are both transparent and properly enforced. The main conclusion drawn from recent events where companies have found parts of their operation, supply chain or end user chain under the spotlight over human rights issues is that, in the absence of such policies, significant costs and damage to corporate reputation may be incurred.

Proximity to human rights violations

The extent to which a particular company is exposed to risk depends on where the company operates and the types of activity in which it engages. Many transnational corporations operate in countries with repressive administrations where the rule of law is weak, where the independence of the judiciary is questionable and where arbitrary arrest, detention, torture and extra-judicial executions occur. The government may ban free trade union activity and deny its citizens freedom of association. Factory workers in plants from which companies source their products may be subject to inhuman and degrading working conditions. Companies may be operating in areas of conflict or may be seen by certain ethnic groups to be violating ancestral lands or traditional knowledge. The government, to which a company is paying taxes and resource rents, may be skewing state expenditure in favour of the military and national security, and away from health and education, or in favour of one ethnic group to the detriment of others.

Companies may also find themselves in environments where bribery and corruption permeate society and where they are seen to condone fraudulent distributions of wealth. Each of these situations creates risks that, if mishandled, may lead to litigation, extortion, lost production, sabotage, higher security costs and increased insurance premiums. Other consequences may include restricted access to capital, difficulty in recruiting or retaining the best staff and, above all, reputational damage.

Reputation

Reputation is a vital corporate asset that is inextricably linked to public trust that the company will 'do the right thing'. A significant proportion of the value of many companies is tied up in the reputation of their brands, rather than in tangible assets. This makes companies and their shareholders vulnerable to reputational damage and is why stock exchanges internationally are putting greater emphasis on disclosure requirements and risk management systems that enable identification of all major risks, including those to intangible assets such as brand and reputation. Policies that companies can adopt – and that a growing number of companies are adopting – are set out in *Human Rights: Is it any of your business?*, a joint publication of Amnesty International and The Prince of Wales International Business Leaders Forum.

Any company engaged in any economic activity can face risk through involvement in human rights abuses and the fallout in terms of reputational, operational or financial loss. However, some business sectors are, through the nature of their activities, more vulnerable. In particular, extractive companies, heavy manufacturing and defence companies, infrastructure and utilities companies, pharmaceutical and chemical companies, information technology hardware and telecommunications companies, and food and beverages companies have been the subject of research by Amnesty International and the International Business Leaders Forum. The product of that research is a series of mappings of business risk published under the title *Business and human rights: a geography of corporate risk*, extracts from which have been used as the basis for this chapter. The sector-specific analyses of human rights violation risks and potential consequences set out in the following pages are good examples from which most businesses will be able to draw conclusions relevant to their own situations.

WHY ARE EXTRACTIVE COMPANIES AT RISK?

The drive for new resources can lead extractive firms into association with human rights violations. This is unlike some aspects of political risk, in that companies cannot readily insure themselves against it, except through having effective policies to deal with the human rights issues confronting them. Experience has shown that problems are most likely to arise when resources are located in zones of conflict, in territories with indigenous populations where land rights are contested or inadequately protected, or in countries with oppressive or corrupt governments. There have been a number of instances in which the sector has been heavily criticized for its record on human rights, in particular when operating in less developed countries.

Conflict

Companies are only too aware of their vulnerability in zones of conflict, where high costs may arise from acts of sabotage, lost production, extortion, kidnapping, security provision, higher insurance premiums and reputational damage. There is an emerging consensus that the human rights impact of a company operating in a zone of conflict or under an oppressive government can never be neutral. The need to protect and defend facilities and operations frequently leads to interactions with security forces and armed groups that are party to the conflict or repression. In this way the company may contribute to its dynamics. Oil- and diamond-producing companies in particular have come under scrutiny for their operations in zones of conflict. Nigeria, Colombia, Indonesia, Myanmar, Sudan, Liberia, Sierra Leone and Angola have all been centres of conflict in which oil or diamonds have played an important role. In most cases the key issue is that the extraction and trading of resources have helped fuel conflict, because the income from these resources has been inequitably distributed or has been used to purchase arms. In some cases territorial control of the areas where the resources are extracted has itself been a source of conflict.

There is likely to be growing pressure from a range of stakeholders for companies to consider how their operations may contribute to conflict and human rights violations, and what they might do to avoid this. A central issue is the security arrangements protecting a company's installations and employees, often involving the company in relationships with private security personnel or government forces that have a poor record on human rights. Inadequate handling of security arrangements, real or perceived, underpins many criticisms of the industry's human rights performance.

Corruption

Another key issue is transparency of the use of revenues from resource extraction. The more that corrupt government officials can siphon off the wealth generated from extraction of their country's resources, the more opposition there may be from communities who gain little from the presence of oil and mining companies. This is especially likely to be the case when these communities are faced with the consequences of any environmental damage, and increased presence of security forces, as well as any encroachment on their social and cultural rights.

The lack of transparency in the agreements reached between companies and governments is closely linked to corruption, and represents an area of risk to which extractive companies are particularly exposed. Bribes to smooth business transactions or win favours are common in some countries where oil and mining firms do business. Endemic corruption creates uncertainty, may perpetuate cycles of poverty and bad governance, and can be particularly detrimental to human rights when the police or judiciary are involved. Bribery and corruption can increase the costs of doing business and lead to adverse publicity.

WHY ARE HEAVY MANUFACTURING AND DEFENCE COMPANIES AT RISK?

The world's major heavy manufacturers tend to employ large workforces in developed countries where labour laws, equal opportunities legislation and health and safety regulations are more advanced than in developing countries. This exposes them to human rights challenges beyond those associated with their physical presence in countries featured on the map. In addition to the risk of litigation in their main centres of operation, they also have long supply chains and a responsibility to ensure that there are no abusive labour practices within those chains.

Heavy manufacturing companies, such as those producing steel, motor vehicles, machine tools, ships and military hardware tend to be long established with deep-rooted working cultures. This makes it more difficult for them than for firms in higher-technology industries to catch up with equal opportunities requirements. Consequently, avoiding discrimination against women and ethnic groups poses a particular challenge. It is hardly surprising that there have been a number of discrimination cases against such manufacturers, particularly in the USA and Europe.

Arms trade under scrutiny

The defence industry faces additional risk of association with human rights violations if it is found to export, to oppressive governments and armed opposition groups, equipment that is used to facilitate repression, torture, cruel, inhuman and degrading treatment, extra-judicial executions and other abuses. The trade in such equipment is the subject of growing scrutiny, not only from non-governmental organizations but increasingly also from the European Union and national governments, themselves under pressure to introduce effective export controls and monitor end use. The Ottawa Treaty banning landmines (1997) set a precedent for intergovernmental action.

A political consensus is developing on the need for greater transparency in reporting arms sales, and for controls on both arms brokerage and the licensing of production to overseas subsidiaries and joint venture partners. Some manufacturers have used such licensing agreements to circumvent controls in their own country. Companies that pursue such third-party arrangements will increase their exposure to allegations of complicity in human rights violations. The current focus on countering terrorism is likely to undermine the arguments of 'commercial confidentiality' that have been used to justify secrecy. In future, transactions may become more difficult to conceal.

The European Union's increasing willingness to establish a regulatory framework for arms exports has implications for any companies involved in the manufacture or trade of certain military or security products. In June 1998, the EU Council of Ministers adopted a Code of Conduct on Arms Exports that committed member states to refusing export licences if there is a risk that the arms might be used for internal repression in the countries of destination. In June 2000, the EU tightened controls on the export of dual-use items.

The growth of socially responsible investment funds that screen out arms manufacturers shows that some investors are concerned about activities that contribute to human rights violations. Many ethical investors are particularly concerned about arms exports and the end user chains of companies that manufacture defence equipment.

Litigation

The recent litigation against companies for use of slave labour during the Second World War illustrates that companies may be held accountable for their human rights impact decades after the event. There is a lesson here for all companies that are found to contribute to human rights violations through their relationships with repressive governments – sooner or later, they may be brought to account. This is in part because the desire for redress for past human rights violations endures over long periods among the victims and their families, and also because of the growing body of legal experts who specialize in human rights law and who are willing to challenge corporate malpractice.

WHY ARE INFRASTRUCTURE AND UTILITIES COMPANIES AT RISK?

Infrastructure and utilities companies often operate in countries where human rights violations are prevalent. The nature of their activities, underpinned by contractual agreements with governments, inevitably brings them into close contact with the authorities. In some cases companies may find themselves dealing with repressive governments, depending on them and on security forces with a poor human rights record for the protection of their installations and employees. Doing business in such areas can bring danger to company personnel, higher insurance costs, risk of sabotage, extortion, delays to projects, withdrawal of export credit guarantees and damage to reputation.

A further risk is that of violent conflict that may arise in situations where local communities suffer high costs from a new infrastructure development without benefiting from the services it provides. For example, they may suffer loss of land or livelihoods. Equally, they may be excluded from accessing the services offered by the project due to high pricing structures, inappropriate technologies or inflexible delivery mechanisms. In such situations the private operator may bear the brunt of community anger, resulting in escalating costs and loss of revenue that may undermine the project's sustainability.

Lack of rule of law

Another risk associated with many major infrastructure projects is corruption. Operating in a country where corruption is rife means added costs for companies and greater uncertainty in the decision-making processes on which the company depends. These uncertainties may threaten the viability of a project, and extend its timescale and costs. Corruption and human rights violations are invariably linked, in that both thrive in a political and legal vacuum where the authorities cannot be held to account. The rule of law is a precondition for protecting corporate assets as well as human rights.

Access to finance and export credits

Some infrastructure companies have become the target of international campaigns conducted by NGOs and the media. This is most likely to happen when projects they are involved in are themselves a cause of human rights violations, such as the forced relocation of communities. The Ilisu dam in Turkey, the Narmada dams in India and the Three Gorges dam in China provide high-profile examples of this. Some governments and intergovernmental bodies are increasingly reluctant to back major construction projects, such as dams, roads or bridges, with export credit guarantees, and now seek an assessment of the likely social and environmental impact before taking a decision. The World Bank took the significant step of reviewing its funding of dam construction projects in response to a report of the World Commission on Dams. The UK government's Export Credits Guarantee Department has adopted human rights principles to ensure that it 'does not contribute to human rights abuses in providing cover for any project or investment'. In keeping with these principles, it commissioned a report to help it decide whether to underwrite a UK company's participation in construction of the Ilisu dam. The report predicted that 60,000 people and many historical sites will be affected. Many local people will have to be resettled, historical and religious sites will be submerged, and the environment will be damaged. The dam might also raise regional tensions in the Middle East over control of water supplies.

As more rigorous human rights screening procedures are applied to infrastructure projects as a condition for export credits, the onus will be on companies to conduct their own pre-investment risk assessments. Those that fail to take human rights issues into account may find themselves incurring considerable planning and tendering costs for projects from which they are subsequently compelled to withdraw, because they have not met the required standards. Even if the projects proceed, ongoing protests and disruption may result in the absence of consultation with local communities and adequate safeguards to ensure that their fundamental rights are protected.

WHY ARE PHARMACEUTICAL AND CHEMICAL COMPANIES AT RISK?

Pharmaceutical and chemical companies face human rights challenges beyond those associated with their physical presence in countries with poor human rights records. Foremost among these for the pharmaceutical sector are calls to make essential drugs and treatments more available and accessible to combat disease in developing coun-tries, especially life-threatening diseases. Where relevant treatments exist, the industry has been criticized for high prices and the restrictive effects of patents. Criticism may also hit the industry if it is deemed to invest insufficiently in the research and devel-opment of treatments for so-called 'unprofitable' diseases, such as malaria and tuberculosis, which are prevalent in poor countries and do not yield sizeable profits.

A key point of contention is whether the products of the pharmaceutical industry should be viewed as private goods to be accessed through the market, or public goods to which citizens have a right. The right to health is expressly proclaimed in the Universal Declaration of Human Rights and in Article 12 of the International Covenant on Economic, Social and Cultural Rights. While responsibility for complying with UN protocols lies primarily with governments, companies are under increasing pressure to act to enhance access to medicines and to address issues around pricing, patents, infrastructure, distribution and public policy.

Intellectual property rights

Underpinning this dilemma is the issue of intellectual property rights, and in partic-ular the WTO Agreement on 'Trade Related Aspects of Intellectual Property Rights' (TRIPS) that was negotiated as part of the Uruguay Round of GATT in 1995. The TRIPS Agreement sets out detailed minimum standards for the protection and enforcement of intellectual property rights, and includes 20-year patent restrictions that enable pharmaceutical companies to recover their research and development costs on new medicines. The agreement has been criticized for serving to restrict access to essential medicines, leading to a clarifying declaration from the WTO Conference in Doha in November 2001 that it 'does not and should not prevent members taking measures to protect public health'. A 2001 report by the UN High Commission on Human Rights (UNHCHR) also criticized the TRIPS Agreement for overlooking the need to protect the cultural heritage and technology of local com-munities and indigenous peoples. According to the UNHCHR report, TRIPS fails to make intellectual property protection relevant to indigenous communities, and runs against the spirit of the Convention on Biological Diversity (1993).

Clinical trials

Pharmaceutical or health companies may also be subject to human rights risk in rela-tion to allegations over poorly conducted or unregulated clinical trials, particularly on people in developing countries who may not be adequately protected from abuse. Many countries in the developing world do not have powerful regulatory mechanisms to protect citizens such as those that exist within the US. Any company seen to exploit this situation is likely to come under pressure from campaign groups, the media or shareholders. A key issue is whether the company has obtained the informed consent of trial participants, as required under international laws and treaties governing clinical trials, such as the Nuremberg Code (1947), which was enacted in part to prevent a recurrence of the medical experimentation associated with the Holocaust.

End use of products

The reputation of the chemical sector has suffered significant damage over a number of years as a result of legal action and allegations of negligence over the effects on health of its products and operations. The risks may be particularly acute in some developing countries where occupational health and safety standards are weak or enforcement is lax. Chemical companies have come under pressure to control the end use of their products and to avoid harmful effects of misuse, for example of pesticides on farms. Litigation in the US shows that companies may be held accountable for the damage to health caused by their products many years after they have left the factory gates. The actions of the chemical industry today could have major repercussions for shareholders in future and are thus a risk management issue.

WHY ARE INFORMATION TECHNOLOGY HARDWARE AND TELECOMMUNICATIONS COMPANIES AT RISK?

Information technology hardware and telecommunications corporations (ICT companies) are exposed to a wide spectrum of human rights challenges. As with other industries that source raw materials and components from developing or transitional economies, ICT companies may be associated with child labour, poor working conditions and other human rights abuses through their supply chains. Though they may benefit from reduced labour costs and local expertise within high-technology manufacturers in countries such as China and Taiwan, large companies may also find themselves sourcing from factories where international labour standards are not recognized or are poorly enforced.

Companies may also find their end user chains subject to scrutiny, especially if repressive governments are found to use their products to manipulate public opinion, facilitate censorship, curtail freedom of expression or violate rights to privacy.

Surveillance technology that enables monitoring of e-mails and the internet may be particularly contentious where that technology is used in support of other forms of repression.

Coltan

Within the framework of human rights risk, the use of Coltan in printed circuit boards, mobile phones, computer games equipment and similar products has become a reputational issue for firms in this sector. Coltan (Colombo Tantalite) is an exceptionally temperature-resistant conductor, widely found in many of today's electrical components. Much of the world's Coltan reserves are believed to lie in Africa, with a large concentration in the war-torn Democratic Republic of Congo. The trade in Coltan is considered to be a source of conflict and is believed to be one reason why armies from several neighbouring states have a presence in the country, killing and displacing large numbers of civilians in the process. In April 2001, a report commissioned by the UN Security Council (S/2001/357) established that proceeds from the sale of Coltan were funding the armies of Rwanda and Uganda in their prosecution of the conflict. Subsequent reports by a UN panel of experts, published in 2002 and 2003, identified business enterprises from outside the region that the panel believed to be implicated in the conflict.

Digital divide

Commentators from both the private and public sector have remarked on the inherently democratic nature of new technologies and their capacity to open up previously closed societies. The internet is increasingly indispensable to human rights activists across the globe in helping to communicate their messages. Text messaging facilities are credited with mobilizing the pro-democracy demonstrations that helped force Filipino President Joseph Estrada from office in January 2001. Yet despite the enormous potential to empower ordinary people and enhance information flows vital to participatory democracy, companies that manufacture and supply ICT goods face immense human rights challenges.

Collaboration

There is little consensus even among the governments of the developed world on how to regulate the new technologies to balance the demands of law enforcement and the protection of public morals, with rights under international law to privacy and the freedom of information and expression. Australia and several EU countries have passed legislation that requires internet service providers (ISPs) to remove or monitor offensive material and assist in police or intelligence operations. The authorities in China, Saudi Arabia, Singapore and the United Arab Emirates employ so-called proxy servers to block access to certain sites or filter internet use for subversive data. Companies may be caught in the middle of such policies and find themselves subject to accusations that they are collaborating with governments to repress human rights.

WHY ARE FOOD AND BEVERAGES COMPANIES AT RISK?

The food and beverages industry has until recently avoided the kind of challenges to company reputations that have affected other sectors. However, the conditions under which agricultural commodities are produced have now come under increased public and media scrutiny, particularly in relation to the sourcing of foodstuffs (such as raw agricultural produce) from developing countries. Major manufacturers source products from an extremely complex network of agricultural producers in the developing world, which generally consist of a combination of large plantations and family smallholdings. Companies may find that human rights standards, such as the ILO conventions concerning freedom of association and forced and child labour, are not always well observed by producers, and that, in the case of family smallholdings, workers are unlikely to be afforded the protection of formal labour associations. What this means in terms of the risk to the multinational company is that their products may be associated with malpractice, as evidenced by media allegations of the complicity of chocolate manufacturers in child slavery in the West African cocoa industry.

Supply chains

Many corporations have developed codes of conduct to help them meet the human rights dilemmas to which they are exposed, such as child labour, forced labour, poor working conditions or constraints on freedom of association. However, the effectiveness of codes of conduct depends on the extent to which they are being enforced. Enforcement presents complex challenges to companies, which vary significantly from commodity to commodity and with the degree of influence the company can exert over its supply chain. As the experience of the garment industry (which faces some of the same questions) indicates, in the absence of adequate monitoring and auditing procedures companies may have serious difficulty convincing their critics that their policies are being implemented.

Impact on health

There are additional areas of human rights risk to which food and beverages companies may be exposed that are not directly tied to corporate presence in countries identified as giving rise to human rights concerns or where the conditions for human rights violations exist. Impact on health is an area that has attracted particular public attention, illustrated by consumer product boycotts relating to genetic food modification and the improper marketing of breast-milk substitutes, where companies are accused of misinforming mothers over the health benefits of bottle versus breast milk. This illustrates the need for adequate implementation mechanisms to safeguard against breaches of the code of conduct devised by the World Health Organization (WHO) for the marketing of breast-milk substitutes.

SUMMARY

As the above analysis shows, companies cannot escape from their human rights obligations by sourcing their products from or shifting their operations to areas of the world where human rights are routinely abused. The trend towards outsourcing makes it more difficult for some companies to assert management control over the circumstances in which human rights violations occur. This is why they should take steps to integrate human rights into their relationships with suppliers, subcontractors and joint venture partners. This can be achieved by viewing human rights as a quality control issue. Just as companies will, as a matter of course, hold suppliers and subcontractors to account for the quality of goods and services provided, so they should also use their contractual leverage to ensure that their subcontractors conduct their operations in conformity with internationally accepted human rights standards.

Moving production to locations where it will be carried out in conditions that would be unacceptable in the company's home country puts its reputation at risk. This is why it is essential for businesses not only to understand the human rights context of their operations, but also to ensure that they have an adequate human rights policy framework in place that is properly enforced right across the company's global functions and operations.

WORK–LIFE BALANCE: A SENSIBLE BALANCE BETWEEN WORK AND LIFE CAN HELP RETAIN THE BEST WORKERS

Glynn Yarnall, Management Consultant

Social responsibility

Most senior executives understand and accept that their corporate responsibility goes beyond the bricks and mortar that is their business, whether it is pollution management, a decent working environment or contributing to the local community.

But to limit a company's efforts to these areas is to miss out on a more fundamental 'audience' that is central to any organization – its employee base. Without a contented workforce, all the sponsored fun runs, crèches and restaurant facilities will fail to satisfy today's demanding employee.

At times of high employment, staff are clearly in the driving seat and can choose the employer that most closely matches their individual needs, in terms of both the job description and how the role will affect their personal life.

With 70 per cent of all sickness absence in the UK workplace being stress related – equating to £370 million in lost business – it has never been more critical that businesses track the success of their personnel policies. If we then recognize that more than a third of absenteeism is due to work–life imbalance, then it becomes apparent that we need regular ongoing reviews on how to improve or evolve the approach to work–life balance.

Everyone recognizes that inefficient use of time is a major source of stress for staff but it is not just the effect it has on their professional workload. Every time people are asked to undertake out-of-hours activities, it is not just their work diary that needs to be rescheduled but also their personal life, often impacting upon the plans made by family and friends.

It is not working long hours in itself that is necessarily the problem. After all, most of us occasionally put in the extra time when we have to meet an urgent deadline. Imbalance, on the other hand, happens when such long hours at work become the norm or you cannot take time out to address home needs.

Employers must recognize that staff have a life outside of work – including both social interests and family responsibilities – and any organization that understands this can create a better environment that leads to extended benefits into the community. It can take many forms, from allowing individuals to develop their interest in a sport or charity work through to just simply spending more quality time with their dependants. Considering that one in five women who are in employment also have to care for both their children and elderly parents, there is a large part of the population who, like it or not, have to balance their job with far more than the school run and trips to the supermarket.

Build in the fact that childcare is with us on average for 16 years and eldercare takes around 22 years, and we have a serious amount of juggling to do! From this, it is obvious that any employer that can help reduce this burden will be contributing to the quality of life far beyond the immediate employee base.

If a contented staff makes a productive team, then a realistic work–life balance strategy provides the perfect opportunity really to make a difference by embracing the needs of the workforce and, indirectly, the other members of their families. With an employee base of say 250, an employer can make a direct impact – negative or positive – that can reach over 1,000 people within days.

For example, if without consultation a decision is made to make even minor changes to shift patterns, staff and their partners may be forced to adapt their childcare timetables and associated schedules to suit the employer. If this results in increased costs and ongoing conflict with partners' home life, the job quickly becomes less attractive, causing workers to feel less valued and likely to consider changing jobs.

Work–life balance – myth or reality?

A company that has achieved full work–life balance for its staff will benefit from more than just the well-publicized reduction in attrition and its related recruitment and retraining costs. It will be moving towards a less stressful and happier environment in which to work. The outcome is a workforce that not only finds time to relax at home, but also becomes an excellent ambassador for the company.

So, what is work–life balance? Experts describe it as a 'journey', rather than items to tick off a list that, once achieved, mean work–life balance has been implemented. While any attempt to improve work–life balance is to be applauded, it will only produce the more major benefits over a longer period of time and with the cooperation and commitment of the workforce.

As a leading expert in work–life balanc, Lynne Copp, Managing Director of Marlborough-based The Worklife Company, sees the two separate elements placing different demands on the individual. As she explains, 'In the work environment, balance is all about productivity, prioritizing, communicating and improving assertiveness. Many of these areas are driven by each individual's circumstances, such as their employer's goals and expectations. By contrast, balance in your home life is more to do with finding time for yourself, developing relationships, building your own self-worth, self-belief and confidence.'

While most organizations have over the years continued to push productivity up and bring costs down, how many have considered the impact these business improvements have had on the personnel? With today's fluid labour market, staff attrition will have a visible effect on the profit and loss through recruitment and retraining costs but we often ignore the truth behind the high employee turnover, preferring to accept the departing employee's stock reason of 'They offered me more money.' By looking beyond this throwaway comment, we are more likely to uncover the often-shared grievances that are never raised at the leaving party. After all, *they* are leaving so why would they rock the boat for their friends who will still be there come Monday morning?

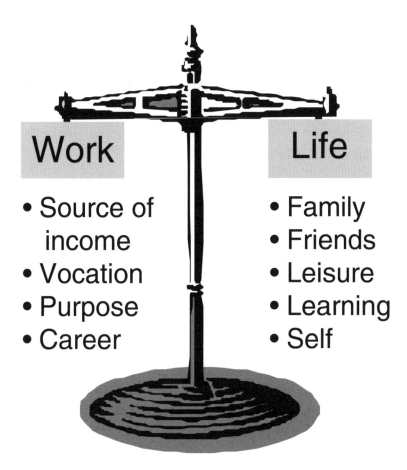

Figure 10.1 Work–life balance

Flexibility – a two-way commitment

A feature of work–life balance is providing staff with options on how to deal with the occasional family crisis or school meeting. One case in point is Stroud and Swindon Building Society, which found that managers and part-timers were the most likely candidates to be working extra hours, while over a quarter of their staff were responsible for family dependants.

An in-depth staff survey revealed that the relatively high levels of inflexibility, absence and attrition were generally due to four areas of staff concern – dependant care, long hours, education and childcare. The research led Sara Phelps, HR Administration Manager for the society, to the conclusion that 'we had a general challenge to educate managers and staff in adopting a flexible approach'.

To achieve this, the company set up a 'work–life focus group', consisting of a single father, someone who cares for both of her elderly parents, and other similarly challenged employees. The result is a set of policies specifically focusing on staff leave for dependant care, emergencies, paternity, parental and career breaks.

As Stroud and Swindon's CEO, John Parker, sees it, 'I am committed to ensuring that we provide staff with the working flexibility they need.' This enlightened attitude will continue to benefit employer and employee beyond the initial implementation phase as both parties learn to work together.

Making the company fit the employee

A second example is at Somerset-based Perfecta, a supplier of high-quality ingredients to the food industry. The nature of the business meant the workforce was typically women with family commitments, and Perfecta's owner, Dr Peter Roberts, recognized that many workers would 'prefer to work when it fitted around their family and other commitments'.

After reviewing their current practices, the company began to identify that the issues staff felt were important were mostly health-related benefits, combined with a willingness to allow staff to work around their external responsibilities. This created a 'pool' of workers who could be called upon, based around their own personal needs and availability.

The outcome is that the company has now attracted twice the number of packers, as the local community begin to appreciate the benefit the company provides to working parents. The flexibility has also helped other departments; for example a recently divorced mother of two, who joined as a laboratory technician, was surprised to find such a company geared towards the employee's needs.

An informal approach to authority

With staff turnover running at up to 25 per cent, Sheffield Chamber of Commerce and Industry realized it had to adopt a work–life initiative if it was to reverse the trend. As with Stroud and Swindon, a staff survey was used to expose the root of the problem. In this case, it was a lack of communication between management and the workforce and, as Sue Williams, the chamber's Personnel Manager, recalls, 'We didn't think we had ever actually refused time off to anyone for personal or domestic reasons. The problem was we didn't have a culture where it was OK to ask.'

After consultation with the staff, it was agreed that a formal flexitime scheme would be difficult to implement. Instead, the simple decision to give all managers the authority to use their discretion in these circumstances has resulted in a significant reduction in staff turnover. The chamber has learnt that communicating reg-ularly overcomes issues early on, and Williams believes that 'work–life balance has already catalysed some very significant changes for the better.'

Ignore work–life balance at your peril

From the above projects the Worklife Company has undertaken, Lynne Copp believes reluctance to embrace work–life balance is often because the business assumes that employees will take advantage of the new policies. Copp adds, 'This attitude engenders a "fear" culture where there is a high level of mistrust and poor communication across the board. For example, in such an environment, an employee with a sick child is more likely to take a day sick leave than actually explain what the problem really is for fear of being seen as an uncommitted or disloyal worker.'

This lack of communication and cooperation simply means that the organization loses a day's productivity, when it need only have lost a couple of hours while the employee made alternative childcare arrangements.

Compare this scenario to any of the case studies mentioned and it is obvious that, far from being costly and unproductive, work–life balance can reduce stress for both parties – the individual feels valued and trusted while the employer has a more reliable workforce.

But if none of this appeals to you, consider the situation from a purely business perspective – if your nearest competitor has implemented work–life balance and is benefiting from a stable employee base, how long will it be before word gets out and you start losing some of your key staff to your competitor? Prevention is certainly cheaper than cure.

11

Waste management and recycling

John Hancock

Much of this book is concerned with things that companies make or do (goods and services) and the activities that accompany the production and marketing of those goods and services. However, many products or services involve a great deal more than the inputs, processes and outputs on which companies build their reputations. Like catalysts in a chemical process, there are materials used in manufacturing that never become part of the final product. For instance, most industrial processes use a greater weight of water than the weight of the product being manufactured. Even services often create paperwork that will be discarded once an application has been completed. Indeed, waste products are the largest single source of the economically active world's impact on the rest of the world. This is why some of the highest-profile campaigns of recent times have been about environmental issues of which waste is half of the story, the other half being the extraction or depletion of non-renewable resources to supply raw materials for the manufacturing process. Of course, the twin strands of waste and resources go very closely together as good management of the one (waste) can reduce the need for the other (virgin raw materials).

Also, waste is an emotive subject, and pictures of small children playing and growing up among the squalor of a business's waste can have many times more impact on an audience than any number of charts, tables and 'proofs' that the business is playing by the rules. And when a disaster is caused by the mismanagement of waste or the waste that is consequent upon the mismanagement of a process, in most cases the company will suffer in terms of its reputation and, in an increasing number of jurisdictions, in financial terms when a 'polluter pays' penalty is levied. It has even been demonstrated that share prices can fall following any environmental disaster where the culprit can be identified.

These days, waste is a big subject, but it was not always the case.

FROM A SLOW START...

For a long time, during the period following the first industrial revolution (from the 18th century onwards, many would say), economic progress seemed to be predicated on the assumption that the world was, to all intents and purposes, an infinite source of materials and energy to fuel the economy with an infinite capability to absorb what the economy did not use or had finished with.

As a result, human activities continued with little regard to the impact that they had on the world and what remained after a process such as, say, mining or manufacturing was simply dumped near to the extraction site or the plant. The world, it was reasoned, was a big place that could easily cope with the relatively small impact of industrial societies. That attitude prevailed throughout the industrialization of the 19th century and, with only a small portion of the world industrialized and only a small proportion of the population in even those places able to afford the products of industrialization, the environment probably did appear to be coping, whether or not that actually was the case.

...TO INCREMENTAL DAMAGE

However, during the 20th century, industrialization spread as emerging nations saw it in terms of national pride to have their own industrial economies. Meanwhile, in the developed economies, the rise of the consumer meant that demand for the products and services that had once been the preserves of the wealthy fuelled continued industrial expansion on a scale far greater than had ever been seen before. After the Second World War, that consumer-driven expansion took all economies to record levels of production but also to record levels of waste generation. And, because nobody was seriously thinking about what to do with that waste, the problem of disposal sites just grew incrementally.

A FINITE WORLD

In the last quarter of the 20th century people began to listen to those who had, for some time, been insistently pointing out that ours is a finite world. This meant that consumption and waste generation on a potentially unfettered scale would eventually fully deplete its resources and poison its environment with the spent waste of profligacy. People and organizations began to consider what to do with waste and even to devise schemes that would make it tolerable. But, if the problem was to be tackled properly, the same planning and implementation of strategies through policy had to be applied to dealing with waste as was applied to the processes that generated it. Waste was as much a part of the economic process as the goods and services that process provided and needed to be treated as such. Waste management is as important to any process as production management, marketing management, human resources management, financial management, IT management and all the other management disciplines that together make the modern economy tick.

WHAT IS WASTE?

A substance falls within the legal definition of waste when:

- it has been discarded;
- there is an intention to discard it; or
- there is a requirement to discard it.

The first one is easy to understand. Anything that we throw away or allow to escape into the environment is waste. But, that may be too simple a definition and it would certainly be a difficult one on which to base any waste management programme. After all, once something has served its purpose and has no other purpose, waste management is really about disposal, the easiest way to add it to the sum of the earth's burdens. That would be the management of an output whereas we can exercise much more control if we manage inputs, which is why the definition goes further. It considers waste to arise when there is an intention to discard it. So we must start to think about how we will handle waste as soon as we have decided that an item is to become waste. That means that, when a new machine is ordered, as much as planning its arrival and installation, the business must plan the removal of its predecessor and its own eventual demise. But it goes even further than that.

Some things are manufactured with the intention that they should become waste. Their purpose is not related to the performance of a product or service in the role for which it has been created but rather is a temporary function that may play its part but will not contribute to the job that the product has to do. Perhaps it will be easier to understand with an example, the most obvious of which is packaging. Most packaging does a job that is not directly important to the function of what it contains. Its purpose is to protect the contents until they are needed and sometimes to dispense them.

However, packaging has become much more than a simple container. It has become a sales and marketing tool, a piece of advertising, a measure of quality judged solely on external appearance. But, whatever it has become, when packaging is made there is an intention for someone to discard it.

There will also be a number of products that simply have to be discarded. Usually, a requirement to discard will have legal connotations. For instance, when a motor tyre no longer meets the legal requirement for a minimum tread depth, there is a legal requirement to discard it. Equally, when food has passed its 'sell by' date and especially its 'use by' date, there is a legal and functional requirement to discard it, and when a product has done its job or worn out there is a functional and economic requirement to discard it.

As with management of all processes, understanding what happens and what outcome is desired or required is an important first step to managing the generation and disposal of waste. Equally, not all waste is solid or a spent product. Liquid and gaseous wastes are, if anything, even more damaging than solid and spent product wastes because they are so much more difficult to contain, collect and control and can quickly pollute a large area simply by spreading into it.

Of course, almost everything is made with the ultimate intention that it should be discarded even if, for practical purposes in the case of, say, buildings, that event will be well beyond the lifetime of the person making it. This means that waste management, although it is about safe disposal, is even more about planning at the outset for a specification, a design, a process, a method of use and, yes, a disposal that will create least impact on the environment by minimizing the amount of waste with which that environment has to cope.

Perhaps today our definition of waste should be: something for which no further productive or useful application can be found. If we take that as the definition then the challenge of waste management is to minimize the amount of waste because if no productive or useful application can be found then waste becomes a dead weight on the environment, something that ties up one or all of space, energy, cost and amenity with no commensurate return. Not good business.

A WASTE STRATEGY

This reality is not lost on the UK government, which established 'Waste Strategy 2000 for England and Wales' in order to pull together objective setting and effort on a national scale and in a coordinated manner to address the problem of waste management.

On a smaller scale than that of the government, the same approach will be required in every organization throughout the economy, from the largest government organization such as the National Health Service right through to the small and medium enterprises (SMEs) driving the economy forward.

Like any economic and commercial activity, waste management must be planned, must be the responsibility of a manager (and team in the larger businesses) and must be accorded the same status as other business activities. There has to be a corporate commitment to waste management as an equal component in the overall management of the business; otherwise it will not be able to secure the resources and authority needed to ensure that the business does not fall foul of an increasing list of laws. And even without a law specifically aimed at every sector, there is already a general duty of care that is set out in the Waste Strategy 2000.

DUTY OF CARE

The duty of care applies to anyone who imports, produces, carries, keeps, treats or disposes of waste or, as a broker, has control of it. Everyone subject to the duty of care must take all such measures as are reasonable in the circumstances to:

- prevent contravention by any other person of the waste management provisions of the 1990 Act;
- prevent the escape of the waste from his or her control or that of any other person;
- ensure that waste is transferred only to an authorized person, such as the holder of a waste management licence, a person operating under the terms of a licensing exemption registered with the Environment Agency or a registered waste carrier;
- ensure that a written description is transferred with the waste.

Everyone to whom the duty of care applies has a legal obligation to comply with it and there are severe penalties for failing to do so, for example an unlimited fine on conviction in a Crown Court.

Neglected, waste will soon start to cost the business in terms of tax, in terms of fines, in terms of litigation from anybody affected by poorly managed waste and, if the management has to be carried out under pressure to somebody else's timetable, in terms of resources diverted to this unproductive task that could otherwise be engaged in more productive activities. Badly managed waste can also damage those core intangible assets, reputation and trust. And while such intangibles can be lost in an instant, their regaining, like their original gaining, may take years or prove impossible. Properly managed, the issue of waste can take its place in the plan and utilize the business's resources at the time most convenient to the business, save costs and improve the image of the business, even provide a marketing edge. And if common sense were not incentive enough to tackle the issue, government-inspired changes in what can be done with waste will mean that businesses that have thought about the subject will be in a stronger position than those that wait until forced into action in response to changes taking place around them that could easily have been predicted and actions built into normal business plans.

Planned reductions in the use of landfill over the next 15 years will require careful planning. Of course, some waste can be incinerated but incineration is also a regulated activity and some substances cannot be safely incinerated without very expensive safeguards, the costs of which will be passed on to users, ie those generating the waste. Also, some substances simply will not incinerate.

The need for change is readily apparent. We can look at the government's vision in Waste Strategy 2000 for England and Wales as a guide because, although it refers to national objectives rather than the objectives for an individual business, the principles hold good at any level in the economy. The extract has been edited to reflect progress to date and annotated – italicized comments in square brackets – to show how the strategy may be translated into the daily life of a business.

The vision, aims and objectives of the waste strategy

The key messages of the waste strategy are:

- England and Wales produced 106 million tonnes of commercial, industrial and municipal waste in 1999, most of which was sent to landfill.
  [*How much waste did the business produce last year and where did it go?*]
- At the heart of government strategy lies the need to tackle the growth in our waste.
  [*This would be true of a business just as much as it is true for the whole country.*]
- We need to maximize the amount of value we recover from waste through increased recycling, composting and energy recovery.
  [*Are there any plans in the business to identify where value recovery is feasible and viable and then to do this?*]
- The strategy sets challenging targets for better waste management:
  - to recover value from 45 per cent of municipal waste by 2010, at least 30 per cent through recycling or composting;
  - to recover value from two-thirds of municipal waste by 2015, at least half of that through recycling and composting, and to go beyond this in the longer term.
  [*Has the business set any targets for waste management through recycling or its accompanying policies of reduction in consumption and reuse of used products?*]

- We need to develop new and stronger markets for recycled materials. The Waste and Resources Action Programme (WRAP), a not-for-profit company, was launched in November 2000 and it began work in January 2001. It was established by government and the devolved administrations, with an initial three-year funding allocation of £40 million jointly provided by the Department for Environment, Food and Rural Affairs (Defra), the Department for Trade and Industry (DTI), the Scottish Executive, the Welsh Assembly government and the Northern Ireland Executive. WRAP's aim is to promote sustainable waste management by working to create stable and efficient markets for recycled materials and products and removing the barriers to waste minimization, reuse and recycling. Over the last year WRAP has undertaken a considerable additional programme of work funded by Defra.

  [What ideas does the business have for marketing spent and recycled products from its range or products that it uses in its processes? How are these notions being carried into the specification design and production processes?]

- Producers must increasingly expect to arrange for recovery of their products – in particular, new targets for more collection and recycling of direct ('junk') mail were agreed in July 2003 . The government and industry have signed an agreement intended to reduce the amount of direct mail delivered to British homes and to increase the amount that is recycled.

  [Does the business know how its products will be dealt with when their useful life is over and has anybody recently audited what goes into direct mail packs, who it goes to and what is the response from that form of marketing?]

- The amount of waste sent to landfill must be reduced substantially. The 1999 EC Landfill Directive requires the UK to reduce substantially the amount of biodegradable municipal waste it sends to landfill. Following a series of consultations, the government will launch the Landfill Allowance Trading Scheme in England on 1 April 2005. This scheme is designed to allow local authorities to reduce the amount of biodegradable municipal waste they send to landfill in the most cost-effective way. Each waste disposal authority will be allocated a decreasing number of landfill allowances for each year between 2005/06 and 2019/20. They can then trade allowances with other authorities, borrow forward 5 per cent of their next year's allocation or bank unused allowances for use in future years. These flexibilities will enable local authorities to match their reductions to their individual waste diversion plans. Waste will only count towards allowances or targets if collected by or on behalf of a local authority to come under the biodegradable waste definition. If collected by a commercial contractor and not on behalf of a local authority, it would then count as commercial or industrial waste depending on the nature of the business producing the waste.

Businesses will not have allowances or permits for their biodegradable waste output; the only allowance will be that of the local authority.

[*Does the business understand what biodegradable waste it produces and from which parts of the business processes that arises? If not, why not and, if so, how can those levels be reduced or eliminated in any revision, redesign or updating of the process or outputs?*]

While businesses can no longer plan to continue with current policies on waste, unless those policies are already in line with government thinking, there are many positive aspects to waste management. These will manifest as increased efficiency in the business, cost reductions (albeit sometimes in the long term) and the USP of being a company whose business philosophy is in tune with the times and the public mood (let alone the government's commitment) in this area. Also, last but not least, businesses will be working towards a better world, and why not? The incorporation of a moral component in business practice has a long, honourable and profitable tradition going back into the Quaker-run corporate giants of the 19th century.

WASTE MANAGEMENT

There are a number of mechanisms that waste managers can use to minimize the waste stream, but three favoured by the government and all those working in this area on a national and continental level are known as the three 'Rs':

- Reduce consumption of materials (including fuel).
- Reuse items and materials wherever possible.
- Recycle items and materials that cannot or can no longer be reused.

There is a fourth 'R', which is the recovery of energy from waste (EfW), usually through burning it to release the calorific value of the material as heat, which is converted to electricity. There are also some schemes that capture the methane produced when organic waste is composted and use that gas as the basis for a fuel.

And, for fans of alliteration willing to stretch a linguistic point in order to make a business point, we can even add a fifth 'R' to the list for the responsible disposal of irreducible waste. This includes the principle of proximity that says that waste should always be disposed of as near as possible to where it has been generated, subject to there being a suitable and licensed facility able to handle the waste in question.

WHY ALL THE FUSS?

It is a perfectly legitimate question for those who are faced with government-inspired or -imposed tasks to ask why those tasks have been framed in the first place. In this case, there are a number of legitimate reasons why individuals, government departments, local authorities and businesses large or small should take steps to minimize waste.

The well-publicized and discussed greenhouse effect, in which emissions resulting from all sorts of human activities rise into the atmosphere and deplete or break down the ozone layer that protects the earth from the more harmful of the sun's rays, has been increasingly blamed for climatic disasters that have devastated various parts of the world in recent times. The avoidance of such emissions (the gaseous waste from various manufacturing and energy production processes as well as the methane generated from the decomposition process that takes place in most landfill sites) will help to reduce or reverse that effect.

On a planet of finite size, everything must be finite including the resources that make up the planet and that are used as material from which the products that society demands have to be made and fuel for the processes that make them. The use of non-renewable resources causes a direct reduction in what remains and a consequent imbalance of the earth's biosphere with long-term consequences, the nature of which we can only guess.

The alternative is to use renewable resources such as wood for manufacturing and wind power for electrical generation or to reuse and recycle resources that have already been used so that they can once again enter the economic chain with a minimum impact on the earth's ecology. Whether the resource itself is actually incorporated into another product or whether its disposal is through incineration from which heat can be extracted to generate electrical energy without the need to use virgin resources such as coal or oil, there is still a net saving to the planet and, often, a cost saving to the businesses involved. Also there is a good economic and business case for getting the most value from anything, whether coffee cups or computers, which has required expenditure of the business's resources to acquire it.

MAKING MARKETS

Businesses can only flourish where there is a market for their outputs, and there are parts of the world where, while there are large numbers of people who could be a potential market, the economy, for one reason or another, just cannot get started. To lift an economy from the third world to a developing market requires injections of resources that often cannot be afforded and so some potential markets simply do not develop. If used items from the developed world can be made available at low or no cost as a means of kick-starting those markets, that will ultimately benefit everybody, including the businesses that may have given the items in the first place and that will now see a new market for their main outputs. A number of aid-related charities have organized such recycling programmes to cascade earlier generations of Western tech-nology to places where there is currently no technology. And it need not only be third world countries that benefit. Plenty of charities will recycle used items to help the economically less well-placed members of our own society to start their own enter-prises, which will, in turn, bring them back into the economically active society and add them to the home market.

BETTER TO THINK AHEAD AND GET AHEAD

The EU regularly discusses waste-related matters, the results of which discussions will no doubt find their way into EU directives and on into legislation in member countries, including the UK. For instance, the end-of-life directives regularly formu-lated in Brussels for translation into national legislation make manufacturers respon-sible for the quality of disposal and recycling of their products whose useful life is finished. It will only be possible to comply with the directive applicable in a given business sector by incorporating consideration of reduction, reuse and recycling at the earliest stages of product specification. Some areas, especially where hazardous substances are involved and with regard to packaging, which is viewed as mainly a use of resources for no added value (except where it performs a safety or product protection role), are already the subjects of specific legislation and charges.

Even if businesses are not yet deluged with waste-related regulations, they soon will be and, as with any bureaucratic process, this one will be easier to deal with if the business already has an established policy of how to handle the matter.

The worst policy is denial: 'It hasn't affected us yet and so we see no reason to act until it does.' This policy falls down, because if the business does not know how it is performing in terms of waste management it may not realize when it is in breach of one of the growing number of regulations in the area. But, as always, ignorance is no excuse in the eyes of the law and a business that does not know how it is doing on waste disposal runs the risk of facing an unexpected and unbudgeted fine as well as the need to incur other related remedial costs.

A better policy is to have a positive approach to waste management, including it as one of the business's core management disciplines with management information, performance targets and action plans in the annual business plan as well as regular reporting and results, just as with any other function in the business. That way, there will be no nasty surprises and there may well be savings and new, more efficient ways of doing things identified that will save cost as well as waste. It may also be possible to improve the products or services that the business provides, thus generating a further marketing edge over and above the 'halo' of a progressive and forward-thinking approach that attaches to businesses perceived by the public to be acting in an environmentally responsible manner.

The best policy is to start now incorporating waste management into product and especially packaging design. The best companies with the best reputations and brands to uphold have realized that and have already taken the lead. End-of-life directives specify that manufacturers will be held accountable for their products right up to and including final disposal of the life-expired item or its component parts. It is no coincidence that BMW is one of the first motor manufacturers to have met this requirement and to have licensed breakers to dispose of or recycle its life-expired products in a way in which they were designed to be. Waste disposal and recycling are not afterthoughts in business; they need to be at the heart of any business that wishes to be seen as a responsible corporate citizen.

12

Environmental risk management

John Hancock

PREVENTION IS BETTER THAN CURE

There is always risk in life but, in a civilized society, we do not have to accept that risk and its consequences are inevitable. We have the resources to take a better view and to apply to risk the same enterprising and creative spirit that has made our society the comfortable place it is today. But, as with any task, before we tackle risk we need to know what it is we are tackling.

As the growing demands of modern society began to put ever more pressure on the earth's ecosystems, some scientists and others began to realize that, on a finite planet, there was an absolute limit to how much damage the ecosystem could sustain from both disasters and long-term degradation. At the same time, the idea that it was somehow acceptable to harm some people if the cost of avoiding that harm seemed too high was wholly discredited. A new model for handling environmental damage and disaster was needed that would, for any given activity, consider where, how and to what extent it impacted on the environment both at the time the activity was under way and through any residual legacy of waste or environmental change that it generated. The new model would also have to be able to devise and implement alternative processes or remedial activities to avoid or mitigate that damage. Thus environmental risk management was born to apply the same forward planning and activity monitoring to environmental risk as was already applied to the other activities of businesses.

And neither is it any longer acceptable to suggest that such a model requires resources to be diverted from profit and growth to non-revenue-generating tasks because the reality is that somebody has to pick up the bill for environmental failure and that somebody has, historically, been the taxpayer at large. The taxpayer through governments elected to manage tax spending has drawn a line and, with so many other and more legitimate demands on the already hard-pressed expenditure budgets of any nation, has chosen not to divert resources that could be used in building, say, a better health service to cleaning up after what are now regarded as avoidable environmental disasters and damage. The new attitude can be summed up in the term 'make the polluter pay' but also stretched to encompass the new readiness to sue organizations that have conducted activities harmful to people, and that has changed the business economics with regard to environmental impact of human activities. What it means is that the costs associated with any activities (including those costs associated with any pollution or erosion or other environmental damage caused by waste resulting from the activity) should be borne by those who expect to profit from those activities.

In the light of this new thinking, it is now far better business practice to consider building managing environmental risk into the business's activities alongside marketing, production, distribution and all of the other processes that make up the modern business model.

SO, WHAT IS ENVIRONMENTAL RISK?

It is the likelihood or possibility that an activity or process in the business will degrade, devalue or destabilize the environment in such a way as to:

- damage the environment itself and lead to further damage as a result;
- harm employees of the business;
- harm other people in the society at large;
- damage the long-term prospects for the business.

It is also possible that changes or events in the environment might damage the business and this also should be built into an environmental risk management model.

SOME COMMON EXAMPLES OF RISK AND CONSEQUENCES

Just as there is nothing new about environmental risk, there is also nothing new about its management; it is simply that we have not used the term until recent times.

If, however, we call it 'common sense', then there are plenty of examples to draw upon from the familiar world around us:

- Household waste, if not properly stored and/or disposed of, will attract vermin and produce conditions in which disease will flourish. In order to manage that risk, we have devised waste storage and collection systems as well as sanitary waste disposal systems that minimize the opportunity to attract vermin or promote disease. We prefer to manage the risk rather than deal with the outcomes.
- When water lands on a large impermeable surface, it all runs to the lowest point before running off the surface at that point. House roofs are an excellent example of this effect and, to avoid a concentrated flow of water leaving the roof from its lowest point and risking eroding the ground on to which it falls, guttering is fitted to channel the flow into a drainage gully. It is easier to build risk management into the design of the building than to have to cope with the effects of water erosion.
- People who spray cars have to work in an environment that is highly polluted with toxic fumes. In order to protect them from the effects of those fumes, employers provide masks with various filters and ensure that powerful extractor fans remove most of the fumes from the spray shop to a safe container. As well as being morally correct, this proper management of the risk will help avoid prosecution from the health and safety authorities as well as removing the grounds on which an employee might bring a civil case against the business.
- In workplaces where smokers and non-smokers share space, non-smokers (who, remember, have chosen not to inhale tobacco smoke) may find themselves subject to passive smoking and may use that as the basis for a claim against their employer for not providing a safe or healthy working environment. Setting aside areas where smokers can smoke is a sensible form of risk management.
- Where a factory is sited near to a water course that is fished or provides water for drinking or recreational activities, no waste should be discharged into it from the factory because it could harm other users of it. Sensible storage, treatment and disposal of waste are simple risk management processes.

At this stage, the reader will understand the point that environmental risk management has been practised for centuries but it was always passive or reactive, ie people took steps to deal with risks whose consequences they had already experienced, cleared up after the problem or simply moved on and left the problem behind, not resolved but 'out of sight, out of mind'. That model seemed to work (many would now dispute whether it actually worked) in a world where relatively few new processes or associated risks existed. However, our modern world is one where new processes abound (as much as older ones are abandoned) and where we are forever pushing out the envelope of our impact on the environment. If we simply waited for a disaster to occur or only dealt with risks whose consequences had already been felt, we would be forever coping with environmental damage and disaster. And for businesses in particular, that model would expose them to many and costly risks.

ENVIRONMENTAL DAMAGE AS A BUSINESS RISK

Almost any human activity can be said to incur a risk and, if one looks far enough and hard enough, almost any business activity can be found to incur an environmental risk. But, of course, there is a need to retain a sense of proportion, and so most of the issues which businesses have to address will be their contribution to the larger risks to the environment and, most importantly, the risk to people as a result of any environmental damage. Also, some balance has to be struck between the activity in question and what the alternative means. So, while a heat exchange unit might well add some pollution to the atmosphere, it may well be that the alternative, a heating unit and an air-conditioning unit, will do far more damage. The key is for the business to look at all of its activities and the links between them as well as any processes outside of the business that precede or follow those activities, ie suppliers and customers, to see what environmental impact they have and the extent of that impact. Then consider other possibilities and assess whether they would make things better or worse.

And when any project is being evaluated and planned, the environmental risk needs to be factored in along with all other inputs (just the same as, say, financial risk) and, where necessary, avoidance or restoration programmes designed from the outset. For some businesses that is very obvious. For instance, a quarrying company knows that its activities will wreak great damage upon the environment but, because the output is a commodity in great demand, it would be economically unacceptable not to quarry, and any alternative supplies would simply move the environmental risk to another part of the world.

So, instead, quarrying companies go to great lengths to move rivers and habitats where that is feasible, and create alternative habitats during the time that quarrying takes place, and they are obliged to restore the land, not to its original state but to an acceptable state, when they have finished their extraction work. Also, like any other businesses using water as part of the process, they must ensure that no toxic or degrading pollutants get returned to the water supply after the process. Sometimes that can be achieved with filters, sometimes with treatment and sometimes by altering the process to minimize or eliminate the need to pollute water.

Environmental risk management is about that part of the process and every bit as important a part as the extraction, collection and distribution of the material extracted from the quarry.

THE PRECAUTIONARY PRINCIPLE

The UK government's attitude to risk management is based upon the Rio Declaration adopted by governments at the 1992 United Nations Conference on Environment and Development where the precautionary principle was stated as: 'Where there are threats of serious or irreversible damage, lack of full scientific certainty shall not be used as a reason for postponing cost effective measures to prevent environmental degradation.'

But also there is a note of realism in the approach, as the UK government's own guidelines go on to say:

> At the same time, precautionary action must be based on objective assessments of the costs and benefits of action. The principle does not mean that we only permit activities if we are sure that serious harm will not arise or there is proof that the benefits outweigh all possible risks. That would severely hinder progress towards improvements in the quality of life.

This recognizes the reality that all human progress will have some impact on the environment. Also, risk management cannot be a one-off action but must accept that, just as the environment itself changes, so the risks can change or their impact can change or our knowledge of their impact can change.

THE CONSEQUENCES OF GETTING IT WRONG

The consequences of failing to manage environmental risk fall into several areas:

- statutory and regulatory;
- civil actions from employees;
- civil actions from the public;
- moral opprobrium;
- loss of business.

Perhaps they deserve some expansion.

Statutory and regulatory

The scope of environmental damage and the ways in which the damage can be done fall under several areas of law and regulation related mainly to waste management, recycling and sustainability, and health and safety legislation for which there is a range of penalties including substantial fines and temporary or permanent closure of the business, and ranging up to imprisonment for directors or executives judged responsible for any incident or damage.

Civil actions from employees

Gone are the days when workers would accept health degradation or injury or even discomfort as 'part of the job'. Nowadays, an employer who does not consider the likely impact of any environmental risk on the workforce is almost certain to end up in court facing an expensive civil action that, even if the insurance company ends up footing the bill, will still be a costly affair in terms of the administrative burden (when insurance companies fight a case, they expect absolute support from their policy-holder) and the increased premiums or, worse still, exclusion clauses in future insurance policies, if cover can be obtained at all.

Civil actions from the public

It is surprising how many people may claim against a business for injuries, other health problems or loss of amenity that they feel have been caused by environmental degradation arising from the activities of that business. If smokers can claim that they did not know that the habit would be bad for their health then it is unlikely that any claim will be considered too fanciful to reach court. Even if it is successfully contested, a court case can cost money and still leave the business looking bad. Proper and well-documented risk management processes may avoid a spurious case from ever reaching court and, where the case is well founded, may help at least to demonstrate the business's good intent.

Moral opprobrium

In some senses, whether or not a case can be brought or won is less important than the reputation of the business. Some years ago, in a case that revolved around the quality of their products, McDonald's fought and won in court against two environmental activists. However, the spectacle of the global corporation bringing the full might of its financial and legal muscle to bear on two apparently well-meaning and honestly motivated protestors did nothing of value for the firm's reputation.

Loss of business

The buying public can be fickle and the merest suggestion that a business's activities have not been above reproach in environmental terms (currently the environment is a fashionable cause) could have repercussions on sales, which in turn could mean the difference between the business thriving or failing. Long-term marketing and expansion plans usually include some sales assumptions and, if those assumptions are not met, then the result can be at least salutary but, at worst, disastrous.

WHAT IS RISK ASSESSMENT?

Before any function or factor can be managed, it is necessary to quantify it in all of the key measurement characteristics. So, before starting a journey, we require to know where we are now, our chosen destination, its direction from where we are and how far away it is. Before structuring a marketing plan we need to know the size of the market, the strength of the competition, ie its levels of market penetration, and whether the product or service we plan to market is likely to be acceptable to the market. The first is a route assessment, the second a market assessment, and a risk assessment is not that different.

Risk can be assessed in three stages:

● what might happen as a result of the activity being assessed;
● the severity of the consequences if the risk became a reality; and
● the probability of the risk becoming a reality.

Risk assessment is the measurement of the key components of risk and is the only starting point for any risk management programme.

Putting a value on risk

But how does a business put a value on a risk? Government Guidelines for Environmental Risk Assessment and Management offer an excellent tool that any business could adapt. The first step is to ask a number of questions about an activity or process:

- What impacts to the environment may occur as a result of the activity? These might range from fumes into the atmosphere to pollution into the water supply or from dust particles that could harm eyes and kill vegetation to inability of materials used in a product to be safely disposed of at the end of its life.
- How harmful are these impacts to the environment? This might range from the dispersal of cooling water into a river (extra weeds growing at the outfall but controllable) to rendering land unusable through chemical pollution or putting lives at risk with the emission of toxic fumes.
- How likely is it that these impacts will occur? Where proper filters, containers, controls and safety measures are in place, it may be unlikely. It may also be unlikely where the impact will only occur *in extremis*, ie where a safety device allows pollutant to escape in order to protect the system from overheating or exploding. However, where the materials or events likely to impact on the environment are released or occur as a routine part of the process, then impact is more likely.
- How frequently and where will these impacts occur? It may be possible to use past data to discover how often situations leading to environmental damage have occurred and, taking account of any improvements in the process since, the likely frequency of occurrence in the future.
- How much confidence can be placed in the results of the risk assessment? This is not an exact science but the more information that can be brought to bear, the better the assessment will be.
- What are the critical data gaps and can these gaps be filled? Where information is missing it may be possible to extrapolate it from other data sources or it may be possible to start collecting it from now on.
- Are any further iterations of the risk assessment needed? In a changing world, very little information collected today will be of use in even a few months' time. It will be as well to set future dates when the assessment will be conducted again.

Background to risk assessment

When evaluating any strategy, it is necessary to evaluate the various risks attendant upon the strategy and the actions needed to deliver the objectives of the strategy. Soldiers are well used to risk assessment in its cruellest manifestation: how many casualties will this action incur and how many of those will need medical treatment or simple removal from the field? This risk assessment applied to the number of fighting troops will give some idea of what resources will be required behind the lines to deal with casualties.

In business also, risk assessment is nothing new. Whenever a strategy is built into the plan, the simple question 'What can go wrong?' ought to be asked so that alternative game plans can be devised to avoid the business being caught on the back foot should events not go to plan or outside factors move the goalposts. Even when planning an event, some risk assessment will be called for if the event has been insured; the insurance company will consult past records to assess the risk and set the premium. Sports managers undertake a risk assessment using information about past games to determine how likely the opposition is to make particular moves and what steps the team can take to deal with those moves.

However, environmental risk management is a relatively new version of the discipline that has evolved as concerns have grown about the environment and the impact of human activities upon that environment. Probably first used by campaigning groups such as Friends of the Earth and Greenpeace in the 1970s and 1980s, the idea was incorporated into government thinking in the Department of the Environment's 1991 'Policy appraisal and the environment', which highlighted the need to examine the environmental impacts of policy options within the decision process. In 1995, the same department's 'A guide to risk assessment and risk management for environmental protection' looked at the place for risk assessment in the UK's Sustainable Development Strategy. Since then, a whole raft of government papers and reports from government and various think-tanks and pressure groups has looked in detail at the application of risk assessment in most areas of human activity.

A lot of development of the type of assessment methodology that can be applied to environmental risk is carried out by those concerned with health and safety aspects of working life and, in this, trade unions have contributed a great deal of work in pursuit of their members' well-being. Equally, the Health and Safety Executive and the various safety bodies addressing the needs of the railways, airlines and other sectors have also developed a number of risk assessment models that can be adapted for environmental risk assessment.

Looked at in this way, environmental risk assessment can be seen as a further application for a tried-and-tested management tool.

The European dimension

As with many other aspects of life today, this one has taken on a European dimension. The issue of pollution and its control or reduction is seen as a matter best addressed across the European Union as a whole to avoid any variations in approach in different countries, which might in turn encourage polluters to move their business to the least legislatively demanding location rather than tackling the problem of their pollution and the environmental impact it has. The 1996 EU directive, Integrated Pollution Prevention and Control (the IPPC Directive), set out to harmonize pollution control across the union although, aware of the negative impact on jobs that too rapid an adoption of the policy could cause, the directive allowed 11 years for implementation in EU businesses that were operating at the time of the directive. New businesses after 1999 have had to comply from the outset. The presence of IPPC has added some measurable targets to the risk assessment and management process, as part of the risk will be not achieving the IPPC standards while part of the management will be ensuring that those standards are achieved.

IPPC requires that all installations must have a licence from the relevant agency of their national, regional or local government to operate after the time that the directive comes into force for them. The licence will only be granted to installations that can demonstrate the application and operation of best available techniques (BAT) in regard to the whole environmental performance of the plant, including:

- emissions to air, water and land;
- generation of waste;
- use of raw materials;
- energy efficiency;
- noise;
- prevention of accidents;
- risk management.

These IPPC performance areas offer a useful guide for the business new to this process of areas in which to look when assessing environmental risk. Also, the directive and its translation into UK law are good reasons to carry out a risk assessment although there are other good business reasons, as covered above.

Ranking risks

Risks can be ranked according to a matrix. One is offered in the government's Guidelines for Environmental Risk Assessment and Management but that has been slightly amended in this book to offer specific measurable rankings based on the magnitude of consequences should a risk become reality and the probability of that happening (see Table 12.1). Each risk that has been identified in each of the operational areas identified should be applied to the matrix to assess a single risk value.

For these purposes, severe consequences would include death of personnel or members of the public and permanent destruction of some element in the environment, while negligible would mean that the damage was very little and/or would be

Table 12.1 A matrix to quantify risk (risk values)

Probability that risk will be realized	Magnitude of consequences should risk be realized			
	Severe: Value 6	Moderate: Value 4	Mild: Value 2	Negligible: Value 0
High: Value 4	24	16	8	0
Medium: Value 3	18	12	6	0
Low: Value 2	12	8	4	0
Negligible: Value 1	6	4	2	0

likely to be self-restoring. However, the particular definitions will vary for each business. Do, though, remember that there will be no point in minimizing the magnitudes because, should a risk be realized and the incident investigated or even should the agency regulating the business conduct a routine check, magnitudes are unlikely to be minimized. The same goes for the probability that a risk might be realized. Having assessed the risks and quantified them on the matrix, it will be possible to rank them in order of magnitude of risk.

The next task will be to prioritize the risks, which may be as simple as tackling the highest-value risk first and then down through the rankings. However, more often than not, the management of some risks will require specific work to be undertaken on plant or processes and, in those circumstances, while the long-term project to manage the more difficult risks is being put in place, the business should go for the quick kills of risk management programmes that can be implemented immediately. There is no point in delaying getting to grips with the lower risks while waiting for the implementation of a more complex programme for the higher risks.

RELATIONSHIP TO OTHER MANAGEMENT SYSTEMS

Environmental risk management should be just as much a part of the business's management process as accounts management, marketing management, development management or any of the other disciplines that make up the management function of a business. In particular, the management of environmental risks and the management of the environment itself are closely connected in that risk management is part of environmental management. But, across the board, environmental risk assessment and management should be part of every plan in the business. From production to marketing to distribution and transport, the environmental impact of the business is important and should be just as well measured, documented and projected as every other impact. The environmental risk assessment should rank alongside the financial audit as a key indicator of the health of the business because a business that is able to work with the environment, minimize its impact on the environment and operate in a sustainable manner will be likely to prosper in the current and future cultural and legislative climate.

Notwithstanding all of the above, readers will have already concluded that environmental risk management is really little more than applied common sense, albeit with a number of preordained parameters. Of course, the opportunity to avoid fines or litigation costs that might arise from environmental damage is a strong incentive but a negative one. The real reason to put environmental risk management at the heart of the business is that it is good for business to be ahead of the game in this area as much as in marketing, product design or even the allocation of budgets. And a business that incorporates the disciplines of thinking ahead in this context might well discover other useful information about the future that could confer a competitive edge or ensure that the allocation of resources over the next few months or years is governed by the business needs of the company, not compliance-driven regulatory needs.

13

Corporate social responsibility as part of the business and its relationships[1]

Deborah Saw, Managing Director, Citigate Dewe Rogerson

The list of corporate excesses of the last few years is long and still fresh in everybody's mind; aggressive accounting methods and unrealistic valuation models, executive greed and numerous examples of management incompetence have led to a massive build-up of debt and value-destroying acquisitions. With boards appearing to be 'asleep at the wheel', unethical and even criminal business practices surfaced at a number of high-profile companies, and auditors seem to have failed to detect risks and irregularities.

These events led to a dramatic loss of investor confidence, heightened shareholder and public scrutiny of executive pay levels, increased regulation and a sharp rise in shareholder activism. Companies responded to these changes and pressures by starting to improve levels of overall transparency and disclosure and by retreating to simpler and more transparent business models.

With corporate governance still making the headlines almost every day, issues such as board composition, management remuneration and director independence are receiving continued attention from investors and companies alike. In response to the significant damage to investor confidence of recent years, the work has begun to rebuild trust and to adopt better standards of corporate governance. Both investors and companies have made enormous efforts to understand what is expected of them and what corporate governance is meant to achieve.

There is general agreement among companies and investors today that corporate governance is vitally important and that improvements have to be made in areas such as financial disclosure, board independence and transparency of management compensation. In most cases, guided by legal advice, companies are already implementing the required changes in order to comply with the relevant national code of corporate governance. This, however, is where many companies stop. By strictly complying with the respective codes, corporates aim to ensure that they have 'covered their back'.

Top players, however, are moving beyond the strict minimum of passive compliance to address actively the concerns and issues relevant to the investment community. The task for companies therefore is to develop communication strategies that are based on a thorough understanding of those issues and to communicate effectively their corporate governance to shareholders.

Thinking along these lines, we instigated a survey of investor relations officers (IROs) and asset managers (AMs), which was conducted in December 2003. The thrust of the survey was to capture the views of those in the vanguard of corporate governance developments, so that we could evaluate current practice in this area and its impact on the investment process. We also wished to examine how the practice and communication of corporate governance issues might evolve in the near term. Guidelines relating to corporate governance are relatively newly established in a number of countries. Many companies are still getting to grips with the implications of these guidelines.

Investors, too, vary in their level of activity in this field. In targeting IR professionals, the sample base for the survey was drawn from those who had been named and ranked highly for the quality of their corporate governance practice within the previous two years. The institutional sample was based on major European-based investors, ranked by assets under management. A total of 40 participants took part in the survey, comprising 19 leading European companies and 21 major European asset managers. The survey was qualitative in nature. This gave us the advantage of speaking in depth with many experienced individuals within major European companies and investing institutions.

Interviews were conducted either in person or by telephone and typically lasted around one hour. The participants were senior individuals within their respective organizations. A list of the participant organizations is shown in Tables 13.1 and 13.2. Report commentary and findings have been compiled on a non-attributable basis. Some quotes have been included, also on a non-attributable basis, to illustrate typical and pertinent comments on particular issues and topics made by participants, and are reproduced in italics.

It is important to note that the individuals interviewed were not aware of the identity of the other participants. Where either type of respondent has made comments about companies or institutions (as appropriate), they were not specifically commenting about each other.

Table 13.1 List of participants: IR professionals

Company	Sector	Country
Aegon	Insurance	Netherlands
Air Liquide	Speciality chemicals	France
Allianz	Insurance	Germany
Amadeus	Travel and leisure	Spain
Aviva	Insurance	United Kingdom
Axa	Insurance	France
Bayer	Chemicals and healthcare	Germany
Buhrmann	Paper and packaging	Netherlands
DaimlerChrysler	Automobile	Germany
Deutsche Bank	Banking	Germany
Endesa	Utilities	Spain
ENI	Oil and gas	Italy
Erste Bank	Banking	Austria
Friends Provident	Insurance	United Kingdom
HypoVereinsbank	Banking	Germany
ING Banking	Insurance	Netherlands
Repsol	Oil and gas	Spain
San Paolo	Banking	Italy
ThyssenKrupp	Engineering	Germany

OVERALL TRENDS AND FINDINGS

- Both investors and IROs see good corporate governance as a decisive factor in the competition for global capital.
- Investors who were not previously associated with shareholder activism are becoming more involved with the companies in which they are invested.
- While the majority of participating institutions see the primary objective of corporate governance as ensuring long-term shareholder value creation and financial stability, the IROs who took part tended to stress independent board structures and overall transparency.
- Only a quarter of the IROs believed that remuneration of top management was a major investor concern, whereas more than 70 per cent of the investors felt it was.
- Financial and governance reporting are expected to be increasingly integrated.
- Although corporate governance is acknowledged to be a key investment criterion, IROs do not have a prominent role in governance issues.

Table 13.2 List of participants: investing institutions

Institution	Participant's area of expertise	Country
ABP Investments	Corporate governance	Netherlands
Artemis Fund Managers	Fund manager	United Kingdom
Barclays	Fund manager	United Kingdom
BNP Paribas	Fund manager	France
CDC IXIS	Fund manager	France
Co-operative Insurance Society	Corporate governance	United Kingdom
Credit Suisse AM	Corporate governance	United Kingdom
Deutsche Bank AM	Fund manager	United Kingdom
DWS	Corporate governance	Germany
Gartmore	Corporate governance	United Kingdom
Henderson	Corporate governance	United Kingdom
Hermes	Corporate governance	United Kingdom
Insight Investment	Fund manager	United Kingdom
ISIS	Corporate governance	United Kingdom
JP Morgan	Corporate governance	United Kingdom
M&G Investment	Fund manager	United Kingdom
Merrill Lynch	Fund manager	United Kingdom
Morgan Stanley	Corporate governance	United Kingdom
Morley Corporate	Governance	United Kingdom
Nomura	Fund manager	United Kingdom
Robeco	Corporate governance	Netherlands

Institutions

- Over 40 per cent of the institutions have a dedicated corporate governance department. A further third of the institutions have corporate governance specialists integrated into their asset management teams. In practically all institutions, corporate governance is now part of a fund manager's job. *'From today's investment viewpoint, looking at the board should be as routine as looking at the balance sheet.'*
- The majority of institutions see the primary objective of corporate governance as ensuring long-term value creation and financial stability. Investors are increasingly willing to engage with company management and want their rights as owners to be better recognized by the company. *'Companies have to be run in the interests of shareholders in the long run. There is no point in maximizing shareholder value in the short term if it leads to the destruction of the company in the long run.'*
- Nearly three-quarters of investors demand a clear link between executive remuneration and performance targets.

- Corporate governance has become a marketing tool. Asset managers increasingly see a dedicated internal corporate governance function as a prerequisite for winning new pension fund business. *'At every beauty parade we go to these days, we have to demonstrate that we have resources in the area of corporate governance. Our potential clients want to be reassured that their assets are safe with us.'*

- Nearly three-quarters of investors are unsure as yet about the benefits of including corporate governance into valuation models. Factors that are hard to quantify such as trust and integrity are as important as more quantifiable factors such as board composition and CEO remuneration. *'We don't include [corporate governance] ratings at the moment, as it is still very much qualitative information. But I think in the future, it will probably be taken into account, via a risk premium, for instance.'*

- The overwhelming majority of investors agree that corporate governance and share price performance are linked, at least to some extent. *'No doubt there is a correlation between good corporate governance and financial performance. Companies that perform well over the long term have the right structures in place; they've got the right people sitting on their boards.'*

- Investors demand earlier consultation and more systematic involvement in issues such as board appointments and remuneration. *'When companies are not clear about what they are trying to do, they will get opposition because we don't have time to try and understand when it is too complicated.'*

- Investors see considerable scope for increases in transparency and disclosure. Investors want more information to be provided online, and find legalistic boilerplates confirming compliance with governance codes of little relevance. Very high on investors' agenda is the need for more details on the functioning of board subcommittees and performance criteria linked to management pay.

- Investors would welcome IR teams that are more informed about and involved in corporate governance issues. Institutions' overall impression is that most IROs are uncomfortable talking about corporate governance issues. *'Most of those IROs to whom I have spoken have not devoted much time to it. Corporate governance is increasingly a focus of investors, so IROs should come to grips with the issues involved.'*

Investor relations officers (IROs)

- In nearly 40 per cent of the companies, there is no formal link between the investor relations and corporate governance functions.
- The majority of IROs see the primary objectives of good corporate governance as ensuring independent board structures and overall transparency and disclosure.
- Over half of the IROs said that the main reason for actively engaging in corporate governance was to enhance their reputation and their brand value. Other reasons

included good governance being part of the company's overall philosophy and responding to shareholder pressure. *'Corporate governance and firm value are clearly related. We take corporate governance seriously because we take shareholder value seriously.'*

- Over two-thirds of the IROs felt that good corporate governance enhances share price.
- IROs are unclear about the influence that corporate governance ratings have on the investment process. Investors as well as rating agencies are perceived to be not very transparent about how ratings influence their investment opinion. *'We never get any feedback as to what the impact of our governance information is that we give out. It would be good if the rating agencies and fund managers would apply to themselves the same rules they apply to us. So far, information flows only in one direction.'*
- Perhaps surprisingly, two-thirds of the IROs say they have not conducted any formal evaluation of their corporate governance or actively sought investor feedback.
- Key challenges companies are facing include the explanation of national particularities to international audiences and the need to address aggressive shareholder activists in a better way.
- Management remuneration is also perceived to need more explanation and justification. Sarbanes-Oxley is a major concern for European companies with an NYSE listing. The conversion to IFRS is also creating problems for some companies. *'Our major problem is the German two-tier system. For most countries this is unusual and therefore it is a challenge for us to explain what it is and make this better understood.'*

INVESTMENT INSTITUTIONS

Corporate governance within investment institutions

Responsibility for corporate governance issues

More than 40 per cent of all participating institutions have a dedicated department dealing with governance issues. However, corporate governance considerations are found to be increasingly integrated into the investment approach. Even in those institutions where a specialist department acts as a first line of contact and centre of expertise, it is often part of every analyst's and fund manager's job to pay attention to governance criteria.

In one-third of cases, corporate governance specialists were integrated into the asset management division, and 14 per cent said that analysis of corporate governance issues was part of everybody's job. Only 10 per cent of respondents explained that they would deal with governance issues only if the need arose.

Selected quotes

- *'Although we have two dedicated people for corporate governance, our work is pretty much integrated. Every research note has a section on corporate governance that we discuss together.'*
- *'We have nobody in particular looking at corporate governance on a full-time basis. It is pretty much part of everybody's job right now.'*
- *'Our corporate governance team are not as integrated as they should be. But there is a rising importance of corporate governance within our investment process.'*
- *'We have increased the team and added to their responsibilities, partly in response to client questions. Since corporate governance has taken a higher profile, it requires more specialists. Now it requires talking both to companies – in which we invest – and to clients about what is happening. Therefore it needs more resources devoted to it.'*

Establishment of specialist function/department

The vast majority of institutions are not newcomers to corporate governance and established a dedicated governance function more than four or five years ago, which indicates that corporate governance was already an issue for investors before Enron, WorldCom and the like. The majority of asset managers have therefore been paying attention to governance for a long time and have developed considerable expertise. Owing to recent scandals and increased pressure to avoid similar events in the future, governance departments and asset management teams have considerably expanded their governance resources and broadened the scope of their analysis.

Selected quotes

- *'We had corporate governance on our radar screen for a long time. Because of the growing demands of our clients and the increasing amount of information to go through, we had to hire two more people to do the job properly.'*
- *'In the past, corporate governance was quite narrowly defined. We feel that it is becoming much broader and we need to look at issues that influence the long-term competitiveness of firms such as environmental and economic sustainability, the way risk is managed. CSR is also becoming part of the governance picture.'*

Reporting line of corporate governance within investment institution

The increased importance of corporate governance is also visible in internal reporting lines. The vast majority of staff with corporate governance responsibility report directly to the chief investment officer. The remaining respondents report to either senior portfolio managers or the managing director for equities, or heads of equity research.

Responsibilities of corporate governance function

The scope of responsibilities varies and ranges from company analysis, voting and engagement with companies to external as well as internal training sessions to promote higher standards of governance.

Support from third parties and research agencies

Whereas all institutions rely first and foremost on their own internal intelligence, a variety of third-party providers is used to complete information or to provide an independent and complementary opinion. Others are used to help an overstretched in-house governance team. In order of frequency, the following external organizations were mentioned:

- ABI – Association of British Insurers;
- NAPF – National Association of Pension Funds;
- ISS – International Shareholder Services;
- PIRC – Pensions Investment Research Consultants;
- Deminor;
- IRRC – Investor Responsibility Research Center;
- GMI – Government Metrics International;
- Manifest;
- IVIS – Institutional Voting Information Service.

Dimensions of good corporate governance

Meaning and objectives of corporate governance

Shareholders increasingly see the achievement of long-term stability and the long-term creation of shareholder value as the overriding objectives of corporate governance. While many investors insist that their rights as owners have to be better recognized by company management, they also acknowledge that it is their duty to get more involved and engaged with company management.

Many investors pointed to the necessity of having the right culture in place and ensuring transparency and integrity throughout the organization. They take governance increasingly seriously and see it as a means to an end and not an end in itself. The parameters of governance have expanded to include additional issues such as succession planning and risk management. Only very few investment institutions are sceptical and associate corporate governance with 'box ticking'.

The following key objectives of corporate governance were mentioned:

- Ensure long-term financial stability.
- Contribute to long-term improvements in value.
- Protect shareholder rights.
- Closely align shareholders' and management's interests.
- Ensure transparent disclosure.
- Reduce financial and operational risk.
- Provide right culture, right focus.
- Ensure consistency between words and actions.

Selected quotes

- *'Companies have to be run in the interest of shareholders in the long run. There is no point of maximizing shareholder value in the short term if it leads to the destruction of the company in the long run.'*
- *'Good corporate governance should avoid centralizing too much power in one individual and promote fair treatment of all shareholders.'*
- *'When you are managing millions of employees' money for their old age, you want a system to be stable and to last. You have a long-term perspective and you are looking for long-term, trustful relationships with companies. Corporate governance is a key to all that.'*
- *'I see it as taking an active involvement in all issues that the shareholders have an influence over, for example voting on board appointments and management remuneration.'*

Key parameters of good governance

Selected quotes

- *'The board has to function properly. Board directors must have the necessary knowledge and power to properly oversee management, to put on the brakes when the CEO is on a big ego trip.'*
- *'It is about structural processes by which companies are run and you want to see that this is in the interest of shareholders. The business model has to be sustainable in the long run and not only generate profits over a short period of time.'*
- *'It all comes down to risk management. We have to protect our clients' assets from unnecessary risks.'*
- *'Nobody has complained too much about people being well paid. What they have complained about is the extremely high pay for not delivering or even destroying value.'*

Excellent corporate governance

When asked which companies represented best corporate governance practice, BP was by far the most frequently mentioned. BP and the other top-ranked companies were praised particularly for:

- high-quality board;
- strong board independence;
- excellent reporting;
- open lines of communication;
- long-term focus;
- going beyond compliance with codes, taking proactive steps;
- integrity and quality factored into overall business culture.

The most frequently named companies that represent governance best practice were:

- BP;
- Unilever;
- Shell;
- ENI;
- Air Liquide;
- ThyssenKrupp.

Common characteristics

Investors stressed that companies operating in politically sensitive sectors such as oil, gas, chemicals, etc, were the first to pay attention to corporate governance. Owing to high reputational risk and greater scrutiny from the media and governments, these companies had to put structures in place that enabled them to engage with various stakeholders and take their concerns into consideration. A willingness to communicate and a strong sense of accountability to shareholders as well as other stakeholders are common characteristics.

Further common denominators of top-performing companies are seen in their long-term approach and their focus on building lasting relationships based on trust and mutual understanding.

Selected quotes

- *'Companies that have been constantly challenged tend to be good, and challenge makes you think.'*
- *'Companies that are proactive, where accountability and openness come naturally and not through pressure.'*

- *'Usually it's companies with a long-term approach, companies whose horizon goes beyond the next quarter, companies that invest into their future and do not make short cuts to boost profits in the short term.'*
- *'Openness and willingness to talk is important. If people are proud of what they are doing, they are happy to discuss all sorts of issues. I always assume that, if somebody doesn't want to talk about something, he might not be so proud of it; maybe he prefers the world not to know.'*
- *'Long-term relationships with shareholders are key, the build-up of mutual understanding and trust.'*

Impact on investment process

Importance of corporate governance criteria

Three-quarters of all institutions polled acknowledge that corporate governance is 'important' or 'very important' and consider it a fundamental criterion in evaluating companies. This is not only the view of the heads of corporate governance but also of the majority of fund managers we have spoken to. In the overall investment process, corporate governance criteria are key not only in the selection process of a stock, but also for ongoing engagement with a company.

Only 15 per cent of the interviewees believe that corporate governance has a moderate or low importance. These institutions tend to associate corporate governance mainly with 'box ticking' and are somewhat sceptical of its performance benefits. Several fund managers have acknowledged the need to establish a dedicated corporate governance resource in order to respond to concerns of governance-conscious pension fund clients.

Selected quotes

- *'From today's investment viewpoint, when we are looking at the company, looking at the board should be as routine as looking at the balance sheet.'*
- *'If companies can't give a toss about corporate governance, then we wouldn't buy the stock or in extreme cases would sell it. Good corporate governance is increasingly a decisive factor in the competition for global capital.'*
- *'After Enron and WorldCom, the market now assumes corporate governance as an investment criterion at least on a par with business quality, market position, quality of balance sheet, etc.'*
- *'If I'm going to present for a local authority fund, unless I can demonstrate to them that I have some resource devoted to corporate governance I will stand no chance of winning the pitch. It is a kind of prerequisite. Nowadays, the average pension fund sends out a*

questionnaire, inviting the fund manager to tender. Having a governance resource is a prerequisite.'

- *'It is variable and depends on the fund manager. For the socially responsible funds, the integration of this type of criterion is systematic, for the others not yet, but it is becoming increasingly important.'*

- *'At every beauty parade we go to these days, we have to demonstrate that we have resources in the area of corporate governance. Our potential clients want to be reassured that their assets are safe with us.'*

Interaction between corporate governance specialists and fund managers

Although half of all participating investors have a dedicated and separate corporate governance department employing specialized staff, corporate governance considerations are found to be increasingly integrated into the investment approach throughout. The establishment of a special corporate governance team is no indication of its separation from the asset management process.

Although governance and financial issues have been evaluated separately in the past, more and more investment professionals are convinced that it is more appropriate to look at these issues jointly. Acceptance is growing that governance has an impact on investment performance; therefore corporate governance specialists and fund managers tend to work increasingly in an integrated way. Integration of governance issues in stock evaluation is further facilitated in institutions where the head of corporate governance has previously been a fund manager or continues to be a fund manager alongside his or her responsibility for governance issues. We have found this to be the case in more than a quarter of institutions we interviewed.

Selected quotes

- *'Everyone sits around a table and views are assimilated. We do not have formal score cards, nor do we tick boxes; corporate governance is not black or white.'*
- *'We regard it as fundamental that the decision on the weighting of individual stocks is taken by the fund manager. We are here to alert him to critical, potentially dangerous issues.'*
- *'We have always seen corporate governance as an integral part of the investment process. I am a fund manager with an added-on function of corporate governance; we don't have separate teams.'*
- *'Historically, governance and financial considerations have been separated. In fact, the two go together. We are now closely working with fund managers; we train them so that they know what to look out for. They have to understand corporate governance issues because they will affect their investment.'*

Inclusion of governance ratings into valuation models

Nearly three-quarters of all institutional investors are as yet unconvinced whether it is beneficial to include formal corporate governance ratings into valuation models. Participants pointed to the complexity of corporate governance and stressed that factors such as trust and integrity are as important as board composition and CEO remuneration, yet much harder to quantify. Therefore, it appears that corporate governance enters the valuation process much more as a qualitative criterion, judged on a case-by-case basis.

Although some institutions have made attempts formally to weigh and incorporate individual governance criteria into their models, there is a strong feeling among investors that a purely quantitative approach is bound to go wrong. One shareholder recalled that some of the biggest corporate bankruptcies had excellent corporate governance ratings while another participant argued that ratings would be included in the future where a low rating could lead to a higher risk premium.

Selected quotes

- *'They are not explicitly included, but good corporate governance tends to be reflected through valuation multiples at a premium against a company's peers.'*
- *'There is an indirect link; if the company is less transparent and there is no willingness to communicate, then inherently you are going to think more negatively of that.'*
- *'Not for the moment, as it is still very much qualitative information. But I think in the future, it will probably be taken into account, via a risk premium, for instance.'*
- *'GMI [Governance Metrics International] ratings are in the process of being integrated formally; there is a rising importance of corporate governance ratings in the selection process of stocks.'*

Link between corporate governance and stock performance

The overwhelming majority of investors agreed that corporate governance and share price are linked, at least to some extent. Although most respondents had difficulties in quantifying the premium they would give, some investors had very precise views on the share price discount companies that violate recognized governance guidelines are suffering. Investors identified both short-term and long-term implications of bad or poor governance. While an inappropriate appointment can lead to immediate discounts on the grounds of increased operational risk, the right corporate structures and a beneficial culture are associated with long-term rewards. A number of asset managers stressed that the presence of activist shareholders monitoring management closely is the best guarantee for excellent performance and increasing returns.

Selected quotes

- 'A badly run company cannot produce excellent or good results over a longer period of time!'
- 'There is evidence, especially from the activist funds, that they are making a difference to performance. They don't go in and ask whether they comply with the Combined Code. They go in and say: "We are here, we are watching you and you had better know what you are doing."'
- 'We are here to make money for our clients and that's why we look at corporate governance. So corporate governance is a means to an end rather than an end in itself. The end is improved value in our clients' holdings.'
- 'No doubt there is a correlation between good corporate governance and financial performance. Companies that perform well over the long term have the right structures in place; they've got the right people sitting on their boards.'
- 'It is difficult to pick one single criterion, to say this is it. Does a separated CEO/chairman role improve share price? I don't think so. Does a certain number of independent directors increase share price? I don't think so. What makes the difference is active shareholders who get involved.'

Communicating on corporate governance

Areas of improvement

In relation to communicating on governance issues and improvements, a variety of comments and suggestions for improvement was made. Generally, investors demand higher levels of disclosure and wish to be informed earlier and more frequently on important issues such as new appointments and changes in the board structure. Companies are criticized for not being proactive enough in involving the shareholders at an earlier stage. Several respondents expressed the view that public debates and fights could be avoided if the shareholders had been consulted earlier on critical issues.

It was also suggested that more information could be provided online to interested parties in a user-friendly and systematic way. The information in the annual report could also be expanded beyond the strict disclosure requirements and include more detail on individual people or committee structures. Investors pointed out that wordy and legalistic boilerplates confirming compliance with a certain governance code is of little relevance to them. Instead, they would prefer to have easy access to relevant and up-to-date information and, if necessary, to top management and board directors. Finally, an IR team that is more informed about and involved in governance issues would equally be welcomed.

Selected quote

- *'Companies have to communicate much more about their governance, give us updates on appointments, changes in remuneration, etc. Putting it once a year in the annual report is no longer enough. It has to be integrated in the regular financial reporting.'*

Increased disclosure in specific areas

A variety of investors appears to be interested in companies' own definitions of corporate governance and what they aim to achieve by given sets of mechanisms and structures. Very high on the agenda are details on the functioning of specific board subcommittees and an adequate explanation of bonuses and pay package details. It is not always the total amount of remuneration that appears to be of major concern but the structure of the pay package and the performance criteria linked to top management pay. For example, the grant of share options should be accompanied by a clear statement on the time horizon to demonstrate that management are incentivized to increase shareholder value in the long term.

The need for clear and comprehensible proposals for the annual general meeting (AGM) was emphasized several times. Owing to the increased workload and the lack of time, shareholders sometimes have no other choice but to oppose an AGM proposal because it is unclear and ambiguous. If companies presented their AGM proposals in a clearer and more transparent way, several fund managers felt that companies would meet less resistance. Share option plans or new appointments to the board, for example, need to be explained in more detail, providing clear performance targets and comprehensive biographical information.

Selected quotes

- *'When companies are not clear about what they are trying to do, they will get opposition because we don't have the time to try to understand when it is too complicated. If they are proposing a share plan and they have not consulted us beforehand and we don't like the things we read, it will be a "no" vote. That's the reality; what we don't understand, we vote no.'*
- *'There has to be better disclosure on AGM proposals. Proposals for share option programmes have to spell out which performance targets have to be met. Sometimes, we don't even get enough information on the biographies of directors who are up for election.'*
- *'All the requests to complete corporate governance questionnaires are driving companies crazy at the moment. I would advise companies to post the relevant information on their website and get some independent agency as intermediary to provide a sense of objectivity.'*

- *'Most annual reports have a section on corporate governance, which is very much a boilerplate saying that they comply with such-and-such code. Very boring and tells us nothing. They should make intelligent statements on their own understanding of corporate governance, what they want to achieve and how they apply the principles to their company.'*
- *'There is a lot of hot air around. The reports are riddled with wordy statements; whether they achieve a great deal is another matter. Every company says "our aim is to attract highly talented managers and pay the appropriate rate". But what does this actually mean?'*

Corporate governance and investor relations

The overall impression is that most IROs are not comfortable talking about governance issues and their impact on stock performance. As fund managers have to come to terms with the reality of corporate governance, it was suggested that IROs should equally 'do their homework'. With the general feeling that financial reporting will include governance reporting in the future, more learning needs to be done on both sides. This is valid not only for IROs but also for top management visiting investment institutions during their roadshows. Some fund managers expressed their surprise that top management appeared to be ill prepared for obvious questions on remuneration or succession issues, for example. Moreover, several investors stressed that corporate governance was not a distinct and separate issue, but an integral part of the equity story.

Selected quotes

- *'My experience is that most of those [IROs] to whom I have spoken have not devoted much time to it, which surprises me. Corporate governance is increasingly a focus of investors, so IROs should come to grips with the issues involved.'*
- *'IR people don't tend to be that well informed. We mostly talk straight to the chairman or the directors but often this doesn't filter down to the IR person. So he is no wiser about what he should be doing or saying.'*
- *'I think in the future financial reporting and governance reporting will be much more closely linked.'*
- *'Companies should be better prepared to talk to us about their governance structures during investor meetings. They will have the same questions thrown at them each time.'*
- *'IR people should be better equipped to communicate the whole picture of the company to the financial community. They should make sure they understand the key issues and how they apply to their company. Good governance is increasingly part of the equity story.'*

Outlook

Corporate governance in five years

Almost all institutional investors are convinced that corporate governance is not only 'here to stay' but that it will be of vital importance going forward. Indeed, recent shareholder activism and increasing public pressure show that companies will have to take shareholder concerns more seriously. Asset managers are under threat from regulatory intervention and feel pressured to put procedures in place to monitor the governance regimes of all companies in which they are invested. This should enable them to intervene more rapidly in poorly governed firms. Governance will increasingly be evaluated as a mainstream investment criterion since it represents a major investment risk. It is further expected to become broader in definition and to include issues of social responsibility and environmental accountability.

Companies, in turn, will have to make a stronger commitment to corporate governance and become more transparent in their governance structures and practices. Disclosure about governance standards is expected to improve both in breadth and depth, while non-executive directors are encouraged to have a higher profile and to show more involvement. However, several respondents also pointed to the dangers of 'bureaucratic overload', arguing that Higgs has gone too far, and warned that companies might be hitting back. Some investors felt that the optimum of interference from shareholders has already been reached.

Selected quotes

- *'Some argue that a market recovery will leave corporate governance considerations behind. I don't think it will. I think corporate governance is here to stay.'*
- *'I am convinced corporate governance will be fully integrated in mainstream asset management.'*
- *'Companies will have to get better at communicating what they are actually doing to a wider and more diverse audience: pressure groups, shareholder activists, SRI funds...'*
- *'Shareholders will be more educated and demanding. There will be more scrutiny; companies will have to disclose much more about their internal structures, how they are run and why they are run that way.'*

Convergence of standards and codes

Most participants agree that, despite the large number of national codes, there already is some degree of convergence in practical terms, as many companies tend to follow international best practice and not local regulation. Several respondents pointed out that most codes expressed very similar objectives, and that the overriding principles of corporate governance are universal. Consequently, most participants believe that there is a chance of an eventual convergence towards one standard of international best practice, although this is expected to happen slowly, given the differences in national regulation and culture. The OECD and ICGN (International Corporate Governance Network) principles are understood to be the guideline for a common European code. EU directives should encourage this type of convergence in Europe. The UK standards are universally judged to be the highest. Several respondents have voiced the opinion that imposing a single set of codes from the UK or the US on Europe or Japan would not be appropriate and potentially counterproductive. However, as one respondent observed, it might be worth considering the adoption of US or UK governance structures if the company is actively seeking to broaden its shareholder base in those markets.

Selected quotes

- *'It looks like Europe is going the way of voluntary codes rather than heavy legislation like Sarbanes-Oxley in the States. These codes will converge more and more.'*
- *'I think that international differences will remain but on a European level. EU directives should encourage convergence to some extent.'*
- *'It is more appropriate to have broadly agreed principles and have different markets work out the details. It wouldn't make sense to impose the UK blueprint on other markets. But if companies want to attract capital from certain markets, they might well need to adapt to those structures.'*
- *'I expect a broad agreement on many principles but law and local practice will be slow to converge.'*

Company compliance and investor confidence

The overwhelming majority of investors are convinced that compliance with principles of best practice will help restore investor confidence. The remaining participants are more sceptical and argue that it is not just compliance that will enhance value and confidence but actual better behaviour. The view of some of these investors is coloured by the feeling that simple compliance with codes and guidelines can be a meaningless, box-ticking exercise. On this, virtually everybody agrees; corporate governance assessments must not become a mere ticking of boxes but must involve a proper and sound review of all vital oversight and reporting functions.

Selected quotes

- *'Corporate governance codes are a good way of promoting good behaviour. Compliance should definitely help.'*

- *'The question is not compliance. You can comply with a code and still be greedy and unethical; you can tick all the boxes but oversight is just exercised on the surface. The behaviour is what counts.'*
- *'The focus is turning away from compliance with codes and towards investor responsibility.'*

Driving force for corporate governance improvements

Virtually all investors hope and expect that corporate governance improvements will be driven by the market and not by government legislation. All UK and European investors insisted that adherence to a voluntary code of best practice is far more appropriate than heavy and rigid regulation as in the US. It is expected that, driven by increased shareholder activism and public pressures, self-regulation from companies will avoid the threat of 'government interference'.

Selected quotes

- *'With institutional investors becoming more interested, these are the best-placed people to do the job.'*
- *'The government will encourage shareholder activism. They already encourage investors to intervene earlier on.'*
- *'It will be a combination of the carrot and the stick. The carrot would be the potential of increasing firm value and reducing risk. The stick might come in the form of regulatory bodies and legislation.'*
- *'Investor pressure and rising public expectations will be the key drivers.'*
- *'The UK doesn't like legislation; you can't legislate behaviour. People will always find a way around it. Guidelines and codes established and accepted by all market participants are much better.'*

IR PROFESSIONALS

Corporate governance and IR function

Responsibility for governance issues

It appears that responsibility for corporate governance is shared by a large variety of people in a company. Only one of the companies we spoke to has an in-house corporate governance specialist. In a third of the companies, responsibility for corporate governance tends to be with a group of people operating as a cross-functional team, including staff from investor relations and public relations, as well as the finance and legal departments. In a number of companies, however, the responsibility for corporate governance tends to be with the board as a whole or an individual such as the company secretary, the chairman or the in-house lawyer.

Selected quotes

- *'We have a corporate governance officer and he works in the legal department.'*
- *'We have a specific person looking after corporate governance. He works closely with specialists in our legal and audit department.'*
- *'We have a cross-functional team, including the legal department, compliance, compensation, accounting, investor relations and corporate communication.'*
- *'No specific department or individual is responsible for governance issues but several people with high responsibility dedicate a substantial amount of their time to this subject.'*

Reporting lines

In nearly half of the cases, the corporate governance responsibility, whether it is being exercised by an individual or a department, reports to an executive member of the board, usually the CFO. In a fifth of cases, the governance function reports to the chairman of the board, who is not at the same time the CEO. In a further fifth of cases, the reporting line may lead to the overall board. A few companies have a structure in place where the corporate governance function reports to the in-house legal team.

In some companies the investor relations department is not a part of the corporate governance cross-functional team. In those cases, regular interaction and the level of liaison with the investor relations department is still very high.

Selected quotes

- *'The reporting line for the company secretary is the chief executive. But on governance he reports specifically to the chairman. This is done deliberately to raise the profile of governance over and above the executive management.'*
- *'Our corporate governance person reports into the legal department. For us, corporate governance is mainly a legal issue.'*
- *'The governance person is part of the CFO's team and reports directly to him.'*

Liaison with investor relations

In more than half of the companies we spoke to, the level of liaison between the corporate governance function and the investor relations department is relatively high and interaction between the two functions is regular. In one case, the corporate governance function is integrated into the IR department.

In more than one-third of the companies, there is no official link and meetings are only set up on demand. In these cases, the frequency of contact varies largely depending on the situation and necessity, and few regular meetings take place.

Selected quotes

- 'The company secretary drives it. When there is an issue, we all sit around the table to sort it out. I would be involved on specific issues on an ad hoc basis; we don't have regular and formal meetings.'
- 'We give each other internal updates on an informal basis, but there are no formal structures.'
- 'Sometimes we get queries on corporate governance by e-mail and we forward them on to the company secretary to answer.'
- 'The relationship we have with our shareholders is one of our most important assets; therefore I would say that corporate governance is something we all care about.'
- 'There is a lot of liaison, official and unofficial meetings, working groups and project teams that come together when special projects arise but also on an ongoing basis.'

Dimensions of good corporate governance

Meaning and objectives

For the majority of IROs, good corporate governance is associated with independent board structures and an appropriate composition of the board. The overall transparency of the company including clear responsibilities and a transparent business model as well as the quality of financial reporting is seen to be the mainstay of good governance. Equal treatment of all shareholders and the protection of shareholder rights were also regarded as essential parts of the corporate governance concept. Some respondents felt that corporate governance should be an essential part of a company's philosophy. Others expressed the view that corporate governance can be an asset securing the brand value for the future.

Only very few respondents saw corporate governance issues as separate from business issues and stated that governance was only an issue in poorly performing companies. The following key objectives of corporate governance were mentioned:

- to ensure independent board structures;
- to provide overall transparency and clarity;
- to guarantee quality of financial reporting;
- to ensure equal treatment of shareholders/shareholder rights;
- to establish trust and accountability;
- to represent an essential part of company philosophy;
- to secure and enhance brand value.

Selected quotes

- 'I think it is good brand value. I think it is goodwill in our company and it is money in the bank.'
- 'For us, it is like a safety net.'
- 'Good governance is more than fulfilling restrictions and regulations. It has to be an essential part of a company's philosophy.'
- 'We should never forget that the most important thing is how you improve the economics, how you drive growth, how you create shareholder value – the sideshow is governance. It's an issue because some people don't do it very well.'

Perceived concerns of investors

Participating IROs were asked about their understanding of investor concerns. The main area of interest for investors is perceived to be the company's board structure and independence. The two other areas of perceived investor concern are overall corporate transparency and disclosure as well as the independence of audit committees and the reliability of the audited figures. Risk management issues and remuneration of top management were seen to be of average concern. The company's ownership structure, especially when there are controlling shareholdings or cross-holdings, shareholder rights and relations with other stakeholders were named last.

Several IROs pointed to differences between the concerns shared by investors and those shared by the media: the media are perceived to be highly interested in the remuneration of top management while investors are believed to pay less attention.

Selected quotes

- 'I guess all they care about is that there is a general system in place to assure the compliance with corporate governance. Only the pure existence of a system is important for them, not specific issues. For the media it's different; they are obviously more interested in remuneration but investors don't pick anything in particular.'
- 'Investors want to know who sits on the board and what their background is, how they are remunerated. The focus is very much on the board and the subcommittees.'
- 'I would say their main concern is board independence and management credibility. Honesty and integrity have become fashionable again.'
- 'Investors want to have more information on top management pay, why they receive what they receive and when. They are interested in share option programmes and how they are tied in overall.'
- 'Increasingly, investors are mindful. When they see companies wanting to pay huge remuneration and golden handshakes, they will vote with their feet.'

Reasons for active engagement in corporate governance

The main reason why companies place significant emphasis on corporate governance is to enhance their reputation and increase their brand value. A significant number of respondents equally felt that meeting high standards of quality and behaviour has always been part of their corporate philosophy. Shareholder activism and increased investor interest in governance issues are further reasons. Several participants stressed that they had been at the forefront of the governance movement, initiating changes and raising standards prior to the introduction of corporate governance codes.

Several companies pointed to the link between governance and value creation and referred to studies and reports that demonstrated that share price performance benefits from sound governance structures and processes. One IRO added that corporate governance is a way of meeting investor expectations and that corporate governance was part of a company's equity story. For some companies, a lower risk profile was the main driver in becoming attentive to governance issues.

Selected quotes

- 'The concept of corporate governance came from the Anglo-Saxon world and it filtered through to us quite early. We were asked by shareholders about our approach and so we took the initiative.'
- 'Good governance acts as a differentiator and helps you stand out of the crowd if you are setting the standard in one area.'
- 'It's a combination of all those factors which in our opinion would lead to an overall improved performance and allow us to win over the market's perception – not just as a marketing tool but as a tool to meet investor expectations.'
- 'It is part of our culture to try and adopt the most demanding standards in whatever field we operate in. Also, we have clearly been pushed to it by our highly international and very US-focused investor base.'
- 'Corporate governance and firm value are clearly related. We take corporate governance seriously because we take shareholder value creation seriously.'
- 'We think that corporate governance is of essential importance to the modus operandi of a company in its entirety. We want to be a modern company: accordingly, our corporate governance system should be modern too.'

Corporate governance and share price performance

When IROs were asked about the extent to which good corporate governance would enhance share price or market valuation, more than 50 per cent felt that it had an influence, but to a limited extent or not directly. A few participants were convinced that good corporate governance can influence the share price to a great extent. Many expressed the view that the positive link may not be very clear, but that there is a stronger correlation and greater negative effect on the share price if corporate governance is poor. Several respondents said that, in their opinion, corporate governance was only a part of a combination of factors and had no direct influence on the share price. However, the share price could be increased as a consequence of enhanced trust and transparency, which are fostered by good corporate governance.

Selected quotes

- *'The McKinsey study suggested a 20 per cent premium for well-run companies. If you are an investor and you have two companies you are considering investing in – one with good governance and the other one with poor – there is no doubt that the one with good governance would be favoured.'*
- *'I do think that, if you are recognized as having poor governance, then it will have an adverse effect. If you have bad governance, you are definitely going to suffer.'*
- *'I don't think it would have such an impact.'*
- *'It definitely helps. It helps shed light on our strategy and performance; it makes aims and targets more comprehensible to investors. It is basically a device to make the shareholders understand our strategy.'*
- *'At present, stocks that lack transparency are clearly penalized by the market. In a similar way, companies that are not able to demonstrate an adequate governance policy will be penalized in the future.'*

Communicating on corporate governance

Channels of communication

A dedicated section in the annual report and online communication (that is, the corporate governance section on the corporate website) seem to be the most popular way used by companies to 'spread the word' to investors about their corporate governance efforts. News releases came third. The inclusion of corporate governance information in investor presentations and participation in conferences and round-table discussions on corporate governance issues were further named means. Increasingly, companies are preparing separate corporate governance reports and expanding corporate governance sections in their annual report to complement their online communication. A few use events throughout the year, particularly the AGM, to get their corporate governance message across.

However, there is also a tendency among companies to 'keep quiet' about their performance and to avoid active communication on governance issues. These companies prefer to keep a low profile and only react to shareholder or media enquiries.

Selected quotes

- *'We have a section in the annual report and we have started to publish a governance report once a year, which is also posted on the web. We also take up any publicity opportunity that comes along such as this survey.'*
- *'This is an issue we do not proactively communicate unless we are being asked to do so.'*
- *'We are and always have been a discreet company about what we do. We try to act and keep our shareholders satisfied; we don't talk about what we do.'*
- *'We are very active in communicating that we have nothing to hide. This year we have independent reports for corporate governance in our annual report package. Also, our website is in the process of review and we intend to expand the section on corporate governance.'*
- *'We don't think it is necessary for us to spread the word. We have established our reputation on corporate governance over a hundred years. We think that if we keep up with our standards and always comply with new regulation, we don't need to proactively communicate on our governance policy.'*

Current focus

Sarbanes-Oxley, the Public Company Accounting and Investor Protection Act of 2002, is a major concern for European companies that have a listing in the US. There is still significant uncertainty about the implications of Sarbanes-Oxley on investor relations in the US. Also, participants are striving to improve their performance against their sector peers and 'best practice' players. Better measurement and enhanced communication on corporate governance are additional areas companies are working on. Some IROs felt that they had no particular focus at the moment and were working hard on various fronts.

For the immediate future, most companies we have spoken to are concentrating their efforts on compliance with local and international regulation and codes of best practice. The communication of a corporate governance track record is in current and future plans. Further improvements are sought in the area of remuneration disclosure, more detailed communication of corporate governance structures, and appropriate explanations of non-compliance with relevant codes.

Selected quotes

- *'Right now, our focus is driven by external pressures. We have to make sure we comply with the latest legislation, and also Sarbanes-Oxley gave us a deadline to implement a number of changes, so we are working on that right now.'*
- *'We are integrating "corporate governance" as a key message in our equity story. Also, we will add an informative corporate governance section on our website. We also want to be in a position to have an official audit of our corporate governance system to get a formal and independent rating.'*
- *'I'm afraid we do not focus on anything in particular at the moment. It is difficult enough to keep pace with all the international developments going on right now.'*
- *'In the past, we have been implementing all the new standards on the subject. Now I would say it's about making everything run efficiently and telling our shareholders about it.'*
- *'We need to monitor new regulations that could apply to non-US companies listed in the US.'*

Perceived use of rating agencies

When asked about how investors are using corporate governance ratings to make investments and proxy decisions, most IROs felt that, although these ratings play a part in the decision-making process, they are certainly not the most important criterion. However, participants thought that positive reports and the willingness to be officially rated added to market confidence and trust in a company.

Several respondents warned that negative ratings had a far greater impact than positive reports. Others argued that ratings can have a harmful effect if used on a stand-alone basis or in a mechanical way. They stressed that a governance rating should never replace an honest discussion with company management. Generally, it was felt that the impact of governance ratings on investment decisions is hard to judge. Investors and rating agencies are perceived to lack transparency on this issue. Investors as well as agencies should be equally open and transparent and inform companies how scores and ratings are used.

Selected quotes

- *'There are so many rating providers out there that it is difficult to make a judgement. They all have different methodologies, look at slightly different factors. Some are based on substance, like Deminor and Standard & Poor's. Others are more based on forms and box ticking. You can't compare them.'*
- *'Corporate governance ratings are definitely part of investors' decision-making process but I would say that it is only one element out of many to form their investment opinion.'*

- *'There are two different types of investors: those who use corporate governance ratings intelligently and those who don't. You cannot take decisions based on the basis of this type of information only.'*
- *'How am I supposed to know? Investors are not very open about that. The only thing I can guess is that some investors use the information and others don't.'*
- *'We wanted to do a proper assessment and got S&P in. They did a very thorough job and talked to a lot of people here. We wanted to have somebody like S&P to comment on our governance to demonstrate to investors that we are serious about corporate governance.'*

Guidance on corporate governance issues

Lawyers were the preferred choice with regard to guidance on corporate governance issues. Auditors came second. The professionalism and high quality of advice offered by these two groups were praised; however, the associated costs were mentioned as a drawback. Also, it was acknowledged that their advice was inevitably of a rather legalistic nature. It was mentioned that useful guidance on corporate governance matters can also be obtained from shareholder and industry associations.

A significant proportion of respondents used mainly their in-house resources that closely monitored international practice as it evolves. The UK and the US markets are perceived to be at the forefront of governance reform and best practice.

Selected quotes

- *'We are very internationally driven. We implement what is coming in terms of best practice from the outside world.'*
- *'We try to keep lawyers and auditors out at all cost; otherwise you spend forever clocking up huge fees.'*
- *'Outside expertise is quite helpful as we don't have this kind of knowledge internally.'*
- *'Lawyers and auditors play a decisive role. But the problem here is that the priority in this context is often compliance without taking questions of business practice and comprehensibility into consideration. Advisors who also cover these areas will be interesting for us in the future.'*
- *'We are very keen to be a best-practice player. We certainly look at Sarbanes-Oxley and Higgs to gather ideas about what we could do to keep our shareholders even more satisfied.'*
- *'Being both a listed company and an institutional investor offers us great opportunities in developing our own views on corporate governance issues. In addition, issues proposed by investors, shareholders' associations and industry associations are a great stimulus in this matter.'*

Investor feedback

Approximately two-thirds of the IROs we interviewed have not conducted any form of formal evaluation of their corporate governance, nor have they actively sought investors' feedback. Others felt that conducting a perception survey among investors was redundant because they believed their rating agencies provided them with necessary market feedback. Almost a quarter of the participating companies gather feedback through informal contacts and discussions while only a small minority conduct formal perception studies to evaluate how their efforts are perceived by the investment community.

Selected quotes

- 'We are normally very active in communicating our corporate governance. But we have not been asking the investors what their opinion is so far.'
- 'We periodically conduct a perception study to assess the opinion of the financial community. One of the topics included is corporate governance.'
- 'We only get feedback in an informal way, mainly through discussions with investors.'
- 'Our policy is not to do any perception studies. We feel we have a good enough contact with our analysts and investors and they give us feedback, including the negative.'
- 'This is something the rating agencies do already, so why should we proactively focus on that?'
- 'No, we have never done that in a formal way. If shareholders have problems with our governance or have questions about something, they will come up and tell us about it.'

Outlook

The ongoing review of international guidelines, national regulation and codes forces companies to concentrate their resources on understanding and complying with the new standards. Key areas of concern are the Sarbanes-Oxley Act in the United States and its implications on European companies with an NYSE listing. The conversion to International Accounting Standards (IAS) or International Financial Reporting Standards (IFRS) also appears to be causing problems and uncertainties among European companies.

Key challenges companies are facing include the explanation of national particularities to international audiences and the need to address aggressive shareholder activists in a better way. Especially the area of remuneration is perceived to need more explanation and justification. Some IROs find it a very complex task to provide a comprehensive picture of their governance structures and feel it difficult to communicate effectively to audiences who are learning themselves how to evaluate governance-related issues properly.

Key concerns

- *'Everyone is nervous about Sarbanes-Oxley. We have a listing in the US and it appears to me that, under Sarbanes-Oxley, you can end up with a more severe sentence for shredding important e-mails than for attempted murder.'*
- *'Remuneration at AGMs is becoming a bigger issue: fat-cat Britain. I don't know if it's jealousy when somebody is paid a lot. It's just typical of the British nation, when managers have huge salaries, they get criticized for it. It's easy to be affected by those tabloid journalists.'*
- *'We never get any feedback as to what the impact of our governance information is that we give out. It would be good if the rating agencies and fund managers would apply to themselves the same rules they apply to us. So far, information flow only goes in one direction.'*
- *'IAS is a nightmare. Particularly for insurance groups, there is going to be a lot of water going under the table. It has been handled badly and there is a lot of concern there.'*

Key challenges

- *'Our major problem is the German two-tier system. For most countries this is unusual and therefore it is a challenge for us to explain what it is and make this better understood.'*
- *'We have to be more proactive with investors, explaining our remuneration, how we justify our bonuses. There is a lot of interest in pay packages at the moment.'*
- *'The design of presentations on corporate governance activities is a challenge. Where do you start? Where do you end? It is so complex.'*
- *'We are still in a situation of very poor communication from British companies on board issues. Most people have no idea what a board of directors does. Often I hear from smaller investors that directors are all fat cats, these non-execs doing nothing, getting paid millions. There is a lot of ignorance here. This is why we get hijacked all the time.'*

CONCLUSION

Good corporate governance is increasingly seen as a decisive factor in the competition for global capital and a risk management system protecting companies from operational, financial and reputational risk. With growing acceptance that there is a significant link between governance standards and company value, there is reason to believe that financial and corporate governance reporting will become more closely linked in the future.

In order to satisfy an increasingly demanding shareholder base, it is no longer enough simply to comply with the codes of corporate governance and to react to changes to the regulatory framework. Top performers are moving beyond the strict minimum of passive compliance and actively addressing the concerns and issues relevant to the investment community. The task for companies therefore is to develop communication strategies that are based on a thorough understanding of those issues and to determine the best way to present and communicate governance messages.

Note

[1] Based on a pan-European survey of investor relations officers and asset managers conducted in December 2003 by Citigate Dewe Rogerson.

14

Responsibility – or what well-led companies do naturally: a pattern for the future

Mark Goyder, Director, Tomorrow's Company[1]

Imagine a world in which companies felt able to admit mistakes and deal with failure as a fact of life. AGMs would be looked forward to as occasions when you could learn from criticisms and suggestions of shareholders. Annual reports would faithfully track the ups and downs of the company on its long-term journey. On or near the front page there would be, among other things, a statement and accompanying graph showing the ratio between the lowest- and highest-paid person in the organization, with accompanying commentary explaining changes in the distribution of rewards.

A core of long-term owners of shares would regularly challenge the CEO about performance and progress towards the targets. Acquisitions would be rare but not unknown, and always accompanied by rigorous due diligence not only on the financial health of the company being bought, but also its cultural strengths and weaknesses.

Instead of payments for failure, the likeliest punishment for a CEO who had made a mess of things would be to stay on for a year, helping to dig the company out of debt, working out the notice period supporting the successor and passing on the most valuable lessons of all – those that come from past failure. There would be no pretence that the arrival of a new CEO heralded the beginning of history: continuity would be valued, and the inheritance from the past, good and bad, would be acknowledged and discussed.

Companies would undertake surveys of their customers and then invite them to presentations at which they shared the feedback, good, bad and ugly, with employees and customers together. Long-term supplier relationships would be based on a foundation of trust, which started from a clear declaration of the way the two or more parties would do business with and behave towards each other. Office and shop-floor employees, well trained in defect prevention, would regularly phone their opposite numbers to discuss new ideas for quality improvement.

Leaders would not be remote figures, hiding behind the tinted glass of their limousines, as they were swept away from an AGM bilious with impotent protest. For a week every year they would go out into the front line with service engineers or undertake a spell of community service. This humility and accessibility would earn them the trust of colleagues who would then see them take management teams away on retreat to rethink where the business was going.

Boards too would be accessible and self-critical groups. They would review their own performance and give their own CEO and chairman marks out of 10, making it easy for the rest of the organization to deal with 360-degree feedback. The unscripted appearance of an independent director at one of the plant's premises to sit in on some meetings and take a bowl of canteen soup with a random group of employees would be unsurprising: as a result, when employees had serious doubts about the ethics of a new directive from on high, they would know that *in extremis* they could e-mail or phone a board member without fear of reprisal because openness always won over hierarchy.

Idealistic? Yes. A fantasy world? No, actually. With only one exception, the examples I have given are based on real life. There is no one company doing all of these things. But there are companies involved with Tomorrow's Company, some in the UK and some in the rest of the world, doing each one of them and attributing a significant part of their profitability to the fact that they are doing them.

They are exemplars of what Tomorrow's Company would call 'an inclusive approach' to enduring business success.

WHAT IS CORPORATE SOCIAL RESPONSIBILITY?

The terms 'social responsibility' and 'CSR' are overused and in great danger of provoking cynicism.[2] If we strip the words back to their essentials, the word that really counts is the word 'responsible'. 'Corporate' simply means 'as applied by or to organizations'. 'Social' means 'towards society'. Corporate social responsibility is the responsibility we expect companies and other organizations, including governments, the EU, religious organizations and NGOs for that matter, to show in being part of society. It means, in short, that we expect companies, like other organizations, at the very least to behave responsibly, not only towards their shareholders, but in all their relationships with people, the natural world and the planet. Nor is this simply a matter of passive duty. A well-led organization will always seek to create the optimal value in all its relationships. In a way, that is simply good leadership. The most impressive corporate leaders have always been those whose vision of a successful business stretches beyond the product and the profits to their positive impact on the world around them.

Nothing new there! Society's expectations of business have been changing for centuries. The best businesses have adapted voluntarily to those changing expectations and have shown leadership by example. Others have dragged their feet, until compelled by law. The Factories Acts in the 19th century and the equal opportunities legislation in the second half of the 20th century offer examples from the UK.

SOCIAL PUSH AND LEADERSHIP PULL

Corporate progress towards greater responsibility has always been the result of both push and pull. Visionary leaders in business pull their organizations to higher standards: people like Gottlieb Dutweiler in Switzerland, Karl Zeiss in Germany, Robert Owen, the Cadburys, the Levers and the Rowntrees, or John Spedan Lewis in the UK, the Schwartz family who founded Timberland, the de Prees of Herman Miller in the USA, and more recently Ricardo Semmler in Brazil.

The push comes from society, from anti-slavery campaigners like William Wilberforce, from leaders of trade unions, from consumer leaders like Ralph Nader and from environmental activists like Greenpeace.

The current debate on CSR therefore represents a particular milestone in the timeless tension between pull and push.

So what has changed? The new interest in CSR arises because corporate responsibility now takes place in a context in which business is more:

- international;
- powerful;
- visible and accountable through the media;
- under pressure for results from institutional shareholders;
- mistrusted by large parts of the general public; and
- under pressure from powerful NGOs.

One of the easiest ways of understanding this has been the concept of the 'licence to operate' (see Figure 14.1). Think of the company as occupying a bounded space. The boundaries for its actions are set, not simply by laws and regulations, but by the combined attitudes of all those people with whom it has contact. If the company communicates its purpose and its values and increases trust in all its relationships, its room for manoeuvre grows. If it disregards the feelings of its stakeholders, its freedom

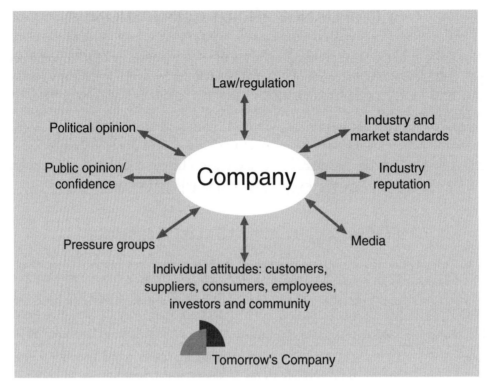

Figure 14.1 The licence to operate

of action is reduced. This is true, at a micro-level, of the individual company. But it is also true, at a macro-level, of the whole population of companies. Earn more trust through your behaviours, and there will less regulation and political interference. Forfeit trust and there will be more. For individual businesses, and for the population of businesses as a whole, the licence to operate is the space within which the pull of business leadership and push of social pressure are played out. The more effectively business pulls, the less it will need to pushed. That is the value of the leadership by example shown by business-led organizations such as Business in the Community and the World Business Council for Sustainable Development.

The 'licence to operate' can be a very good way to stimulate the process of thinking about CSR. It focuses on risk rather than opportunity. It is a language that investors find easy to connect with their own sense of self-interest.

What the best companies have always done is to go further than this. They are not just talking about 'aligning stakeholders'. CSR is, to these companies, a natural and practical expression of values for which they have always stood: provided that they stick to these values they are confident that they will continue to earn the trust that is essential to their ability to compete.

COMPLIANCE VERSUS CONVICTION

This takes us to the heart of the question about what we mean by CSR. To some people, CSR is no more than a set of external behaviours by which a company ensures that it fits society's template and thereby earns and retains its licence to operate. This is compliance CSR.

TOMORROW'S COMPANY: AN INCLUSIVE APPROACH

Tomorrow's Company…

- Clearly defines its *purpose and values*, and communicates them in a consistent manner to all those important to the company's success;
- Uses its stated purpose and values, and its understanding of the importance of each *relationship*, to develop its own *success model* from which it can generate a meaningful framework for performance measurement;
- Values reciprocal relationships, understanding that by focusing on and learning from all those who contribute to the business, it will best be able to improve returns to shareholders;
- Works actively to build reciprocal relationships with customers, suppliers, and other key stakeholders, through a partnership approach;
- Expects its relationships to overlap and acts, with others where necessary, to maintain a strong 'licence to operate'.

From the RSA Inquiry, Tomorrow's Company, 1995, p 1

To others that is not enough. They use the term 'CSR' to describe their approach to business leadership as a whole. To these people, CSR is synonymous with what Tomorrow's Company would call an 'inclusive approach' to business – an approach in which every behaviour flows naturally from the company's purpose and values.

CSR used in the first sense – minimizing risk and aligning stakeholders – will quickly lose its appeal, and be looked back upon rather cynically as a passing fashion. CSR in the second sense – having convictions and having the courage to act on these in all your relationships – is not new but will always be important. One tell-tale sign of a company that is acting more out of compliance than conviction is the weight it places on the business case for particular actions.

IS THERE A BUSINESS CASE FOR CSR?

There is a business case for CSR. But it is not in the superficial form that is often claimed. The convincing and enduring business case, set out below in seven steps, sees corporate responsibility as one of the outputs you can expect from a well-led company. But, while particular companies in particular circumstances may enjoy business benefits from particular CSR programmes, you cannot make the leap that somehow argues that because companies adopt CSR programmes or practices they will as a result be more successful. There is, on the other hand, evidence to support the view that well-led companies that are clear about their purpose and values will create more shareholder value than companies that simply and expediently talk about making money.[3]

Seven steps in the real business case

The real business case goes like this:

1. Companies are started by entrepreneurs. In their early years that drive may come from one individual leader. But if companies are to grow and last, and retain that entrepreneurial drive, the qualities of the entrepreneur need to be embedded in the habits and attitudes of the whole organization.
2. In every company that is built to last, a common outlook develops, which makes it easy for people to work together and trust and challenge each other. New people who join see quickly by example what is expected of them. A culture is developed. The personal qualities of the leader still matter. But the organization takes on its own personality.
3. Every company needs to create economic value to distribute to its shareholders. But the creation of that value happens through the relationships the company develops with customers, employees, suppliers, communities and shareholders. Companies are only as successful as the quality of these relationships. The relationships overlap, and much of the value that is created is at the interface between relationships – for example, in the impact that loyal employees have upon the customers they meet, or the impact that excellent community activities have upon the motivation and skill levels of employees.
4. You cannot have successful relationships unless you have clear purpose and clear values. The first role of the leader is to ensure that, in all the relationships of the business, there is a clear and consistent idea of why the company exists and what it stands for. This is how trust and loyalty are created. This is how leaders influence the achievements of thousands of employees in different relationships without personally being present in every conversation. It is this combination of clear purpose and values and a focus on relationships as the foundations for success that is described as an inclusive approach.

5. Because relationships overlap, the messages cannot be compartmentalized. You cannot send one message to the shareholders and another to other stakeholders. One of the prime tasks of leaders is to ensure that the behaviours and the messages remain consistent at a time when shareholders and society are making strong and often inconsistent demands. This can include saying no to today's shareholders in the interest of tomorrow's, and saying no to other stakeholders – be they demanding customers, employees who feel they should be paid more, neighbourhoods or NGOs making demands the company cannot afford or does not agree with.

6. Responsible business practice is an important part of the inclusive approach because it helps strengthen relationships and build trust. Responsible corporate behaviour in all relationships is one aspect of a well-led company. The others include its overall strategy, the quality of its products and its marketing, the effectiveness of its investment and innovation, and its ability to learn and adapt faster than its competitors to changing conditions. Just as you can tell a lot about a person from his or her friends, you can tell a lot about a company from its relationships.

7. The adoption of CSR practices is, therefore, not a predictor of business success. Effective leadership, based upon clear purpose and values that permeate an organization and its relationships, is. A close examination of a company's relationships is essential to the assessment of its leadership, and therefore of its future ability to generate economic value.[4]

You cannot understand a company by taking one isolated slice of its behaviours. You have to get under its skin. You have to find ways of distinguishing the companies that are 'faking it' from the companies for which responsible behaviour is important. That means the 'behavioural audit trail' and learning to detect how the purpose and values of the organization work in practice.[5] Outside the organization, that is becoming the new challenge for analysts, rating agencies and all those who need to understand the hidden potential of companies, and the hidden risks. Inside the company, the same task falls to the board, which can no longer afford to rely solely on the numbers that are put in front of it. This is the new agenda for governance, which is necessitated not only by the demands of society but also by the painful learning about risk that results from recent corporate failures.

THE NEW BOARD AGENDA

One of my favourite – and wisest – public company chairmen used to say, 'You can tell a lot about a CEO by looking at his diary.' He was right. Today, he might well add: 'You can tell a lot about a board by looking at how they spend their time.'

You are a new independent director on two boards. Company A does things in style. You dine well with your fellow directors. The board meeting the next day is dispatched efficiently by the chairman. There is a general feeling things are going well. And the CEO and the FD seem to be competent people. You are relatively new. You feel proportionately able to ask one, maybe two, questions.

Before you get near a board meeting at Company B you have had several stages of induction. The chairman explains that your role is not simply to oversee the current reports of performance in the business, but to identify risks and opportunities and hold the business to account against its original purpose and values.

You visit the operations, take lunch in the staff canteen with a mixed group of employees. You meet one of the NGOs that opposed the company. You learn about the major business risks. You meet some major investors. Your induction covers your own ethical position, and how to deal with potential conflicts of interest. You are shown how the company's business principles are communicated to every employee in the world. The company secretary explains that you always have the right of independent access to information. You discuss your own professional development towards achieving chartered director status.

At the end of the induction, you hope that can describe yourself as an independent director: you would no longer describe yourself as 'non-executive'. And, you ask yourself, how in limited time do you keep your finger on the pulse?

A company is a living entity, not a machine. If we want to help people to stay lean and healthy, we have to do more than merely take their pulse. We have to understand the risks to their health, and their motives, and characteristics that may put at risk our attempts to make them healthier.

The accounting and audit systems are useful sources of information about the health of a company. But on their own they provide no guarantee of that health.

Two companies may have similar financial performance. In the first, shareholders may find nothing to lose sleep over; in the second they may find a disaster waiting to happen. The differences are human. Who dominates whom? What are the pressures to massage the results? Who dares to ask embarrassing questions? What are we here to achieve – the earnings we promised this year or value in the long term? What is the way we all behave round here?

I was recently visiting a large quoted company, which was involved in an acquisition that had recently turned seriously sour. I asked a director what he had learnt from the experience. He told me that he was dissatisfied by the way they had gone about their due diligence. The questions they should have asked, which they never asked, were about the ethics of the organization and the appetite for bad news. Failure to ask those questions cost shareholders hundreds of millions of pounds.

A common feature of nearly every corporate disaster is that, afterwards, you will find good people inside the organization who will say, 'If anybody had asked me I could have told them something was not right.' It was true in Parmalat, in Ahold, in Marks & Spencer, in Maxwell, in Christies, and it was true in Enron where the *Financial Times* tells us that executives kept asking how on earth the rest of the company could be making money if it was managed as their part was managed.

Back in 1995, the RSA Tomorrow's Company Inquiry proposed a list of questions that should be asked by any director. They covered the organization's purpose and values, its understanding of the risks and opportunities inherent in all its relationships, and, crucially, its systems of measurement and reward. Directors were challenged to ask whether the company practised what it preached, rewarded behaviours that matched its values, and was able to anticipate the risks of failure through all its key relationships:

- **Company purpose and values:**
  - Have we adopted a clear statement of purpose?
  - Have we adopted an explicit statement of values, which indicates how the company will conduct business and behave in its key relationships?

- **Key relationships**:
  - Do we know which relationships are crucial to the success of the business?
  - How do we ensure that the company is maintaining consistent and open two-way communications with people in all relationships?
  - How do we ensure that the risk of failure is being managed?

- **Success model:** Have we adopted a success model for the company, which demonstrates how value is added?
- **Measurement:** Do we review the company measurement system annually against its ability to support our goals, purpose, values and key relationships?
- **Reward system:**
  - Do we review the reward system against its ability to reinforce business goals and motivate the right behaviours? Do we monitor positive behaviours such as team working and empowering?
  - Do we seek reports on levels of behavioural risk in key areas of the business?

- **Fiduciary responsibilities:** Are we satisfied as fiduciaries that we are acting in the interests of the general body of shareholders as it exists from time to time and not simply current shareholders?

These questions are not technical. They are common sense. They point to a behavioural audit trail. They ask: what do we demand of people? How do we know if we are getting it? What kind of performance are we looking for? If it is purely financial, what is our protection against fiddling and fraud? The subtext is: never mind the fine words, what kind of behaviours actually get people bonuses and promotion round here? Never mind the carefully honed numbers that keep fund managers happy.

What is really going on in the business and how robust is it? Non-executive directors need to know what kind of behaviours get rewarded in the business. They need to have their own ways of connecting with the real DNA of the business. How often did any non-executive director in Enron ask a question such as:

- Can we say that respect (one of the stated values of the company) is one of our key values?
- How do we audit whether we live by that value?
- Can I see the recruitment criteria for senior positions?
- Are the values reflected there?
- Can I see the criteria used by the performance review committee?
- Are the values reflected there? Or are they simply words?
- What is the secret to getting on in your career in this organization?

A non-executive director in Marks & Spencer five years ago, before the collapse in the company's share price, could, if he or she had asked the right people, have discovered that the HR department wanted to do an employee attitude survey, but felt unable to do so, because it feared that it would not be allowed to publish the results if these were unfavourable. These are the danger signs in organizations that have become too complacent or too narrow in their view of success.

The truth is that purpose, values and relationships are the leading indicators that tell you something is wrong before it hits the bottom line. If you focus on financial indicators, you will be too late. The Enron story reminds us that many people inside the business know that things stink long before the whistle is blown. And people on the edge of the business have the opportunity to manage their risk by following the behavioural audit trial. Of course we need proper protection against conflicts of interests, and greater seriousness and independence in the conduct of the audit committee. But as long as we see governance in narrow terms and seek new technical rules to guard our companies against fraud, these things will continue to happen. We need a values-based, as well as a compliance-based, approach to governance, based on what Tomorrow's Company calls the 'virtuous circle of governance'[6] (see Figure 14.2).

THE SUBVERSION OF SHAREHOLDER VALUE

Part of the reason for failures like Enron is that our investment system is losing its grip on the concept of long-term shareholder value. The investment community has shifted the emphasis from shareholder value to share price. Companies can be congratulated for increasing shareholder value when all they have done is (often temporarily)

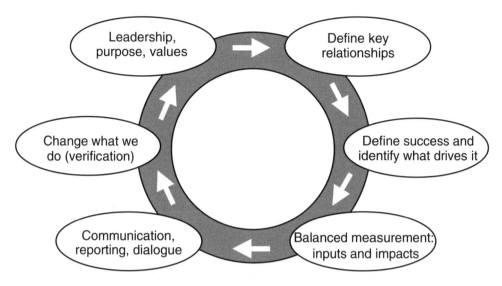

Figure 14.2 The virtuous circle of governance

boosted the share price. Companies can be accused of destroying shareholder value when the share price goes down. Yet, as the technology boom reminds us, the share price is heavily influenced by opinion, assumptions, sentiment and investors' beliefs about which way other investors will jump. It has become an increasingly poor indicator of the underlying health of the business.

There can be no better example of this subversion of shareholder value than the Marconi case. A few months ago, Marconi's former finance director gave an account of his actions in the *Financial Times*. He produced figures to demonstrate that, in terms of total shareholder return during his term of office, the company had really done quite well. His biggest regret, he went on to say, was that he had failed the board by not selling the company to someone else when the share price had gone down to £7, well off its high of £12 but long before it collapsed to under 20p. In other words, the value-destroying decision to put all the eggs in the telecoms basket was not the biggest mistake. The real failure was not cashing in at the right time by finding someone else willing to take on this basket case. This is what is sometimes described as the 'greater fool' school of shareholder value: it does not matter how foolish your strategy, as long as you can find a greater fool to take it off your hands.

This is a corrupted view of shareholder value. It concentrates not upon the organic capacity of a company to create future value, but on the potential to come out ahead after undertaking a series of transactions. It is instructive to observe the difference between Marconi and BAE Systems, the company formed from the acquisition by British Aerospace of all the GEC Marconi defence operations. Here are two companies that restructured themselves. In BAE Systems there was a leadership that believed in making profound changes in the attitudes and the competence of the people running the business, so that the new company was ready for the challenges that lay ahead. In Marconi the attention was on reshuffling the portfolio and not on the development of the capabilities of those running the business.

The primary pressures to which most business leaders have to respond are the perceived shareholder pressures. Without an inclusive approach, the risk is that what shareholders will get is what Enron gave them – earnings today and nothing tomorrow.

There is an expectations and timescale problem. As a German working in the USA put it to me: 'You Anglo-Americans are all the same. You want the harvest at Easter.' Research last year by *Fortune* magazine showed that, of the top 150 US companies over the last 40 years, only three or four have been able to sustain earnings growth at an average of 15 per cent a year for a 20-year period. But, as Terry Smith has pointed out (*FT Business News*, 3 February 2002), this does not stop many CEOs from claiming that they will double earnings within five years, equivalent to compound growth of 15 per cent a year. CEO tenure has shortened. Rewards for executive performance are increasingly linked to share price over periods significantly shorter than the investment cycle of the industry or the time taken to effect cultural change or to implement strategy. And, of course, we have stopped rewarding CEOs for long-term performance. More and more we are giving them stock options – an incentive for them to manipulate upwards the price of the business rather than its ultimate value. Tomorrow's Company has been working for the last four years on creating a new investment agenda to complement the new board agenda described here.[7]

Some questions for...

So here is the agenda that I would like to offer to the many bodies that will play a part in ensuring that companies are ready for the connected demands of greater responsibility, better governance and better risk management.

... chairman, CEO and the board

You are ultimately the company's ethics, risk and responsibility committee. Clear your agenda so that there is time for the serious examination of corporate values and the gap between what is preached and what is practised in your company. It may tell you more than the report of the audit committee. Ask repeatedly what kind of behaviours and what kind of managers get on round here. Do the answers fill you with confidence? If not, dig deeper.

… institutional shareholders

Re-examine your time horizons. What kinds of performance are you rewarding and how durable is it? Are you incentivizing people to boost the share price without regard to the future? Challenge the remuneration. Is it one-dimensional? If it is, how can you be sure that what you are getting is real or cosmetic improvements?

Question CEOs about the kind of atmosphere and culture they seek to create in their companies. See if they are managing the risks that go with big rewards for performance. You are right to invest a lot of credibility in CEOs and teams who deliver what they promise. But how much do you trust the earnings reported to you? What about cash and what about the underlying health of key relationships in the business? Are you encouraging a game of presentation, rather than underlying substance?

Are you leaving responsibility in the ghetto occupied by the SRI or governance specialist? Or does it form part of your overall evaluation of a company?

… pension trustees

Question the more active of your fund managers. What are they doing to promote the underlying health of the businesses they invest in and to manage the risk around values, culture and governance? How are they rewarded? Are they encouraging an approach that delivers expected numbers at the expense of building value for the future? Is this what you want?

… company secretaries

Open up the AGM. Encourage awkward questions as an insurance policy and a sign that the CEO and chairman of your company are role models for open behaviour.

… the remuneration committee

Is your approach to performance one-dimensional? If it is focused on total shareholder return, over what timescale is that measured? How are you protecting tomorrow's shareholders against today's creative accounting? Where in the remuneration system are you sending signals that results are not to be achieved at any price to the values and integrity of the organization?

... business journalists

How often do you ask the CEOs you profile about the things they are doing to ensure the business is still robust in 10 years' time? Do you ask them about the ethos of the business? Is the emphasis exclusively on performance and the next few quarters' earnings? What about following the behavioural audit trail? Do you talk to employees and customers about the underlying health of the organization that is expected to continue delivering these results?

CONCLUSION: AN INCLUSIVE APPROACH TO GOVERNANCE AND RISK MANAGEMENT

The company is a living system. Employees are its lifeblood. Management is the heart that keeps the blood pumping. Strategy is the brain, and measurement and communication the central nervous system. Culture is the DNA. Leadership and continued entrepreneurial energy are its soul and spirit. Governance and accountability are its rhythms and disciplines, like exercise a means of keeping this living organism fit and lean. Unless we understand social responsibility in this wide context, we will continually fail to manage risk, sustain performance and earn trust.

Notes

1 Tomorrow's Company is a business-led think-tank whose vision is of a business future that makes as much sense to staff, shareholders and society. See www.tomorrowscompany.com. Mark Goyder is the author of *Living Tomorrow's Company* (Gower, 1998).
2 For a more detailed discussion of these ideas, see Tomorrow's Company (2003) *Redefining CSR*, Tomorrow's Company, London.
3 For a summary, see Tomorrow's Company (1998) *The Inclusive Approach and Business Success*, Tomorrow's Company, London.
4 For a fuller version of this case, see Mark Goyder (1998) *Living Tomorrow's Company*, Gower, Aldershot.
5 Mark Goyder (2002) *Lessons from Enron*, Tomorrow's Company, London.
6 Tomorrow's Company (2000) *The Corporate Reporting Jigsaw*, Tomorrow's Company, London, p 5.
7 See Tomorrow's Company (2004) *Twenty-first Century Investment*, Tomorrow's Company, London.

Appendix 1

FTSE4Good

FTSE4GOOD INDEX SERIES: BACKGROUND, PHILOSOPHY AND INCLUSION CRITERIA

Introduction

FTSE launched the FTSE4Good Index Series in July 2001 in response to the increasing focus on corporate responsibility by investors as a method of identifying and measuring the non-financial risk of a company and its impact on shareholder value.

In addition, the increasing recognition of the impact of multinational companies on the global economy and the communities where they operate has been a catalyst in encouraging many business leaders to demonstrate a real commitment to corporate responsibility. Far from harming companies' prospects, commitments to the principles of corporate responsibility enhance their reputations and reduce their business risks. The growth of socially responsible investment (SRI) policies and the increasing interest in corporate governance by many large global investment institutions has also given impetus to the need to understand the relationship between corporate responsibility and governance and shareholder value.

Today, many codes of practice, and increasingly legislation, provide a starting point. However, well-designed, well-constructed and widely followed indices can provide the framework and encouragement for companies to adopt the best practice that lawmakers and regulators cannot.

It is this 'best practice' that the index seeks to identify and capture while performance-specific indicators are being developed.

FTSE4Good Index Series: key objectives and features

Key objectives

- To provide a tool for socially responsible investors to identify and invest in companies that meet globally recognized corporate responsibility standards. These companies are best positioned to capitalize on the benefits of superior non-financial risk management, and the opportunities brought by good corporate responsibility.
- To provide asset managers with a basis for socially responsible investment products (such as tracker funds and structured products), as well as a benchmark for all socially responsible investment products.
- To contribute to the development of responsible business practice around the world.

Key features

- Evolving selection criteria to reflect changes in globally accepted corporate responsibility standards and codes of conduct over time.
- Criteria are challenging yet achievable to encourage companies to strive to meet them.
- Higher-impact companies have to meet higher standards.
- Transparent criteria and methodology.
- Criteria based on respected codes and principles.
- New criteria drawn up by experts following widespread consultation.

FTSE4Good: principles of corporate responsibility

The principles of corporate responsibility have developed rapidly in recent years and are still evolving. Many governments and organizations have contributed to the discussion and have undertaken extensive international research and consultation in order to arrive at these basic principles.

Sources

FTSE has identified the common themes from a set of widely followed declarations and international conventions drawn up by governmental bodies, non-governmental organizations and business organizations. The themes that these groups have identified have been used to create the criteria used by FTSE in selecting companies to be included in the FTSE4Good Index Series. The philosophy and criteria of FTSE4Good are based on the principles outlined by the following organizations and documents.

The full texts of these principles can be found through links available at http://www.ftse.com/ftse4good/index.jsp.

The governmental principles are:

- **The Universal Declaration of Human Rights (1948).** Agreed in 1948, this declaration of the General Assembly of the United Nations provides the foundation for all subsequent human rights agreements, including those more directly aimed at business.
- **The OECD Guidelines for Multinational Enterprises (1976).** Adopted by 33 countries, these guidelines cover the issues of disclosure, employment and industrial relations, environment, combating bribery, consumer interests, science and technology, competition and taxation.
- **The UN Global Compact (1999).** Implemented in 1999, this compact was a result of consultation between the United Nations and business to uphold nine principles in the area of human rights, labour standards and environmental practices.

The non-governmental/business principles are:

- **CERES (Coalition for Environmentally Responsible Economies) (1989).** A coalition of environmental, investor and advocacy groups working together for a sustainable future, CERES has issued nine guidelines for sustainability including: protection of the biosphere, environmental restoration and management commitment.
- **Amnesty International Human Rights Principles for Companies.** This set of nine principles includes health and safety, freedom from slavery, and security, and is closely linked to the Universal Declaration of Human Rights.
- **The Caux Round Table Principles for Business (1994).** A coalition of business leaders from Europe, Japan and the United States, the Caux Round Table believes that the world business community must play an important role in improving economic and social conditions around the world. The Caux Round Table is concerned with the general principles of human dignity and how to apply them practically.
- **The Global Sullivan Principles (1977).** Based on self-help, these principles are acknowledged to be one of the most effective efforts to increase corporate social responsibility throughout the world.
- **Ethical Trading Initiative (ETI) – The Base Code (1998).** The ETI is an alliance of companies, NGOs and trade union organizations committed to working together to identify and promote good practice in the implementation of codes of labour practice.
- **Social Accountability 8000 (SA8000) (1997).** Based on a number of existing international human rights and labour standards, SA8000 provides 'transparent,

measurable, verifiable' standards for certifying the performance of organizations in nine areas: 1) child labour; 2) forced labour; 3) health and safety; 4) compensation; 5) working hours; 6) discrimination; 7) discipline; 8) free association and collective bargaining; and 9) management systems.

FTSE4Good: The Model of Best Management Practice for Corporate Responsibility

As the principles of corporate responsibility have been developed, agreement on the practical application of those principles has emerged. Companies face a challenge to incorporate and integrate these principles into their existing framework of governance. Many have made considerable progress towards meeting this challenge.

Building on the principles and on the experience of companies committed to corporate social responsibility, a model of the best practice for companies abiding by these widely accepted principles has been developed. The key elements are:

- **Understanding:** Companies should understand how they affect the environment and the society in which they operate, both for better and for worse.
- **Policy:** Companies should establish broad goals and boundaries to reflect their responsibility for and guide their behaviour with respect to social and environmental challenges. They should set appropriate objectives and targets for improved performance.
- **Management systems:** Companies should establish processes and structures at the operating level to ensure that policies are implemented and risks are managed effectively.
- **Performance and monitoring:** Companies should continually improve their social and environmental performance in line with the objectives and targets set by their policies, and should monitor their success in doing so.
- **Reporting:** Companies should effectively and clearly communicate their understanding of their impacts, policies, management systems and performance with regard to social and environmental issues. Reports should be independently verified where practicable.

This model for best practice is gaining acceptance as the best way for companies to address the challenges of corporate responsibility. The successful application of these principles might be expected to result in the better performance of companies willing to meet those challenges. A company's performance can be judged in terms of:

- comparison with the company's past performance;
- comparison with appropriate peer groups;

- the expectations of society as expressed in legislation, codes of conduct, declarations and international conventions;
- emerging public expectations of corporate conduct.

FTSE considers that those companies incorporating best practice into the fabric of their business will most effectively mitigate and manage the non-financial risks that business faces both today and in the future.

Index management and criteria development consultation process

FTSE will be concentrating on reviewing and increasing the amount of information available to assess and confirm performance in relation to the principles in the Model of Best Governance Practice for Corporate Responsibility. Although the principles can be universally applied, some companies can be considered to have a higher social and environmental 'impact' or 'footprint'. These companies will be subjected to greater challenges in adhering to the principles of corporate responsibility.

It is understood that the availability, quality and comparability of information about performance is not always sufficient for use in the selection criteria at present. In these cases, the criteria actually used are intended as alternatives until such time as actual performance data are available.

Finally, the standards required for inclusion in the FTSE4Good Indices will continually evolve. At the moment, many of the criteria are proxies for future standards that the committee hopes to introduce. It should also be noted that presently the FTSE4Good Indices do not reflect all the issues identified in the accepted Codes for Corporate Responsibility. The FTSE4Good Advisory Committee intends to develop and publish a forward-looking plan to identify new areas of enquiry and to refine the process and the criteria for the future. This document will be available on the FTSE4Good web pages.

Controversial cases

No system of criteria can anticipate every eventuality. The indices may occasionally include companies who are involved in controversy surrounding the social responsibility of their business practices. From time to time this may give rise to questions about their inclusion in the FTSE4Good Indices. Any major events or controversies will be considered as and when they arise. However, it is the opinion of the advisory committee that such occasions will be rare and when they do arise they will indicate a criteria area that requires further development. Decisions regarding the inclusion or exclusion of companies in light of any exceptional events or controversies will only be made at the time of the semi-annual index reviews.

FTSE4Good: key themes

FTSE4Good criteria are broadly based upon three themes acknowledged as essential in assessing or developing corporate responsibility practices:

- working towards environmental sustainability;
- developing positive relationships with stakeholders;
- upholding and supporting universal human rights.

The FTSE4Good Index Series provide a workable means of meeting the complex needs of socially responsible investment. FTSE4Good also offers practical guidelines for companies that desire to be committed to or increase their existing commitment to corporate responsibility. The following themes, drawn from the documents and declarations listed above, reflect widely held views on what constitutes a socially responsible company.

Working towards environmental sustainability

Companies should:

- work to prevent, diminish and control serious environmental damage from their operations;
- continually seek to improve their environmental performance by: adopting environmentally beneficial technologies; developing products/services that have no undue environmental impacts and are energy and resource efficient, reusable, recyclable and can be disposed of safely; promoting higher awareness among customers of environmental implications of their products/services; and researching ways to improve environmental performance over the long term;
- protect the biosphere, use natural resources in a sustainable manner, reduce and dispose of wastes, conserve energy, produce safe products and services, and restore the environment;
- focus on the following – risk reduction, informing the public, management commitment, reports and audits.

Developing positive relationships with stakeholders

Companies should:

- develop and apply effective self-regulatory practices and management;
- treat stakeholders (ie customers, employees, owners/investors, suppliers, competitors and local communities) with dignity, fairness and respect;

- ensure that employees and other people with whom they work are entitled to rights such as: freedom from discrimination; the right to life and security; freedom from slavery; freedom of association; the right to collective bargaining; and fair working conditions;
- take adequate steps to prevent accidents and injury to health by minimizing, so far as is reasonably possible, the causes of hazards inherent in the working environment;
- not engage in or support forced or child labour;
- encourage human capital formation, through creating employment and facilitating training;
- act in accordance with fair business, marketing and advertising practices and take all reasonable steps to ensure the quality of their goods and services;
- provide stakeholders with reliable and relevant information on social issues (as well as environmental and economic) that fosters dialogue, inquiry and accountability;
- enhance transparency of their activities in the fight against bribery and extortion;
- support and uphold good corporate governance principles.

Upholding and supporting universal human rights

Companies should:

- ensure that core labour standards are met as they are enshrined in the various conventions of the International Labour Organization that have been signed by the vast majority of governments;
- respect the human rights of those affected by the company's activities;
- cooperate in creating an environment where human rights are understood and respected. Human rights by their nature are universal and cannot be considered an encroachment on national sovereignty;
- accept their responsibility to use their influence to try to stop violations of human rights by governments or armed political groups in the countries in which they operate.

Criteria development programme

With the aid of the FTSE4Good Advisory Committee, FTSE aims to revise its criteria regularly to move step by step towards an evaluative framework reflecting continuous improvement in evolving consensus on good management and performance with regard to corporate responsibility.

The criteria will continue to be challenging but achievable for companies.

Table A1.1 Action programme

Issue	Criteria development programme	Date*
Human rights	Implementation of revised human rights criteria.	2003-05
Supply chain labour standards	Consultation and implementation of criteria for labour standards in companies' supply chains.	2003-04
Bribery and corruption	Consultation and implementation of criteria for bribery and corruption.	2004

*Subject to change.

Specific areas of current development

Table A1.1 shows the action programme that has been identified, which will necessarily be subject to change owing to evolving SRI/CSR priorities.

Industry exclusions

The FTSE4Good Advisory Committee wishes to examine industry sectors that are presently excluded from FTSE4Good, with a view to introducing specific perfor-mance criteria that will allow companies in these sectors to aspire to entering the FTSE4Good Indices. At appropriate points in time, the committee intends that sector exclusions will be removed, and will be replaced with suitable and measurable performance criteria specifically for these industries.

To become and remain a constituent of FTSE4Good, unlike other FTSE indices, companies need to meet a set of increasingly challenging corporate responsibility standards.

Table A1.2 Tackling exclusions

Issue	Criteria development programme	Date*
Exclusions	Investigating the removal of exclusions where suitable and substantial key performance indicator criteria can be developed with which to replace them:	Ongoing
	– breaches of the breast-milk marketing code – public consultation in summer 2003;	2003
	– uranium mining.	2004

*Subject to change.

FTSE4Good inclusion criteria

For inclusion in the FTSE4Good Index Series, companies must be constituents of one of the starting universes: FTSE All Share Index (UK), FTSE Developed Europe Index, FTSE US Index and FTSE Developed Index (Global).

Companies in the starting universe need to satisfy criteria based on three principles:

- working towards environmental sustainability;
- developing positive relationships with stakeholders;
- upholding and supporting universal human rights.

Excluded companies

Companies that have been identified as having business interests in the following industries are currently excluded from the FTSE4Good Index Series:

- tobacco producers;
- companies manufacturing either parts for, or whole, nuclear weapons systems;
- companies manufacturing whole weapons systems;
- owners or operators of nuclear power stations;
- companies involved in the extraction or processing of uranium.*

*The removal of this exclusion is currently being reviewed.

Environmental criteria

Companies are assigned a high-, medium- or low-impact weighting according to their industry sector. The higher the environmental impact of the company's operations, the more stringent the criteria it needs to meet to be included in the index.

New entrants to the FTSE4Good Index Series

Companies wishing to be added to the FTSE4Good Index Series will need to meet all the new criteria for their impact category.

Social and stakeholder criteria

To qualify for inclusion, companies must be disclosing information that meets at least two of the seven indicators in Table A1.7 either globally or in their home operating country.

To warrant inclusion in the indices, companies must not have breached the infant formula manufacturing section of the International Code on Marketing of Breast Milk Substitutes according to the International Baby Food Action Network. The removal of this exclusion is currently being reviewed.

Table A1.3 Environmental impact weighting

High-impact sectors	Medium-impact sectors	Low-impact sectors
Agriculture	DIY and building supplies	Information technology
Air transport	Electronic and electrical	Media
Airports	equipment	Consumer/mortgage finance
Building materials	Energy and fuel distribution	Leisure not elsewhere
(includes quarrying)	Engineering and machinery	classified (gyms and gaming)
Chemicals and	Financials not elsewhere classified	Property investors
pharmaceuticals	Hotels, catering and facilities	Research and development
Construction	management	Support services
Major systems	Manufacturers not elsewhere	Telecoms
engineering	classified	Wholesale distribution
Fast food chains	Ports	
Food, beverages	Printing and newspaper	
and tobacco	Property developers	
Forestry and paper	Public transport	
Mining and metals	Publishing	
Oil and gas	Retailers not elsewhere classified	
Pest control	Vehicle hire	
Power generation		
Road distribution		
and shipping		
Supermarkets		
Vehicle manufacture		
Waste		
Water		

Note: the business sectors indicated above are determined and classified by EIRIS. For more information on these classifications, go to www.eiris.org.

Human rights criteria

On 10 April 2003 FTSE announced changes to the FTSE4Good Index Series selection criteria relating to upholding and supporting universal human rights. The new criteria outlined below were formed on the basis of a broad public human rights consultation during 2002. This involved taking into account almost 200 responses from corporations, fund managers, non-governmental organizations and private investors.

In the same way as for the new environmental criteria, companies have been divided into groups according to their potential impact. The higher the potential human rights impact of the company's operations, the more stringent the criteria it needs to meet to be included in the index. Companies currently have been divided into three groups:

Table A1.4 What do companies need to do in order to meet the environmental criteria?

	High-impact companies	Medium-impact companies	Low-impact companies
Policy	Policy must cover the whole group and either meet all five core indicators plus at least one desirable indicator, or four core plus two desirable indicators.	Policy must cover the whole group and meet at least four indicators, at least three of which must be core.	Companies must have published a policy statement including at least one commitment indicator.
Management	If environmental management systems (EMS) are applied to between one- and two-thirds of company activities, all six indicators must be met, and targets must be quantified. If EMS are applied to more than two-thirds of company activities, the company must meet at least five of the indicators, one of which must be documented objectives and targets in all key areas. ISO certification and EMAS. registrations are considered to meet all six indicators and are assessed on that basis.	EMS must cover at least one-third of the company and meet at least four indicators. If there is less than one-third coverage, the company must meet six indicators, including quantitative objectives and targets. ISO14001 certified or EMAS registered systems are considered to meet all six indicators.	No requirement.
Reporting	Report must have been published within the last three years, cover the whole group, and meet at least three of the four indicators. Corporate reports that do not cover the entire global operations of the listed company must meet either all four core indicators or three core indicators together with two desirable indicators.	No requirement.	No requirement.

Table A1.5 What are the criteria indicators?

Policy	Core indicators	Desirable indicators
	Policy refers to all key issues.	Globally applicable
	Responsibility for policy at board or	corporate standards.
	department level.	Commitment to stakeholder
	Commitment to use of targets.	involvement.
	Commitment to monitoring and audit	Policy addresses product
	or service impact.	Strategic moves towards
	Commitment to public reporting.	sustainability.
Management	Presence of environmental policy.	
	Identification of significant impacts.	
	Documented objectives and targets in	
	key areas.	
	Outline of processes and responsibilities,	
	manuals, action plans, procedures.	
	Internal audits against the requirements	
	of the system (not limited to legal	
	compliance).	
	Internal reporting and management	
	review.	
Reporting	Text of environmental policy.	Outline of an EMS.
	Description of main impacts.	Non-compliance, prosecution,
	Quantitative data.	fines, accidents.
	Performance measured against targets.	Financial dimensions.
		Independent verification.
		Stakeholder dialogue.
		Coverage of sustainability issues.

Table A1.6 When do companies have to meet the environmental criteria requirements?

Company deadline	Low-impact company requirements	Medium-impact company	High-impact company requirements requirements
1 August 2003	No requirement.	Basic policy (to low-impact requirement).	Meet medium-impact policy/EMS requirements.
1 February 2004	No requirement.	Policy proper.	Meet all requirements.
1 August 2004	No requirement.	EMS.	
1 February 2005	Policy requirement.		

Table A1.7 Inclusion criteria for new entrants

	Indicators
Policy	Adopting an equal opportunities policy and/or including a commitment to equal opportunities or diversity in the annual report or website.
	Adopting a code of ethics or business principles.
Management	Providing evidence of equal opportunities systems including one or more of: monitoring of the policy and workforce composition; flexible working arrangements and family benefits (meaning at least three of flexible working time, childcare support, job sharing, career breaks, and maternity or paternity pay beyond the legal requirements); and more than 10 per cent of managers being women or the proportion of managers who are women or from ethnic minorities exceeding two-fifths of their representation in the workforce concerned.
	Providing evidence of health and safety systems including one or more of: awards; details of health and safety training; and published accidents rates.
	Providing evidence of training and employee development systems including one or more of: annual training reviews for staff (more than 25 per cent of those staff where figures are available); and providing significant data on time and money spent on training.
	Providing evidence of systems to maintain good employee relations including union recognition agreements or other consultative arrangements (covering more than 25 per cent of staff where figures are available).
Practice/ performance	Making charitable donations in excess of £50,000; operating payroll giving schemes; providing gifts in kind or staff secondments to community schemes or assigning responsibility for charitable donations or community relations to a senior manager.

1. **Global resource sector**. The group of companies identified as potentially having the highest human rights impact are companies in the global resource sector (oil, gas and mining). This sector is defined more specifically in the 'Definitions' section below. The FTSE4Good Advisory Committee proposes to extend the higher requirements over time to other sectors, such as textiles and apparels, pharmaceuticals, chemicals, agriculture, banking and finance. Details of the criteria and implementation timetable are given below.

2. **Significant involvement in countries of concern.** Companies with significant involvement in countries with the greatest human rights concern have been identified as potentially having a significant impact although in general having a lower human rights impact than the global resource sector. Therefore these companies are required to meet an intermediate level of criteria. Details of the criteria and implementation timetable are given below.

3. **All other companies.** In recognition that human rights issues are relevant to all companies every constituent must demonstrate at least a basic policy in relation to either equal opportunities or freedom of association.

New entrants to the index

Companies wishing to be added to the FTSE4Good Index Series will need to meet the new criteria according to the same deadlines as the current constituents.

Definitions

- **Global resource sector** is defined as companies with global involvement in oil and gas and mining including upstream operations.
- **Global** is defined as operations that extend to non-OECD countries.
- **Upstream operations** are exploration and production that includes companies such as rig operators and contract drillers.
- **Downstream operations** include refining, marketing and selling and are not included for these criteria.

What are the human rights criteria for the global resource sector?

Table A1.8 Policy criteria for the global resource sector

New criteria	Details
Public policy	The company has published policies covering human rights issues that are clearly communicated globally (in local languages where appropriate).
Board responsibility	The strategic responsibility for the human rights policy or policies rests with one or more board members or senior managers who report directly to the CEO.
ILO core labour standards or UN Global Compact/ SA8000/OECD Guidelines	A statement of commitment to respect all the ILO core labour standards globally. The core conventions relate to: equal opportunities, freedom of association/collective bargaining, forced labour and child labour. Alternatively, signatories to the UN Global Compact or SA8000, or companies whose policy states support for the OECD Guidelines for Multi-national Enterprises are considered to meet this requirement.
UDHR	A clear statement of support for the Universal Declaration of Human Rights.

(continued)

Table A1.8 *(continued)*

New criteria	Details
Guidelines on armed security guards	Guidelines governing the use of armed security guards based on UN Basic Principles on the Use of Force and Firearms by Law Enforcement Officials or the Code of Conduct for Law Enforcement Officials. Alternatively signatories to the Voluntary Principles on Security and Human Rights meet this requirement.
Indigenous people	A stated commitment to respecting indigenous people's rights.

Table A1.9 Management systems criteria for the global resource sector

New criteria	Details
Implementing policy criteria and monitoring	Monitoring the implementation of the human rights policy including the existence of procedures to remedy any non-compliance.
Employee human rights training	Training for employees globally in the human rights policy.
Stakeholder consultation	Consulting with independent local stakeholders in the countries of concern.
Human rights impact assessment	Evidence of a human rights impact assessment, which includes the company identifying the major human rights issues it faces and integrating human rights concerns into its risk assessment procedures.

Table A1.10 Reporting criteria for the global resource sector

New criteria	Details
Produce a human rights report	Reporting on the human rights policy and performance to the public in a published format.
Cover policies and management systems	As a minimum, covering policies and management systems.

What are the human rights criteria for companies with a significant presence in countries of human rights concern?

Definitions

- **Significant presence** is defined as having 1,000-plus employees or £100 million in turnover or assets in these countries through a 20 per cent-plus equity stake in subsidiaries or associates incorporated there.

- **Countries of concern.** The list is drawn up and reviewed each year by EIRIS in the light of human rights developments using a variety of sources. EIRIS uses the latest Freedom House list of 'not free' countries to identify those with significant levels of corporate investment and then amends that list in the light of further information including the annual reports from Human Rights Watch and Amnesty International.

The company must meet at least two of the four criteria set out in Table A1.12.

Since the creation of the index some two years ago, increasing numbers of companies are stepping up to the plate and meeting the challenge posed by the expectations of a wide range of global investors as expressed in the FTSE4Good index criteria.

What is also clear is that many NGOs, investors and other followers of CSR are continually seeking answers to the question of how companies are responding to the demands of society. One indicator that can help is the future programme of development and tightening of the FTSE4Good index criteria, as this creates an irresistible challenge that most companies in the index today appear willing to meet.

FTSE GLOBAL CLASSIFICATION SYSTEM AND UK BENCHMARK DATA

Table A1.14 lists the largest 300 UK companies that had passed the FTSE4Good screen as at 10 June 2004. This table will prove useful to readers if they seek out in it businesses that are similar to their own. For that you will need to first look down the classification system in Table A1.13 and identify which economic group, sector and subsector best describe your business. You can then obtain a copy of that company's annual report and look for the section on CSR or, in some cases, the company may produce a separate CSR report – all publicly available documents. Another place to look for CSR information is on the company's website or you can even contact the company and ask to speak to whoever is in charge of CSR. While nobody will wish to share commercially confidential material with an outsider, most companies are only too proud to discuss their CSR credentials and the activities and structures that they feel have enabled them to pass a CSR screen such as that used to identify businesses with the potential to be listed in the FTSE4Good Index. The market capitalization columns in Table A1.14 will help to identify companies nearer to your own in size. The two columns represent the actual value of the business 'before investibility weighting' and the value of the business adjusted to reflect how liquid and available for investment the stock is, ie whether a majority of the shares are held by one investor and whether the shares are usually available on the market. This latter column represents the value 'after investibility weighting'. The overall result should be to enable you to

Table A1.11 Human rights policy criteria for companies in countries of concern

New criteria	Details
ILO core labour standards or UN Global Compact/ SA8000/OECD Guidelines	A public statement of commitment to respect all the ILO core lab our standards globally. The core conventions relate to: equal opportunities, freedom of association/ collective bargaining, forced labour and child labour. Alternatively, signatories to the UN Global Compact or SA8000, or companies whose policy states support for the OECD Guidelines for Multi-national Enterprises are considered to meet this requirement.
Board responsibility or UDHR or global human rights communication	The strategic responsibility for the human rights policy or policies rests with one or more board members or senior managers who report directly to the CEO. Alternatively, a clear statement of support for the Universal Declaration of Human Rights. Alternatively, communication of the human rights policy to employees globally.

see how other businesses similar to yours are dealing with CSR and even managing to leverage their CSR performance to generate a marketing plus and to impress the growing band of institutional investors for which a strong CSR record is a prerequisite to being included in their list of stocks in which they can invest their fund members' money. While the programmes that others employ may not be exactly correct for your business, they will certainly provide you with some strong pointers as to what will work in circumstances akin to those in which you operate.

Table A1.12 Human rights management systems criteria for companies in countries of concern

New criteria	Details
Implementing policy criteria and monitoring	Monitoring the implementation of the human rights policy including the existence of procedures to remedy any non-compliance.
Employee human rights training	Training for employees globally in the human rights policy.
Stakeholder consultation	Consulting with independent local stakeholders in the countries of concern.
Human rights impact assessment	Evidence of a human rights impact assessment, which includes the company identifying the major human rights issues it faces and integrating human rights concerns into its risk assessment procedures.

Table A1.13 FTSE Global Classification System

Economic groups	Sectors	Subsectors
00 Resources	**04 Mining**	**043 Gold mining** Prospectors for, extractors and refiers of gold-bearing ores. **045 Mining finance** Finance houses engaged in financing and developing mining interests or deriving an income from mining interests. **048 Other mineral extractors and mines** Companies engaged in the exploration, extraction and/or refining of minerals other than gold.
	07 Oil and gas	**073 Oil and gas – exploration and production** Companies engaged in exploration for, and production of, mineral oil and gas. **075 Oil – services** Providers of services, including drilling, for oil and natural gas exploration and production. (NB: As distinct from 'Gas distribution' in the Utilities economic group – 773.) **078 Oil – integrated** Companies engaged in the exploration for, production, refining, distribution and supply of mineral oil and gas products.
10 Basic industries	**11 Chemicals**	**113 Chemicals – commodity** Producers of commodity and industrial chemicals, industrial gases and fibres. **116 Chemicals – advanced materials** Producers of cellular polymers and specialist plastics. Manufacturers of polystyrene and other plastic packaging materials. **118 Chemicals – speciality** Producers of fine chemicals, dyestuffs and chemicals for specialized applications.
	13 Construction and building materials	**131 Builders' merchants** Wholesalers of building materials and timber importers. **132 Building and construction materials** Producers of materials used in the construction and refurbishment of buildings and

(continued)

Table A1.13 *(continued)*

Economic groups	Sectors	Subsectors
		structures (eg cement, glass and flooring materials other than carpets not classified in 'Furnishings and floor coverings '– 342 in the Cyclical Consumer Goods economic group) and refractory materials.
		134 House building
		Constructors of residential buildings.
		137 Other construction
		Constructors of non-residential buildings. Infrastructure contractors and providers of services to construction.
	15 Forestry and paper	**153 Forestry**
		Owners and operators of timber tracts, forest tree nurseries and sawmills.
		156 Paper
		Producers, converters and merchants of all grades of paper.
	18 Steel and other metals	**186 Non-ferrous metals**
		Metal traders or producers of primary non-ferrous metal products, encompassing all processes from smelting to alloying, rolling and drawing.
		188 Steel
		Steel stockholders or manufacturers of primary iron and steel products, encompassing all processes from smelting in blast furnaces to rolling mills and foundries.
20 General industrials	**21 Aerospace and defence**	**215 Aerospace**
		Manufacturers and assemblers of aircraft, equipment and aircraft parts primarily used in commercial or private air transport.
		216 Defence
		Producers of components and equipment for the defence industry.
	24 Diversified industrials	**240 Diversified industrials**
		Industrial companies engaged in three, or more, classes of business that differ substantially from each other, no one of

(continued)

Table A1.13 *(continued)*

Economic groups	Sectors	Subsectors
		which contributes 50 per cent, or more, of pre-tax profit, nor less than 10 per cent.
	25 Electronic and electrical equipment	**252 Electrical equipment** Producers and distributors of industrial electrical components and equipment. **253 Electronic equipment** Producers and distributors of industrial electronic components and equipment not classified elsewhere (eg in 'Aerospace and defence' – 215 and 216, 'Household appliances and housewares' – 345, or the 'Hardware' sector of the Information Technology economic group – 932, 936 and 938).
	26 Engineering and machinery	**263 Commercial vehicles and trucks** Manufacturers of commercial vehicles, railway rolling stock and heavy agricultural and construction machinery and their parts. **264 Engineering – contractors** Designers, manufacturers and installers of industrial plant and pollution control equipment. **266 Engineering fabricators** Producers of castings, pressings, welded shapes; fabricators and erectors of structural steelwork. **267 Engineering – general** Engineering companies not classified elsewhere, making or distributing a variety of products.
30 Cyclical consumer goods	31 Automobiles and parts	**311 Automobiles** Companies that manufacture and assemble passenger automobiles and motorcycles. **313 Auto parts** Manufacturers and distributors of auto parts other than those classified elsewhere (eg in 'Tyres and rubber' – 317).

(continued)

Table A1.13 *(continued)*

Economic groups	Sectors	Subsectors
		317 Tyres and rubber Tyre manufacturers and distributors. Tyre treaders for automobiles, trucks, tractors and aircraft. **318 Vehicle distribution** Distributors, sellers and/or servicers of vehicles.
	34 Household goods and textiles	**341 Clothing and footwear** Manufacturers or wholesalers of all types of clothing and footwear, including those for sportswear. **342 Furnishings and floor coverings** Manufacturers and distributors of furniture (including office furniture) and furnishings, carpets andother materials for covering floors. **343 Consumer electronics** Manufacturers or distributors of consumer electronic and electrical equipment. **345 Household appliances and housewares** Manufacturers or distributors of domestic appliances, lighting, tools for use in the home, hardware, cutlery, tableware, giftware, jewellery and watches. **347 Leisure equipment** Manufacturers or distributors of leisure equipment not classified under 'Clothing and footwear' – 341. **349 Other textiles and leather goods** Manufacturers or distributors of textile materials and goods other than clothing and of leather goods other than footwear. Processors of hides and skins.
40 Non-cyclical consumer goods	**41 Beverages**	**415 Beverages – brewers** Manufacturers and shippers of malt and malt liquors such as beer, ale and stout. (NB: Brewers are classified in 'Beverages – brewers' – 415, or in the 'Restaurants

(continued)

Table A1.13 *(continued)*

Economic groups	Sectors	Subsectors
		and pubs' subsector – 539 of the Cyclical services economic group.)
		416 Beverages – distillers and vintners
		Distillers, blenders and shippers of alcoholic beverages such as whisky, brandy, rum, gin and liquors. Producers of wine and cider.
		418 Soft drinks
		Manufacturers of non-alcoholic beverages including carbonated mineral waters.
	43 Food producers and processors	**433 Farming and fishing**
		Crop growers, excluding forestry. Companies that raise livestock, commercial fishers and manufacturers of livestock feeds. Owners of plantations.
		435 Food processors
		Processors and wholesalers of food.
	44 Health	**443 Health maintenance organizations**
		Owners and operators of health maintenance organizations.
		444 Hospital management and long-term care
		Owners and operators of hospitals, clinics, nursing homes, rehabilitation and retirement centres.
		446 Medical equipment and supplies
		Manufacturers of medical equipment, devices and eyecare products.
		449 Other healthcare
		Diversified and other healthcare companies not classified elsewhere (eg 'Education, business training and employment agencies' – 583).
	47 Personal care and household products	**475 Household products**
		Producers and distributors of detergents, soaps and polishes.
		477 Personal products
		Producers and distributors of toiletries, cosmetics and hygiene products.

(continued)

Table A1.13 *(continued)*

Economic groups	Sectors	Subsectors
	48 Pharmaceuticals and biotechnology	**482 Biotechnology** Companies, the majority of whose research and development involves the use of living material as the means of drug discovery and diagnostics development. The majority of their revenue is derived from either the sale or licensing of these drugs and/or diagnostic tools. **486 Pharmaceuticals** Companies involved in drug research, development, exploitation and distribution other than those classified elsewhere (eg 'Biotechnology' – 482).
	49 Tobacco	**490 Tobacco** Cigarette or tobacco manufacturers and wholesalers.
50 Cyclical services	**52 General retailers**	**524 Discount and super-stores and warehouses** Shops concentrating on mass distribution of both hardlines and soft goods at discounted prices due to volume. **525 Retailers – e-commerce** Retailers conducting the majority of their business on the internet or other electronic systems (eg digital TV). Retailers also conducting business by traditional means will be classified under other retailing subsectors until published figures reveal that over 50 per cent of their business, as measured by profit or turnover, is derived from e-commerce-related activities. **526 Retailers – hardlines** Shops and wholesalers concentrating on the sale of a single class of goods, not classified elsewhere. **527 Retailers – multi-department** Retail outlets with more than one department, selling a varied range of goods not classified

(continued)

Table A1.13 (*continued*)

Economic groups	Sectors	Subsectors
		elsewhere (eg 'Discount and super-stores and warehouses' – 524).
		528 Retailers – soft goods
		Shops concentrating on the sale of a single class of soft goods – clothing, etc.
	53 Leisure and hotels	**532 Gambling**
		Providers of gambling and casino facilities.
		536 Hotels
		Hoteliers and hotel service companies.
		538 Leisure facilities
		Providers of leisure facilities.
		539 Restaurants and pubs
		Operators of restaurants and pubs, including integrated brewery companies.
	54 Media and entertainment	**542 Television, radio and filmed entertainment**
		Independent radio and television contractors, not classified elsewhere (eg 'Subscription entertainment networks' – 543). Companies providing facilities and/or programmes for contractors. Film production.
		543 Subscription entertainment networks
		Providers of television, media services and programming facilities driven by subscriptions.
		545 Media agencies
		Advertising, marketing and public relations agencies and consultancies.
		546 Photography
		Manufacturers of photographic equipment for use by the general public. Operators of photographic studios and film development companies.
		547 Publishing and printing
		Publishers of information via printed or electronic media. Printers or distributors of printers' requisites and artists' materials.

(*continued*)

Table A1.13 *(continued)*

Economic groups	Sectors	Subsectors
	58 Support services	**581 Business support services** Providers of non-financial services to a wide range of industries, which could have been provided 'in-house', excluding those activities classified elsewhere. **582 Delivery services** Couriers and providers of non-contractual mail and package delivery services. **583 Education, business training and employment agencies** Providers of education, business and management training courses and employment services. **584 Environmental control** Providers of solid and hazardous waste management, recovery and disposal services. Funeral directors, cemetery and crematorium operators. **587 Transaction and payroll services** Providers of financial administration services. **588 Security and alarm services** Companies installing, servicing and monitoring alarm systems and those providing security services.
	59 Transport	**591 Airlines and airports** Air transport companies and operators of airports and related facilities and services. **596 Rail, road and freight** Land transport and related facilities and services, including road and tunnel operators, vehicle rental and agencies that undertake the transportation of goods from shippers to receivers. **597 Shipping and ports** Water-borne transport and related services and terminal facilities.
60 Non-cyclical services	**63 Food and drug retailers**	**630 Food and drug retailers** Retailers of food and drug products.

(continued)

Table A1.13 *(continued)*

Economic groups	Sectors	Subsectors
	67 Telecommunication services	**673 Fixed-line telecommunication services** Operators of fixed-line telecommunications networks. **678 Wireless telecommunication services** Operators of mobile (cellular and satellite broadcast) telecommunications networks.
70 Utilities	**72 Electricity**	**720 Electricity** Generators and distributors of electricity.
	77 Utilities – other	**773 Gas distribution** Distributors of natural and manufactured gas. **775 Multi-utilities – other** Companies where the majority of total profits arise from the provision of utilities, where no single utility accounts for more than 80 per cent of the profits arising from utilities. **778 Water** Companies responsible for the provision of water and the removal of sewage.
80 Financials	**81 Banks**	**810 Banks** Banks providing a broad range of financial services, with significant retail banking and money transmission.
	83 Insurance	**833 Insurance brokers** Insurance and life assurance agencies. **834 Insurance – non-life** Companies engaging principally in accident, fire, marine and other classes of insurance business not classified elsewhere. **837 Re-insurance** Re-insurance companies. **839 Other insurance** Insurance companies with life assurance, non-life insurance and re-insurance interests, no one of which predominates.
	84 Life assurance	**840 Life assurance** Companies engaging principally in life assurance and/or disability business.

(continued)

Table A1.13 *(continued)*

Economic groups	Sectors	Subsectors
	85 Investment companies	**850 Investment companies (eligible for index inclusion)**
		Companies engaged primarily in owning stakes not giving control in a diversified range of companies, which are FTSE Index eligible subject to passing the relevant entry criteria.
	86 Real estate	**862 Real estate holding and development**
		Companies specializing in the ownership and/or development of property assets not classified elsewhere.
		864 Property agencies
		Estate agents and surveyors.
	87 Speciality and other finance	**871 Asset managers**
		Asset managers.
		873 Consumer finance
		Credit card companies, providers of personal finance services (ie personal loans) not classified under 'Mortgage finance' – 877.
		875 Investment banks
		Banks providing a range of specialist financial services, primarily to corporate clients and stockbrokers.
		877 Mortgage finance
		Institutional providers of mortgages and mortgage insurance not engaging in other types of retail or commercial banking.
		879 Other financial
		Financial holding companies, security and commodity exchanges and companies engaged in financial activities not specified elsewhere.
	89 Investment entities	**890 Investment entities (ineligible for index inclusion)**
		Companies ineligible for inclusion in FTSE Indices due to their being engaged primarily in owning stakes not giving control in a diversified range of companies. These

(continued)

Table A1.13 *(continued)*

Economic groups	Sectors	Subsectors
		include open-ended investment companies, currency funds and split capital investment trusts in which two or more classes of capital have different entitlements to assets and/or income after meeting the requirements of any other capital classes or borrowings.
90 Information technology	**93 Information technology hardware**	**932 Computer hardware** Manufacturers and distributors of computers and associated electronic data-processing equipment and accessories. **936 Semiconductors** Semiconductor capital equipment, wafer and chip manufacturers and distributors. **938 Telecommunications equipment** Manufacturers and distributors of digital equipment used in telecommunications, including mobile telephones, exchanges and microwave systems.
	97 Software and computer services	**972 Computer services** Providers of computer services. Consultants for information technology not classified elsewhere (eg 'Education, business training and employment agencies' – 583). **974 Internet** Access providers, internet software, online service providers. **977 Software** Producers, and distributors of computer software.

Table A1.14 FTSE4Good UK benchmark data as at 10 June 2004

Name of company	Economic group	Sector	Subsector	Market capitalization £ million before investibility weighting	after investibility weighting
		(See Table A1.13 Classification system)			
ARM Holdings	90	93	936	1,245	1,245
AWG	70	77	778	867	867
Abacus Group	20	25	253	127	127
Abbey National	80	81	810	6,989	6,989
Aberdeen Asset Management	80	87	871	187	187
Aegis Group	50	54	545	973	973
Aga Foodservice Group	20	26	267	297	297
Aggregate Industries	10	13	132	1,098	1,098
Aggreko	50	58	581	418	418
Alliance & Leicester	80	81	810	3,992	3,992
Alliance UniChem	40	48	486	2,225	1,669
Allied Domecq	40	41	416	5,137	5,137
Alpha Airports Group	50	59	591	140	105
Amlin	80	83	834	614	614
Amvescap	80	87	871	2,945	2,945
Antisoma	40	48	482	51	38
Arla Foods UK	40	43	435	366	183
Arriva	50	59	596	787	787
Ashley (Laura) Holdings	50	52	528	101	30
Ashtead Group	50	58	581	81	81
Associated British Ports Hldgs	50	59	597	1,471	1,471
AstraZeneca	40	48	486	43,186	43,186
Autologic Holdings	50	59	596	124	124
Avis Europe	50	59	596	581	291
Aviva	80	84	840	12,370	12,370
Axis-Shield	40	48	482	81	81
Axon Group	90	97	972	65	49
BAA	50	59	591	5,766	5,766
BBA Group	50	59	591	1,160	1,160

(continued)

Table A1.14 *(continued)*

Name of company	Economic group	Sector	Subsector	Market capitalization £ million before investibility weighting	after investibility weighting
		(See Table A1.13 Classification system)			
BG Group	0	7	78	12,127	12,127
BHP Billiton	0	4	48	11,279	11,279
BOC Group	10	11	113	4,528	4,528
BP	0	7	78	106,431	106,431
BPP Holdings	50	58	583	182	182
BSS Group	10	13	131	208	208
BT Group	60	67	673	16,386	16,386
BTG	50	58	581	164	164
Barclays	80	81	810	32,277	32,277
Berkeley Group	10	13	134	1,148	1,148
Bespak	40	44	446	141	141
Biocompatibles International	40	44	446	67	67
Blacks Leisure Group	50	52	526	180	180
Bloomsbury Publishing	50	54	547	173	173
Body Shop International	50	52	528	338	169
Boots Group	50	52	527	5,014	5,014
Bovis Homes Group	10	13	134	616	616
Bradford & Bingley	80	81	810	1,824	1,824
Brambles Industries	50	58	581	1,563	1,563
Brammer (H)	50	58	581	65	65
Brewin Dolphin Holdings	80	87	875	149	149
Britannic Group	80	84	840	686	686
British Airways	50	59	591	2,808	2,808
British Land Co	80	86	862	3,360	3,360
British Polythene Industries	50	58	581	75	75
British Sky Broadcasting Group	50	54	543	12,162	9,122
Brixton	80	86	862	777	777
Brown (N) Group	50	52	528	303	227

(continued)

Table A1.14 *(continued)*

Name of company	Economic group	Sector	Subsector	Market capitalization £ million before investibility weighting	after investibility weighting
		(See Table A1.13 Classification system)			
Bunzl	50	58	581	2,119	2,119
Burberry Group	50	52	528	1,974	592
Cable & Wireless	60	67	673	3,097	3,097
Cadbury Schweppes	40	43	435	9,469	9,469
Cambridge Antibody Tech Group	40	48	482	202	202
Capita Group	50	58	587	2,103	2,103
Capital & Regional	80	86	862	313	313
Capital Radio	50	54	542	380	380
Care UK	40	44	444	148	148
Carillion	10	13	137	371	371
Carnival	50	53	538	5,232	5,232
Cattles	80	87	873	1,050	1,050
Celltech Group	40	48	482	1,519	1,519
Centrica	70	77	773	9,330	9,330
Chesnara	80	84	840	89	89
Chloride Group	20	25	253	117	117
Chrysalis Group	50	54	542	305	229
Close Brothers Group	80	87	875	1,151	1,151
Colt Telecom Group	60	67	673	1,311	983
Communisis	50	58	581	149	149
Compass Group	50	58	581	7,425	7,425
Computacenter	90	97	972	765	574
Corus Group	10	18	188	1,508	1,508
Countryside Properties	10	13	134	174	174
Countrywide	80	86	864	462	462
Courts	50	52	526	150	112
Crest Nicholson	10	13	134	383	383
Croda International	10	11	118	380	380
DTZ Holdings	80	86	864	85	85
Danka Business Systems	50	58	581	155	155
Datamonitor	50	54	547	92	28

(continued)

Table A1.14 *(continued)*

Name of company	Economic group	Sector	Subsector	Market capitalization £ million before investibility weighting	after investibility weighting
		(See Table A1.13 Classification system)			
Davis Service Group	50	58	581	753	753
De La Rue	50	58	581	597	597
De Vere Group	50	53	536	502	502
Derwent Valley Hldgs	80	86	862	460	460
Diageo	40	41	416	22,453	22,453
Dimension Data Holdings	90	97	972	413	413
Dixons Group	50	52	526	2,989	2,989
Domestic & General Group	80	83	834	216	216
Domnick Hunter Group	20	26	267	123	123
EMI Group	50	54	547	1,787	1,787
Egg	80	81	810	1,267	380
Electrocomponents	50	58	581	1,600	1,600
Emap	50	54	547	1,908	1,908
Emblaze	90	97	974	157	78
Enodis	20	26	267	353	353
Eurotunnel/ Eurotunnel SA	50	59	596	298	298
Exel	50	59	596	2,156	2,156
Expro International Group	0	7	75	171	171
FKI	20	26	267	663	663
Findel	50	52	528	323	323
First Technology	20	25	253	217	217
FirstGroup	50	59	596	1,117	1,117
Forth Ports	50	59	597	546	546
Freeport	80	86	862	132	132
Friends Provident	80	84	840	2,442	2,442
Future Network	50	54	547	209	209
GUS	50	52	527	8,501	8,501
GWR Group	50	54	542	324	243

(continued)

Table A1.14 *(continued)*

Name of company	Economic group	Sector	Subsector	Market capitalization £ million before investibility weighting	Market capitalization £ million after investibility weighting
		(See Table A1.13 Classification system)			
Games Workshop Group	30	34	347	212	212
GlaxoSmithKline	40	48	486	68,195	68,195
Gleeson (MJ) Group	10	13	137	112	112
Go-Ahead Group	50	59	596	611	611
Great Portland Estates	80	86	862	519	519
Greggs	60	63	630	398	398
HBOS	80	81	810	27,833	27,833
HHG plc	80	87	871	1,078	1,078
HSBC Hldgs	80	81	810	90,460	90,460
Halma	20	26	267	576	576
Hammerson	80	86	862	1,908	1,908
Helical Bar	80	86	862	246	246
Helphire Group	80	87	879	237	237
Heywood Williams Group	10	13	132	72	72
Hilton Group	50	53	536	4,204	4,204
Hiscox	80	83	834	462	462
Hitachi Capital (UK)	80	87	873	84	34
Holidaybreak	50	53	538	247	247
House of Fraser	50	52	527	276	276
Huntleigh Technology	40	44	446	191	143
IMI	20	26	267	1,311	1,311
ISIS Asset Management	80	87	871	268	80
ITV	50	54	542	4,496	4,496
Imperial Chemical Industries	10	11	118	2,636	2,636
Incepta Group	50	54	545	164	164
Inchcape	30	31	318	1,306	1,306
Intec Telecom Systems	90	97	977	133	40
InterContinental Hotels Group	50	53	536	3,965	3,965

(continued)

Table A1.14 (*continued*)

Name of company	Economic group	Sector	Subsector	Market capitalization £ million before investibility weighting	after investibility weighting
		(See Table A1.13 Classification system)			
International Power	70	72	720	1,581	1,581
Invensys	20	25	253	938	938
iSOFT Group	90	97	977	896	672
Itnet	90	97	972	211	211
iTouch	50	54	547	103	31
JJB Sports	50	52	528	615	461
Jardine Lloyd Thompson Group	80	83	833	951	713
Jarvis	50	58	581	128	128
Johnson Matthey	10	11	118	1,920	1,920
Johnson Service Group	50	58	581	226	226
Johnston Press	50	54	547	1,598	1,199
Kelda Group	70	77	778	1,877	1,877
Kesa Electricals	50	52	526	1,611	1,611
Kidde	20	26	267	1,002	1,002
Kingfisher	50	52	527	6,852	6,852
Kingston Comms	60	67	673	253	190
Laing (John)	50	58	581	383	383
Land Securities Group	80	86	862	5,488	5,488
Lavendon Group	50	58	581	47	47
Legal & General Group	80	84	840	5,965	5,965
Lloyds TSB Group	80	81	810	24,566	24,566
LogicaCMG	90	97	972	1,386	1,386
London Merchant Securities	80	86	862	440	440
London Merchant Securities (Dfd)	80	86	862	150	112
London Scottish Bank	80	87	879	176	176
London Stock Exchange	80	87	879	1,102	1,102
Lonmin	0	4	48	1,365	1,365
Luminar	50	53	539	332	332
MFI Furniture Group	50	52	526	979	979
MITIE Group	50	58	581	393	393

(continued)

Table A1.14 *(continued)*

Name of company	Economic group	Sector	Subsector	Market capitalization £ million before investibility weighting	Market capitalization £ million after investibility weighting
		(See Table A1.13 Classification system)			
Maiden Group	50	54	545	101	50
Man Group	80	87	879	5,053	5,053
Manchester United	50	53	538	644	644
Marks & Spencer Group	50	52	527	8,105	8,105
Marylebone Warwick Balfour Group	80	86	862	57	29
Matalan	50	52	528	817	409
McAlpine (Alfred)	10	13	137	293	293
Menzies (John)	50	58	581	243	182
Mersey Docks & Harbour Co	50	59	597	540	540
Michael Page International	50	58	583	647	647
Millennium & Copthorne Hotels	50	53	536	920	460
Minerva	80	86	862	404	404
Misys	90	97	977	1,204	1,204
Mitchells & Butlers	50	53	539	1,360	1,360
mmO2	60	67	678	8,345	8,345
Morgan Sindall	10	13	137	179	134
Morse	90	97	972	159	120
Mothercare	50	52	527	264	264
NXT	20	25	253	92	92
National Express Group	50	59	596	981	981
National Grid Transco	70	77	775	13,247	13,247
Nestor Healthcare Group	40	44	449	113	113
Next	50	52	528	3,944	3,944
Northern Rock	80	81	810	3,159	3,159
Northgate Information Solutions	90	97	972	318	318

(continued)

Table A1.14 *(continued)*

Name of company	Economic group	Sector	Subsector	Market capitalization £ million before investibility weighting	Market capitalization £ million after investibility weighting
		(See Table A1.13 Classification system)			
Old Mutual	80	84	840	3,775	3,775
Oxford Instruments	20	25	253	109	109
PSD Group	50	58	583	58	58
Pace Micro Technology	30	34	343	120	120
Paragon Group of Companies	80	87	873	426	426
Peacock Group	50	52	528	273	273
Pearson	50	54	547	5,317	5,317
Peninsular & Oriental Steam Nav Co	50	59	597	1,623	1,623
Pennon Group	70	77	778	919	919
Photo-Me International	50	54	546	335	251
Phytopharm	40	48	482	62	62
Porvair	10	11	116	40	40
Premier Farnell	50	58	581	896	896
Premier Oil	0	7	73	425	425
Provident Financial	80	87	873	1,609	1,609
Prudential	80	84	840	9,178	9,178
Quintain Estates and Development	80	86	862	518	518
RAC	50	58	581	810	810
RM	90	97	977	119	119
RMC Group	10	13	132	1,532	1,532
RPC Group	50	58	581	167	167
RPS Group	50	58	581	236	236
Reckitt Benckiser	40	47	475	10,625	10,625
Reed Elsevier	50	54	547	6,692	6,692
Regent Inns	50	53	539	49	49
Reliance Security Group	50	58	588	126	38
Renishaw	20	25	253	338	169
Restaurant Group	50	53	539	175	175
Reuters Group	50	54	547	5,362	5,362
Rexam	50	58	581	2,434	2,434

(continued)

Table A1.14 (continued)

Name of company	Economic group	Sector	Subsector	Market capitalization £ million before investibility weighting	after investibility weighting
		(See Table A1.13 Classification system)			
Rotork	20	26	264	339	339
Royal & Sun Alliance Insurance Group	80	83	834	2,263	2,263
Royal Bank Of Scotland Group	80	81	810	52,141	52,141
Royalblue Group	90	97	977	174	174
SABMiller	40	41	415	6,736	6,736
SHL Group	50	58	583	67	67
SMG	50	54	542	349	349
SSL International	40	44	446	583	583
SVB Holdings	80	83	834	150	150
Sage Group	90	97	977	2,326	2,326
Sainsbury (J)	60	63	630	5,359	4,019
Savills	80	86	864	275	275
Schroders	80	87	871	1,380	1,035
Schroders N/V	80	87	871	392	392
Scottish & Newcastle	40	41	415	3,839	3,839
Scottish & Southern Energy	70	72	720	5,919	5,919
Scottish Power	70	72	720	7,263	7,263
Scottish Radio Hldgs	50	54	542	306	230
Senior	20	26	267	120	120
Severn Trent	70	77	778	2,823	2,823
Shaftesbury	80	86	862	342	342
Shanks Group	50	58	584	277	277
Shell Transport & Trading Co	0	7	78	38,933	38,933
Shire Pharmaceuticals Group	40	48	486	2,382	2,382
Signet Group	50	52	526	1,963	1,963
Slough Estates	80	86	862	1,788	1,788
Smith & Nephew	40	44	446	5,375	5,375
Smith (WH) Group	50	52	528	865	865
Spectris	20	25	253	583	583

(continued)

Table A1.14 *(continued)*

Name of company	Economic group	Sector	Subsector	Market capitalization £ million before investibility weighting	Market capitalization £ million after investibility weighting
		(See Table A1.13 Classification system)			
Speedy Hire	50	58	581	177	177
Sportech	50	53	532	73	36
St James's Place Capital	80	84	840	733	293
Staffware	90	97	977	117	87
Stagecoach Group	50	59	596	1,111	1,111
Standard Chartered	80	81	810	10,603	10,603
Stanley Leisure	50	53	532	603	603
Synstar	90	97	972	112	112
THUS Group	60	67	673	351	351
Tate & Lyle	40	43	435	1,537	1,537
Taylor Nelson Sofres	50	54	547	923	923
Telewest Communications	60	67	673	23	17
Tesco	60	63	630	19,866	19,866
Tomkins	20	26	267	2,010	2,010
Topps Tiles	50	52	526	393	294
Town Centre Securities	80	86	862	154	116
Travis Perkins	10	13	131	1,533	1,533
Tribal Group	50	58	581	158	119
Trifast	50	58	581	46	46
Trinity Mirror	50	54	547	1,943	1,943
Ulster Television	50	54	542	220	165
Unilever	40	43	435	15,268	15,268
Unite Group	80	86	862	204	204
United Business Media	50	54	547	1,584	1,584
United Utilities	70	77	778	3,063	3,063
United Utilities A Shs	70	77	778	1,086	1,086
Vanco	60	67	673	135	41
Vardy (Reg)	30	31	318	316	237
Vernalis	40	48	482	73	73
Viridian Group	70	72	720	785	785
Vitec Group	20	26	267	141	141
Vodafone Group	60	67	678	87,075	87,075

(continued)

Table A1.14 *(continued)*

Name of company	Economic group	Sector	Subsector	Market capitalization £ million before investibility weighting	after investibility weighting
		(See Table A1.13 Classification system)			
WPP Group	50	54	545	6,641	6,641
WSP Group	50	58	581	124	124
Wagon	30	31	313	96	96
Warner Estate Hldgs	80	86	862	260	195
Wellington Underwriting	80	83	834	435	435
Wembley	50	53	538	295	295
Wetherspoon (JD)	50	53	539	577	577
Whatman	40	44	446	272	272
Whitbread	50	53	539	2,450	2,450
Wolverhampton & Dudley	50	53	539	594	594
Woolworths Group	50	52	527	635	635
Workspace Group	80	86	862	271	271
Wyevale Garden Centres	50	52	526	206	206
Xansa	90	97	972	289	289
Yule Catto & Co	10	11	118	353	265

Appendix 2

Understanding intangible value: rating and comparing social responsibility performances

When investors need to quantify and compare the financial value of one business with another, there are a number of well-established criteria that can be applied to a similarly well-established set of performance categories. These are generally understood measurements based on generally understood principles, enabling those who have to (or who wish to) analyse and understand businesses to do so using a universally accepted set of tools to create a like-for-like assessment of each business. This makes it possible to compare different businesses with each other in respect of their traditional financial value and performance. However, there are not, as yet, comparable criteria, tools and categories to analyse and understand the intangible value of businesses for assessment and comparison purposes. Nonetheless, to satisfy the demand for such information from investors and investment fund managers, a number of organizations are now endeavouring to standardize and quantify intangible values so that they can be incorporated in judgements and investment decisions about businesses in the same way that financial values always have been incorporated.

Of course, there is a certain commercial value in this knowledge and so no provider of information on intangible values would wish to see all of their commercial value published within the price of even this book. Nevertheless, we have secured examples of intangible value assessment reports produced by Innovest Strategic Value Advisors in respect of five UK companies. These illustrate the type of report that investors are looking for when considering the intangible values (corporate citizenship, integrity, sustainability and forward thinking) of businesses in which they may invest their funds.

By better understanding what it is that investors are looking for, readers should be more prepared when approaching their own objective-setting efforts for the CSR element in their business plan. As has been said many times in this book, CSR is not simply about ticking the boxes to achieve minimum compliance with whatever regulations apply but rather it is about building a CSR plan as strong, well supported, seriously regarded and assiduously driven by the business as are all other plans, ie financial, marketing, sales, etc. Reading these reports will show how the intangible aspects of business performance are viewed and judged by those to whom investors turn for reliable information and assessment of a potential investment.

Innovest
STRATEGIC VALUE ADVISORS

www.innovestgroup.com
New York: +1 212 421-2000
London: +44 (0) 20 7073 0470
Toronto: +1 905 707-0876
Paris: +33 (0)1 44 54 04 89

Intangible Value Assessment

Jan–04

AstraZeneca Plc

Country:	Great Britain
Ticker Symbol:	AZN.L
Industrial Sector:	Pharmaceuticals
Combined IVA Rating:	A (A IVA- AA EV)
Rank:	IVA:6 of 31; EV:5 of 45
Sub-Factors:	
Strategic Governance:	7
Human Capital:	8.3
Environment:	6.4
Stakeholder Capital:	7

Analyst: Aled Jones / Cecile Lamotte
(+44) 20 7073 0470
ajones@innovestgroup.com
clamotte@innovestgroup.com

Intangible value comprises a growing percentage of companies' market capitalization. Innovest's IVA™ ratings analyze relative corporate performance on intangible value drivers related to the strength and sustainability of companies' competitive advantage. By assessing differentials typically not identified by traditional securities analysis, IVA™ ratings uncover hidden risks and value potential for investors. Ratings range from AAA (best) to CCC (worst). Scores on sub-factors range from 10 (best) to 0 (worst).

PERFORMANCE / ALPHA INTENSITY MATRIX

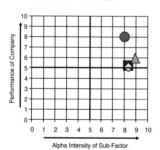

Alpha Intensity of Sub-Factor

■ Strategic Governance ▲ Human Capital
● Environment ◇ Stakeholder Capital

This matrix situates the four key intangible value drivers along 2 dimensions: 1. How well or poorly the company performs on each of the 4 key factors. 2. How much impact that particular factor has on financial performance in that industry sector; its "alpha intensity".

COMPANY OVERVIEW

Core Business: Astrazeneca is engaged in the research and development of prescription medicines for serious health conditions. It focuses on areas of healthcare such as gastrointestinal, cardiovascular, oncology, respiratory and inflammation, central nervous system, pain control and infection.

Geographic Focus: The company's principal manufacturing facilities are in the UK, Sweden, US, Australia, Brazil, China, France, Germany, Italy, Japan and Puerto Rico. Revenue Breakdown: 2002 revenues of US$17,840m came entirely from healthcare sales.

Operations: AZN has manufacturing sites in 20 countries and sells products in 100 countries.

Workforce: 58,000 employees worldwide with some 10,000 R&D personnel.

INDUSTRY DRIVING FORCES

Patent Expiry and Thin Pipelines: Two parallel issues threatening the entire pharmaceutical industry are that of expiring patents on blockbusting drugs and a lack of new drugs coming to market. As patents are lost, generic competition opens up, normally with major implications for sales of branded drugs. Further deepening this problem is that company product pipelines are worryingly thin.

Industry Consolidation: Increasing consolidation within the industry is a response to rising cost pressures (especially in R&D) and the combination of generic competition and the difficulties of raising drug prices to maintain margins. Investors are now wary as no major new products have been announced, and expiring patents may gradually erode the initial benefits of consolidation. However, partnerships with small biotech research firms may provide input to the pipeline process, benefiting from the capital of the large companies and from the innovative potential of smaller ones.

AREAS OF POTENTIAL RISK

Governance: Some concerns voiced by shareholders in 2002 over the election of the current chairman, who has in the past attracted criticism for his own approach to governance standards, otherwise the company has a good record.

Product Safety: Share price dropped when safety concerns rose regarding AstraZeneca's new cholesterol treatment currently in advanced trials. Another new cancer treatment has also been struggling to gain US FDA approval after fears were raised in Japan over possible links between a number of deaths and patients using the drug.

AREAS OF COMPETITIVE ADVANTAGE

AstraZeneca's new sustainability strategy shows promise. Strong sustainable governance systems in place, for management of both environmental and social responsibility issues.

Focus on "wellbeing" creates financial benefits. AstraZeneca claims that its programs to reduce employee stress and improve general wellbeing have significant productivity benefits. The group estimates for every $1 invested. it gains $4 in improved productivity and decreased sick leave.

In parallel with this policy, AstraZeneca is also amongst industry leaders in terms of Health & Safety management.

STRATEGIC PROFIT OPPORTUNITIES

AstraZeneca has begun efforts to tackle infectious diseases, despite historically not focusing on such conditions. The company is also part of a new UK scheme using biotechnology to identify toxins in industrial waste such as textiles and paper.

Over the last two years the industry has begun to realize that the issue of 'access to medicines' is a major reputational issue, and many companies are now beginning to offer their expertise and assistance e.g. in providing discounted HIV/AIDS treatments to countries with infection rates now at epidemic status.

The R&D conducted into diseases such as TB in a new Indian facility is one example of how the company is addressing such concerns.

RATING OUTLOOK: POSITIVE

Astrazeneca has been at the forefront of corporate sustainability initiatives for some time, and continues to improve its strategy and implementation of CSR policies and initiatives.

Innovest
STRATEGIC VALUE ADVISORS

Intangible Value Assessment

STRATEGIC GOVERNANCE: 7
Trend: Steady

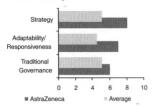

- ▪ AstraZeneca ▪ Average

Strategy: AstraZeneca is amongst the leaders in its industry on sustainability performance, and is in a strong position to remain at this level. Comprehensive CSR policies and principles have been drawn up, complementing those for HSE (health, safety and environment). The result is that AstraZeneca now has a clear global strategy on environment, health, safety, labor issues, bioethics, and purchasing. The only omission appears to be a company position on how it deals with potential reputational issues in emerging markets where, for example, labor standards are less stringent. AstraZeneca is looking at the possibility of assigning full executive responsibility for CSR.

Adaptibility/Responsiveness: Astra-Zeneca's efforts to promote CSR and HSE throughout the company appear to be extensive. The new CSR strategy and policies, drawn up in 2001 (and using 2000 as a baseline) were communicated to employees during 2002 using a variety of online and published media. Disclosure to shareholders and external stakeholders is excellent. AstraZeneca produces a summary report of CSR and HSE activities, and more detailed information can be accessed on the company website. AstraZeneca follows GRI guidelines for disclosure.
A cross-functional CSR committee is in charge with implementing and reviewing CSR policies and procedures while HSE issues are addressed by separate teams. Management of both CSR and HSE is also the responsibility of site and facility managers.

Traditional Governance Factors: The company has a 13-member board, eight of whom are non-executive directors, including the chairman. Three of the non-executive directors are women. The board is supported by nominations, remuneration and audit committees, all of which are chaired by non-executive directors. The board adheres to the principles of good governance outlined in Section 1 of the UK Combined Code. Current non-executive chairman, Percy Barnevik did attract some criticism while at ABB, in relation to a pension payment that was regarded as excessive and controversial during the mid-1990s.

HUMAN CAPITAL: 8.3
Trend: Steady

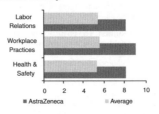

- ▪ AstraZeneca ▪ Average

Labor Relations: Due in part to AstraZeneca's efforts to promote workforce diversity, employee satisfaction and wellbeing, labor relations at AstraZeneca appear to be good. AstraZeneca has received criticism from previous employees in its Australian division over the handling of dismissals, but the company has also received an award from the Australian Human Resources Institute.

High-Performance Workplace Practices:
AstraZeneca considers itself to be an employer of choice, and the evidence seems to support this. Employees are considered a key stakeholder group and AstraZeneca devotes time and resources to ensuring that personal development, access to management, employee diversity and 'wellbeing' are high on the policy agenda.
Convinced that focusing on all of these factors will ultimately improve its bottom line performance, the company has reaped satisfying results so far, estimating that efforts to reduce stress have made a significant contribution to productivity - every $1 invested generates $4 in reduced sick leave and increased productivity.

Health & Safety: AstraZeneca is amongst industry leaders in terms of H&S management. New management systems were set up in 2001 and now include the development of indicators, regular reporting (2002 onwards) and auditing of company facilities to ensure ongoing compliance. Accident and illness rates have actually risen, due to more in-depth and accurate reporting, but the key test will be the accident rate trend over the next few years. The fact that AstraZeneca appears keen to improve and demonstrate genuine improvements to its stakeholders is encouraging.

ENVIRONMENTAL PERFORMANCE: 6.4
Trend: Up

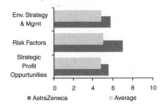

- ▪ AstraZeneca ▪ Average

Environmental Strategy & Management: In 2002, environmental management was included into the overall mission and strategy of the company and in the CSR document. The EMS is guided by the ISO 14001 standard. A sector laggard with only 4 plants ISO14001 certified to date. No system in place yet for environmental cost accounting. As regards environmental reporting, HSE is not specified in detail. Basic indicators available but only from 2000. Progress on updating KPIs is expected thanks to new indicators and a new database to capture worldwide information. Supply chain purchasing principles developed to encourage and support the suppliers in embracing CSR standards.

Risk Factors: AZN has below average environmental burden risks associated with global warming, ozone depletion, and smog forming emissions. Best in class in CO_2 reduction, the issue remains a number one priority for the group. Although AZN is currently replacing CFCs in propellants with HFCs, HFCs are greenhouse gases, so they are not the most desirable alternative. No direct biotechnology risks. Regarding the endocrine disrupting chemicals issue, AZN is likely to encounter risks from its products for the treatment of cancer that work by modulating the endocrine system. To track down toxins, the company is working on biosensors capable of detecting harmful chemicals in the environment.

Eco-efficiency Initiatives: AZN demonstrates above average performance in eco-efficiency. Best in class in energy efficiency, top tier in material use efficiency and water efficiency. But as noted the group has no environmental cost accounting in place to track the economic benefits achieved. However, AZN records on-going improvement thereby reducing production costs significantly. By developing a new process, AZN succeeded in reducing the use of solvent for the manufacturing of its key product Zeloken ZOC by 1,000 tons per year, thus cutting costs and reducing photochemical ozone creation potential.

STAKEHOLDER CAPITAL: 7

Innovest
STRATEGIC VALUE ADVISORS

Intangible Value Assessment

Trend: Steady

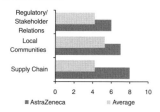

- AstraZeneca
- Average

Stakeholder relations:

Regulator: Significant regulatory or compliance issues facing AstraZeneca include on-going investigations in the USA over alleged marketing misconduct and price-fixing. AstraZeneca is facing significant potential liabilities from investigations into improper marketing of Zoladex (a prostate cancer treatment). It is alleged that the company conspired to receive payments for drug samples that were provided free to doctors. Settlements could be significant for these charges (a company paid US$875m in a similar case).

Shareholders: AstraZeneca states that it holds "frequent discussions" with shareholders on financial matters, but does not state whether it also engages with institutional shareholders on non-financial issues. Customers: it is not clear from CSR policy statements how customer concerns are addressed.

Local Communities: Overall, the company's efforts are impressive and show a clear commitment to 'corporate citizenship'. At a local level, AstraZeneca has site-based community liaison groups acting as a communication channel between the company and the communities in which it operates. On a national /international level AstraZeneca has given its commitment to the 'Global Health Initiative', a voluntary initiative with the World Economic Forum. AstraZeneca also has programs in developed economies to promote access to healthcare e.g. the 'Patient Assistance' program in the US or the creation of a fund supporting school-based/educational science projects in the UK. In addition to the above programs, AstraZeneca provides donations in the form of monetary gifts and by encouraging employees to volunteer their time to local schemes.

Supply Chain: AZN has a set of purchasing principles. The guidelines provide screening criteria on social and environmental standards.

EMERGING MARKETS: Strategy: has no apparent strategy for assessing and reacting to non-financial risks in overseas markets where it has a major presence, such as China and Brazil. Potential risks may include lack of adequate worker protection or union rights, less stringent legislation regarding health, safety and environmental standards and human rights abuses. Whilst a company like AstraZeneca may have little exposure to some of the more serious of these risks, it would benefit from greater transparency and disclosure with regards its overseas operations.

Human Rights: The pharmaceutical industry is not typically associated with human rights abuses. For the most part labor is skilled, and production facilities are often located in Europe or N America. AstraZeneca does have facilities in countries that have a history of human rights abuses (e.g. China), but no examples of poor practice were found involving AstraZeneca.

Oppressive Regimes: As mentioned above, AstraZeneca does have operations in countries with a history of human rights abuses e.g. China, Brazil, and where there may be a lack of personal freedom.

SRI NEGATIVE SCREENING INFORMATION

The following information is provided for investors who for various ethical or social reasons may wish to avoid investments in companies involved in the following business areas. Innovest's IVA product uses a positive screening approach to identify superior management. Beyond assessing potential market risks, involvement in the following businesses does not impact our ratings.

SCREEN

Alcohol - N/A
Animal Testing - AstraZeneca uses animals during its R&D activities. In its `Bioethics' policy, the company sets out the standards by which it operates in these instances e.g. animals are to be treated humanely, alternatives will be sought whenever possible and when animals must be used, experiments are designed so as to minimize the suffering of the animals in use.
Contraception - N/A
Gambling - N/A
Genetically Modified Organisms - AstraZenaca does not use biotechnology but it does use GMOs during the R&D process, including transgenetic animals, which the company claims reduces the need for animal testing in later stages.
Nuclear Power - N/A
Pornography - N/A
Tobacco - N/A
Weapons Production – N/A

COMPETITIVE SET

Pharmaceuticals

ABBOTT LABORATORIES
ALLERGAN
ALTANA AG
ASTRAZENECA PLC
AVENTIS
BIOVAIL CORP.
BRISTOL MYERS SQUIBB
CHUGAI PHARMACEUTICAL COMPANY LTD.
DAIICHI PHARMACEUTICAL
EGIS RT
EISAI CO
ELAN CORP.
ELI LILLY & CO
FOREST LABORATORIES
FUJISAWA PHARMACEUTICAL COMPANY LTD.
GALEN HOLDINGS
GLAXOSMITHKLINE
H. LUNDBECK
JOHNSON & JOHNSON
KAKEN PHARMACEUTICAL COMPANY LTD.
KING PHARMACEUTICALS INC.
KYOWA HAKKO KOGYO COMPANY LTD.
MERCK & CO INC.
MERCK KGAA
NOVARTIS
NOVO NORDISK
ORION CORP.
PFIZER INC.
PHARMACIA CORP.
RICHTER GEDEON RT
ROCHE HOLDING AG
SANKYO COMPANY LTD.
SANOFI-SYNTHELABO
SCHERING AG
SCHERING-PLOUGH CORP.
SHIONOGI & CO
SHIRE PHARMACEUTICALS GROUP PLC
SKYEPHARMA PLC
STADA ARZNEIMITTEL AG
TAISHO PHARMACEUTICAL
TAKEDA
UCB
WATSON PHARMACEUTICALS INC.
WYETH LABORATORIES
YAMANOUCHI

Figure A2.1 Intangible value assessment: AstraZeneca

Innovest
STRATEGIC VALUE ADVISORS

www.innovestgroup.com
New York: +1 212 421-2000
London: +44 (0) 20 7073 0470
Toronto: +1 905 707-0876
Paris: +33 (0)1 44 54 04 89

Intangible Value Assessment

Jan–04

Aviva

Country:	Great Britain
Ticker Symbol:	CGNU.L
Industrial Sector:	Insurance – UK & Ireland
Combined IVA Rating:	**AAA**
Rank:	**1 of 11**
Sub-Factors:	
Strategic Governance:	9
Human Capital:	9
Environment:	8
Stakeholder Capital:	7.6

Analyst: Beth Ambrose
(+33) 1 44 54 04 89
bambrose@innovestgroup.com

Intangible value comprises a growing percentage of companies' market capitalization. Innovest's IVA™ ratings analyze relative corporate performance on intangible value drivers related to the strength and sustainability of companies' competitive advantage. By assessing differentials typically not identified by traditional securities analysis, IVA™ ratings uncover hidden risks and value potential for investors. Ratings range from AAA (best) to CCC (worst). Scores on sub-factors range from 10 (best) to 0 (worst).

PERFORMANCE / ALPHA INTENSITY MATRIX

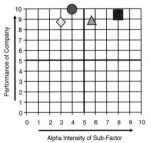

Alpha Intensity of Sub-Factor

■ Strategic Governance ▲ Human Capital
● Environment ◇ Stakeholder Capital

This matrix situates the four key intangible value drivers along 2 dimensions: 1. How well or poorly the company performs on each of the 4 key factors. 2. How much impact that particular factor has on financial performance in that industry sector; its "alpha intensity".

Innovest Strategic Value Advisors, Inc.

COMPANY OVERVIEW

Core Business: Aviva plc (formerly CGNU plc) is the holding company of a group that provides life insurance, general insurance and long-term savings products, as well as managing investments.

Geographic Focus: The company is the seventh largest insurer worldwide, (ranked first in the UK) and is ranked as the top life and pensions provider in Europe. Aviva has 25m customers worldwide.

Revenue Breakdown: In 2002, operating profit before tax was £1.798m, of which general insurance accounted for £959m. Continental European businesses accounted for 43% of worldwide life and pensions sales and 49% of life achieved operating profit. Aviva has £208bn in assets under management.

Operations: the group includes Norwich Union and Morley Fund Management in the UK, Hibernian in Ireland, the Delta Lloyd group in the Netherlands, Commercial Union in Poland, Aviva France, Aviva Europe, Aviva International, Aviva Asia, Aviva USA and CGU Canada among others.

Workforce: 59,000 staff employed worldwide.

INDUSTRY DRIVING FORCES

Consolidation of services: The boundaries between banking and insurance services are increasingly blurred. This can lead to redundancies when mergers are processed.

Market Conditions: Poor economic conditions, as well as the estimated losses of $35-55bn resulting from the 2001 terrorist attacks, have adversely affected the insurance industry. Insurers have therefore reassessed their rates, resulting in higher premiums and a reduction in capacity. They have also reduced their risks with more stringent underwritings and are striving to cut costs. Customer services are now addressed with more care than before to prevent loss of custom.

New Insurance risks: new risks that have emerged, such as terrorist threats, asbestos liabilities, cyber and financial crime and the increase in natural catastrophes have increased purchase costs of insurance.

AREAS OF POTENTIAL RISK

Consolidation: Sustainability issues related to consolidation include significant workforce reductions, community disruptions due to office closures and declining customer service levels. Failure to manage these issues proactively can lead to a tarnished image and reduced sales.

New regulations: the financial problems at Equitable Life and the failure of Independent Insurance have led to a crisis of confidence that is being addressed by the strengthening of insurance regulations.

Climate Change: the increased likelihood of natural catastrophes in areas with a high proportion of insured property makes the potential of losses so high (e.g. Hurricane Andrew) that insurers are viewed as having an important role to play in helping society to cope with such events.

AREAS OF COMPETITIVE ADVANTAGE

Aviva sets the standard for best practice in nearly every aspect of Corporate Social Responsibility (CSR) in the insurance industry. Particularly noteworthy is the expansion of the CSR program throughout the corporation and the company's involvement with social issues in emerging markets. As stakeholders become more concerned about social performance and as sustainability issues have growing financial impact on firms, Aviva will be able to improve its market positioning as a result of its activities.

Aviva is one of three companies in the sector that has made significant efforts to broaden the availability of insurance to the low the income population through development of schemes such as "Insurance with Rent". Efforts in this area not only improve the social performance of the company but also allow the company to access an unsaturated market.

STRATEGIC PROFIT OPPORTUNITIES

Emerging markets represent a major growth opportunity for insurance companies. Along with this potential gain of market share there is the potential for social responsibility to transfer significant knowledge and skills to the local people and businesses, engage local government and industry regarding sustainable investments and practices in the area and encourage governments to provide compensation to those affected by large-scale catastrophes.

RATING OUTLOOK: POSITIVE

Aviva has been at the forefront of corporate sustainability initiatives for some time, and continues to improve its strategy and implementation of CSR policies.

Innovest
STRATEGIC VALUE ADVISORS

Intangible Value Assessment

STRATEGIC GOVERNANCE: 9
Trend: Steady

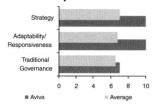

Strategy: Aviva has a comprehensive corporate social responsibility (CSR) strategy in place, with policies covering eight elements: environment, community, health and safety, workforce, human rights, suppliers, customers and standards of business conduct in place at the corporate level. These elements are addressed within a framework of corporate values. Almost all of the group businesses have embarked on CSR implementation, but are at different stages, partly due to the different national perceptions of CSR. Reporting of progress is consolidated at the corporate level.

A vital aspect of CSR for an insurance company pertains to its investment strategy. Aviva's asset management division, Morley Fund Management, implements a strong SRI strategy as an institutional investor. The company also encourages business partners and members of the wider community to reduce their own impacts.

Adaptibility/Responsiveness: The CSR policy was approved in January 2002, and began to be rolled out across the group in the following month.

The Aviva board reviews the CSR policy and program progress annually, with the CEO charged with overall responsibility for the CSR program. The director of CSR at the corporate level is responsible for environmental management, standards of business conduct, public reporting and communication with the CEO. At the business level, CSR responsibilities remain with the relevant manager.

CSR reports are submitted to the executive committee and for the purposes of external public reporting.

The CSR steering group meets quarterly to discuss implementation progress, to share best practices. The CSR review group carries out an annual review of policy, plans and progress which includes participation from NGO partner organizations. The CSR risk profile is audited annually by the CSR team and group risk and bi-annual external assurance is carried out.

CSR-related activities are regularly communicated to staff via the intranet as well as staff magazines.

Traditional Governance Factors: The board currently comprises seven non-executive directors including the chairman, and six executive directors. There is one female non-executive director. The nomination committee annually reviews directors' interests that may be potential conflicts of interest. The remuneration and audit committees comprise non-executive directors, in compliance with the UK combined code on corporate governance. Aviva has a policy prohibiting political donations.

HUMAN CAPITAL: 9
Trend: Steady

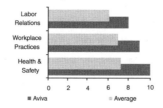

Labor Relations: Minimizing the impacts of structural changes includes redeployment, relocation and the involvement of those affected at the earliest possible stage. Outplacement programs are offered via third party suppliers. The acquisition of ICS Singapore resulted in redundancies. In an effort to deal responsibly with this issue, Aviva contributed to the Insurance Union's training fund to enhance re-training and redevelopment of redundant staff.

There are plans to move all call center staff to India, the process was discussed with Amicus - the financial services union - prior to the formal announcement.

High-Performance Workplace Practices: Employee surveys and workshops are an integral part of a two-way communication process.

The corporate workforce policies include the implementation of programs to improve employee motivation and encourage development, especially through comprehensive training.

Aviva is a member of Opportunity Now and the Employers' Forum on Disability. The group encourages and actively promotes diversity and equal opportunities with a dedicated program. As a result, the proportion of senior female staff has risen significantly.

Health & Safety: Health and safety is the responsibility of the head person of the unit concerned. The corporate health and safety policies are designed to ensure a healthy working environment for all staff and close stakeholders. The policy also covers the promotion of awareness of these issues. New employees receive information and training on health and safety matters and provide access to an occupational health service and confidential counseling and help to promote a healthy lifestyle by meeting costs of sporting activities.

ENVIRONMENTAL PERFORMANCE: 8
Trend: Up

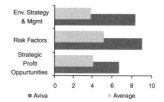

Strategy & Management The company is concerned about having good environmental performance. The four main objectives of the environmental program in place are the integration of environmental considerations into business decisions, implementation of eco-efficiency initiatives, employee training and the promotion of best practice amongst clients and the broader community. The director of environmental management reports to the company secretary who then reports to the board. Business units are responsible for the development of local programs, supervised by a CSR manager. The specialist managers have an environmental reward/incentive package. An extensive EMS is in place and an annual consolidated report is published with interim updates on the web-site.

Risk Factors: Attention is given to environmental considerations in underwriting, to reduce environmental risks associated with property insurance. Aviva has also established an environmental risk consulting unit for small to medium sized businesses. In addition, EMS minimizes the possibility of internal operational inefficiencies. All property acquisitions are subject to environmental assessments. All new property developments are audited using the BREEAM method.

Eco-efficiency Initiatives: All businesses have a range of eco-efficiency initiatives in place. A strategy for improving building management is underway in the UK. Some entities are switching to renewable energy while others are promoting energy conservation. Recycling programs are being phased in, including paper reduction initia-

Innovest
STRATEGIC VALUE ADVISORS

Intangible Value Assessment

tives. Car travel was significantly reduced in 2002, partly due to increased use of video conferencing. The company is improving and extending indicator measurement.

STAKEHOLDER CAPITAL: 7.6

Trend: Steady

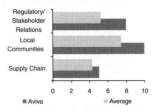

Regulators: The company chairs the FORGE group of insurers and banks which has produced two sets of guidance, one on environmental and another on CSR management and reporting published in 2002. It is also a signatory to the UNEP finance initiative and a member of the Institute of Business Ethics (IBE), established to encourage high standards of corporate behavior and the sharing of best practice. Other partners include BITC, an organization comprising 700 UK companies (77% of the FTSE 100), WWF-UK and the Amnesty International Business Group.

Local Communities: a five-year community sponsorship strategy and program has been implemented. The corporate community policy is designed to implement programs that will ensure positive interaction between Aviva businesses and local communities. Implementation and data collection occurs at the business unit level with specific charities chosen by each business. Employees are encouraged to support community activities. The company's activities can be classified under the headings of health and welfare, crime prevention and youth development

Supply Chain: Businesses across the group are increasingly requiring evidence of supplier CSR performance. Suppliers are required to state an environmental policy and are helped to gain environmental accreditation. The sourcing process now includes questions on further CSR elements as well as environmental issues.

EMERGING MARKETS: Strategy: Aviva has funded insurance seminars and study centers at finance colleges in Beijing, Guangzhou and Shanghai and set up an Insurance Accounting Masters program at the South Western University of Finance and Economics in Chengdu. Shareholder pres-

sure and positive SRI engagement from Morley and other stakeholders influenced Balfour Beatty's decision to pull out of the Ilisu dam project in Turkey, which had been linked to ethnic cleansing.

Human Rights: Aviva supports the Universal Declaration of Human Rights and is signatory to the Global Compact and has a corporate-wide policy covering the area. The responsibility for this is split between the director of purchasing, the director of HR and the director of CSR, as the company is able to exercise responsibility through purchasing as an employer as well as through investment policies. For example, three of the businesses are building human rights based questions into their sourcing.

Oppressive Regimes: Aviva's major investments in China are The China Index Fund and China Capital Partners. It has established representative offices in four major Chinese cities: Beijing, Shanghai, Guangzhou and Chengdu. China Capital Partners, which is a 50/50 joint venture between CGU and CDC, operates with the aim of investing $100m through equity stakes in the private sector in China; its investments are guided by strict socially responsible investment criteria and performance is monitored.

Morley Fund Management joined forces with a group of financial institutions to launch a formal statement outlining the concerns associated with the military dictatorship in Burma (Myanmar) and highlighting the risks to shareholders of investing in companies that have interests in the country.

SRI NEGATIVE SCREENING INFORMATION

The following information is provided for investors who for various ethical or social reasons may wish to avoid investments in companies involved in the following business areas. Innovest's IVA product uses a positive screening approach to identify superior management. Beyond assessing potential market risks, involvement in the following businesses does not impact our ratings.

SCREEN

Alcohol - The company is not directly involved in this line of business, but does make investments in companies that are.
Animal Testing - The company is not directly involved in this line of business, but does make investments in companies that are.
Contraception - The company is not directly involved in this line of business, but does make investments in companies that are.
Gambling - The company is not directly involved in this line of business, but does make investments in companies that are.

Genetically Modified Organisms - The company is not directly involved in this line of business, but does make investments in companies that are.
Nuclear Power - The company is not directly involved in this line of business, but does make investments in companies that are.
Pornography - The company is not directly involved in this line of business, but does make investments in companies that are.
Tobacco - The company is not directly involved in this line of business, but does make investments in companies that are.
Weapons Production – The company is not directly involved in this line of business, but does make investments in companies that are.

COMPETITIVE SET

UK Insurance

AMLIN PLC
AVIVA PLC
BRITANNIC PLC
BRIT INSURANCE HOLDING PLC
FRIENDS PROVIDENT PLC
HISCOX PLC
IRISH LIFE & PERMANENT PLC
LEGAL & GENERAL GROUP
PRUDENTIAL PLC
ROYAL & SUN ALLIANCE GROUP
ST JAMES'S PLACE CAPITAL

Figure A2.2 Intangible value assessment: Aviva

Innovest
STRATEGIC VALUE ADVISORS

www.innovestgroup.com
New York: +1 212 421-2000
London: +44 (0) 20 7073 0470
Toronto: +1 905 707-0876
Paris: +33 (0)1 44 54 04 89

Intangible Value Assessment

Jan–04

BAA PLC

Country:	Great Britain
Ticker Symbol:	BBA.L
Industrial Sector:	Surface Transport
Combined IVA Rating:	**AAA**
Rank:	▆▆▆▆
Sub-Factors:	▌
Strategic Governance:	8.3
Human Capital:	7.3
Environment:	7.4
Stakeholder Capital:	7.6

Analyst: Andy White
(+44) 20 7073 0470
awhite@innovestgroup.com

Intangible value comprises a growing percentage of companies' market capitalization. Innovest's IVA™ ratings analyze relative corporate performance on intangible value drivers related to the strength and sustainability of companies' competitive advantage. By assessing differentials typically not identified by traditional securities analysis, IVA™ ratings uncover hidden risks and value potential for investors. Ratings range from AAA (best) to CCC (worst). Scores on sub-factors range from 10 (best) to 0 (worst).

PERFORMANCE / ALPHA INTENSITY MATRIX

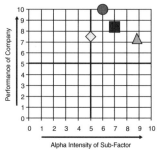

■ Strategic Governance ▲ Human Capital
● Environment ◇ Stakeholder Capital

This matrix situates the four key intangible value drivers along 2 dimensions: 1. How well or poorly the company performs on each of the 4 key factors. 2. How much impact that particular factor has on financial performance in that industry sector; its "alpha intensity".

Innovest Strategic Value Advisors, Inc.

COMPANY OVERVIEW

Core Business: BAA is the world's largest commercial operator of airports, running seven in the UK. It is also a property owner, operates rail links between central London and its airports, and is the world's leading travel retail specialist, with activities including shops/duty free, catering, financial services, car parks, car hire and advertising.

Revenue Breakdown: revenue in 2003 was £1.91 billion with £1.37 billion from UK airport operations. Of UK airport revenues in 2003, airport/traffic charges accounted for 49%; retail activities, 29%; property/operational facilities, 19% and other, 3%.

Workforce: BAA serves over 200 million passengers worldwide, 128 million in the UK alone and employs just under 12,000 staff.

INDUSTRY DRIVING FORCES

High level of impact: Airport operations can be very unpopular with local residents and campaign groups. They have major impacts in terms of noise, energy use, land use and pollution.

Security costs: Since the events of September 11th the threat of terrorist activity or a terrorist attack hangs over all companies connected to the transport industry. Employees, customers and the public face the possible risk of violence, injury or death from terrorist action.

Compensation: Remuneration of senior management needs to be sensitive to the significant health and safety issues in this sector.

AREAS OF POTENTIAL RISK

Social and environmental impacts: Gatwick and Heathrow are two of the busiest airports in the world and will expand considerably over the next 20 years. The challenge for BAA is to manage this expansion with the minimum of disruption to local communities and its strategy to date suggests that it is sensitive to and well prepared for the concerns of the large number of stakeholder groups.

AREAS OF COMPETITIVE ADVANTAGE

Sector leader for sustainability approach, BAA has a progressive and integrated sustainable development strategy.

The company is tuned in to government objectives in the areas of promoting growth, tourism, regeneration, integrated transport infrastructure and community welfare.

BAA has aligned its objectives with those of government and this is a sensible strategy given that it is government which ultimately decides on transport policy and aviation requirements in particular. The company is developing its own economic regeneration programs and these will help both local communities and the company in the long run.

The company reports on its performance in very transparent fashion and follows GRI guidelines and the AA1000 process model.

BAA has a long list of stakeholders and these different communities all take a keen interest in airport operations and can shape the way the business develops. BAA's stakeholders have concerns about the impacts of the business, particularly noise, local air quality, road congestion around the airports, waste and the effects aviation has on climate change.

BAA conducts regular stakeholder dialogue and aims to continually improve its understanding of its impacts and ability to address them.

BAA can be regarded as being at the leading edge of research and development in the field of transport security.

STRATEGIC PROFIT OPPORTUNITIES

BAA's business strategy is to develop core airport management competencies and its property and retail potential. It aims to grow the value of non-regulated business and develop its business globally. Capital investment is an important part of this strategy and BAA wants to become excellent in the use of information technology. By doing this the company considers it will continuously improve the profitability, quality and growth prospects of a prudently financed business adept at managing a diversity of tasks.

Given that air traffic is projected to grow considerably and given that aviation contributes over £10 billion each year to the UK economy, BAA is very well positioned to benefit from both its role as a leading airports operator and its strong awareness of the sustainable development agenda.

RATING OUTLOOK: <u>POSITIVE</u>

BAA has been at the forefront of corporate sustainability initiatives for some time, and continues to drive innovation in many areas. The company is now likely to manage the expansion of London's airports with a minimum of disruption to the local communities, one of its most challenging objectives in the years ahead.

Innovest
STRATEGIC VALUE ADVISORS

Intangible Value Assessment

STRATEGIC GOVERNANCE: 8.3
Trend: Steady

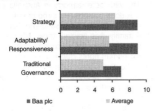

- ▮ Baa plc
- ▮ Average

Strategy: Currently the company has four integrated goals, informed by the government's sustainability agenda, which are social progress, environmental protection, prudent resource use and steady growth. It now has a sustainable development policy in place, rather than merely stating a commitment, a positive step that follows on from stakeholder feedback. BAA identifies its full range of impacts, sets out some clearly stated goals and understands the potential benefits, opportunities and changing operating environment. This approach puts BAA at the top of its peer group. BAA has secured approval to expand its airports at Gatwick, Heathrow and Stansted - an important achievement with demand for air travel set to double over the next 20 years and one that reflects the company's good understanding of sustainable development issues. The company has instigated a number of mitigation measures in the construction of terminal 5 at Heathrow.

Adaptibility/Responsiveness: There are two management frameworks which the company has developed to support the implementation of strategy. One is an organizational effectiveness model (OEM) and the other is a sustainable development framework (SDF). The OEM is an enabling tool, bringing the business components together within a sustainable development agenda, while the SDF is an operational tool. The BAA system is progressive, in that it is comprehensive and integrated, with the board ultimately responsible for its implementation. Board directors sit on the 'corporate responsibility board' and there is representation from 'local sustainability boards'. Further reflecting a best practice approach, BAA has developed a thorough stakeholder feedback mechanism and reports according to GRI guidelines. External verification takes place and there is input from Forum for the Future.

Traditional Governance Factors: The board considers that it has complied fully with the best practice provisions of the combined code. The roles of chairman and chief executive are separate. Auditors' fees for non-statutory work were higher than for basic audit fees. All non-executive directors are considered independent by the company

and the board has a strong independent element, with none of the non-executives having served for more than five years. Performance-related pay is targeted to account for 40-45% of directors' remuneration packages. In line with best practice, BAA provides graphics to show how it has performed against its comparator group. Performance criteria for the various bonus and option schemes are relatively narrow, do not include non-financial targets and are not as stretching as some would advocate, but they are fairly in line with those used by similar companies. As well as the audit, remuneration and nominations committees, there is an ethics committee, HSE and security committee and charitable donations committee. BAA has adopted a code of ethics for all employees.

HUMAN CAPITAL: 7.3
Trend: Steady

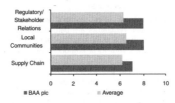

- ▮ BAA plc
- ▮ Average

Labor Relations: Industrial relations do not always run smoothly in the transport sector and during 2002 BAA's unions threatened strike action over the annual pay increase for the period. Other issues were also affecting staff such as the working environment, uniforms, recognition and communication and BAA worked also on these issues. Staff belong to two of BAA's recognized trade unions, TGWU and Amicus, two of the most powerful UK unions. At each airport there is a framework for consultation and discussion of collective issues. The aim is for matters to be resolved quickly and at local level. All airports have written grievance procedures and individual grievances are handled by the immediate supervisor. A specific policy is in place to address complaints of bullying and harassment.

High-Performance Workplace Practices: BAA's approach to employment issues is comprehensive and policies cover equal opportunities, fair rewards, flexible working and family needs, occupational health, remuneration, learning and development and redeployment. In line with good practice in the UK, BAA is a member of the Employers Forum on Disability and the Employers Forum on Age as well as Race for Opportunity.

BAA ran an Inland Revenue-approved Sharesave scheme that encouraged a degree of employee loyalty, other leading UK companies offer employee schemes which provide for the award of free or matching shares.

Staff turnover is low and this reflects positively on BAA's employment practices, particularly since many jobs will require manual or unskilled labor. While 34% of management staff are women, this proportion falls to just 18% at the senior management level. While statistics show that the company could do more to help ethnic minorities progress to senior management levels, its approach indicates that BAA is on the right track.

Health & Safety: Growth of the business, including the construction of terminal 5, presents BAA with constant challenges in the management of health and safety. BAA understands that good performance in health and safety is essential in this sector to achieve a profitable business and aims to integrate health and safety into every business process. Following implementation of a health and safety management system (SMS) in 1996 the company has benefited from consistent improvement in its health and safety performance (e.g. declining injury rates to staff). In 2002 BAA launched a five year targeted strategy. BAA has a very sound approach to managing risks in this area of its business. It assesses and manages risks through audited best management systems. Performance is reviewed by the health, safety, security and environment board and BAA works closely with regulators including the Department for Transport (DfT), Health and Safety Executive, local authorities, CAA and fire services. The BAA board has overall responsibility for managing business risks and its key role is to guide, endorse and support the implementation of health and safety, security and environmental (HSSE) policy and strategy for the BAA group. Board members also have individual responsibilities for HSSE within BAA and these responsibilities are clearly defined.

ENVIRONMENTAL PERFORMANCE: 7.4
Trend: Steady

Innovest
STRATEGIC VALUE ADVISORS

Intangible Value Assessment

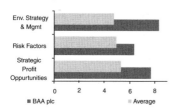

Env. Strategy & Mgmt / Risk Factors / Strategic Profit Oppurtunities

■ BAA plc   ■ Average

STAKEHOLDER CAPITAL: 7.6
Trend: Steady

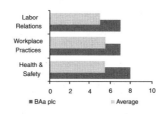

Labor Relations / Workplace Practices / Health & Safety

■ BAa plc   ■ Average

Environmental Strategy & Management: BAA demonstrates a commitment to operating responsibly and has progressive stance towards sustainable development. The environment is addressed through BAA's comprehensive sustainability policy and management framework. Particular emphasis is given to climate change, local air quality, noise, surface transport and waste with good mechanisms in place to monitor and improve performance. BAA endeavors to set the standard for best practice, supported by a number of policies, initiatives and partnerships. A board member has overall responsibility, supported by various senior level managers. Two sustainability-focused committees exist which include board representatives. Airports develop EMS in line with ISO14001, led by stakeholder consultation as to the priority they place on formal certification. BAA produces a number of sustainability and environmental reports at all major locations. Reporting follows GRI core indicators and is verified externally.

Risk Factors: Environmental issues are critical to achieving expansion plans. Materials and construction policy in place to minimize impact, including reusability focus in design and recycling materials. As regards waste, regulations may push up disposal costs if landfill remains a primary disposal route. In 2002, BAA was subject to investigation for three pollution incidents. It faces challenges in meeting UK National Air Quality objectives as there is risk of a potential aviation fuel tax. NOx objectives not met. BAA is aiming to reduce GHG emissions and to increase renewable energy use by 10% by 2010. Currently 20% of company's vehicle fleet runs on alternative fuels (target of 40% by 2005).

Eco-efficiency Initiatives: Aims to recycle/compost 80% of waste by 2020. Installation of environmentally preferable equipment, building efficiency, local renewable energy schemes is under way. BAA is working with Carbon Trust to implement climate change strategy and educate 1,300 employees to promote energy efficient culture. 215 ha managed for conservation, and works with organizations to achieve biodiversity aims. Member of London Sustainable Construction Initiative, and set up BAA Environment Construction Awards.

BAA has developed and maintains good two-way relationships based on dialogue and understanding. BAA is reviewing its stakeholder engagement processes against AA1000 (an accountability standard designed to establish a systematic process for stakeholder engagement which is integrated into daily operations).

Regulators: Good relations with government and regulators are particularly important for BAA and the company aims to share objectives with local authorities at an early stage to give them the chance to influence development plans before BAA tables them formally for planning permission. By understanding the strategic objectives of local authorities BAA is able to develop plans which support them.

Local Communities: The aim of its own charity, the BAA 21st Century Communities Trust, is to directly benefit the people living in the areas immediately around its airports. Additional funds are raised through noise fines and other airport sources such as foreign coin collection boxes and money-spinners.

Employees are encouraged to become involved in their local communities and this helps the company by fostering team building and closer links to its local neighborhoods. Employees can invest up to six days of paid time in community projects.

Supply Chain: The outlay on BAA's supply chain is £1 billion per annum. During the past year BAA has undertaken a strategic risk management approach to address sustainability across the supply chain. This has included dialogue with other interested parties and companies and a consultation exercise to profile the sustainability impacts and risks of categories of goods and services procured. This has generated a list of 30 areas and supply chain managers responsible for these areas are required to meet specific targets.

EMERGING MARKETS: Strategy: BAA's main airport operations are in the UK and the US, with other airports in Australia and Italy. It does operate two airports in Oman. This country is a small sultanate but the royal family has invited tribal leaders to serve in its cabinet. The country does have a basic human rights charter and labor laws. While human rights observers have highlighted some restrictions on political and personal freedoms, including limits to freedom of association, there are no reports of state sponsored torture, repression or severe human rights violations, practices which are alleged to take place in other Gulf states.

Although BAA does not have an explicit policy covering human rights, its other policies in areas such as health and safety and employment are reported to extend to the whole group.

Human Rights: see above

Oppressive Regimes: see above

SRI NEGATIVE SCREENING INFORMATION

The following information is provided for investors who for various ethical or social reasons may wish to avoid investments in companies involved in the following business areas. Innovest's IVA product uses a positive screening approach to identify superior management. Beyond assessing potential market risks, involvement in the following businesses does not impact our ratings.

SCREEN

Alcohol - see comments below
Animal Testing – N/A
Contraception - see comments below
Gambling – N/A
Genetically Modified Organisms – N/A
Nuclear Power – N/A
Pornography - see comments below
Tobacco - BAA has its own specialist travel retail company, World Duty Free, which is a direct retailer of alcohol and tobacco products. Revenues in 2002/03 were £352m, around 18% of total turnover. In addition, other retailers, bars, cafes and restaurants are located at BAA's airport and will also sell alcohol and tobacco products. Some newsagents may sell adult magazines. Gaming areas which have slot machines are also a feature of many airports.
Weapons Production – N/A

COMPETITIVE SET
Surface Transport

ABERTIS

Innovest
STRATEGIC VALUE ADVISORS

Intangible Value Assessment

COMPETITIVE SET

Surface Transport

ALGOMA CENTRAL RAILWAY
AP MOLLER-MAERSK
ARRIVA PLC
ASSOCIATED BRITISH PORTS HOLDINGS PLC
AUCKLAND INTERNATIONAL AIRPORT
AUTOROUTE DU SUD FRANCE
AUTOSTRADE
AVIS EUROPE PLC
BAA PLC
BBA GROUP PLC
BRISA-AUTO ESTRADAS SA
BURLINGTON NORTHERN SANTA FE CORP.
CANADIAN NATIONAL RAILWAY CO.
CANADIAN PACIFIC RAILWAY LTD.
CENTRAL JAPAN RAILWAY CO.
CMB
CNF INC.
COMFORTDELGRO
CP SHIP LTD.
CSX CORP.
D/S NORDEN AS
DSV
EAST JAPAN RAILWAY COMPANY
EUROTUNNEL PLC
FIRST GROUP PLC
FLUGHAFEN WIEN AG
FORTH PORTS PLC
FRAPORT AG
GATX COPR.
HOPEWELL HOLDINGS LIMITED
KAMIGUMI COMPANY LIMITED
KANSAS CITY SOUTHERN INDUSTRIES INC
KAWASAKI KISEN
KEIHIN ELECTRIC EXPRESS RAILWAY COMPANY
KEIO ELECTRIC RAILWAY CO LTD.
KINKI NIPPON RAILWAY COMPANY LTD.
KOBENHAVNS LUFTHAVNE
LAIDLAW INC
MACQUARIE INFRASTRUCTURE GROUP
MITSUBISHI LOGISTIC LTD.
MITSUI OSK LINES LIMITED
MTR CORP.
NATIONAL EXPRESS GROUP PLC
NEPTUNE ORIENT LINES LTD.
NIPPON EXPRESS COMPANY LTD.
NIPPON YUSEN KK
NORFOLK SOUTHERN CORP.
NORTHGATE PLC
PATRICK CORP
PENINSULAR AND ORIENTAL STEAM NAVIGATION
RYDER SYSTEM
SALVESEN (CHRISTIAN) PLC
SEINO TRANSPORTATION COMPANY LTD.
SEIMBCORP LOGISTICS LITD.
SMFT CORPORATION
STAGECOACH GROUP PLC
THE GO-AHEAD GP PLC
THE MERSEY DOCK & HARBOUR COMPANY
TOBU RAILWAY COMPANY LIMITED

COMPETITIVE SET

Surface Transport

TOKYU TRANSURBAN GROUP
TOLL HOLDINGS LTD.
TRANSURBAN GROUP
UNION PACIFIC CORP.
WEST JAPAN RAILWAY

Figure A2.3 Intangible value assessment: BAA

Innovest
STRATEGIC VALUE ADVISORS

www.innovestgroup.com
New York: +1 212 421-2000
London: +44 (0) 20 7073 0470
Toronto: +1 905 707-0876
Paris: +33 (0)1 44 54 04 89

Intangible Value Assessment

Jan–04

Scottish Power plc

Country:	Great Britain
Ticker Symbol:	SPW.L
Industrial Sector:	Electric Utilities – Intl
Combined IVA Rating:	BBB(IVA) AA(EV)
Rank:	7 of 30
Sub-Factors:	∎
Strategic Governance:	9.3
Human Capital:	6.6
Environment:	6.9
Stakeholder Capital:	8.3

Analyst: Trina Chattoraj
212 421 2000
tchattoraj@innovestgroup.com

Intangible value comprises a growing percentage of companies' market capitalization. Innovest's IVA™ ratings analyze relative corporate performance on intangible value drivers related to the strength and sustainability of companies' competitive advantage. By assessing differentials typically not identified by traditional securities analysis, IVA™ ratings uncover hidden risks and value potential for investors. Ratings range from AAA (best) to CCC (worst). Scores on sub-factors range from 10 (best) to 0 (worst).

PERFORMANCE / ALPHA INTENSITY MATRIX

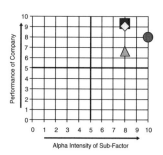

■ Strategic Governance ▲ Human Capital
● Environment ◇ Stakeholder Capital

This matrix situates the four key intangible value drivers along 2 dimensions: 1. How well or poorly the company performs on each of the 4 key factors. 2. How much impact that particular factor has on financial performance in that industry sector; its "alpha intensity".

COMPANY OVERVIEW

Core Business: The principle activities of Scottish Power group cover electricity generation, transmission and distribution, trading and supply both in the UK and US. In Great Britain, Scottish Power also supplies gas whilst the company's US activities extend to coal mining.

Geographic Focus: In the UK, there is a regulated Infrastructure Division (6% of revenue) and a competitive energy business, the UK Division (41% of revenue). In the US, Scottish Power has a regulated electricity business, PacifiCorp (47% of revenue), and a competitive energy business, PacifiCorp Power Marketing Inc, PPM (5% of revenue).

Revenue Breakdown: Revenue in 2002 was £5.3 billion.

Workforce: Scottish Power has about 14,000 employees.

INDUSTRY DRIVING FORCES

Deregulation: Deregulation is causing utilities in many regions to face competition, often for the first time. As a result, firms are working aggressively to improve customer service and retain customers in their 'home' territory. Many gas and electricity companies, for example, have launched expensive and aggressive sales and marketing campaigns.

Mergers and Acquisitions: Substantial M&A activity has occurred in the electrical utility sector in North America and Europe over the past several years. The quest for scale economies in administration, operations, marketing and customer service is expected to drive continued M&A activity among electric and natural gas companies. M&A activity has led to thousands of lay-offs in this industry, which can lead to lower employee morale, weaker labor relations, and disruptive economic consequences.

AREAS OF POTENTIAL RISK

Climate Change: Within the wider energy industry, natural gas holds an advantageous position as the cleanest and most efficient of the fossil fuels. The issue of climate change is stimulating demand for renewable sources of energy and natural gas as a means to reduce current emissions while also providing a "transition" fuel between the so-called carbon-economy and a lower or zero-emissions economy of the future. Concerns about climate change are projected to contribute to rapid growth of gas fired and renewable energy generation relative to fossil fuels.

Public Health Concerns: Depending on the fuel mix of power plants, the emissions into air and water can have a large negative impact on public health, including premature deaths, asthma attacks, acute bronchitis. Another recent report by the California Department of Health Services links electric magnetic fields (EMF's) and childhood leukemia, adult brain cancer, Lou Gehrig's disease and miscarriage. Public health concerns are placing growing pressure on owners of coal-fired power plants and transmission and distribution lines to lower public health risks.

AREAS OF COMPETITIVE ADVANTAGE

Scottish Power is a leader in its sector in reporting on sustainability, which is beneficial to attracting and strengthening relationships with stakeholders.

SP is the UK's second largest generator of wind power. The company is proactively committed to the community and positive social change.

STRATEGIC PROFIT OPPORTUNITIES

PacifiCorp has an aim of acquiring 1,400 MW of renewables by 2013 and PPM aims to have 2,000 MW by 2010.

RATING OUTLOOK: POSITIVE

Scottish Power is a leader in its sector for its sustainability management system. The company is strongly committed to customer service, environmental issues, and relationships with other key stakeholders.

Despite its robust system, Scottish Power's performance does lag in certain areas such as health and safety, labor relations and R&D. The company is therefore noted for its strong overall programs but a lack of progress on some performance indicators lower its overall rating.

Innovest

STRATEGIC VALUE ADVISORS

Intangible Value Assessment

STRATEGIC GOVERNANCE: 9.3
Trend: Steady

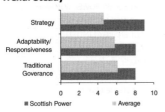

- Strategy
- Adaptability/Responsiveness
- Traditional Goverance

0 2 4 6 8 10

■ Scottish Power   ■ Average

Strategy: Scottish Power is a leader in its sector for sustainability management systems. For example, the CEO has stated the company's commitment to customer service, environmental issues, and relationships with other stakeholders. Through its rigorous sustainability reporting, the company clearly shows that it proactively identifies opportunities to achieve economic, environmental, and social profitability. What the company calls a hierarchal model portrays how all decisions will affect economic, environmental, and social considerations. Scottish Powers' strong sustainability programs and policies are increasingly pushed through the company and in spite of relatively low ranking in terms of performance on H&S, labor relations and R&D it is likely that the company will experience significant financial and strategic benefits from its overall approach.

Adaptibility/Responsiveness: In an initiative to achieve best practice in sustainability reporting, Scottish Power has published, in response to stakeholder demands, comprehensive data pertaining to environmental and social issues through an environmental report, a community report, web based reporting and a Health and Safety report to come.
In 2002/03, Scottish Power formed the Corporate Social Responsibility Steering Committee, which consists of executives responsible for governance, human resources and corporate communications and staff with environmental and community responsibilities. It meets monthly to review sustainability issues, comment on reporting, and make recommendations to the Executive Team. The board also has an Energy and Environmental committee and a Health and Safety Executive committee.

Traditional Governance Factors: There is separation between the Chairman and the CEO roles. There are three executives and seven non-executive directors, including the Chairman. Individual executive directors have specific responsibilities for matters such as health and safety, environment and regulation. The Committees are Audit (only non-execs), Remuneration (only non-execs), Nomination (CEO and three non-execs), and Executive Team.

External auditors are prohibited from also supplying general consultancy services.
Intending to manage, rather than eliminate risk, there is a Group Risk Management Committee, which is comprised of members of the Executive Team. It meets monthly and identifies any major exposures and mitigating actions, provides a consolidated view of the risk profile of the company and embeds a risk awareness culture throughout the group.

HUMAN CAPITAL: 6.6
Trend: Steady

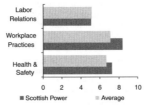

- Labor Relations
- Workplace Practices
- Health & Safety

0 2 4 6 8 10

■ Scottish Power   ■ Average

Labor Relations: The threat of strike action has been a feature of labor relations in the past two to three years. In March 2002, Scottish Power announced 500 job cuts (5% of staff). The firm's spokesperson hoped that redundancies would be achieved through voluntary long-term service agreements and through the non-renewal of temporary contracts. The cuts were blamed on the Government's 'chaotic' energy policy.

High-Performance Workplace Practices: The company has established a single corporate human resources team, which is intended to recruit, motivate, and retain high quality staff in a planned, systematic manner. Its Group Leadership and Business Leadership programs identify staff who demonstrate the potential to do well and groom them, through training, guidance, mentoring and project work, for higher levels of responsibility.
Set up in the UK in 1996 to support learning within the company and within the community, Scottish Power Learning runs the Open Learning initiative. Open Learning Center courses provide training in Health and Safety, languages, and computer skills to thousands of staff. This model was successfully transferred to eight sites in five states in the US. Access is easy with desktop and home access as well as Learning Centers. More than 15,000 courses were accessed last year.
During 2001/02 Scottish Power was among the UK's top 100 companies to introduce an All Employee Share Ownership Plan to employees in the UK which gained the 2001 ProShare Award for the best new employee share ownership plan. Three-quarters of the UK staff subscribe to one or both share ownership plans.

The downside is that in the pension schemes, Scottish Power matches employee contributions with its own shares, in which case employees are threatened by market downturns since the plans do not seem to be appropriately diversified.

Health & Safety: Health and Safety (H&S) strategy and policy are managed by the Group H&S Executive Committee, chaired by the Group Director of Human Resources. A special emphasis is laid on safety by the implementation of safety management system. In spite of a 29% improvement in lost time accident incidence rate, in 2002/03 and 3 main power stations awarded level 5 in RoSPA's for their quality safety, two people died in 2002 and there is limited disclosure on how they died and what is being done to prevent such accidents from happening again.

ENVIRONMENTAL PERFORMANCE: 6.9
Trend: Steady

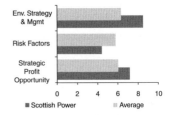

- Env. Strategy & Mgmt
- Risk Factors
- Strategic Profit Opportunity

0 2 4 6 8 10

■ Scottish Power   ■ Average

Environmental Strategy & Management: Scottish Power is rated above average in its environmental management relative to peers. It is increasing its renewable generation capacity, investing in environmental protection for its coal-fired plants, and achieving lower levels of CO_2/GWh to combat global climate change. SP conducts thorough reviews for compliance, business, and image risks. The Corporate Environment Director provides an overview of the key issues facing the US & UK. Key Performance Indicators measure progress towards achieving strategic environmental goals. All coal-fired plants of PacifiCorp have achieved ISO 14001 certification.

Risk Factors: With a higher than average coal contribution in its generation (15.5% gas, 78% coal, 5% hydro, and 1% renewable), Scottish Power has high risk exposure to increasing air regulations. However, it is proactive in abatement for NOx, SO_2, CO_2, dust and ash. US authorities and Scottish Power representatives are in debate about whether the 10 million pounds of toxic materials issued in 2000 were all contained, recycled, or left to the environment and public health to absorb. SP built Europe's largest sludge drying plant to create dry granular fuel from sewage sludge. The fuel

Innovest
STRATEGIC VALUE ADVISORS

Intangible Value Assessment

is then burned with coal at Longannet power station to generate electricity.

Eco-efficiency Initiatives: Works with customers to promote energy efficiency. The Customer Energy Challenge Program, offered by PacifiCorp, gives residential customers credit on their bill for reducing energy consumption. Its renewable energy products, such as Blue Sky Tariff have 21,000 customers. Lets Do the Bring Thing Utah energy efficiency program engaged 5,500 students and 150 teachers, reducing their utility bills by $100-$200 per month. The Green Tariff in the UK, where customers pay a premium to fund the Green Energy Fund, enables investment in renewable energy products.

STAKEHOLDER CAPITAL: 8.3
Trend: Steady

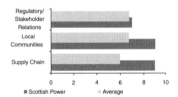

■ Scottish Power   ■ Average

Stakeholders:

Regulators: Partly driven by regulations, SP takes an active role in alleviating fuel poverty. The company does not give political donations. Customers: The company has a wide range of retail customers, including large industrial and commercial businesses and individual householders. Although Scottish Power has specific performance targets, i.e. interruptions, restoring power supply, answering customer calls, Scottish Power received the third highest number of complaints from customers, according to Energywatch. But SP was able to attain 150,000 more customers in the past year and reduced churn rate by 4%.

Local Communities: Scottish Power is very proactive in its relationship with local communities. The company recently commissioned Business in the Community to conduct a social impact audit of US and UK activities and is now implementing its recommendations. In 2002/03, cash donations, staff time and support in totaling £8.5 million (72% Leadership and Partnership, 20% Employment and Education, 6% Environment, and 2% Economic Development) and 55,000 employee volunteer hours. SP is strongly involved in education programs either to engage disinterested youth in education or to help young people enhance their employability.

In the US, PacifiCorp partnered with local non-profit agencies to offer free auditing and energy efficiency services to low-income households. The PacifiCorp Foundation is dedicated to childhood literacy programs. In the UK, Scottish Power partners with the Energy Action Grants Agency to help homeowners to replace old or inefficient equipment with modern combined systems with manageable payment.

Supply Chain: Scottish Power provides training and briefing material for suppliers and checks compliance with its requirements through regular audits. The company has an Environmental Supplier Initiative, including a Supplier Environmental questionnaire. Its ultimate objective is to ensure a good cultural fit with those who work closely with the company, to minimize risk and ensure a consistent approach.

EMERGING MARKETS: Strategy: Currently, there are no operations in emerging markets nor are there plans to expand in these areas in the near future.

Human Rights: N/A

Oppressive Regimes: N/A

SRI NEGATIVE SCREENING INFORMATION

The following information is provided for investors who for various ethical or social reasons may wish to avoid investments in companies involved in the following business areas. Innovest's IVA product uses a positive screening approach to identify superior management. Beyond assessing potential market risks, involvement in the following businesses does not impact our ratings.

SCREEN

Alcohol – N/A
Animal Testing - N/A
Contraception - N/A
Gambling - N/A
Genetically Modified Organisms - N/A
Nuclear Power - It sells nuclear power by contract, but does not generate any nuclear power on its own.
Pornography - N/A
Tobacco - N/A
Weapons Production – N/A

COMPETITIVE SET
Surface Transport

BRITISH ENERGY PLC

COMPETITIVE SET
Surface Transport

CHUBU ELECTRIC POWER COMPANY INC
CLP HOLDINGS LTD
CONTACT ENERGY LIMITED
E.ON AG
ELECTRABEL SA
ELECTRICIDADE DE PORTUGAL, SA
ELECTRICITE DE FRANCE
ENDESA SA
ENEL SPA
FORTUM CORP.
GRANINGE AB
HONG KONG ELECTRIC HOLDINGS LIMITED
IBERDROLA SA
INTERNATIONAL POWER PLC
KANSAI ELECTRIC POWER COMPANY INC
KYUSHU ELECTRIC POWER COMPANY INC
NATIONAL GRID GROUP PLC
PUBLIC POWER CORPORATION
REPOWER SYSTEMS AG
RWE AG
SCOTTISH AND SOUTHERN ENERGY PLC
SCOTTISH POWER PLC
TOHOKU ELECTRIC POWER COMPANY INC
TOKYO ELECTRIC POWER COMPANY INC
TRANSALTA CORPORATION
UNIFIED ENERGY SYSTEM OF RUSSIA RAO
UNION ELECTRICA FENOSA
VERBUND AKT
VIRIDIAN GROUP PLC

Figure A2.4 Intangible value assessment: Scottish Power

Innovest
STRATEGIC VALUE ADVISORS

www.innovestgroup.com
New York: +1 212 421-2000
London: +44 (0) 20 7073 0470
Toronto: +1 905 707-0876
Paris: +33 (0)1 44 54 04 89

Intangible Value Assessment

Jan–03

Unilever NV / plc

Country:	Netherlands / UK
Ticker Symbol:	UN / UNVR.L
Industrial Sector:	Food Products
Combined IVA Rating:	**AAA**
Rank:	**1 of 49**
Sub-Factors:	▮
Strategic Governance:	9
Human Capital:	9
Environment:	7.1
Stakeholder Capital:	8

| Analyst: | Katharine Preston
905 707 0876
kpreston@innovestgroup.com |
|---|---|

Intangible value comprises a growing percentage of companies' market capitalization. Innovest's IVA™ ratings analyze relative corporate performance on intangible value drivers related to the strength and sustainability of companies' competitive advantage. By assessing differentials typically not identified by traditional securities analysis, IVA™ ratings uncover hidden risks and value potential for investors. Ratings range from AAA (best) to CCC (worst). Scores on sub-factors range from 10 (best) to 0 (worst).

PERFORMANCE / ALPHA INTENSITY MATRIX

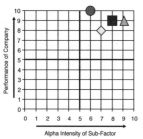

■ Strategic Governance ▲ Human Capital
● Environment ◇ Stakeholder Capital

This matrix situates the four key intangible value drivers along 2 dimensions: 1. How well or poorly the company performs on each of the 4 key factors. 2. How much impact that particular factor has on financial performance in that industry sector; its "alpha intensity".

COMPANY OVERVIEW

Core Business: Unilever N.V. (NL) and Unilever PLC (UK) each own half of Unilever, one of the world's largest packaged consumer goods firms. Unilever is the second largest food company in the world. Unilever is split into two business units: Food Products and Home & Personal Care. Unilever has a single board of directors and operates as a single entity, although the stocks are listed separately.

Geographic Focus: Sales are from 150 countries and are split regionally: 40% in Europe, 26% in North America, 16% in Asia & Pacific, 11% in Latin America and 7% in Africa, Middle East & Turkey.

Revenue Breakdown: Sales in 2002 were nearly U.S $51 billion of which 57% are in Foods, 43% in Home and Personal Care.

Workforce: company employees numbered 265,000 at the end of 2001.

INDUSTRY DRIVING FORCES

Genetically Modified Organisms: The issues surrounding the use of the genetic modification of seeds to make the plants resistant to pests are new and long-term impacts to both the environment and to human health and are not entirely known. There is a growing concern among consumers that GE food could be harmful, lead to allergic reactions, and have significant negative impacts on the environment. Consumers are therefore demanding more comprehensive food labeling so that they can choose whether to eat food containing GMOs. Firms in this industry are exposed to reputational risks if they do not engage stakeholders and respond to consumer concerns over GMOs. Financial repercussions have been significant and include billions in losses due to lost export markets, impacts from consumer boycotts and recall costs from contamination.

Globalization of sourcing: With the increase in globalization, food products companies are increasingly sourcing raw materials from countries around the world. In some emerging markets, agricultural operations are often the site for human rights abuses. Until conditions can be adequately monitored firms operating in these regions are exposed to reputational and productivity risk as well as the threat of consumer boycott. As a lot of food products are traded as commodities in international markets, farmers have little control over prices and see large fluctuations in income. Leading companies are addressing this issue by initiating fair-trading practices.

Nutrition and Food Safety: Due to lifestyle evolution, food must be often prepared and this requires more processing, more pre-servatives, more packaging and as a result may offer less nutrition for consumers. In addition, long transportation distances can expose food to epizootic diseases. The risk of contamination can be highly damaging for businesses in the sector.

AREAS OF POTENTIAL RISK

As described above, the industry's driving forces are also closely related to areas of potential risk the companies in the sector can face, depending on their strategy and responses to these issues. GMOs, emerging markets and Public Health issues are the main issues industry has to cope with.

Unilever's Board of Director's is limited in its gender and ethnic diversity. Given the scale of its global operations, the company is potentially falling behind its peers when it comes to representing more of its market at the supervisory level.

AREAS OF COMPETITIVE ADVANTAGE

Unilever is the sector leader in demonstrating its commitment to sustainable development and corporate social responsibility. The strength of this commitment to CSR strategy significantly enhances shareholder value.

Unilever has been a sector leader in its response and approach to using GMOs in its food products. The company commits to including stakeholders in the GMO discussion and will not use them where consumers are opposed.

STRATEGIC PROFIT OPPORTUNITIES

Unilever's leadership in driving sustainable development initiatives is raising the bar in the industry. Given the size and global reach of the organization, Unilever can drive these initiatives throughout its supply chain and potentially that of its industry peers and partners. Both the business and shareholders will benefit from the value added by these activities.

RATING OUTLOOK: POSITIVE

Unilever is a sector leader in most of the sustainability related issues screened. Its progressive approach and continual efforts to improve the scope of its policies and processes stand the company in god stead to cement its leading postion.

Innovest
STRATEGIC VALUE ADVISORS

Intangible Value Assessment

STRATEGIC GOVERNANCE: 9
Trend: Steady

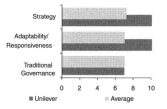

Strategy: Unilever has been the industry leader in integrating sustainable development into its business practices. The company has sustainability goals and targets in three key areas; sourcing all fish from sustainable stocks by 2005, ensuring that all crops used are gown in a sustainable way, and water care. Unilever has been measuring and reporting on environmental indicators for five years. The company sets eco-efficiency targets and reports on its progress annually. Unilever has a Code of Business Principles that outlines expectations of employee ethics and transparency. It published its second annual Social Review in 2002. Signatory to the UN Global Compact, the company commits to nine principles on human rights, labor and environmental practice.

Adaptability/Responsiveness: The Code of Business Principles sets out the operational standards for all employees worldwide and covers issues such as standards of behavior, health and safety, quality assurance and commitment to the environment. This Code is updated regularly and simultaneously offers a full training program for all employees, suppliers and business partners. The Unilever Boards (directors and advisory) are responsible for ensuring these principles are communicated to, understood and observed by all employees. Board committees in a supportive role include the Audit Committee of the Board and the Corporate Risk Committee. Day-to-day responsibility is delegated to the senior management of the regions and operating companies. The individual operating companies are responsible for implementing the Code. Unilever is quick to respond to any adverse situation as witnessed by its response to Mercury leaks in India.

Traditional Governance Factors: Unilever has both a Board of Directors and an Advisory Board. The Board of Directors consists of eight members of the Unilever executive while the Advisory Board includes 12 non-executives from a variety of backgrounds. There is little ethnic diversity and only one female member among the 20 member combined group, however nine nationalities are represented. There is a fair

degree of independence of oversight, given the large size of the advisory board and that all chairs of the board committees are non-executives.

Unilever neither supports political parties nor contributes to the funds of groups whose activities are calculated to promote party interests.

HUMAN CAPITAL: 9
Trend: Steady

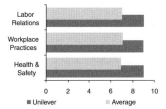

Labor Relations: Unilever has announced a restructuring plan as part of a new brand focus and the planned synergy savings from the Bestfoods integration. In 2000 the company announced a 5-year restructuring that will lead to a reduction of 33,000 workers worldwide (about 10% of its total employees). There is a very comprehensive program to assist in re-employment for any laid off staff. Unilever representatives can spend up to a year assisting in training, education, and job hunting to ensure all employees find new employment. The company seeks to mitigate personal impact on employees by promoting the long-term employability and claims that remuneration packages typically exceed both the minimum required by law and the collective agreements with trade unions.

High-Performance Workplace Practices: Remuneration systems were recently redesigned to reward exceptional achievement and delivery of shareholder value. This year Unilever ran a series of international events for both rising and established managers. For example, the 'Leaders in Action' program focuses on building leadership capability and enabling moves into senior management roles. An International Management Training College in the UK runs 21 courses for managers worldwide covering topics as diverse as enterprise skills, advanced marketing, managing integrated supply chains. Unilever has also successfully launched 'open job posting'. By communicating management vacancies company-wide, this system ensures that selection is fair and transparent. Unilever is committed to diversity within the workplace but the non-discrimination policy does not include sexual orientation. There is a Diversity Board that currently exists only in the UK but is being used as a pilot program that may be rolled out globally. Freedom of as-

sociation is respected. Benefits include extended healthcare in developing regions. The company uses many channels for employee dialogue such as regular workplace briefings, newsletters, intranets and obtains the views and concerns of employees. Unilever has telephone 'carelines' to connect with customers and offer advice on issues such as water conservation. The company has a share option scheme for all staff, in 15 countries, as well as a matching program for executives.

Health & Safety: Unilever is committed to a high standard of health and safety for all employees. Unilever's Safety, Health and Environment Action Committee (SHEACO) aims for continuous improvement performance towards zero accidents. The committee operates worldwide and is staffed by specialists in risk management to ensure that their decisions and support are independent of commercial considerations. Unilever has shown a consistent decline in accident frequency since 1996, however in 2001 the Worldwide accident rate increased. H&S indicators have been expanded.

ENVIRONMENTAL PERFORMANCE: 7.1
Trend: Steady

Environmental Strategy & Management: Unilever attempts to quantify the environmental impact of the company in a global economy via lifecycle analysis. All sites are required to develop an EMS based on ISO 14001 and report on both corporate and facility-established environmental performance indicators. Almost all sites are ISO 14001 certified. Environmental strategy is integrated throughout the company via SHEACO, the Unilver External Environmental Advisory Group and a partnership with Forum for the Future. The biannual Corporate Environmental Report is audited by an outside consultancy.

Risk Factors: According to an outside audit, most environmental impacts associated with Unilever and its products are outside the company's control. As a result, extensive supplier certification programs and supply chain management initiatives are in place. Its specialty chemicals group was sold in 1997, but substantial Superfund liability remains. As the world's largest buyer of frozen fish, the company has a partnership with the WWF and Marine Stewardship

Innovest
STRATEGIC VALUE ADVISORS

Intangible Value Assessment

Council for environmentally responsible and economical fishing practices. The company's emissions of SOx, hazardous and non-hazardous wastes, and CO2 have been on the decline per unit of production since 1997. The company advocates an open debate on the role and safety of GMOs.

Eco-efficiency Initiatives: To conduct eco-efficiency and detailed analyses of waste, Unilever supports a purpose-built laboratory. Processes and packing machines are observed. Projects on waste reduction have been expanded from pilot initiatives to cover multiple sites. A facility in Indonesia achieved $200,000 annual savings in energy, water and waste minimization through this process.

STAKEHOLDER CAPITAL: 8
Trend: Steady

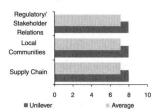

Regulators: Unilever cooperates with governments and other organizations, both directly and through bodies such as trade associations, in the development of proposed legislation and other regulations that may affect its business interests.

The company engages with Business for Social Responsibility, GRI, and continues to work with the UN Global Compact.

Local Communities: Unilever commits to investing 1% of pre-tax profits in community programs through voluntary contributions. The focus for Unilever's stakeholder relationships is on initiatives with long-term societal importance like healthcare and education. For example, Unilever is a partner in the African Comprehensive HIV/AIDS Partnership in Botswana. Unilever has been actively educating its employees and their communities about HIV/AIDS for more than a decade.

Supply Chain: Unilever's updated Code of Business Practices requires that all suppliers follow it as well. The company has extensive systems in place to monitor and audit supplier performance on a range of issues.

Unilever is working with farmers and growers under the Sustainable Agriculture Initiative, with other industry leaders, to ensure the sustainability of raw materials. The company is also working on a Unilever Sup-

plier Code that will include measures for diversity and health & safety.

EMERGING MARKETS: Strategy: Unilever's products already reach most corners of the globe. Unilever involvement in emerging and developing markets is extensive given its agricultural input requirements and the company often has direct contracts with farmers in these regions. The company has made small, affordable packets of its products for these markets.

Unilever has always been involved in skill transfer programs to these regions. A growing percentage of managers are from the local area.

Human Rights/ Child and Forced Labor: Policy fully supports the ILO convention on minimum working age and child labor. The company claims to not use any form of forced, compulsory or child labor. Unilever is involved in numerous countries with HR abuses according to Amnesty International. Given Unilever's exposure in these markets, to avoid increasing the risk to investors, the company must ensure it is adequately monitoring and auditing these facilities.

Oppressive Regimes: Unilever has operations in numerous countries that are not considered 'Free' by Freedom House. Unilever still has operations in Saudi Arabia where it is illegal for women to work. Some stakeholders and investors may be opposed to or sensitive to the company's presence there.

SRI NEGATIVE SCREENING INFORMATION

The following information is provided for investors who for various ethical or social reasons may wish to avoid investments in companies involved in the following business areas. Innovest's IVA product uses a positive screening approach to identify superior management. Beyond assessing potential market risks, involvement in the following businesses does not impact our ratings.

SCREEN

Screen	
Alcohol - N/A	
Animal Testing – Yes, but extent is not disclosed.	
Contraception - N/A	
Gambling - N/A	
Genetically Modified Organisms – Uses them outside EU.	
Nuclear Power - N/A	
Pornography - N/A	
Tobacco - N/A	
Weapons Production – N/A	

COMPETITIVE SET
Metals & Mining

AJINOMOTO COMPANY LIMITED
ARCHER-DANIELS-MIDLAND COMPANY
ARIAKE JAPAN COMPANY LIMITED
BARRY CALLEBAUT
DANISCO AS
DEAN FOODS CORP.
FUTURIS CORP. LIMITED
GEEST PLC
GREENCORE GROUP PLC
HOUSE FOODS CORP.
INDOFOOD SUKSES MAKMUR
KATOKICHI COMPANY LIMITED
KERRY GROUP PLC
KIKKOMAN CORPORATION
KRAFT FOODS INC
LINDT & SPRUNGLI
MEIJI DAIRIES CORP.
MEIJI SEIKA LIMITED
NICHIREI CORPORATION
NIPPON MEAT PACKERS INC
NISSHIN SEIFUN GROUP INC
NISSIN FOOD PRODUCTS COMPANY LIMITED
OSTASIATISKE KOM
PARMALAT
QP CORP.
SNOW BRAND MILK PRODUCTS COMPANY
SUEDZUCKER AG
TATE & LYLE PLC
TOYO SUISAN LIMITED
UNIQ PLC
WIMM-BILL-DANN FOODS
YAKULT HONSHA COMPANY LIMITED
YAMAZAKI BAKING COMPANY LIMITED

Figure A2.5 Intangible value assessment: Unilever

Appendix 3

A selection of profiles of contributing organizations

INTRODUCTION

The following pages include profiles of a number of the organizations from which our experts have contributed their chapters. As with the FTSE4Good Index material earlier, these profiles will give readers some guidance as to places where they could start to develop practical and achievable CSR policies. Perhaps the strongest message to have come out of all contributors to this book is that CSR is not a box-ticking exercise to see what is the least one can get away with while satisfying the requirements of legislation and avoiding the costs of litigation. CSR is a creative opportunity to inject a new energy into the business, to start to think of profit, yes, but of long-term profitability and contribution to the communities that support any business. Like any shrewd investment, an investment of time, people and money into the development of responsible and sustainable business plans and programmes will pay strong dividends in a continuity of high-quality supplies, a loyal workforce and a positive image in the marketplace – in short, brand. And a resilient, trusted and sustainable brand is something that every business aspires to. It is no coincidence that the companies in the FTSE4Good Index include some of the strongest brands around; well-run businesses know that operating responsibly, operating in a manner that does not leave the business a hostage to fortune but rather operating in a manner of which the business can always be proud and for which it is prepared to be known, is the surest way to long-term success and profitability.

PROFILE: CORPORATE CITIZENSHIP AT ACCENTURE

Our firm

Accenture is a global management consulting, technology services and outsourcing company. Committed to delivering innovation, Accenture collaborates with its clients to help them become high-performance businesses and governments. Accenture employs over 83,000 people in 48 countries around the world and we consider ourselves very much to be a 'people' business.

Our philosophy

Our understanding and knowledge are evolving the whole time but we have developed and maintained a strong philosophy towards being a responsible corporate citizen. The approach Accenture has adopted is one that takes it beyond traditional concepts of corporate philanthropy and 'giving something back' to a new, positive management of relationships with key stakeholders, based on mutual benefit. We recognize that we have many stakeholders – our marketplace, the environment, our workforce and the local communities in which we work and live – and managing the balance between their differing interests and goals is good for business now and will ensure the long-term sustainability of our organization.

The approach

There are four key strands to Accenture's approach to delivering meaningful benefits through corporate citizenship:

- **Focus on core skills and assets.** Part of the evolution of our thinking has been that real success is driven from a strong focus on utilizing the core skills and assets within our firm and of our people. Accenture has a great many people with deep business expertise ranging from strategy development through to complex systems implementation and human performance. At the same time, we have a number of technical and physical assets that we can call on. By doing things that we are already good at, we have much greater impact because we tend to deliver much more effectively. At the same time, it is easier to manage as part of our ongoing business and, in many cases, working directly on a corporate citizenship initiative is likely to directly benefit the business and the employees, as the skills developed are valuable to normal business operations.

- **Creating and maintaining synergistic partnerships.** Given the focus on core skills, we have realized that to deliver successful initiatives we cannot do it by ourselves. Therefore, we need to create synergistic partnerships with groups and organizations that share the views and interest in specific activities. To be effective the net must be thrown much wider than in normal business circumstances and Accenture has looked to develop long-term partnerships with other companies, governments, academic institutions, think-tanks and non-governmental organizations (NGOs) as well as community-based organizations. Each group brings different elements and each is vital to successfully delivering meaningful benefits.

- **Strong leadership.** Successful corporate citizenship in Accenture has to be led from the top. Accenture's International Chairman chairs a global Corporate Citizenship Council, which is made up of senior partners from around the world. This group is responsible for defining and refining the philosophy as well as for the management of Accenture's Foundation and the oversight of all our corporate citizenship activities. The personal commitment and drive of the members, along with the mandate of the council, ensures that the right level of attention and focus is given to corporate citizenship activities and that this is driven down into the organization.

- **Action.** In the end, delivering benefits to society and our business does not come about by having a strong philosophy or a clear strategy. It is realized through taking action – this is where we spend the majority of our time. Accenture is delivering its pledge to be a responsible corporate citizen in different places and through different methods around the world, and the following are examples of some of them:

  - **Accenture Development Partnerships (ADP)**. Accenture in the UK has recognized the strong demand from non-profits wanting high-value consulting but unable to pay for it. At the same time, there is strong demand from some of our best performers to be able to provide their skills to the non-profit and development community. Therefore, ADP was created to provide high-value, lower-cost consulting to non-profits and the development community, to help NGOs and donors achieve their social and economic development goals while providing an inspirational opportunity for Accenture people. ADP is able to provide these services by hand-picking the highest performers who demand the opportunity to work for up to six months in development environments around the world, asking them to take a significant pay cut and dropping Accenture's margin to zero. ADP is being piloted very successfully from the UK and, to date, has undertaken projects in a number of countries ranging from the Balkans to Vietnam and from India to Namibia.

  - **Enablis:** helping to create digital opportunities. We believe that the digital divide is a direct reflection of the socio-economic divide and that the support and creation of enterprises (specifically small and medium-sized enterprises) that develop, build and/or utilize ICTs in an innovative way (digital opportunities) will lead directly to the long-run improvement in the socio-economic environment. Enterprise and ICTs are at the core of Accenture's business and success. Therefore, following our involvement in the G8 Digital Opportunities Task Force, Accenture has partnered with HP and Telesystem to create a new, commercially minded, non-profit organization called Enablis. Enablis supports entrepreneurs through providing them with debt financing, business and technical support and networking as well as advice on policy and regulatory environments. Enablis has seed funding from the government of Canada and has opened its first operating unit, for southern Africa, in South Africa. Accenture has committed significant human and technical resources to the development of Enablis while building strong relationships in G8 governments, our partners and the non-profit sector organizations we are working with.

 – **World Links for education.** The Accenture Foundation made its first ever global grant to World Links to support education and entrepreneurial activities in India, Brazil and China and, at the same time, Accenture is providing resources on a volunteer and pro bono basis. The two main projects have been: the conversion of five school computer labs into dual-use community learning and entrepreneurship centres in both India and Brazil, and the establishment of a pilot World Links programme in China.

The Corporate Citizenship Council has ensured that each of the relevant Accenture country managing directors leverage their local expertise to maximize the benefit of this relationship to both sides by ensuring that the mechanisms are in place to allow staff engagement locally. Again, the programme has looked to use Accenture's core skills and we have provided knowledge regarding business and enterprise development and, critically, helping to make the school-based telecentres self-sustaining in the medium and long term.

PROFILE: THE AMNESTY BUSINESS GROUP

Established in 1991, the Amnesty International UK Business Group comprises people with expertise in the socially responsible investment industry, law, social auditing and reporting, academia and ethical investment. The group works with members of staff employed in this area, to encourage companies to:

● be aware of the human rights impact of all aspects of their operations;
● use their legitimate influence in support of human rights, in all countries in which they operate;

- give effect to the Universal Declaration of Human Rights;
- avoid complicity in human rights violations committed by other parties;
- include a specific commitment to human rights in their statements of business principles and codes of conduct;
- make their human rights policies explicit, ensuring they are integrated, monitored and audited across all functions.

Key milestones of the Business Group

Below is a list of some of the key milestones of the Business Group since its inception:

- **1997:** Business Group organizes first ever UK conference specifically on the theme of Business and Human Rights.
- **1997:** *Human Rights Guidelines for Companies* published and distributed; widely used by companies and by the socially responsible investment (SRI) industry.
- **1998:** Several UK major corporations acknowledge for the first time the relevance of the Universal Declaration of Human Rights to business, referring to their responsibilities for human rights in their statements of business principles.
- **1998:** Business Group publishes first edition of its newsletter, 'Human rights and business matters'.
- **1999:** Richard Howitt MEP speaks at AIUK's AGM on the European Parliament's landmark resolution to create a legally binding framework for regulating transnational corporates.
- **1999:** AIUK submit comments to the Department of Trade and Industry's Review of Mission and Status of Export Credits Guarantee Department.
- **2000:** Publication of *Business and Human Rights in a Time of Change* and *Human Rights – Is It Any of Your Business?* Both publications receive media reviews and are used as course texts in leading business schools.
- **2000:** Publication of *Business Briefing on Saudi Arabia* – AI's first country-specific business briefing. Picket held outside Investing in Saudi conference – gains media coverage.
- **2000:** Launch of AIUK's Socially Responsible Investment Campaign, with publication of *Human Rights Guidelines for Pension Fund Trustees*; receives coverage on TV and radio and in the press. AIUK members and local groups mobilized to take action.
- **2000:** AIUK make a submission to UK government's Company Law Review.
- **2001:** AIUK submission to EU Green Paper on Corporate Social Responsibility.
- **2002:** AIUK is a founder member of the Corporate Responsibility (CORE) Campaign Coalition. The campaign's goal is to 'improve the environmental, social and economic performance of companies by requiring greater transparency

and accountability to stakeholders'. The coalition is seeking to achieve this through a Corporate Responsibility Bill.

- **2002:** Launch of 'Geography of corporate risk'. Business briefings held in London, New York, Brussels and Stockholm; TV, radio and press coverage received.
- **2003:** Publication by AIUK of a human rights' checklist for companies entitled 'The human rights responsibilities of companies', reproducing work undertaken within the UN Sub-Commission on Human Rights.
- **2003:** Launch of 'Human rights on the line report' into the Baku–Tbilisi–Ceyhan oil pipeline project and the Host Government Agreement between BP and the Turkish government.

The Corporate Responsibility (CORE) Campaign

The Corporate Responsibility (CORE) Coalition was formed in response to the government's failure in the Modernising Company Law White Paper to specify rules requiring companies to be more transparent and be held accountable to their wider stakeholders. Although the White Paper represents the most radical overhaul of UK company law in 150 years, the government failed to take advantage of this unique opportunity and its proposals fell short of requiring companies to consider the wide-ranging impact they have on people's lives and to reflect stakeholder concerns alongside shareholder interests.

The founding members of CORE included Amnesty International UK, Christian Aid, Friends of the Earth, New Economics Foundation and Traidcraft. The coalition is now supported by over 50 organizations, including NGOs, church groups and trade unions. The primary focus of the campaign is the Corporate Responsibility (CORE) Parliamentary Bill. The Bill presents key principles of corporate responsibility to be made law, proposing greater transparency through company reporting in terms of social, environmental and economic impacts and for companies to be accountable to a wider group of affected individuals.

Advocacy

Over the past 10 years, members of the AIUK Business Group have been visiting companies to discuss concerns about their potential or actual human rights impacts and to give advice on appropriate policies. Our strategy is one of constructive but critical engagement:

- We hold face-to-face meeting with companies to urge them to address the human rights context of their operations by developing effective policies and implementation mechanisms.

- We produce materials in the form of reports, briefings and guidelines to give companies the terms of reference to understand how to safeguard human rights and how to avoid contributing to violations. Some of these materials are general; others relate to specific industrial sectors and countries.
- We also participate in workshops, seminars and conferences to communicate our messages to key constituencies within business, government, the media and the investment community.

Human rights policies for companies

We always urge that a company's human rights policy be based on a commitment to the Universal Declaration of Human Rights (UDHR), explaining that it calls on 'every individual and every organ of society' to play their part in securing the observance of the rights contained within it.

This not only means that companies should support and respect the protection of human rights within their sphere of influence but also that they should make sure they are not complicit in human rights abuses (for instance, when operating in a country where governmental abuse of human rights is prevalent). This latter point is still hard for some companies to accept and a major reason for the publication of the 'Geography of corporate risk'.

To assist companies in developing their human rights policies, AIUK has published a checklist for companies, 'The human rights responsibilities of companies', based on work undertaken within the UN Sub-Commission on Human Rights.

However, the real test lies in companies' implementation of their human rights policies throughout their global operations, which means having in place the monitoring and auditing systems necessary to ensure compliance.

For further information about the work of the Business Network, please contact: Business Team, Amnesty International United Kingdom, 99–119 Rosebery Avenue, London EC1R 4RE (tel: 020 7814 6200; e-mail: business@amnesty.org.uk).

PROFILE: CENTRICA, A BUSINESS THAT PROFITS FROM RESPONSIBILITY

Corporate responsibility (CR) generates challenges in all aspects of a business's operations, and Centrica has accepted those challenges. Responsibility is embedded in our strategy and as such helps to underpin our success. It covers such areas as minimal environmental impact, operational transparency, positive treatment for workers, a fair deal for customers, excellent returns for shareholders and commitment to the wider community. Applying corporate responsibility principles in all of these areas and others means that, for Centrica, CR is a driver of economic value.

In order to establish a responsible business we must:

- know our starting point;
- know our objectives;
- know who will do it;
- know how it will be done;
- do it; and
- monitor results.

Know our starting point

To establish independently Centrica's starting point in terms of corporate responsibility, we commissioned the SMART Company to conduct a CR audit. The outcome was feedback in six core areas where responsibility has an impact:

- employment practice and human rights;
- supply chain management;
- community investment and investment policy and corporate governance;
- environmental management;
- investment and corporate governance; and
- reporting and communication.

That feedback set out Centrica's CR achievements to date and the further challenges faced by the business if it is to achieve the high CR standards that we have set as our objective. All of this was set in the overall positive context of the SMART Company's summary reporting that:

- Centrica is well advanced in both its thinking and its approach towards social responsibility.
- Centrica has areas of strength to celebrate; for example, its policies and practice in community investment are exemplary.
- It performs well in both meeting current legislative standards and considering future expectations.
- Centrica has established practices and policies in a number of key areas. However, there would appear to be areas for further consideration; for example, the company has targets for reducing emissions of hazardous substances but is not yet tracking their recycling systems.

While it was gratifying to hear how well we were doing in most areas, of equal value was to know where we needed to improve. For instance, in tracking recycling systems, we since have established data reports of our recycling performance, details of which can be found on our website, www.centrica.com/responsibility.

Know our objectives

Our CR targets in all key operational areas are not simply wish lists. As with any meaningful targets, CR objectives need to be specific and measurable. A good example would be our Resource Efficiency Goals for improvements by 2005 compared to a 2000 baseline:

- **Energy** – reduce energy use in our buildings by 15 per cent.
- **Fuel** – reduce fuel use per mile by 13 per cent.
- **Waste** – reduce waste sent to landfill by 15 per cent and increase the recycling rate in our offices to 50 per cent.

Know who will do it

The Centrica Corporate Responsibility Committee has been established to set the strategy and direction for our CR programme and reports annually to the board. The committee is also charged with ensuring appropriate and effective communication of the CR strategy, identifying and prioritizing areas of group activity where there are acknowledged weaknesses in performance and ensuring that group-wide initiatives support the agreed CR framework and complement brand activity. Particular programmes such as our community programmes are the responsibilities of specific committee members.

Centrica brands are charged to implement the CR framework in a manner appropriate to the markets or countries in which they operate to ensure that group principles are put into practice in the most effective manner everywhere that Centrica operates. Brands are also responsible for relationships with their own stakeholders and must support the wider CR strategy.

Know how it will be done

We have already instituted a number of programmes across the Centrica group and brands to ensure that our CR policy objectives become achievements. There is a commitment for all businesses to have systematic environmental management in place by 2005 and, for our 'higher-impact' businesses, we are taking the steps to achieve external accreditation to ISO14001. This will apply to all five power stations, the Morecambe Bay and Rough gas fields, AA patrol force and service centres and British Gas engineers. With an environment policy, quantitative goals and public reporting in place since 2000, Centrica has already established robust means through which CR will be delivered.

Do it

With solid achievements to date, such as 6,000 tonnes of CO_2 emissions saved in just 18 months, an 11 per cent improvement in vehicle fuel efficiency in 2002 compared with 2000 and a 90 per cent overall waste recycling rate (40 per cent in offices), we know that a businesslike approach to CSR adds bottom-line value.

There are also many achievements on a more human scale. We have a positive employment policy towards disabled people, which has brought benefits to those involved and helped raise awareness of the prejudices faced by disabled people in the employment market. British Gas has also formed a partnership with Help the Aged to tackle the havoc that cold-related illnesses wreak in our senior population during winters, while the British Gas 'Here to Help' programme works with local authorities, housing associations and charities to tackle fuel poverty wherever it may be. And for the longer term, our award-winning 'Think Energy' programme has the ambitious aim of using education and awareness of energy efficiency to encourage better understanding across the population so that future energy users will be better informed as to the real cost of energy and how to minimize that cost.

Monitor results

With a proper CR model operating in the business, performance in the key CR areas is an integral part of Centrica's management information provision, which coupled with the audits by the SMART Company will ensure that we do not simply do the right things but that we know enough about them to be able to tell all of our stakeholders what we are doing, how well we are doing it, what our future CR plans entail and how that will impact on their involvement with the business.

In short, we are building social responsibility into the foundations of Centrica.

Further information is available from Simon Henderson (tel: 01753 494071; e-mail: simon.henderson@centrica.co.uk) or on the website, www.centrica.com.

PROFILE: DIAGEO, PROUD OF WHAT WE DO

Diageo is the world's leading premium drinks business with a collection of brands across spirits, wine and beer categories. Operating in 180 countries around the world,

Diageo is listed on both the London Stock Exchange and New York Stock Exchange. It has taken over two centuries to create the Diageo brands that the company designates as global priority brands – for example, Justerini & Brooks, the creator of J&B, can trace its origins back to London in 1749.

Diageo has focused its business on those global priority brands: Smirnoff, Johnnie Walker, Guinness, Baileys, J&B, Captain Morgan, Cuervo and Tanqueray. These brands hold the strongest positions in the best-performing markets. The company's four major markets – North America, Great Britain, Ireland and Spain – make the largest contribution to the business and generate nearly 60 per cent of operating profit.

Social responsibility

Diageo believes that all the communities in which it operates should benefit from its presence. That is why the company gives priority to areas where its impact is greatest. The single biggest area of impact is social responsibility and alcohol.

Alcohol is the company's main product and the company strives to tackle the causes of irresponsible consumption. Its approach is based on three principles:

- Moderate and responsible consumption of alcohol, whether beer, wine or spirits, can be part of a balanced and healthy lifestyle for most adults.
- The industry should work together to promote responsible drinking and ensure that self-regulation of marketing practices is effective.
- Adults should be able to make informed choices about drinking – or not drinking. Young people need appropriate education and guidance from teachers, parents and other role models.

Diageo aims to set standards in responsible marketing. As well as abiding by local and national laws, the company aims to comply with self-regulatory codes drawn up by the drinks industry. On an industry-wide level, Diageo is a signatory of the Dublin principles, which sets out principles of cooperation among the beverage alcohol industry, governments, scientific researchers and the public health community. And as a member of the International Center for Alcohol Policy (ICAP) Diageo has co-funded a range of peer-reviewed research overviews and publications.

In addition to industry codes, Diageo has its own marketing code, first implemented when the company was established in 1998. In 2001, an independent audit of the code was carried out – it examined the promotion of 27 brands in 27 countries, reviewing about 1,000 advertisements, and found a high level of compliance with the code.

The review suggested a number of areas for improvement. Alongside feedback from alcohol policy experts, these suggestions helped form an updated code of practice, which was launched in October 2002. Since then, all Diageo's marketing teams and key agency people have been trained in the use of the code, and new compliance processes put in place in every country.

There is also an increasing trend for Diageo's advertising to carry a specific responsibility message. In the US, 20 per cent of Diageo's broadcast advertising budget is dedicated to branded responsibility advertisements. Smirnoff Ice, Smirnoff, Johnnie Walker Black, Baileys, Captain Morgan and Crown Royal have all developed commercials with a responsibility message.

Not just charitable giving

For Diageo, good corporate citizenship encompasses all the ways in which its business and products interact with society and the natural world, and indicates the balance between the duty to act responsibly and the right to trade freely.

The term 'corporate citizenship' is defined broadly, including within it ethics, governance, relations with employees, customers, consumers and suppliers, communities, health and safety, the environment and many other areas of business activity. In all of these aspects Diageo aspires to leadership in its industry.

For Diageo, being a good corporate citizen is a natural part of doing business. And good corporate citizenship:

- helps create a sustainable business environment;
- builds awareness among Diageo's people;
- builds trust with stakeholders;
- develops team spirit, capabilities and skills;
- enhances the company's reputation and the value of its brands.

To support Diageo's businesses around the world in their community involvement, The Diageo Foundation was established to provide kick-start funding and expertise. The foundation is a registered grant-making charity, legally distinct from Diageo plc.

Measuring investment

Diageo evaluates many of its community investment projects using the London Benchmarking Group (LBG) model. The model puts a monetary value on the 'input' costs of a company's community involvement programmes, whether the contributions are made in cash, in time or in kind. Combining this with the programme management costs, covering the salaries, benefits and overheads of staff involved in community relations, it enables a total cost of community involvement to be calculated. The LBG model also assesses what projects actually achieve – the 'output', defined in terms of the community and business benefit.

Philanthropy

Spirit of America

The Diageo (formerly Guinness UDV) Spirit of America fund was set up for the victims of the attacks on the World Trade Center in 2001. Every dollar contributed to the fund by Diageo employees worldwide was matched dollar for dollar by the company up to a total of $1 million. A special team made up of Diageo North America employees, representing all parts of the business, determined dispersal of these funds. Diageo employees in the UK made donations to the Helping USA Disaster Fund, which was set up to relieve immediate distress and provide ongoing support to those affected. Spirit of America funds contributed to money, services and equipment for fire and ambulance services, as well as to humanitarian airlifts of supplies for hospitals and orphanages in Afghanistan and Iraq. The programme was recognized by the Mayor of New York, as well as by international humanitarian agencies.

Social investment

Alcohol education

The Diageo-supported TIPS – Training for Intervention Procedures – programme teaches bartenders about the responsible serving of alcohol. The Spanish-language version of TIPS has been launched and will run in US cities with large Hispanic populations. Similar schemes will be rolled out in Latin America and the Caribbean.

Water of Life

The purpose of the programme, which was launched by Guinness Nigeria in 2003, is to provide 10 communities with basic clean and safe water. Guinness Nigeria has secured funding from the Diageo Foundation, and is working closely with the Voluntary Services Organization and local organizations that specialize in water management and drilling boreholes. Local communities will be actively involved in the planning, construction and maintenance of their own projects, and opportunities will be created for unemployed people in these areas. The project is being extended to provide 70,000 people with clean water. The business benefits are clear: links have been strengthened with local government and the health community, and employees have felt engaged and proud of the company's work.

Commercially led initiatives

Keep Walking

Launched in 2000, the Keep Walking Fund in Mexico is run in partnership with JEMAC (Jóvenes Empresarios por México AC), which has recently received accreditation from Youth Business International, the international network of the Prince's Trust. The Diageo Foundation has provided £100,000 of funding over three years. In 2002, the Keep Walking Fund allocated 10 grants: 5 to people whose initiatives aim to support the community, and 5 to aspiring entrepreneurs. The community programmes include: a project that provides education, along with nutrition, to families in rural areas (to break the cycle of infantile malnutrition caused by ignorance), a programme to support rural families in areas where deforestation has stripped the land of nutrients, and a scheme to set up a refuge for street children. The entrepreneurial initiatives include: a programme to establish a laboratory to investigate the manufacture of certain chemical agents used in the analysis of blood samples, a micro credit scheme, and the creation of an automated web-based drug dispenser.

The Keep Walking Fund has enabled talented young Mexicans to achieve their career potential. It has been such a success that the programme has also been replicated in other countries. For Diageo, it has also had a significant impact on Johnnie Walker brand awareness in Mexico. The campaign attracted 8,000 grant applications and, in six months, 162 presentations were held across Mexico with 18,000 people taking part.

The environment

Earthwatch is an international environmental charity, which supports scientific field research around the world. Its aim is to fund research that will lead to sustainable conservation of some of the world's more vulnerable creatures and habitats.

Under the Diageo Foundation-funded Earthwatch programme, 15 employees were selected from hundreds of applicants to take part in six two-week Earthwatch research projects. On their return to their home countries, the employees helped to introduce new approaches to biodiversity and sustainability around the business. These include: a biodiversity study to transform a piece of disused land, car sharing, pollution control and water-saving bottling techniques.

Diageo has committed 1 per cent of its pre-tax profits to such community projects – currently worth over £19 million. The Diageo Foundation makes part of this investment. But while financial contributions are important, Diageo believes active involvement can often achieve much more for the community, whether through the time and skills of the company's employees or surplus products and other 'in-kind' resources.

The future

Diageo is proud of its history of community and environmental achievement, and in 2004 it published its first corporate citizenship report, to highlight successes, but also to cast a clear light on areas for improvement. In the words of Diageo's CEO Paul Walsh, 'We see it as a milestone on our journey towards the social, environmental and economic sustainability of our business.'

Further information is available on the website, www.diageo.com.

PROFILE: DLA UPSTREAM

DLA Upstream is the government affairs and media relations practice of DLA, one of the largest law firms in Europe with bases throughout the UK, Europe and Asia.

Our integrated team in London, Brussels and Edinburgh provides incisive communications advice at all political levels. We enable clients to follow and interpret political and regulatory developments in the national and pan-European arenas. Then we help them use this intelligence effectively to engage successfully in shaping developments to protect and enhance their position in the market.

DLA Upstream also has a high level of media relations and crisis management capability, offering the full circle of communications support and strategic advice.

Expertise

The firm advises clients from both the public and private sectors with a wide range of requirements. Our services are complemented by DLA's extensive regulatory expertise across a range of sectors, including:

- financial services, banking, competition and insurance;
- e-commerce, telecommunications, marketing and the media;
- utilities;
- healthcare and pharmaceuticals;
- transport, environment and local government;
- planning, development, property and construction.

Our team

The DLA Upstream team has a proven track record in corporate communications, government affairs, regulatory advice, media relations and crisis management.

Project teams are established and tailored according to the needs of clients. We have extensive experience of advising clients on a wide range of issues and on communications that shape public perceptions. This includes managing relationships with:

- policy makers, regulators and opinion formers in the EU and UK;
- regional, national, international and specialist media;
- business analysts and the City;
- employees, suppliers, customers and other stakeholders.

Corporate social responsibility

Companies are increasingly required to behave in a socially responsible manner. An effective CSR programme should be measurable, achievable and tailored to reflect the activity of the business. DLA Upstream provides a full audit service to identify key areas and develop a CSR strategy that responds to the needs of a client's business and its stakeholders. We understand the commercial context in which businesses operate and we can provide a strategic response that offers a genuine competitive advantage, as well as enabling a business to communicate successfully with key audiences.

Our CSR services

DLA Upstream can assist in understanding the CSR environment in which our clients' businesses operate and in meeting the CSR challenges they face. We offer the following services:

- **CSR issues identification.** We can help identify CSR activity that matches a client's business objectives and commercial activities and that will, over time, contribute to stakeholder relations, brand loyalty and corporate reputation. CSR activity has to be indicative of the actions of the whole company, be directed by key senior personnel and engage all key stakeholders. Priority issues should be identified and addressed, enhancing the company's relations with its key stakeholders.
- **Benchmarking audit.** For clients we assess approach, position and policy on a number of key CSR issues. The aim is to identify areas of strength, highlight areas of potential vulnerability and benchmark performance against other equivalent companies' CSR programmes.
- **Stakeholder relations.** We identify and engage with our clients' key stakeholders. On many occasions the most constructive feedback and identification of issues can come from key stakeholders.

- **Stakeholder communications training.** DLA can assist in training key personnel in how to engage with the most important stakeholders. Each external audience has its own set of issues and priorities. Each requires a different approach. It is important that key senior personnel are prepared for all eventualities.
- **Strategy formulation and implementation.** We help develop, draft and implement a focused CSR strategy, integrated with clients' overall communications programmes. This covers both internal and external audiences, stakeholders and others.
- **Report content.** DLA can work with client companies in identifying and drafting the content of their CSR report.
- **Partnerships.** In some circumstances it may be advisable to engage in partnership activity to further a business's CSR activity. In the context of a CSR report, organizations such as Business in the Environment or Business in the Community may be appropriate partners. DLA works closely with the specialist consultancy, Context, on environmental and social reporting and systems. Depending on a business's requirements, DLA can identify potential partners in the reporting process.
- **External communications.** We help to communicate CSR achievements to key stakeholders and to the wider audience. DLA Upstream can develop an external communications programme, incorporating CSR reports, as well as social and environmental reporting and management systems, including the use of the internet to maximize CSR communications. This is, of course, also the option of using a CSR programme as part of a wider public affairs strategy.
- **Internal communications.** Most companies will have a comprehensive internal communications structure in place. Senior managers and other colleagues across the whole company will understand the relevance and purpose of communicating CSR activities to staff. DLA Upstream is experienced in helping clients make the most of existing means of internal communications. New ideas should always be welcome, and we can offer a significant amount of experience in this area.

Other services

DLA Upstream provides a range of other government relations and strategic communications services. These include:

- **Government affairs:**
  - early warning of public policy developments, with strategic advice and analysis;
  - policy research services;
  - message development and campaign strategy;

  – contact building, briefing and platform building;
  – government affairs training and advice on establishing in-house systems.

- **Corporate communications:**
  – communications audits;
  – stakeholder management and communications;
  – internal communications;
  – financial PR;
  – planning communications.

- **Media relations:**
  – media monitoring;
  – strategic advice on media tactics;
  – journalist contact programmes;
  – media training.

- **Crisis management:**
  – establishing crisis and risk management systems;
  – ongoing support during a crisis.

For further information on DLA Upstream, contact Dr Stuart Thomson, Account Director, DLA Upstream (tel: +44 (0)20 7796 6923; mobile: +44 (0)7971 142 487; fax: +44 (0)20 7796 6139).

PROFILE: EMI

EMI is the world's largest independent music company. Its business is focused on content, with a commitment to quality, long-term artist development and a growing consumer focus as defining features of its strategy.

The basis of its social responsibility programme is the belief that business should be both profitable and beneficial to society. EMI's social responsibility policy embraces the key areas of environment, employment, community, human rights, product values and suppliers and it is against this policy that the company will assess its progress as it moves forward with its CSR agenda.

This profile focuses on two parts of that policy – EMI's work in reducing its environmental impacts, and the music education strand of its community activity.

Greening a music company

EMI first adopted an environmental policy in 1991 because it believed that this was the responsible step to take. It also recognized that an environmental programme could play a role in terms of the company's long-term competitive advantage. Public reporting was introduced in 1993, and EMI found that the annual reporting process itself brought with it a number of benefits:

- It provided a continuous mechanism to raise awareness internally.
- It provided impetus to introduce change and sustain local programmes.
- It enabled better management (equipped with measurement) of key impact areas.

The implementation of environmental management systems in EMI's CD manufacturing facilities also helped bring focus in terms of firm environmental objectives and site-wide engagement with the environmental programme. Over 90 per cent of EMI's CD output now comes from plants certified to ISO14001, and manufacturing operations have worked hard to 'shrink' the environmental impact of CDs. Since 1995 this has resulted in:

- a reduction of 71 per cent in hazardous waste generated per million units produced (puo);
- a reduction of 55 per cent puo in solvent consumption;
- a reduction of 36 per cent puo in polycarbonate (the plastic CDs are made of) scrap.

Improvement programmes have not been limited to the higher-impact side of the business, however. Many EMI offices around the world have successfully reduced energy consumption, cut back on resource use and introduced waste management systems so that increasing amounts of waste are recycled. This includes ensuring that product returns or obsolete stock in the supply chain now gets recycled in all markets where the infrastructure exists to do so.

Reducing energy consumption has been a priority from the beginning, as the company has always recognized its contribution to global warming and climate change as one of its key environmental impacts. More recently, EMI has begun to address its indirect carbon emissions at source, by moving away from electricity supplies that rely on fossil fuels and thereby making a real contribution to the concept of a low-carbon economy. A switch to renewable sources of energy began in the UK in 2000, and by the end of 2002 EMI's UK electricity contracts were 100 per cent 'green'. This has played the major part in a reduction of CO_2 emissions from EMI's UK buildings of nearly 90 per cent in the period. At the beginning of 2003, the company's European manufacturing and distribution facility in the Netherlands also went green, which is providing further reductions in CO_2 emissions. What surprised EMI in both cases was that the switch was not as difficult to achieve as it had thought it might be – renewables need not be the most expensive choice.

Looking forward, EMI and the entire music industry could play an exciting role in the advent of dematerialization, as a shift to direct digital distribution of music reduces the need for physical products, print and transport. To ensure that the company understands the environmental implications of this shift, EMI participated in Forum for the Future's recent Digital Europe project; the challenge now is to ensure that the potential environmental benefits are realized.

Harnessing the power of music

For many years, EMI has been a strong supporter of the performing arts in the UK, and has long-standing relationships with organizations ranging from London's Royal Opera House, the English National Opera and the Royal Albert Hall to Tate Britain and the National Gallery. More recently, the company has tried to broaden the music-related support it provides in its community engagement activities.

As a music company, EMI is fortunate in that its core product involves creativity, relaxation and entertainment. Together with the other arts, music is one of the principal trainers of the imagination, and imagination brings with it a host of benefits from scientific discovery and technological advance to better jobs and improved communities. What EMI now looks for is ways in which it can use its particular strengths – both its products and its people – to make a positive contribution to society that is also in the long-term interests of the company. Improving access to music, particularly for young people, is one of those areas.

EMI's flagship project in the UK is the Music Sound Foundation (MSF), an independent music education charity established in 1997 to commemorate the centenary of EMI Records. MSF's aim is to improve music education and it does this in three ways:

- providing capital funding to schools wishing to become performing arts colleges under the government's Specialists Schools scheme (MSF is the largest single sponsor of performing arts colleges in England);
- providing annual bursaries to six UK music colleges;
- providing grants for instrument purchase to non-specialist schools and students in full-time education, and to music teachers for training.

Continuing engagement with the schools whose performing arts bids it supports is central to MSF's philosophy, and wherever possible it is represented on the board of governors. The charity also plays an active role in the Specialist Schools college community, organizing annual two- and three-day events in London that give both teachers and students of music an inside look at various aspects of arts organizations and the music industry. More recently MSF and EMI have worked together to extend this to workshops with teachers, looking at ways in which the music industry can best support education.

EMI continues to support MSF with an annual donation and by funding its administration costs, which enables the charity to pass virtually 100 per cent of its investment income on to the people and places that most need it.

In 2003, EMI became a founding partner of the new Roundhouse, London's legendary music venue. The vision for the regenerated Roundhouse is to be not just a dynamic performing space, but also an exciting creative centre for young people. The company's partnership will enable it to participate in a variety of learning programmes linked to music and the industry. EMI has also begun to work with The Prince of Wales Arts & Kids Foundation, participating in programmes that provide access to professional arts performances, together with pre-performance workshops, for schoolchildren who might otherwise not have the opportunity.

The company is one of the founding sponsors of Masterprize, a biennial international competition now firmly established as the world's leading prize for composers. Masterprize's outreach work is significant, with a parallel education programme in which numerous UK youth orchestras use the finalists' compositions for workshops and performances.

Finally, the company is fortunate to have been involved in the development of, and is pleased to be a signatory to, the UK government's 'music manifesto' for music education, and looks forward to helping with that agenda for progress over the next few years.

PROFILE: FRIENDS PROVIDENT

Friends Provident was founded in 1832 by Quakers to alleviate the hardship of families facing misfortune. Today, as we pay out millions of pounds every working day, improving the quality of life of our customers and their families remains our aim.

Quaker origins have placed ethics at the heart of our business for 170 years and provide the basis for our long-standing commitment to social responsibility. We recognize that the long-term interests of our stakeholders are best served by acting in a responsible manner. Our success depends on the trust and confidence placed in us by our customers, shareholders, business partners and staff, the communities around us and society at large.

Vision

Our vision of our corporate responsibilities is based on:

- CSR as part of good corporate governance;
- the relative materiality of our different direct and indirect impacts;
- the integration of CSR into routine business planning and decision making;
- balancing CSR with other key business drivers.

In conjunction with our stakeholders we have developed a Statement of Business Principles, which sets out our core values, outlines our responsibilities and explains how we will live up to our principles. Underpinning these principles is a framework of CSR-related policies.

Impact

Friends Provident has both direct and indirect impacts on society. Our direct impacts are:

- environmental management:
  - emissions;
  - energy efficiency;
  - waste;
  - resource use (principally paper);
- labour practices;
- community investment.

Our indirect impacts occur through:

- responsible investment and engagement;
- supply chain management.

Action

Environment

Compared to some industries our direct impact on the environment is low. Our most significant impact is the indirect influence we can exert through responsible investing in its various forms. We are a pioneer of responsible investing in the UK. In 1984 Friends Provident launched the first ethical unit trust, the Stewardship Unit Trust. Our Stewardship range of products, now operated through our asset management business, is still the market leader with 31 per cent of the £4 billion screened fund market in the UK.

And in 2000, the group launched 'reo' (responsible engagement overlay), a state-of-the-art overlay to the investment management system for engaging with companies on a range of social and environmental issues. We believe that companies that change the way they behave to address these issues also enhance their long-term shareholder value.

Finally, in 2004 Friends Provident became the first company fully to disclose the way it votes with the shareholdings held in other companies at those companies' meetings. Records are available from 1 January 2003 and include all votes cast world-wide, for all companies where we have a shareholding. The monthly reports list the way we have voted and include a brief explanation of every vote not supporting the boards' recommendations. Our decision to make this information public is driven by a desire to be open and accountable to our policyholders whose money we are invest-ing and to raise industry standards on this issue.

Despite their relatively low significance, we still have a structured programme for managing our direct environmental impacts. Climate change is probably the biggest environmental issue facing the planet. Friends Provident has reduced its energy-related emissions by 80 per cent over the last three years and fuel-related emissions by more than 50 per cent over the same time period.

We cannot, however, eliminate emissions altogether, so we also look for ways to offset or neutralize them. We have teamed up with Future Forests and Greener Solutions to sponsor an opportunity for people to recycle their old mobile phones and support reforestation by doing so. The phones are used for parts or sold at low cost into the developing world. This generates an income, part of which flows to Future Forests to support their CarbonNeutral forestry programme.

Energy efficiency is tackled through building management systems and education programmes, and the amount of waste sent to landfill and our use of water and paper have all been reduced over recent years by sound environmental housekeeping.

Employment practices

Motivated employees are a key factor in the long-term success of any business, and creating the right culture is crucial to recruiting and retaining the best people. As a result of our responsible employment practices we have been rated as one of the UK's best workplaces three years running. This is supported by our annual employee opinion survey, which shows that overall satisfaction remains despite a period of unprecedented change for the company. We work closely with the union Amicus, with which we liaise on all employee-related matters, and our approach to health and safety has won awards from RoSPA.

Community investment

Our main charitable giving is channelled through the Friends Provident Charitable Foundation, a charity with wide grant-making powers. We facilitate payroll giving and currently have in excess of 10 per cent of employees participating compared to a national average of just 2 per cent. Through payroll giving, as well as being able to support a charity of their choice, employees are also given the option of sponsoring a child in a third world country through a unique link-up with the aid agency World Vision.

To improve the financial literacy of future generations we support 'pfeg' (Personal Finance Education Group). We partner Barnardo's in an initiative called Future Citizens, promoting citizenship to students across the country. Education is also a key theme of our company-wide volunteering programmes for which employees receive paid-time leave.

Supplier chain management

We have a progressive programme for addressing social and environmental issues in our supply chain centred on risk profiles, which we have established for core product areas. Our programme covers both the suppliers themselves and their products.

Process

Friends Provident has a well-developed and integrated CSR management system, which includes the following features:

- main board responsibility;
- a group-wide steering committee chaired by a main board director, which meets quarterly;
- a CSR manager;
- defined roles and responsibilities across the group;
- performance indicators for all main impact areas;
- an objective and target-setting mechanism built into the company's strategic and business planning process;
- an internal education and communications programme;
- an internal verification process.

CSR risks and opportunities are routinely identified through the group's risk management process. Key CSR-related risks that have been assessed include recruitment and retention of key employees; reputational issues; responsible investing; community relations; human rights; mis-selling issues; and bribery and corruption. The main opportunities are strengthening our reputation and the growth of the responsible investment market for both screened funds and engagement services.

To establish our principles, policy framework and performance indicators we undertook a programme of stakeholder engagement and have developed a matrix that maps issues against different stakeholder groups. We continue to talk with our stakeholders and take opportunities to link into existing research programmes to ensure this matrix remains up to date.

PROFILE: INNOVEST STRATEGIC VALUE ADVISORS

Innovest Strategic Value Advisors is an international investment research firm specializing in analysing 'non-traditional' drivers of risk and shareholder value, including companies' performance on environmental, social, and strategic governance issues. Innovest has been recognized recently by several independent commentators as the leading firm in the world in this area.

Founded in 1998, the firm currently has over US$1.1 billion under structured sub-advisory mandates with asset management partners including State Street Global Advisors, ING Investment Management, IDEAM, and ABP Investments.

Innovest also provides custom portfolio analysis and research to more than 30 major institutional investors including Hermes, Schroders, Cazenove, and Rockefeller & Co, as well as to leading pension funds in the United States, the UK, Continental Europe and Scandinavia. Innovest currently has clients in over 20 countries.

The firm's founder, Dr Matthew Kiernan, is a former senior partner with KPMG and was the first director of what is now the World Business Council for Sustainable Development in Geneva. Innovest's chairman Jim Martin was chief investment officer for North America's largest pension fund, TIAA-CREF, for over 15 years. Innovest's advisory directors have also included former senior executives from such leading financial companies as Citibank, a former G7 finance minister, and the former chairman of Royal Dutch/Shell.

Innovest's principal outside investor is ABP (Netherlands), currently the third-largest pension fund in the world, and one of the most highly regarded. Innovest has a professional staff of over 40, with offices in New York, Toronto, London, Paris and Madrid.

Products and services

Industry and company research reports

Industry sector reports
These provide in-depth analysis of over 30 high-risk industry sectors, identifying environmentally driven risks and opportunities for each sector and including detailed profiles on as many as 40 companies per sector.

Company reports

These include EcoValue'21®, Intangible Value Assessment™ and CarbonValue™ environmental/sustainability rating reports, which are detailed profiles of company performance on environmental, social, and strategic governance issues. Over 2,200 global companies in over 50 industrial sectors are followed by Innovest research analysts.

Specialized reports

Innovest has leveraged its analysts' combined financial, environmental and industry expertise, in addition to its proprietary global research database, to provide clients with fresh perspectives on and analysis of the business risks and opportunities presented by a variety of global megatrends.

Clean energy

In our view, a fundamental and irreversible restructuring of the energy value chain is under way, changing the way energy is used, transformed, regulated, distributed and managed. This is presenting compelling new growth opportunities for clean energy delivery systems, fuel cells, renewables, energy management and outsourcing services, GHG abatement solutions, alternative power devices and power 'in-sourcing', advanced industrial materials, and related clean power technologies. Well-informed investors will also note the emerging market for energy and environmental commodities (green certificates, GHG credits, etc), which will assist many clean technology companies achieve their full economic potential.

Carbon finance

The Innovest Carbon Finance Practice was formed to assist our financial sector clients understand the relevance of, and craft appropriate strategic responses to, emerging carbon finance issues in respect of their investment banking, asset management, equity research and risk management activities.

The practice also works with insurance companies interested to estimate their exposure to climate-related risks across the full range of commercial underwriting interests and investment strategies, and industrial corporations aiming to compare their own risk profile and policy position against industry competitors and regional benchmarks as part of their strategic planning activities.

The Innovest carbon-profiling database currently covers several hundred companies from high-impact sectors around the world, and allows comparisons of management strategy and emissions profiles to be drawn among companies on a consistent, systematic basis using the proprietary CarbonValue'21™ platform. Using qualitative management information in tandem with estimated actual and projected

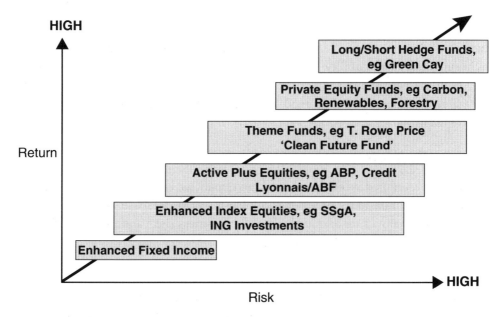

Figure A3.1 The risk/return continuum

emissions performance data, the potential financial costs for different companies to achieve emissions reduction targets can be estimated and expressed in terms of impact to market capitalization, earnings or other financial metrics.

Asset management sub-advisory services

One of Innovest's principal activities is working with our asset management partners and others to design and provide ongoing research support to a variety of 'sustainability-enhanced' funds. Specifically designed as value-added overlays, EcoValue'21®, Intangible Value Assessment™ and CarbonValue™ can be used as complements to, rather than substitutes for, existing investment strategies. They can, therefore, add value and risk-adjusted performance benefits to a wide variety of investment styles and products: active, passive, enhanced index, long-only, long-short, value, growth, sector-focused, and others. This allows Innovest and its partners to tailor a wide variety of products to the specific risk/return objectives of our clients (see Figure A3.1).

Key aspects of Innovest's approach

- We believe that companies' ability to handle political, environmental, labour and human rights risks are powerful proxies and leading indicators for their *overall* management quality – *or* the lack thereof. Management quality, in turn, is the single greatest determinant of companies' financial performance.

- Innovest's analysis is therefore designed primarily to assist our clients to construct and manage portfolios that out-perform *financially.*
- We do *not* screen out entire industry sectors, unless specifically instructed by clients to do so. Our 'screens' are *positive* ones, and seek out sources of value creation and competitive advantage in companies.
- Where necessary to reduce tracking error, we may not even screen out individual *companies* altogether; we simply increase/decrease their weightings in the portfolio.
- We work *with* the asset managers our clients choose; we seek to *add* to their research and analysis, *not* to replace or compete with it.

Further information is available from Dr Matthew Kiernan, Chief Executive (tel: (+) 905 707 0876 extn 204; e-mail: mkiernan@innovestgroup.com) or Mr Peter Wilkes, Managing Director (tel: (+) 212 421 2000 extn 216; e-mail: pwilkes@innovestgroup.com), or on the website, www.innovestgroup.com.

PROFILE: ISIS ASSET MANAGEMENT

Putting our mouth where our money is…

As Europe's leading socially responsible investment (SRI) house, ISIS has more ethically screened assets under management than any other fund manager in the City and more corporate engagement activity under way than virtually anywhere in the world.

This means that having a watertight policy on corporate social responsibility (CSR) is not just desirable, but is part of our identity. Central to our investment approach is our belief that companies run in accordance with socially responsible guidelines are more effective and, ultimately, more profitable entities. That is why we use our influence as a major stakeholder to try to encourage the adoption of up-to-date CSR practices.

This means we have two good reasons for making sure that our own 'house' is in good order when it comes to corporate social responsibility.

Managing the message

In total, ISIS manages £20.4 billion (as at 31 December 2003) of equities for various client investors. Responsible engagement overlay (reo®) – the name given to our process of responsible shareholder voting and engagement on governance and SRI issues – applies to £19.4 billion of this. In addition, ISIS also holds mandates for reo® overlay on a further £3.1 billion of assets not directly managed by the company. In total then, ISIS carries out responsible voting and corporate engagement activity on behalf of £22.4 billion of equity holdings, making us a leading voice on how investee companies should approach sustainability issues such as human rights and climate change.

This is the primary way in which we manage our 'indirect' influence on our surroundings. This, we believe, provides a valuable service to our clients by helping to build the long-term value of the companies in which we invest, benefiting all stakeholders and the wider community. We are able to offer clients access to this type of socially responsible risk management through our range of ethically screened funds and our reo® engagement service.

Direct responsibility for implementing the governance, social, environmental and ethical (SEE) objectives of these products lies with the ISIS governance and socially responsible investment (GSRI) team. This 12-strong team, led by ISIS director Karina Litvack, is the largest of its kind in Europe. The extent of the team's experience in financial markets and environmental and social policy making, and of the operational implementation of CSR initiatives is second to none, ensuring that ISIS remains at the cutting edge of this discipline.

To track the impact of our reo® activity, we measure the numbers of 'milestones' achieved. This is taken to be any occasion when our participation in an issue can be seen to be a significant influencing factor in achieving an improvement in corporate governance or SEE risk management.

In 2003 ISIS set a target of 47 reo® milestones for the GSRI team, which actually succeeded in generating 83 such markers over the course of the year.

Some of our larger milestones

In 2003, ISIS recruited a group of 37 investors worldwide to endorse the Investors' Statement on Transparency in the Extractive Sectors. In total, this group represented US $3 trillion of investor assets – the highest figure ever registered for an initiative of this type – and attracted the support of some of the world's largest and previously uncommitted investors.

The statement called for extractive companies to vouch support for the Extractive Industries Transparency Initiative (EITI), which aims to reduce corruption and the misappropriation of revenues in resource-rich countries. The initiative, which was warmly welcomed by Prime Minister Tony Blair, has since seen 19 companies – including all of the world's largest publicly listed extractive companies – announce their support for the initiative.

Other key initiatives of the last year or so included:

- Work on protecting biodiversity in the form of our ground-breaking research into the sustainability of palm oil sourcing, entitled 'New risks in old supply chains: where does your palm oil come from?'
- 'Waste and workers in the tech sector: benchmarking the ICT giants on supply and disposal chains' dealt with similar concerns, this time in the information, communications and technology sector.
- Our handbook written in partnership with Washington-based NGO Trace, entitled *The High Cost of Small Bribes*, called for tighter corporate guidelines and behaviour over the making of 'facilitation' payments.
- Our 2003 annual review of corporate governance also trod new ground. Producing the guide, which explains the rationale behind how we cast our votes at company AGMs and the trends that we saw emerging as a result, was another industry first and one that is yet to be emulated.

More generally though, successful engagement tends to take the form of a series of small steps in progress as companies acknowledge areas of concern and slowly build up the momentum required to effect real change. For individual examples of how we identify and pursue such opportunities with investee companies, see our contribution to Chapter 7 of this book.

Whatever we might wish of our investee companies in terms of their approach to CSR issues is relevant within our own business. Our performance in the Business in the Community Corporate Responsibility Index is indicative of how we approach such issues. We were particularly pleased that, in 2003, ISIS rated as one of the very top-performing companies in the index.

Similarly, ISIS's leadership in this field was recognized in 2003 through the winning of the Global Pensions SRI Manager of the Year Award and the Sustainable Asset Management 2003 Award from the Corporation of London's Liveable City Awards 2003, run by the Corporation of London. ISIS was able to repeat its success here early in 2004 when it again lifted both the top prize for sustainable and ethical investment and the overall winner prize in the Corporation of London's Liveable City Awards 2004.

Ensuring we make the grade

ISIS operates a corporate governance committee chaired by the company's chief investment officer (CIO), which seeks to ensure that not only do all the companies in which we invest strive for the standards of corporate governance we require, but that ISIS itself matches up to these values.

ISIS operates a structured system of risk management encompassing reputational and other SEE risks through quarterly 'Turnbull' management reporting. It is here that we review existing policies at least annually in light of emerging new standards of best practice.

We also work closely with our majority shareholder, Friends Provident plc, on CSR policies across the group. All individuals responsible for managing aspects of our CSR have such responsibilities detailed in their role profile and, wherever relevant, CSR performance is taken into account in determining performance-related bonuses.

All of our CSR and corporate governance policies are available to view on the company's website at www.isisam.com.

ISIS also participates in widely published CSR performance indices including Business in the Community's (BITC) Corporate Responsibility Index and the FTSE4 Good Index.

During 2003 we were able to strengthen further our internal management of such issues through establishing a SEE workshop or 'groundswell group' made up of representatives from throughout the organization. The group now operates as a think-tank for identifying practical CSR initiatives that complement existing programmes and that can be 'championed' by group members through to full implementation.

We have also implemented a CSR management system that formalizes accountabilities through CSR targets, enabling us to track our performance. This system mirrors that employed by our in-house GSRI team.

Such processes allow us to monitor our own environmental impact in exactly the same way as that which we encourage from investee companies.

For example, we quantify and set MACC2 targets for our environmental impact in areas such as our annual carbon dioxide emissions, use of electricity and gas and the level of paper recycling undertaken each year. Similarly, we have sought ways to reduce the number of business miles travelled by staff, particularly by air. This makes good sense in cost terms as well as benefiting the environment as a whole.

ISIS Asset Management is authorized and regulated by the FSA. All sources are ISIS Asset Management unless stated otherwise. Further information is available on the website, www.isisam.com.

PROFILE: THIS IS MISTRA

The Foundation for Strategic Environmental Research – Mistra – funds and organizes 26 major research programmes whose purpose is to solve strategic environmental problems.

A Mistra programme is a meeting place between two worlds. One is the research community, driven by a desire constantly to advance the frontiers of knowledge. The other world is that of action, where environmental problems are to be solved, where environmentally compatible products, services and production processes are to compete in a market, where legislation can be amended and where conflicting interests should be able to coexist and agreements be reached as a result of international environmental negotiations.

A Mistra programme is intended to supply corporate and public sector users, international negotiators, decision makers at various levels, special interest organizations and lobby groups with the latest scientific findings, regardless of sectoral boundaries. A Mistra programme should also supply the research community with problems defined by users, regardless of the borders between various areas of scientific research.

The board of directors of Mistra and its chairman are appointed by the Swedish government. The Royal Swedish Academy of Sciences (KVA), the Royal Swedish Academy of Engineering Sciences (IVA) and the Royal Academy of Agriculture and Forestry (KSLA) continuously review Mistra's activities.

Mistra's target groups

Mistra exists for:

- Research scientists wishing to study problems whose solution may be of use in the efforts being made to achieve an environmentally sustainable society.
- Swedish companies wishing to be world leaders at developing environmentally compatible products, services or production processes.
- Public authorities and legislators wishing to tighten regulatory frameworks for activities that are potentially harmful to the environment. Stricter regulations must have a sound scientific basis.
- International negotiators endeavouring to achieve global environmental improvements. A Mistra programme must meet the quality requirements of the global scientific community as well as the negotiator's need for specific information.
- Non-governmental organizations and others endeavouring to achieve a sustainable society.

Mistra's approach to quality assurance

To assure quality, each proposed programme is evaluated by Swedish and international experts on the basis of four criteria:

- The proposed environmental problem must be relevant.
- The proposed research programme must be of high scientific quality.
- There must be a plan as to how the research findings will be put to practical use.
- The proposed project management team must possess the requisite documented skills.

Each programme is run by a programme board whose task is to keep the focus on problem solving and practical utility of research findings. Nowadays, the programme board is appointed at the planning stage of the research programme, before Mistra has decided to approve it. The board is then formally responsible for appointing a programme director and for preparing a plan for implementing the programme.

Mistra programmes must also be systematically reported. There are four important criteria:

- a summary of the scientific findings;
- a summary of the practical utility of the research and the use to which it can be put;
- an account of the way competence has been developed and where the researchers have gone to conduct their research;
- a plan for handing over the baton, ie how the research findings are to be put to use.

Mistra actively monitors every programme throughout its existence.

Mistra is now in its 10th year. One way we are marking this anniversary is by reviewing our own operations, by asking and questioning:

- What have we achieved, and how far can we go?
- Are we focusing on the right things and are we doing them in the right way?
- As a small player in a small country (Sweden), is Mistra achieving its aims?

We have a large sum of money at our disposal. How can we best use our resources? Should we invest large amounts in research now with a view to solving problems quickly, or should we make sure that the money lasts for a long time?

Bridging boundaries

Mistra's task is to support research whose findings can be put into practice. Synthesis and interdisciplinary cooperation are keywords. There are technical solutions to many of the major environmental problems of today. But one of the greatest challenges is to change human behaviour.

Climate change is an obvious example. Most people know what causes it and what needs to be done to deal with the problem. But still we carry on as usual, as if the problem did not exist. What can politicians, the corporate sector and organizations do to change the daily habits of individuals?

If research programmes are to bring about real change, greater commitment will be needed from the non-technical sector, from behavioural scientists, city planners and others capable of communicating messages to influence people and their lifestyles. We must achieve better cooperation to solve environmental problems – before it is too late.

PROFILE: NATIONAL GRID TRANSCO, RESPONSIBLE BUSINESS DELIVERING SHAREHOLDER VALUE

About us

National Grid Transco is one of the world's largest utility companies focused on delivering energy safely, reliably and efficiently. What we do is essential to the economies of the countries and regions in which we operate as well as the comfort and well-being of the millions of citizens who depend on our services.

These are long-term responsibilities that must be fulfilled in conjunction with our duty to create value for our shareholders. This depends on the continuing financial success of National Grid Transco, the prudent and effective management of all forms of risk, and the lasting trust of our other stakeholders, including governments, regulatory bodies and the communities in which we operate.

Our Framework for Responsible Business

In a climate where the governance arrangements in large companies are increasingly under scrutiny, our board has implemented a transparent approach, driven by our 'Framework for Responsible Business' and underpinned by a suite of group-wide policies.

Our Framework for Responsible Business has been developed with the help of more than 4,000 stakeholders from a variety of backgrounds in the UK and the USA including employees, government, pressure groups, media, investors, customers and regulators. It is based on three critical business goals:

- sustainable growth;
- profits with responsibility;
- investing in the future.

So, our Framework for Responsible Business is the yardstick by which we are able to ensure that the decisions we take will deliver long-term value. Underpinning our business goals is a series of business values through which we take account of economic, environmental, employee and social considerations.

Sustainable growth

We are constantly looking to expand and grow our business by transferring our skills to new markets. Growth needs to be sustainable if we are to bring long-term value both to our shareholders and to others. So, as we look to grow our business, we aim to:

- contribute to the economic growth of the countries in which we operate through the way in which we manage and invest in our business;
- act with honesty and integrity as we undertake and develop our business;
- protect the future of our business by proactively managing existing and future non-financial and environmental risks;
- employ and develop a talented and diverse workforce;
- employ the right number of people with the right skills for the work we have to do;
- treat our employees fairly;
- act in accordance with all laws and regulations;
- respect human rights.

Profits with responsibility

For our business to be sustainable, we must be profitable. However, increasing our profitability at any cost is neither sustainable nor acceptable. We therefore have to be responsible in the way in which we generate our profits. So we aim to:

- improve our efficiency without compromising the reliability and integrity of our operations;
- maintain a sound system of internal financial control;
- be efficient in our use of natural resources;
- keep our waste to a minimum and increase the economic value of any waste we produce;
- help protect the environment for future generations, including making our contribution to minimizing climate change;
- safeguard each other and those who work with us by operating an injury-free and healthy workplace, and protect the safety of the public through the integrity of our operations;
- help our employees balance work with their other commitments;
- respect our customers and suppliers by conducting our business in a professional manner;
- be open and constructive in the dialogue we have with our stakeholders.

Investing in the future

As a responsible business, our commercial success enables us to invest in the future in a way that benefits our shareholders, our employees, the environment and society. This investment is a reflection of our desire to be a long-term business. So we:

- seek to deliver progressively increasing returns for our shareholders;
- enable others to contribute to economic growth by providing high-quality, dependable services;

- improve, where we can, the environmental status of the land on which we operate;
- contribute to the development of new laws and initiatives aimed at improving the environment and the quality of life;
- develop our employees so that they can add value to the company, to themselves and to society;
- recognize and reward our employees for the contribution they make;
- encourage and support investment in the community both through the activities of our employees and through our financial contributions, with an emphasis on developing partnerships.

The commitment of our board

Our reputation as a company that manages its business in a responsible manner is very important to us. Corporate governance has increasingly focused on the effective management of non-financial risks and the way corporate responsibility is integrated into day-to-day decision making.

The board has overall responsibility for matters of corporate responsibility and has established the Risk and Responsibility Committee chaired by James Ross, our deputy chairman. The Risk and Responsibility Committee has responsibility for reviewing the non-financial risks, strategies, policies, management, targets and performance of the company and, where appropriate, our suppliers and contractors.

Our progress so far

Operating in a responsible manner is a day-to-day activity that permeates our business. We do not have large-scale CSR programmes, preferring instead to drive the business values through everything we do. By taking this approach we believe we can make a lasting difference.

Having started out on this journey in 2002, we are proud of our achievements in this area. So far, we have been listed in the top 20 per cent of the UK Business in the Community's Corporate Responsibility Index and the 'Premier League' of the associated environmental index, while certain fund managers have rated us as an industry leader for our management of environmental and social issues. We are also a constituent of the FTSE4Good and Dow Jones World Sustainability indices.

Our website, www.ngtgroup.com/responsibility, provides further details of the progress we are making in implementing our Framework for Responsible Business.

Appendix 4

Human rights in the global workplace – The UN Human Rights Norms for Business: towards legal accountability

CONTENTS

Introduction

Why do we need the UN Human Rights Norms for Business?

How were the UN Human Rights Norms for Business prepared?

What is the legal status of the UN Human Rights Norms for Business?

What issues do the UN Human Rights Norms for Business cover? (Positive and negative obligations on businesses; Scope of the UN Human Rights Norms for Business; Which businesses are covered by the UN Norms?)

What are the key substantive provisions? (Non-discrimination; Protection of civilians and laws of war; Use of security forces; Workers' rights; Corruption, consumer protection and human rights; Economic, social and cultural rights; Human rights and the environment; Indigenous peoples' rights)

What implementation and enforcement mechanisms are provided by the UN Human Rights Norms for Business?

Why is a legal approach preferable? Do we need more regulation?

Will complying with the UN Norms add costs to companies?

Will the UN Norms add to bureaucracy?

Are the UN Norms too generic?

Will the UN Norms place unrealistic obligations on business?

Will the UN Norms make companies responsible for what governments should be doing?

Will the UN Norms delay the creation of binding regulations or undercut current standards?

What is the relationship between the UN Human Rights Norms for Business and the Global Compact?

Conclusion

Recommendations (To governments; To companies and business associations; To the World Bank, regional banks and other financial institutions; To the UN and OECD; To non-governmental organizations and advocates)

Notes

International human rights standards relevant to business
Commentary on the Norms on the Responsibilities of Transnational Corporations and Other Business Enterprises with Regard to Human Rights

INTRODUCTION

Human rights organizations have addressed concerns to businesses for a number of years. Recognizing that economic globalization has expanded the reach of corporate power, advocates have struggled to ensure that companies, no less than other significant actors, are brought within the framework of international human rights rules. A significant step in this direction was taken in August 2003 by the UN Sub-Commission on the Promotion and Protection of Human Rights when it approved the UN Norms on the Responsibilities of Transnational Corporations and Other Business Enterprises with Regard to Human Rights.

This document provides an introduction to the UN Human Rights Norms for Business. It answers a number of questions about the UN Norms and their legal status, and includes an overview of their development, background on the drafting process, and a description of the content and legal status of the UN Norms. The text of the UN Norms and their Commentary are reproduced on pages 325–51.

In Amnesty International's view, governments, advocates and companies should support the UN Human Rights Norms for Business as offering an authoritative and comprehensive statement of the responsibilities of companies in relation to human rights.[1]

The UN Norms provide clarity and credibility amidst many competing voluntary codes that too often lack international legitimacy and provide far less detail on human rights issues. AI supports efforts to strengthen the legal basis for the UN Norms, and calls on governments, companies and advocates to disseminate and apply the UN Norms.

WHY DO WE NEED THE UN HUMAN RIGHTS NORMS FOR BUSINESS?

The nature and scale of the most recent wave of economic globalization has created a world that is more interdependent than ever before. Since the end of the Cold War there has been an explosion in international trade and financial relationships and a corresponding expansion in the power of large transnational corporations and financial institutions. Capital, labour, technology, and other resources are increasingly directed towards or away from investment destinations based mainly on economic factors. A growing number of businesses operate across boundaries in ways that exceed the regulatory capacities of any one national system. Economically powerful actors may dramatically influence policy – whether for good or ill – and thereby impact on the human rights of millions of people.

There is a well-established body of international human rights rules, dating back over half a century. The UN Charter of 1945 and the Universal Declaration of Human Rights (UDHR) of 1948 spelt out a number of important human rights obligations. In many instances, these obligations have now become customary international law, binding on all states. While primarily addressed to states, the Universal Declaration also calls on 'every organ of society' to respect, promote, and secure human rights – laying the foundation for obligations which apply not only to states but also to non-state actors including private businesses. Additional treaties elaborating the obligations in the UDHR followed. The growing acceptance of international human rights laws and standards made it inevitable that companies would face the question of their responsibilities towards human rights.

While the activities of businesses provide employment for countless millions, a variety of daily business practices may negatively affect human rights. Companies may violate human rights through their employment practices, or through the manner in which their production processes impact on workers, communities and the environment. Companies may also be implicated in abuses through their association with repressive governments or political authorities.

Scrutiny of the activities of global businesses led many companies to adopt codes of conduct during the 1980s and 1990s, and an emerging movement on corporate social responsibility led to numerous voluntary codes. However, voluntary codes of conduct, while a welcome signal of corporate commitment, have proved insufficient. Many codes are very vague in regard to human rights commitments. As far as Amnesty International is aware, fewer than 50 companies even refer explicitly to human rights in their codes. Whether unique to the company, or adopted sector-wide, voluntary codes too often lack international legitimacy.[2] This has resulted in calls for a more detailed, comprehensive, and effective instrument. The UN Human Rights Norms for Business took shape in this context.

> The good news is that there are now tools to help companies with this task. For example, the UN Sub-Commission on the promotion and protection of human rights has recently adopted a set of human rights norms for business, that pull together in one document international human rights standards that are relevant to business – relating to labour issues, health and environmental issues, discrimination issues, security issues, etc.
>
> Mary Robinson, Director, Ethical Globalization Initiative
> Formerly UN High Commissioner for Human Rights

The UN Human Rights Norms for Business set out, in a single, succinct statement, a comprehensive list of the human rights obligations of companies. They highlight best practice and various modes of monitoring and enforcement. In addition to setting a standard that business can measure itself against, the UN Norms are also a useful benchmark against which national legislation can be judged (to determine if governments are living up to their obligations to protect rights by ensuring that appropriate regulatory frameworks are in place). The UN Norms are also an important reference and campaigning tool for non-governmental organizations (NGOs) and grassroots activists.

HOW WERE THE UN HUMAN RIGHTS NORMS FOR BUSINESS PREPARED?

The UN Human Rights Norms for Business were adopted by the UN Sub-Commission on the Promotion and Protection of Human Rights. The Sub-Commission is a body of independent human rights experts within the UN system. The experts are elected from all regions of the world by the UN Commission on Human Rights, which oversees the Sub-Commission's work. The Sub-Commission has drafted a number of human rights documents that have eventually developed into treaties or other UN standards, including the International Convention on the Elimination of All Forms of Racial Discrimination, the UN Declaration on the Human Rights of Non-Nationals, and others.[3]

In 1997, the Sub-Commission prepared a study on the connection between transnational corporations and human rights. The following year a Working Group on the Working Methods and Activities of Transnational Corporations consisting of five Sub-Commission experts was established and in 1999 it began the process of preparing a draft Code of Conduct for companies. Prior laws and codes were researched and an extensive consultation process carried out. The consultation process solicited broad input and heard testimony from relevant stakeholders, including many businesses as well as unions, human rights organizations and other NGOs. After four years' work, the Working Group forwarded the draft UN Human Rights Norms for Business to the Sub-Commission, which unanimously adopted them in August 2003.

The UN Norms include a 'Commentary', which provides useful, authoritative guidance on the meaning of specific terms, the scope of particular provisions, and the legal basis for different obligations (with references to other international standards). When adopting the UN Norms, the Sub-Commission also welcomed the Commentary.[4]

> The Business Leaders Initiative on Human Rights programme is committed to testing the value of [the UN Norms] as a driver for change, and contributing to the work of existing networks and associations committed to promoting human rights in business.
>
> The Business Leaders Initiative on Human Rights
> (ABB, Barclays, MTV Europe, National Grid Transco, Novartis, Novo Nordisk,
> The Body Shop International)

WHAT IS THE LEGAL STATUS OF THE UN HUMAN RIGHTS NORMS FOR BUSINESS?

The UN Norms are not a formal treaty, which states ratify and thereby assume binding legal obligations. On the other hand, the UN Norms are clearly more authoritative than the many codes of conduct adopted by companies, and are a significant advance over other existing standards. For a number of reasons, the UN Norms are likely to have some legal effect:

- International law is not static, and is in a constant process of development. To the extent that the UN Norms command attention and respect, and are used by advocates and companies, they will take on greater force. If national and international tribunals and courts begin to make reference to and apply the UN Norms, their legal effect will increase.
- Unlike codes of conduct (whether adopted by individual companies or sector-wide), the UN Norms result from a formal, UN-authorized, and consultative process. The process leading to the UN Norms is similar to that resulting in other 'soft law' standards, some of which are now seen as part of customary international law.
- In their tone and approach, the UN Human Rights Norms for Business are self-consciously *normative*. Unlike the Organization for Economic Cooperation and Development (OECD) Guidelines for Multinational Enterprises, and the International Labour Organization (ILO) Tripartite Declaration of Principles, the UN Norms are not limited by clauses emphasizing their non-regulatory nature.
- All of the substantive human rights provisions in the UN Norms are drawn from existing international law and standards. The novelty of the UN Norms is to apply these – within the limits of businesses' impact and influence – to private enterprises, but even in doing so to draw on a wide range of international practice (including the practice of companies themselves). The UN Norms, in other words, are well-grounded in law.

Some argue that international law applies only between states, or that human rights obligations apply only to states, and that the UN Norms cannot create legal obligations for companies. This view can no longer be credibly maintained. While the major human rights treaties place obligations on states in the first instance, the substantive obligations those states are bound to enforce include ensuring respect for human rights – not least by non-state actors such as enterprises and individuals. For example, the ILO Conventions follow the formal structure whereby states ensure compliance by companies. However, it is recognized that they place substantive duties such as nondiscrimination and respecting freedom of association directly on companies.

There is growing acceptance that international human rights treaties create obligations – at least indirectly – on companies.[5] For those conventions drafted so as to place liability directly on businesses the issue is beyond doubt.[6]

It is true that because most international human rights treaties were drafted with primary attention to the obligations of states (as opposed to businesses or individuals), the scope of those obligations when applied to companies may appear somewhat uncertain in some contexts. The allocation of responsibilities between government and businesses is evolving and developing, and so is the allocation of responsibilities between enterprises and the individuals running them. All that can be said with certainty is that there is a clear trend to extend human rights obligations beyond states, including to individuals (for international crimes), armed groups, international organizations, and private enterprises.[7] The UN Norms must be seen as part of this development.

> In recent years, a major concern of our organization has been the growing power of transnational corporations at the expense of the capacity of human rights defenders. By setting forth in clear fashion the responsibilities of business leaders and managers confronting these issues, and contemplating mechanisms of monitoring and enforcement, the UN Human Rights Norms and Commentary provide a meaningful first step toward greater corporate accountability.
>
> Human Rights Watch

The Sub-Commission resolution adopting the UN Human Rights Norms for Business transmitted them to the Commission on Human Rights for information and consideration. Amnesty International hopes that the Commission will support the UN Norms, thus strengthening their legal effect (as the Commission is a formal UN body, composed of governments). Action by the Commission on Human Rights is not, however, a prerequisite for the legitimacy of the UN Norms.

WHAT ISSUES DO THE UN HUMAN RIGHTS NORMS FOR BUSINESS COVER?

The UN Human Rights Norms for Business set forth basic, minimal business obligations regarding human rights. They reaffirm that states still bear the primary responsibility for promoting and protecting human rights, but recognize that transnational corporations and other businesses, as organs of society (and collections of individuals), carry responsibilities as well. The first operative paragraph states that the responsibilities apply to businesses 'within their respective spheres of activity and influence'. This principle determines how all the succeeding paragraphs may be read and applied. That is, any duties companies have pursuant to the UN Norms are limited by the reach of their activity and influence.

Positive and negative obligations on businesses

Within their spheres of activity and influence (which vary between large and small enterprises), the UN Human Rights Norms for Business require companies to 'promote, secure the fulfilment of, respect, ensure respect of and protect human rights recognized in international as well as national law'. At a minimum, this requires businesses to *refrain from activities that directly or indirectly violate human rights, or benefit from human rights violations, and to use due diligence* to do no harm. The UN Norms also include the affirmative obligation to promote and work for the full protection of all human rights. The Commentary to the Norms requires businesses to use their influence to help promote and ensure respect for human rights.

To achieve both the negative obligations (to avoid complicity in violations in order to respect human rights) and the positive ones (to promote human rights), businesses can no longer be wilfully ignorant of the circumstances in which they operate; they must become much more aware of and sensitive to those circumstances, and much more engaged in taking actions to influence human rights positively.

Scope of the UN Human Rights Norms for Business

The UN Norms invoke a number of laws and standards that businesses should 'recognize and respect'. These include not only 'applicable' international norms, national laws and regulations, but also more abstract notions including 'the rule of law', the 'public interest', and 'development objectives, social, economic, and cultural policies including transparency, accountability, and prohibition of corruption'. These less precise notions generally attempt to focus corporations on *public* interests, above and beyond *private* interests. The Commentary clarifies that within their resources, businesses should encourage social progress and development by expanding economic opportunities, especially in developing and least developed countries.

> The development of an international normative framework to guide corporate behaviour is a natural step in the development and constitution of a global international society.
>
> Centro de Derechos Humanos y Ambiente (Centre for Human Rights and the Environment), Argentina

Which businesses are covered by the UN Norms?

The UN Norms apply to 'transnational corporations' and 'other business enterprises' and the definitions provided are intentionally broad. A transnational corporation is defined as an economic entity operating in two or more countries. Other business enterprises, including purely domestic enterprises, are also covered in addition to transnational corporations. This prevents transnational corporations being able to avoid the application of the UN Norms by reorganizing their operations as strictly domestic entities, conducting business through independent contracts. In addition to this broad language, the UN Norms confirm explicitly that they should be presumed to apply if the business enterprise has any relation with a transnational corporation, if the impact of its activities is not entirely local, or the activities are so serious that they affect the right to security of life and person.

WHAT ARE THE KEY SUBSTANTIVE PROVISIONS?

Non-discrimination

The prohibition of discrimination is a fundamental human rights principle, and it is included prominently in the UN Human Rights Norms for Business. Non-discrimination provides an example of both the negative obligation to refrain from violations and the affirmative obligation to promote human rights. Businesses are required not to discriminate on grounds unrelated to the job (for example, race, colour, sex, language, religion or political opinion) and as well to promote equal opportunities. The Commentary clarifies that this non-discrimination obligation extends, for example, to health status (for example HIV/AIDS or disability), sexual orientation, pregnancy, or marital status. Physical or verbal abuse in the workplace is similarly prohibited, with businesses obliged to ensure that such abuse will not be tolerated.

Protection of civilians and laws of war

The UN Human Rights Norms for Business make clear that businesses will have to ensure that they do not aid or abet human rights violations, nor benefit from war crimes such as plunder and pillage, crimes against humanity, genocide, torture, forced labour, hostage-taking, or other violations of international human rights or humanitarian law. These have been among the most serious violations in recent years. Moreover, concerns about human rights violations committed in conflict are intensifying. The UN Norms require businesses to exercise due diligence regarding the source or potential uses of goods or services, and in some instances to forego business opportunities in order to avoid complicity in, or encouragement of, human rights violations. For example, the Commentary makes clear that this provision would require businesses supplying arms, or security products or services to 'take stringent measures' to prevent use in connection with human rights violations, which would presumably include due diligence to ensure that their *customers* are not known human rights violators; that appropriate direction and training is provided, and the like. The Commentary also indicates a prohibition on the production and sale of weapons declared illegal under international law, as well as trade known to lead to human rights violations.

Use of security forces

One of the recurring patterns of companies' human rights abuses has stemmed from violations committed by security forces which have neglected local and international human rights standards. This includes, but is not limited to, situations in which extractive, energy, or other businesses have required the services of state security forces who have used excessive force against peacefully protesting indigenous communities or striking workers. Greater attention to these issues is essential, as is compliance with international instruments and due diligence procedures, and prior and ongoing consultation with affected communities. Businesses using security forces should establish policies to ensure that security-related *employees or contractors* are not known human rights violators; to provide adequate training in human rights procedures to security forces; and to incorporate human rights obligations in security contracts.

Workers' rights

Labour rights are an area where companies are likely to have a direct impact on the protection of human rights. The UN Norms and Commentary reiterate, on the one hand, the prohibitions on forced or compulsory labour and against exploitation of children, and on the other hand, the mandates for safe and healthy working conditions, remuneration that ensures an adequate standard of living, freedom of association, and the right to collective bargaining. The Commentary to the paragraph explains that workers shall have the opportunity to leave employment, and that businesses shall take action against debt bondage and contemporary forms of slavery (such as human trafficking). Prison labour is allowed only in accordance with international law, after conviction in a court of law and under public supervision. Except for light work – the definition of which emphasizes work that is not harmful to the health or development of the child – child labour prior to age 15 or the end of compulsory schooling is presumed to be exploitative.

> … The norms provide a new instrument to oblige companies to fulfil a very broad set of human rights guaranteed in different international Declarations and Conventions. The responsibility would cover the whole supply chain of companies and the employers, understood in a broad sense, would be considered liable for the offences made.
>
> WCL (World Confederation of Labour)

There might be some controversy over the provision obliging 'remuneration that ensures an adequate standard of living' – a living wage. Some economists as well as some businesses argue that any floor established for compensation unjustifiably interferes with the free market, creates inefficiencies, and in the end will reduce the number of jobs. But the UN Norms do not attempt to establish an international minimum wage. All they require is fair compensation under local standards. A job that fails to pay such fair compensation is exploitative and a violation of human rights.[8]

Corruption, consumer protection and human rights

Corruption by governmental officials undermines the rule of law, diverts resources that could be used to fulfil human rights commitments, and reinforces poverty and inequality. The UN Norms concisely restate international standards against corruption and bribery. The UN Norms also reaffirm obligations of fair and honest business practices according to consumer protection laws and standards. The UN Norms state that this includes a duty to refrain from producing or marketing harmful or even potentially harmful products. The Commentary clarifies that this is to be understood 'in the context of reasonable usage and custom'.

Economic, social and cultural rights

One result of the ideological divisions of the Cold War was that when the provisions of the Universal Declaration of Human Rights were elaborated, they were split between two treaties: the International Covenant on Civil and Political Rights and the International Covenant on Economic, Social, and Cultural Rights. After the Cold War, it again became possible to view human rights obligations as interdependent. Without protecting basic subsistence rights (such as food, water or shelter), it is difficult to exercise civil and political rights (such as free speech, fair trials or electoral participation). Conversely, the exercise of civil and political rights is often essential to overcoming discrimination and obtaining protection for economic, social and cultural rights.

The UN Human Rights Norms for Business oblige businesses to respect all human rights, and to 'contribute to their realization'. Some UN treaty bodies have already stated authoritatively that their treaties apply directly to businesses in areas including privacy,[9] food,[10] water,[11] and health.[12] The UN Norms similarly emphasize that businesses should do what they can 'within their respective spheres of activity and influence' to uphold the rights to adequate food, drinking water, the highest attainable standard of physical and mental health, housing and education. They also forthrightly support the right to development and the rights of indigenous peoples. The right to development is described as entitling 'every... person and all peoples to participate in, contribute to and enjoy economic, social, cultural and political development in which all human rights and fundamental freedoms can be fully realized'. Businesses globally can play a particularly important role in this regard.

Human rights and the environment

Pursuant to the UN Norms, businesses are obliged to comply with international and national laws, policies, and regulations on preserving the environment. This includes complying with the precautionary principle and conducting their activities so as to contribute to the wider goal of sustainable development. The precautionary principle – to err on the side of caution and refrain from actions indicating unacceptable human rights or environmental risks – may conflict with some businesses' interpretation of an entrepreneurial, risk-taking culture. For example, those companies that do not accept the emerging scientific consensus about climate change will not be receptive to the Commentary's provision that the lack of 'full scientific certainty' should not be used as a reason to delay remedial measures. On the other hand, there is growing acceptance of the precautionary principle, even if its precise meaning is ambiguous, and many companies have stated their commitment to it (for example, in the Global Compact).

> The UN Norms on Transnational Business set an important precedent in the struggle to make corporations accountable and liable for their actions everywhere and anywhere in this planet.
>
> Greenpeace

Indigenous peoples' rights

Numerous provisions of the UN Norms provide safeguards that are important for indigenous people, not least the strong guarantee of non-discrimination and the inclusion of a general commitment to respect cultural rights. The Commentary calls on companies to respect the rights of indigenous communities to own their lands and other natural resources, and their cultural and intellectual property. It specifies that companies should respect the principle of free, prior and informed consent of communities to be affected by development projects. The Commentary also states that companies should not forcibly evict communities 'without having had recourse to, and access to, appropriate forms of legal or other protection pursuant to international human rights law'. Companies should engage in periodic assessment of their compliance with the UN Norms taking into account comments from indigenous communities.

WHAT IMPLEMENTATION AND ENFORCEMENT MECHANISMS ARE PROVIDED BY THE UN HUMAN RIGHTS NORMS FOR BUSINESS?

In addition to setting out the human rights obligations of companies, the UN Norms also give attention to implementation and enforcement.

- The first mode of implementation relies on the business itself creating a more human rights oriented culture. Companies should:
  - Adopt internal operational rules complying with the UN Norms (for example, a human rights policy);
  - Incorporate the UN Norms in contracts and dealings with others;
  - Train all concerned;
  - (Over time) deal only with suppliers and other businesses which follow the UN Norms;
  - Ensure monitoring throughout the supply chain;
  - Establish confidential 'hotlines' and worker complaint mechanisms; and,
  - Periodically conduct self-evaluation, report compliance and implement remedial plans.

- Second, the Norms contemplate that their application could be assessed through external monitoring and verification, for example by existing UN human rights mechanisms. Other bodies such as unions, non-governmental organizations, ethical investment initiatives and industry groups would be encouraged to use the UN Norms as the basis for monitoring, dialogue, lobbying and campaigning activities with businesses.

These norms have been put together by people representing various backgrounds including companies. They clarify companies' social obligations already existing under international law and offer a comprehensive tool and a practical answer to both questions of what are exactly the priorities which companies should have in terms of human rights, right to work and environment and what are the aspects of companies' social management that institutional investors will take into account in their choice of investments. In particular the objective of these Norms is to take a first step towards a common legislation which would define the same rules of the game for everyone. In this respect, they should be a priority for the UN.

Batirente, a financial institution managing the pension assets of different groups of workers in Québec, Canada

● The third method of enforcement is through the state and individuals and organizations using state enforcement mechanisms. This includes publicizing the UN Norms, using them as a model for business activities, and the traditional means of passing, strengthening, and enforcing laws and regulations implementing them, and of course enforcing them in national and international courts and tribunals. Businesses must pay for any damage they cause, and both lawyers and clients can urge national and international courts and tribunals to use the UN Norms to apply damages and criminal sanctions.

WHY IS A LEGAL APPROACH PREFERABLE? DO WE NEED MORE REGULATION?

The most basic objection to the UN Norms is grounded in a resistance to normative or legal frameworks and a belief that voluntary approaches are preferable as they more easily obtain the necessary commitment from companies. This argument ignores the inability of voluntary approaches to reduce persistent abuses and achieve compliance with generally agreed substantive norms. It also ignores the historical reality that some form of legal framework is often necessary to restrain abuses.

Most importantly, perhaps, the argument against regulation ignores the fact that voluntary approaches work best for the well intentioned. Despite the interest in corporate social responsibility, the overwhelming majority of companies have no human rights policy at all, and only a few companies are prepared to make explicit commitments in this area. The UN Norms level the playing field – and particularly if they are a basis for renewed attention by governments to their own responsibilities.

WILL COMPLYING WITH THE UN NORMS ADD COSTS TO COMPANIES?

Some companies and governments object to regulation (of any sort) because they believe compliance will cost too much. In this specific context, there has been an objection to the Commentary provision that, within their 'resources and capabilities', businesses should study the human rights and environmental impacts of their activities. Such a human rights impact statement is increasingly recognized, however, as a prudent and necessary component of risk-assessment. Others have objected to the Commentary's call for companies to make environmental and human health reports publicly accessible – some object to the general call for enhanced transparency and disclosure. Although this challenges the traditional confidentiality in which decisions are made, people have a right to participate in decisions that affect them, and they can only do so if they have access to relevant information. It ought also to be clear that transparency will contribute, in the long term, to better business.

WILL THE UN NORMS ADD TO BUREAUCRACY?

Resistance for fear of bureaucratic regulation is misguided in other respects. First, the UN Norms do not call for onerous or bureaucratic regulation. Second, intelligent laws not only restrain abuses, they can also fulfil an important role in promoting better practices. Indeed, this is historically a key function of international human rights standards – setting benchmarks for national law and acting as a catalyst for progressive reform.

No serious business would argue that laws are never useful; companies depend, in fact, on regulation in many areas in order to operate. The question, therefore, is about the extent and scope of laws. Amnesty International believes that the UN Norms fill an important gap, and do not impose unreasonable demands on companies. Reflecting input not only from human rights and environmental experts and organizations, but also the business sector and unions, the UN Norms balance a normative framework with an acknowledgement of the role business can play in economic development and promotion of human rights.

ARE THE UN NORMS TOO GENERIC?

One argument against the UN Norms is that they adopt a 'one-size-fits-all' approach. This is untrue. The UN Norms are explicit that they apply within the sphere of influence and control of the respective business, and that they need to be operationally tailored by company policies (within the boundaries established by the UN Norms) to reflect the values of a given business. The UN Norms are also explicitly variable depending on resource and capability limitations. However, the value of the UN Norms lies in their universality, and, because they comprise an *international* standard, of necessity they adopt a general approach.

Those who complain about the lack of specificity of the UN Norms, therefore, are missing the point. The UN Norms offer a statement of principles, not a detailed regulatory framework. The UN Norms do not tell companies whether particular investments, in particular countries, or specific business decisions are undesirable – no law of general application could do so. The UN Norms do, however, provide the key points – from a human rights perspective – that need to be considered in making such decisions.

> The UN Norms illuminate the role expected of corporations in today's inter-connected world. They aim to reconcile the claims of shareholders and the rights of stakeholders. Equipped with these comprehensive standards, companies can combine financial efficiency with social responsibility.
>
> OECD Watch

WILL THE UN NORMS PLACE UNREALISTIC OBLIGATIONS ON BUSINESS?

Some opponents argue that the UN Norms place unrealistic expectations on businesses to 'bite the hand that feeds them' by requiring them to criticize host governments. Because the UN Norms call on businesses to take affirmative steps to fulfil their human rights obligations, they will undoubtedly require some firms to act or speak up for human rights, privately or publicly. However, companies cannot be silent witnesses to widespread human rights violations, nor can they hide behind the shield of 'respecting cultural relativism' where violations are concerned. The UN Norms do recognize that less powerful businesses need more leeway in interpreting these obligations than the more powerful.

WILL THE UN NORMS MAKE COMPANIES RESPONSIBLE FOR WHAT GOVERNMENTS SHOULD BE DOING?

Another argument used against the UN Norms is that they attempt to 'replace government with business' by obligating business to provide essential goods or services (such as housing, food, healthcare or education) that are government responsibilities. This argument is misleading, because the UN Norms clearly distinguish between the primarily responsibilities of governments and the secondary responsibilities of business within their respective sphere of influence.

WILL THE UN NORMS DELAY THE CREATION OF BINDING REGULATIONS OR UNDERCUT CURRENT STANDARDS?

The UN Norms have also been criticized by some – including certain NGOs – on the grounds that they fall short of creating binding legal obligations and that a binding, international treaty on this issue is needed. Leaving aside the very real difficulties in achieving such a treaty in the short term, the UN Norms are a key contribution to developing international legal norms in relation to business and human rights. If this development is to include an international treaty, the UN Norms will assist in laying its foundations.

For those who fear that the current status of the UN Norms may undermine existing international legal obligations, it is important to draw attention to the 'savings clause', which is intended to ensure that businesses 'pursue the course of conduct that is the most protective of human rights'. This clause provides that the UN Norms do not diminish, restrict, or adversely affect national human rights obligations, more protective human rights norms, or business obligations in fields other than human rights.

The UN Norms are clearly intended to reinforce the approach that is most protective of human rights, whether that is found in international law, national law, or other sources, now or in the future. The UN Norms make a valuable contribution in clarifying the widespread scope and type of international human rights laws pertaining to global business, and the fact that despite their dramatic improvement over present practice, they are still expressed as 'minimum' standards which businesses are encouraged to exceed.

WHAT IS THE RELATIONSHIP BETWEEN THE UN HUMAN RIGHTS NORMS FOR BUSINESS AND THE GLOBAL COMPACT?

The Global Compact states nine general principles, two of which relate to human rights. The UN Human Rights Norms for Business go into much greater detail, and reference key international instruments that provide much more significant guidance to transnational and other businesses confronting these issues, as well as the individuals and groups affected by and monitoring compliance.

The Draft Norms have already initiated significant educational efforts and we are looking forward to seeing how these efforts could contribute positively to the Global Compact.

Global Compact Office

In Amnesty International's view, the UN Norms are essential for understanding the scope of the general human rights provisions in the Global Compact. Amnesty International believes that the Global Compact office should formally indicate that the UN Norms are an authoritative guide to Principles 1 and 2 of the Global Compact.

CONCLUSION

The UN Human Rights Norms for Business are the first authoritative and comprehensive set of global business standards bearing the UN imprimatur – a powerful symbol of legitimacy and universality. They mark a clear step forward from voluntary codes of conduct towards establishing clear legal obligations in this area.

We welcome the UN Human Rights Norms and Commentary as a valuable road-map for companies, guiding them through the thicket of human rights challenges before them.

International Business Leaders Forum

Companies ought to respect human rights, avoid being complicit in human rights abuses and, within their sphere of influence, do what they can to promote human rights principles. On this there is widespread agreement. The UN Human Rights Norms for Business provide a set of universal principles that set out in further detail what these commitments mean in practice. There is, therefore, a strong moral argument for supporting them.

There is also a strong business case in favour of the UN Norms. Businesses which respect ethics and law, and which have prudent risk management policies, have better prospects of surviving and prospering over the long run than those that do not. As the UN Norms are used and their legal authority continues to grow, they will place businesses on a more level playing field. The UN Norms are a practical device to help reveal risk-management issues and ensure that they are confronted and addressed.

The time has come for a stronger international framework for corporate accountability, and the UN Human Rights Norms for Business are a significant contribution to this. By bringing together in one place all the major international human rights, labour rights, and environmental laws and standards pertaining to global business, and by surveying key international instruments and best practice, the UN Norms provide helpful guidance and leadership opportunities for businesses willing to comply with their legal and ethical responsibilities. They also provide a useful tool for advocates who are engaging businesses on human rights issues.[13]

RECOMMENDATIONS

Amnesty International urges the widest possible use and dissemination of the UN Human Rights Norms for Business. We believe they will be of interest and practical benefit to all those concerned to ensure companies respect human rights and use their influence in ways that promote human rights. We offer the following recommendations.

To governments

- Use the UN Human Rights Norms for Business as a benchmark to ensure domestic legislation is adequate, and to inform the interpretation of the concept of due diligence by domestic courts.
- Establish the necessary legal and administrative framework for ensuring that transnational corporations and other business enterprises abide by the UN Human Rights Norms for Business.

To companies and business associations

- Adopt, disseminate and implement a code of conduct which complies with the UN Human Rights Norms for Business.
- Prepare and implement operational guidelines to apply the UN Human Rights Norms for Business.
- Apply the UN Human Rights Norms for Business in contracts and other dealings with contractors, subcontractors and any other associates.
- Organize training seminars and workshops for staff and facilitate similar events with associates and within industry associations to raise awareness of the UN Human Rights Norms for Business.

To the World Bank, regional banks and other financial institutions

- Evaluate companies in which you invest by using the UN Human Rights Norms for Business as a benchmark.
- Use the UN Human Rights Norms for Business in the development of criteria to assess the human rights impact of potential projects.

To the UN and OECD

- The UN Commission on Human Rights should support the UN Norms, including through a resolution welcoming their adoption. It should assist in efforts to disseminate the UN Norms to all governments.
- The Office of the Global Compact should issue a strong statement of support for the UN Human Rights Norms for Business, and indicate that the UN Norms are to be used as a reference for understanding Compact Principles 1 and 2 (on human rights).
- The Office of the Global Compact should disseminate the UN Human Rights Norms for Business through its networks.
- The OECD should indicate that the UN Human Rights Norms for Business are to be used as a reference for understanding the scope of the human rights clause in the OECD Guidelines for Multinational Enterprises.

To non-governmental organizations and advocates

- Use the UN Human Rights Norms for Business in your monitoring, campaigning and lobbying activities and in your dialogues with companies, governments and other bodies.
- Support the further dissemination and development of the UN Human Rights Norms for Business.

Notes

[1] Available at www.business-humanrights.org.
[2] Voluntary, company-specific codes of conduct are distinct from the International Labour Organization's Tripartite Declaration of Principles concerning Multinational Enterprises and Social Policy, www.ilo.org, or the Guidelines for Multinational Enterprises developed by the Organisation for Economic Cooperation and Development, www.oecd.org.
[3] For example, the Sub-Commission did the first draft on Article 27 (rights of minorities) of the International Covenant on Civil and Political Rights, GA res 2200A (XXI), 21 UN GAOR Supp (No. 16) at 52, UN Doc A/6316 (1966), 999 UNTS 171, entered into force 23 Mar 1976. Also, the International Convention on the Elimination of All Forms of Racial Discrimination, 660 UNTS 195, entered into force 4 Jan 1969. The Declaration on the Protection of All Persons from Enforced Disappearances, GA res 47/133, 47 UN GAOR Supp (No. 49) at 207, UN Doc. A/47/49 (1992) adopted by General Assembly resolution 47/133 of 18 Dec 1992. And the Declaration on the Human Rights of Individuals Who Are Not Nationals of the Country in Which They Live, GA res 40/144, annex, 40 UN GAOR Supp (No. 53) at 252, UN Doc A/40/53 (1985).

4   Available at www.business-humanrights.org.
5   See Beyond Voluntarism: Human rights and the developing international legal obligations of companies, International Council on Human Rights Policy, 2002.
6   These include, for example, the International Convention on Civil Liability for Oil Pollution Damage, 1969, and the Convention on Civil Liability for damage resulting from activities dangerous to the environment, 1993.
7   In addition to state obligations to ensure respect for customary international law norms (for example the prohibition of genocide, torture, or slavery), all major human rights and humanitarian law treaties call on states to ensure that non-state actors respect the human rights obligations therein.
8   See for example, the International Covenant on Economic, Social, and Cultural Rights, Art 11 (right to adequate standard of living).
9   Human Rights Committee, General Comment 16 (Twenty-third session, 1988).
10 Committee on Economic, Social and Cultural Rights, General Comment 12, Right to adequate food, UN Doc E/C.12/1999/5.
11 Committee on Economic, Social and Cultural Rights, General Comment 15, The right to water, UN Doc E/C.12/2002/11.
12 Committee on Economic, Social and Cultural Rights, General Comment 14, The right to the highest attainable standard of health, UN Doc E/C.12/2000/4.
13 Hundreds of non-governmental organizations have already joined Amnesty International in endorsing the Norms. For further information, in addition to Amnesty International's website (www.amnesty.org), see also www.business-humanrights.org, the website of the Business and Human Rights Resource Centre (an independent organization working in partnership with Amnesty International and leading academic institutions).

COMMENTARY ON THE NORMS ON THE RESPONSIBILITIES OF TRANSNATIONAL CORPORATIONS AND OTHER BUSINESS ENTERPRISES WITH REGARD TO HUMAN RIGHTS

UN DOC E/CN.4/SUB.2/2003/38/REV.2 (2003)

Preamble

Bearing in mind the principles and obligations under the Charter of the United Nations, in particular the preamble and Articles 1, 2, 55, and 56, inter alia to promote universal respect for, and observance of, human rights and fundamental freedoms,

Recalling that the Universal Declaration of Human Rights proclaims a common standard of achievement for all peoples and all nations, to the end that Governments,

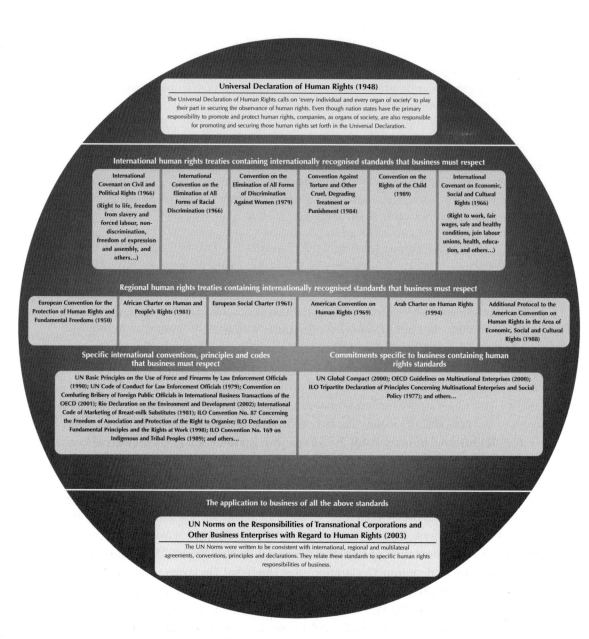

Figure A4.1 International human rights standards relevant to business

other organs of society and individuals shall strive, by teaching and education, to promote respect for human rights and freedoms, and, by progressive measures, to secure universal and effective recognition and observance, including of equal rights of women and men and the promotion of social progress and better standards of life in larger freedom,

Recognizing that even though States have the primary responsibility to promote, secure the fulfilment of, respect, ensure respect of and protect human rights, transnational corporations and other business enterprises, as organs of society, are also responsible for promoting and securing the human rights set forth in the Universal Declaration of Human Rights,

Realizing that transnational corporations and other business enterprises, their officers and persons working for them are also obligated to respect generally recognized responsibilities and norms contained in United Nations treaties and other international instruments such as the Convention on the Prevention and Punishment of the Crime of Genocide; the Convention against Torture and Other Cruel, Inhuman or Degrading Treatment or Punishment; the Slavery Convention and the Supplementary Convention on the Abolition of Slavery, the Slave Trade, and Institutions and Practices Similar to Slavery; the International Convention on the Elimination of All Forms of Racial Discrimination; the Convention on the Elimination of All Forms of Discrimination against Women; the International Covenant on Economic, Social and Cultural Rights; the International Covenant on Civil and Political Rights; the Convention on the Rights of the Child; the International Convention on the Protection of the Rights of All Migrant Workers and Members of Their Families; the four Geneva Conventions of 12 August 1949 and two Additional Protocols thereto for the protection of victims of war; the Declaration on the Right and Responsibility of Individuals, Groups and Organs of Society to Promote and Protect Universally Recognized Human Rights and Fundamental Freedoms; the Rome Statute of the International Criminal Court; the United Nations Convention against Transnational Organized Crime; the Convention on Biological Diversity; the International Convention on Civil Liability for Oil Pollution Damage; the Convention on Civil Liability for Damage Resulting from Activities Dangerous to the Environment; the Declaration on the Right to Development; the Rio Declaration on the Environment and Development; the Plan of Implementation of the World Summit on Sustainable Development; the United Nations Millennium Declaration; the Universal Declaration on the Human Genome and Human Rights; the International Code of Marketing of Breast-milk Substitutes adopted by the World Health Assembly; the Ethical Criteria for Medical Drug Promotion and the 'Health for All in the Twenty-First Century' policy of the World Health Organization; the Convention against Discrimination in Education of the United Nations Educational, Scientific, and Cultural Organization; conventions and recommendations of the International Labour Organization; the Convention and Protocol relating to the Status of Refugees; the African Charter on Human and Peoples' Rights; the American Convention on Human Rights; the European Convention for the Protection of Human Rights and Fundamental Freedoms; the Charter of Fundamental Rights of the European Union; the Convention on Combating Bribery of Foreign Public Officials in International Business Transactions of the Organization for Economic Cooperation and Development; and other instruments,

Taking into account the standards set forth in the Tripartite Declaration of Principles Concerning Multinational Enterprises and Social Policy and the Declaration on Fundamental Principles and Rights at Work of the International Labour Organization,

Aware of the Guidelines for Multinational Enterprises and the Committee on International Investment and Multinational Enterprises of the Organization for Economic Cooperation and Development,

Aware also of the United Nations Global Compact initiative which challenges business leaders to 'embrace and enact' nine basic principles with respect to human rights, including labour rights and the environment,

Conscious of the fact that the Governing Body Subcommittee on Multinational Enterprises and Social Policy, the Committee of Experts on the Application of Standards, as well as Committee on Freedom of Association of the International Labour Organization have named business enterprises implicated in States' failure to comply with Conventions No. 87 concerning the Freedom of Association and Protection of the Right to Organize and No. 98 concerning the Application of the Principles of the Right to Organize and Bargain Collectively, and seeking to supplement and assist their efforts to encourage transnational corporations and other business enterprises to protect human rights,

Conscious also of the Commentary on the Norms on the responsibilities of transnational corporations and other business enterprises with regard to human rights, and finding it a useful interpretation and elaboration of the standards contained in the Norms,

Taking note of global trends which have increased the influence of transnational corporations and other business enterprises on the economies of most countries and in international economic relations, and of the growing number of other business enterprises which operate across national boundaries in a variety of arrangements resulting in economic activities beyond the actual capacities of any one national system,

Noting that transnational corporations and other business enterprises have the capacity to foster economic well-being, development, technological improvement and wealth, as well as the capacity to cause harmful impacts on the human rights and lives of individuals through their core business practices and operations, including employment practices, environmental policies, relationships with suppliers and consumers, interactions with Governments and other activities,

Noting also that new international human rights issues and concerns are continually emerging and that transnational corporations and other business enterprises often are involved in these issues and concerns, such that further standard-setting and implementation are required at this time and in the future,

Acknowledging the universality, indivisibility, interdependence and interrelatedness of human rights, including the right to development, which entitles every human person and all peoples to participate in, contribute to and enjoy economic, social, cultural and political development in which all human rights and fundamental freedoms can be fully realized,

Reaffirming that transnational corporations and other business enterprises, their officers – including managers, members of corporate boards or directors and other executives – and persons working for them have, inter alia, human rights obligations and responsibilities and that these human rights norms will contribute to the making and development of international law as to those responsibilities and obligations,

Solemnly proclaims these Norms on the Responsibilities of Transnational Corporations and Other Business Enterprises with Regard to Human Rights and urges that every effort be made so that they become generally known and respected.

A. General obligations

1. States have the primary responsibility to promote, secure the fulfilment of, respect, ensure respect of and protect human rights recognized in international as well as national law, including ensuring that transnational corporations and other business enterprises respect human rights. Within their respective spheres of activity and influence, transnational corporations and other business enterprises have the obligation to promote, secure the fulfilment of, respect, ensure respect of and protect human rights recognized in international as well as national law, including the rights and interests of indigenous peoples and other vulnerable groups.

Commentary

(a) This paragraph reflects the primary approach of the Norms and the remainder of the Norms shall be read in the light of this paragraph. The obligation of transnational corporations and other business enterprises under these Norms applies equally to activities occurring in the home country or territory of the transnational corporation or other business enterprise, and in any country in which the business is engaged in activities.

(b) Transnational corporations and other business enterprises shall have the responsibility to use due diligence in ensuring that their activities do not contribute directly or indirectly to human abuses, and that they do not directly or indirectly benefit from abuses of which they were aware or ought to have been aware. Transnational corporations and other business enterprises shall further refrain from activities that would undermine the rule of law as well as governmental and other efforts to promote and ensure respect for human rights, and shall use their influence in order to help promote and ensure respect for human rights. Transnational corporations and other business enterprises shall inform themselves of the human rights impact of their principal activities and major proposed activities so that they can further avoid complicity in human rights abuses. The Norms may not be used by States as an excuse for failing to take action to protect human rights, for example, through the enforcement of existing laws.

B. Right to equal opportunity and non-discriminatory treatment

2. Transnational corporations and other business enterprises shall ensure equality of opportunity and treatment, as provided in the relevant international instruments and national legislation as well as international human rights law, for the purpose of eliminating discrimination based on race, colour, sex, language, religion, political opinion, national or social origin, social status, indigenous status, disability, age – except for children, who may be given greater protection – or other status of the individual unrelated to the inherent requirements to perform the job or of complying with special measures designed to overcome past discrimination against certain groups.

Commentary

(a) Transnational corporations and other business enterprises shall treat each worker with equality, respect and dignity. Examples of the other sorts of status on the basis of which discrimination should be eliminated are health status (including HIV/AIDS, disability), marital status, capacity to bear children, pregnancy and sexual orientation. No worker shall be subject to direct or indirect physical, sexual, racial, psychological, verbal, or any other discriminatory form of harassment or abuse as defined above. No worker shall be subject to intimidation or degrading treatment or be disciplined without fair procedures. Transnational corporations and other business enterprises shall establish a work environment in which it is clear that such discrimination will not be tolerated. These responsibilities shall be carried out in accordance with the Code of Practice on HIV/AIDS and the World of Work and the Code of Practice on

Managing Disability in the Workplace of the International Labour Convention (ILO) and other relevant international instruments.

(b) Discrimination means any distinction, exclusion, or preference made on the above-stated bases, which has the effect of nullifying or impairing equality of opportunity or treatment in employment or occupation. All policies of transnational corporations and other business enterprises, including, but not limited to, those relating to recruitment, hiring, discharge, pay, promotion and training, shall be non-discriminatory.

(c) Particular attention should be devoted to the consequences of business activities that may affect the rights of women and particularly in regard to conditions of work.

(d) Transnational corporations and other business enterprises shall treat other stakeholders, such as indigenous peoples and communities, with respect and dignity, and on a basis of equality.

C. Right to security of persons

3. Transnational corporations and other business enterprises shall not engage in nor benefit from war crimes, crimes against humanity, genocide, torture, forced disappearance, forced or compulsory labour, hostage-taking, extrajudicial, summary or arbitrary executions, other violations of humanitarian law and other international crimes against the human person as defined by international law, in particular human rights and humanitarian law.

Commentary

(a) Transnational corporations and other business enterprises which produce and/or supply military, security, or police products/services shall take stringent measures to prevent those products and services from being used to commit human rights or humanitarian law violations and to comply with evolving best practices in this regard.

(b) Transnational corporations and other business enterprises shall not produce or sell weapons that have been declared illegal under international law. Transnational corporations and other business enterprises shall not engage in trade that is known to lead to human rights or humanitarian law violations.

4. Security arrangements for transnational corporations and other business enterprises shall observe international human rights norms as well as the laws and professional standards of the country or countries in which they operate.

Commentary

(a) Transnational corporations and other business enterprises, their officers, workers, contractors, subcontractors, suppliers, licensees and distributors, and natural or other legal persons that enter into any agreement with the transnational corporation or business enterprise shall observe international human rights norms, particularly as set forth in the Convention against Torture and Other Cruel, Inhuman or Degrading Treatment or Punishment; the Rome Statute of the International Criminal Court; the United Nations Basic Principles on the Use of Force and Firearms by Law Enforcement Officials; the United Nations Code of Conduct for Law Enforcement Officials; and emerging best practices developed by the industry, civil society and Governments.

(b) Business security arrangements shall be used only for preventive or defensive services and they shall not be used for activities that are exclusively the responsibility of the State military or law enforcement services. Security personnel shall only use force when strictly necessary and only to the extent proportional to the threat.

(c) Security personnel shall not violate the rights of individuals while exercising the rights to freedom of association and peaceful assembly, to engage in collective bargaining, or to enjoy other related rights of workers and employers, such as are recognized by the International Bill of Human Rights and the Declaration on Fundamental Principles and Rights at Work of the ILO.

(d) Transnational corporations and other business enterprises shall establish policies to prohibit the hiring of individuals, private militias and paramilitary groups, or working with units of State security forces or contract security firms that are known to have been responsible for human rights or humanitarian law violations. Transnational corporations and other business enterprises shall engage with due diligence in investigations of potential security guards or other security providers before they are hired and ensure that guards in their employ are adequately trained, guided by and follow relevant international limitations with regard, for example, to the use of force and firearms. If a transnational corporation or other business enterprise contracts with a State security force or a private security firm, the relevant provisions of these Norms (paragraphs 3 and 4 as well as the related commentary) shall be incorporated into the contract and at least those provisions should be made available upon request to stakeholders in order to ensure compliance.

(e) Transnational corporations and other business enterprises using public security forces shall consult regularly with host Governments and, where appropriate, non governmental organizations and communities concerning the impact of their security arrangements on local communities. Transnational corporations and other business enterprises shall communicate their policies regarding ethical conduct and human rights, and express their desire that security be provided in a manner consistent with those policies by personnel with adequate and effective training.

D. Rights of workers

5. Transnational corporations and other business enterprises shall not use forced or compulsory labour as forbidden by the relevant international instruments and national legislation as well as international human rights and humanitarian law.

Commentary

(a) Transnational corporations and other business enterprises shall not use forced or compulsory labour, as forbidden in the ILO Forced Labour Convention, 1930 (No. 29) and the Abolition of Forced Labour Convention, 1957 (No. 105) and other relevant international human rights instruments. Workers shall be recruited, paid, and provided with just and favourable conditions of work. They shall take all feasible measures to prevent workers falling into debt bondage and other contemporary forms of slavery.

(b) Workers shall have the option to leave employment and the employer shall facilitate such departure by providing all the necessary documentation and assistance.

(c) Employers shall have resort to prison labour only in the conditions spelled out in ILO Convention No. 29, which allows such labour only as a consequence of a conviction in a court of law provided that the work or service is carried out under the supervision and control of a public authority and that the person concerned is not hired out to or placed at the disposal of private individuals, companies or associations.

6. Transnational corporations and other business enterprises shall respect the rights of children to be protected from economic exploitation as forbidden by the relevant international instruments and national legislation as well as international human rights and humanitarian law.

Commentary

(a) Economic exploitation of children includes employment or work in any occupation before a child completes compulsory schooling and, except for light work, before the child reaches 15 years of age or the end of compulsory schooling.

Economic exploitation also includes the employment of children in a manner that is harmful to their health or development, will prevent children from attending school or performing school-related responsibilities, or otherwise is not consistent with human rights standards such as the Minimum Age Convention (No. 138) and Recommendation (No. 146), the Worst Forms of Child Labour Convention (No. 182) and Recommendation (No. 190) and the Convention on the Rights of the Child. Economic exploitation does not include work done by children in schools for general, vocational, or technical education or in other training institutions.

(b) Transnational corporations and other business enterprises shall not employ any person under the age of 18 in any type of work that by its nature or circumstances is hazardous, interferes with the child's education, or is carried out in a way likely to jeopardize the health, safety, or morals of young persons.

(c) Transnational corporations and other business enterprises may employ persons aged 13 to 15 years in light work if national laws or regulations permit. Light work is defined as work which is not likely to be harmful to the health or development of the child, and will not prejudice school attendance, participation in vocational orientation, training programmes approved by competent authority, or the child's capacity to benefit from the instruction received.

(d) Transnational corporations and other business enterprises shall consult with Governments on the design and implementation of national action programmes to eliminate the worst forms of child labour consistent with ILO Convention No. 182. Transnational corporations and other business enterprises using child labour shall create and implement a plan to eliminate child labour. Such a plan shall assess what will happen to children when they are no longer employed in the business and include measures such as withdrawing children from the workplace in tandem with the provision of suitable opportunities for schooling, vocational training and other social protection for the children and their families, for example by employing the parents or older siblings or engaging in other measures consistent with ILO Recommendations Nos. 146 and 190.

7. Transnational corporations and other business enterprises shall provide a safe and healthy working environment as set forth in relevant international instruments and national legislation as well as international human rights and humanitarian law.

Commentary

(a) Transnational corporations and other business enterprises bear responsibility for the occupational health and safety of their workers and shall provide a working environment in accordance with the national requirements of the countries in which they are located and with international standards such as those found in the International Covenant on Economic, Social and Cultural Rights; ILO Conventions Nos. 110 (Plantations, 1958), 115 (Radiation Protection Convention, 1960), 119 (Guarding of Machinery Convention, 1963), 120 (Hygiene (Commerce and Offices) Convention, 1964), 127 (Maximum Weight Convention, 1967), 136 (Benzene Convention, 1971), 139 (Occupational Cancer Convention, 1974), 147 (Merchant Shipping, 1976), 148 (Working Environment (Air Pollution, Noise and Vibration) Convention, 1977), 155 (Occupational Safety and Health Convention, 1981), 161 (Occupational Health Services Convention, 1985), 162 (Asbestos Convention, 1986), 167 (Safety and Health in Construction Convention, 1988), 170 (Chemicals Convention, 1990), 174 (Prevention of Major Industrial Accidents Convention, 1993), 176 (Safety and Health in Mines Convention, 1995), 183 (Maternity Protection, 2000) and other relevant recommendations; as well as ensuring their application under ILO Conventions Nos. 81 (Labour Inspection Convention, 1947), 129 (Labour Inspection (Agriculture) Convention, 1969), 135 (Workers' Representatives Convention, 1971), and their successor conventions. Such a safe and healthy work environment for women and men shall aid in the prevention of accidents and injuries arising out of, linked with, or occurring within the course of work. Transnational corporations and other business enterprises shall also take into account the particular needs of migrant workers as set forth in the Migrant Workers (Supplementary Provisions) Convention, 1975 (No. 143) and the International Convention on the Protection of the Rights of All Migrant Workers and Members of Their Families.

(b) Consistent with paragraph 15 (a), transnational corporations and other business enterprises shall make available information about the health and safety standards relevant to their local activities. The information shall also include arrangements for training in safe working practices and details on the effects of all substances used in manufacturing processes. In particular, and additionally consistent with paragraph 15 (e), transnational corporations and other business enterprises shall make known any special hazards that tasks or conditions of work involve and the related measures available to protect the workers.

(c) Transnational corporations and other business enterprises shall provide, where necessary, measures to deal with emergencies and accidents, including first-aid arrangements. They also shall provide, at their expense, personal protective clothing and equipment when necessary. Further, they shall incur expenses for occupational health and safety measures.

(d) Transnational corporations and other business enterprises shall consult and cooperate fully with health, safety and labour authorities, workers' representatives and their organizations and established safety and health organizations on matters of occupational health and safety. They shall cooperate in the work of international organizations concerned with the preparation and adoption of international safety and health standards. Where appropriate, matters relating to safety and health should be incorporated in agreements with the representatives of the workers and their organizations. Transnational corporations and other business enterprises shall examine the causes of safety and health hazards in their industry and work to implement improvements and solutions to those conditions, including the provision of safe equipment at least consistent with industry standards. Further, they shall monitor the working environment and the health of workers liable to exposure to specified hazards and risks. Transnational corporations and other business enterprises shall investigate work-related accidents, keep records of incidents stating their cause and remedial measures taken to prevent similar accidents, ensure the provision of remedies for the injured, and otherwise act in accordance with paragraph 16 (e).

(e) Consistent with paragraph 16 (e), transnational corporations and other business enterprises shall also: (i) respect the right of workers to remove themselves from work situations in which there is a reasonable basis for concern about present, imminent and serious danger to life or health; (ii) not subject them to consequences as a result; and further (iii) not require them to return to work situations as long as the condition continues.

(f) Transnational corporations and other business enterprises shall not require any worker to work more than 48 hours per week or more than 10 hours in one day. Voluntary overtime for workers shall not exceed 12 hours per week and shall not be expected on a regular basis. Compensation for such overtime shall be at a rate higher than the normal rate. Each worker shall be given at least one day off in every seven-day period. These protections may be adjusted to meet the different needs of management personnel; construction, exploration and similar workers who work for short periods (eg a week or two) followed by a comparable period of rest; and professionals who have clearly indicated their personal desire to work more hours.

8. Transnational corporations and other business enterprises shall provide workers with remuneration that ensures an adequate standard of living for them and their families. Such remuneration shall take due account of their needs for adequate living conditions with a view towards progressive improvement.

Commentary

(a) Transnational corporations and other business enterprises shall provide workers with fair and reasonable remuneration for work done or to be done, freely agreed upon or fixed by national laws or regulations (whichever is higher), payable regularly and at short intervals in legal tender, so as to ensure an adequate standard of living for workers and their families. Operations in the least developed countries shall take particular care to provide just wages. Wages shall be paid, consistent with international standards such as the Protection of Wages Convention, 1949 (No. 95). Wages are a contractual obligation of employers that are to be honoured even into insolvency in accordance with Workers' Claims (Employer's Insolvency) Convention, 1992 (No. 173).

(b) Transnational corporations and other business enterprises shall not deduct from a worker's wages already earned as a disciplinary measure, nor shall any deduction from wages be permitted under conditions or to an extent other than as prescribed by national laws or regulations, or fixed by a collective agreement or arbitration award. Transnational corporations and other business enterprises shall also avoid taking actions to undermine the value of employee benefits, including pensions, deferred compensation and health care.

(c) Transnational corporations and other business enterprises shall keep detailed written records on each worker's hours of work and wages paid. Workers shall be informed in an appropriate and easily understandable manner before they enter employment and when any changes take place as to the conditions in respect of wages, salaries and additional emoluments under which they are employed. At the time of each payment of wages, workers shall receive a wage statement informing them of such particulars relating to the pay period concerned as the gross amount of wages earned, any deduction which may have been made, including the reasons therefore, and the net amount of wages due.

(d) Transnational corporations and other business enterprises shall not limit in any manner the freedom of workers to dispose of their wages, nor shall they exert any coercion on workers to make use of company stores or services, where such stores exist. In cases in which the partial payment of wages in the form of allowances in kind is authorized by national laws or regulations, collective agreements, or arbitration awards, transnational corporations and other business enterprises shall ensure that such allowances are appropriate for the personal use and benefit of workers and their families and that the value attributed to such allowances is fair and reasonable.

(e) In determining a wage policy and rates of remuneration, transnational corporations and other business enterprises shall ensure the application of the principle of equal remuneration for work of equal value and the principle of equality of opportunity and treatment in respect of employment and occupation, in accordance with international standards such as the Equal Remuneration Convention, 1951 (No. 100), The Discrimination in Employment and Occupation Convention, 1958 (No. 111) and the Workers with Family Responsibilities Convention, 1981 (No. 156).

9. Transnational corporations and other business enterprises shall ensure freedom of association and effective recognition of the right to collective bargaining by protecting the right to establish and, subject only to the rules of the organization concerned, to join organizations of their own choosing without distinction, previous authorization, or interference, for the protection of their employment interests and for other collective bargaining purposes as provided in national legislation and the relevant conventions of the International Labour Organization.

Commentary

(a) Transnational corporations and other business enterprises shall respect workers' and employers' freedom of association consistent with the Freedom of Association and Protection of the Right to Organize Convention, 1948 (No. 87) and other international human rights law. They shall respect the rights of workers' organizations to function independently and without interference, including with respect to the right of workers' organizations to draw up their constitutions and rules, to elect their representatives, to organize their administration and activities and to formulate their programmes. Further, they shall refrain from discriminating against workers by reason of trade union membership or participation in trade union activities, and shall refrain from any interference that restricts these rights or impedes their lawful exercise. They shall ensure that the existence of workers' representatives does not undermine the position of the union established consistent with international standards, and that workers' representatives are entitled to bargain collectively only where there is no such union in the company. Where appropriate in the local circumstances, multinational enterprises shall support representative employers' organizations.

(b) Transnational corporations and other business enterprises shall recognize workers' organizations for the purpose of collective bargaining consistent with the Right to Organize and Collective Bargaining Convention, 1949 (No. 98) and other international human rights law. They shall respect the right of workers to strike, to submit grievances, including grievances as to compliance with these Norms, to fair and impartial persons who have the authority to redress any abuses found, and to be protected from suffering prejudice for using those procedures, consistent with the norms contained in the Collective Bargaining Convention, 1981 (No. 154).

(c) Transnational corporations and other business enterprises shall enable representatives of their workers to conduct negotiations on their terms and conditions of employment with representatives of management who are authorized to make decisions about the issues under negotiation. They shall further give workers and their representatives access to information, facilities and other resources, and ensure internal communications, consistent with international standards such as the Workers' Representatives Convention, 1971 (No. 135) and the Communications within the Undertaking Recommendation, 1967 (No. 129) that are relevant and necessary for their representatives to conduct negotiations effectively and without unnecessary harm to legitimate interests of employers.

(d) Transnational corporations and other business enterprises shall abide by provisions in collective bargaining agreements that provide for the settlement of disputes arising over their interpretation and application and also by decisions of tribunals or other mechanisms empowered to make determinations on such matters. Transnational corporations and other business enterprises jointly with the representatives and organizations of workers shall seek to establish voluntary conciliation machinery, appropriate to national conditions, which may include provisions for voluntary arbitration, to assist in the prevention and settlement of industrial disputes between employers and workers.

(e) Transnational corporations and other business enterprises shall take particular care to protect the rights of workers from procedures in countries that do not fully implement international standards regarding freedom of association, the right to organize and the right to bargain collectively.

E. Respect for national sovereignty and human rights

10. Transnational corporations and other business enterprises shall recognize and respect applicable norms of international law, national laws and regulations, as well as administrative practices, the rule of law, the public interest, development objectives, social, economic and cultural policies including transparency, accountability and prohibition of corruption, and authority of the countries in which the enterprises operate.

Commentary

(a) Transnational corporations and other business enterprises, within the limits of their resources and capabilities, shall encourage social progress and development by expanding economic opportunities – particularly in developing countries and, most importantly, in the least developed countries.

(b) Transnational corporations and other business enterprises shall respect the right to development, which all peoples are entitled to participate in and contribute to, and the right to enjoy economic, social, cultural and political development in which all human rights and fundamental freedoms can be fully realized and in which sustainable development can be achieved so as to protect the rights of future generations.

(c) Transnational corporations and other business enterprises shall respect the rights of local communities affected by their activities and the rights of indigenous peoples and communities consistent with international human rights standards such as the Indigenous and Tribal Peoples Convention, 1989 (No. 169). They shall particularly respect the rights of indigenous peoples and similar communities to own, occupy, develop, control, protect and use their lands, other natural resources, and cultural and intellectual property. They shall also respect the principle of free, prior and informed consent of the indigenous peoples and communities to be affected by their development projects. Indigenous peoples and communities shall not be deprived of their own means of subsistence, nor shall they be removed from lands which they occupy in a manner inconsistent with Convention No. 169. Further, they shall avoid endangering the health, environment, culture and institutions of indigenous peoples and communities in the context of projects, including road building in or near indigenous peoples and communities. Transnational corporations and other business enterprises shall use particular care in situations in which indigenous lands, resources, or rights thereto have not been adequately demarcated or defined.

(d) Transnational corporations and other business enterprises shall respect, protect and apply intellectual property rights in a manner that contributes to the promotion of technological innovation and to the transfer and dissemination of technology, to the mutual advantage of producers and users of technological knowledge, in a manner conducive to social and economic welfare, such as the protection of public health, and to a balance of rights and obligations.

11. Transnational corporations and other business enterprises shall not offer, promise, give, accept, condone, knowingly benefit from, or demand a bribe or other improper advantage, nor shall they be solicited or expected to give a bribe or other improper advantage to any Government, public official, candidate for elective post, any member of the armed forces or security forces, or any other individual or organization. Transnational corporations and other business enterprises shall refrain from any activity which supports, solicits, or encourages States or any other entities to abuse

human rights. They shall further seek to ensure that the goods and services they provide will not be used to abuse human rights.

Commentary

(a) Transnational corporations and other business enterprises shall enhance the transparency of their activities in regard to payments made to Governments and public officials; openly fight against bribery, extortion and other forms of corruption; and cooperate with State authorities responsible for combating corruption.
(b) Transnational corporations and other business enterprises shall not receive payment, reimbursement, or other benefit in the form of natural resources without the approval of the recognized Government of the State of origin of such resources.
(c) Transnational corporations and other business enterprises shall assure that the information in their financial statements fairly presents in all material respects the financial condition, results of operations and cash flows of the business.

12. Transnational corporations and other business enterprises shall respect economic, social and cultural rights as well as civil and political rights and contribute to their realization, in particular the rights to development, adequate food and drinking water, the highest attainable standard of physical and mental health, adequate housing, privacy, education, freedom of thought, conscience, and religion and freedom of opinion and expression, and shall refrain from actions which obstruct or impede the realization of those rights.

Commentary

(a) Transnational corporations and other business enterprises shall observe standards that promote the availability, accessibility, acceptability and quality of the right to health, for example as identified in article 12 of the International Covenant on Economic, Social and Cultural Rights, general comment No. 14 on the right to the highest attainable standard of health adopted by the Committee on Economic, Social and Cultural Rights and the relevant standards established by the World Health Organization.
(b) Transnational corporations and other business enterprises shall observe standards which promote the availability of food in a quantity and of a quality sufficient to satisfy the dietary needs of individuals, free from adverse substances, acceptable within a given culture, accessible in ways that are sustainable and do

not interfere with the enjoyment of other human rights, and are otherwise in accordance with international standards such as article 11 of the International Covenant on Economic, Social and Cultural Rights and general comment No. 12 on the right to adequate food adopted by the Committee on Economic, Social and Cultural Rights. Transnational corporations and other business enterprises shall further observe standards which protect the right to water and are otherwise in accordance with general comment No. 15 adopted by the Committee on Economic, Social and Cultural Rights on the right to water.

(c) Transnational corporations and other business enterprises shall further observe standards which protect the right to adequate housing and are otherwise in accordance with article 11 of the International Covenant on Economic, Social and Cultural Rights and general comment No. 7 adopted by the Committee on Economic, Social and Cultural Rights on the right to adequate housing: forced evictions. Transnational corporations and other business enterprises shall not forcibly evict individuals, families and/or communities against their will from their homes and/or land which they occupy without having had recourse to, and access to, appropriate forms of legal or other protection pursuant to international human rights law.

(d) Transnational corporations and other business enterprises shall observe standards that protect other economic, social and cultural rights and are otherwise in accordance with the International Covenant on Economic, Social and Cultural Rights and the relevant general comments adopted by the Committee on Economic, Social and Cultural Rights, paying particular attention to the implementation of norms stated in paragraphs 16 (g) and (i).

(e) Transnational corporations and other business enterprises shall observe standards that protect civil and political rights and are otherwise in accordance with the International Covenant on Civil and Political Rights and the relevant general comments adopted by the Human Rights Committee.

F. Obligations with regard to consumer protection

13. Transnational corporations and other business enterprises shall act in accordance with fair business, marketing and advertising practices and shall take all necessary steps to ensure the safety and quality of the goods and services they provide, including observance of the precautionary principle. Nor shall they produce, distribute, market, or advertise harmful or potentially harmful products for use by consumers.

Commentary

(a) Transnational corporations and other business enterprises shall adhere to the relevant international standards of business practice regarding competition and anti-trust matters, such as The Set of Multilaterally Agreed Equitable Principles and Rules for the Control of Restrictive Business Practices of the United Nations Conference on Trade and Development. A transnational corporation or other business enterprise shall encourage the development and maintenance of fair, transparent and open competition by not entering into arrangements with competing businesses to directly or indirectly fix prices, divide territories, or create monopoly positions.

(b) Transnational corporations and other business enterprises shall observe relevant international standards for the protection of consumers, such as the United Nations Guidelines for Consumer Protection, and relevant international standards for the promotion of specific products, such as the International Code of Marketing of Breast-milk Substitutes adopted by the World Health Assembly and the Ethical Criteria for Medical Drug Promotion of the World Health Organization. Transnational corporations and other business enterprises shall ensure that all marketing claims are independently verifiable, satisfy reasonable and relevant legal levels of truthfulness, and are not misleading. Further, they shall not target children when advertising potentially harmful products.

(c) Transnational corporations and other business enterprises shall ensure that all goods and services they produce, distribute, or market are capable of use for the purposes claimed, safe for intended and reasonably foreseeable uses, do not endanger the life or health of consumers, and are regularly monitored and tested to ensure compliance with these standards, in the context of reasonable usage and custom. They shall adhere to relevant international standards so as to avoid variations in the quality of products that would have detrimental effects on consumers, especially in States lacking specific regulations on product quality. They shall further respect the precautionary principle when dealing, for example, with preliminary risk assessments that may indicate unacceptable effects on health or the environment. Further, they shall not use the lack of full scientific certainty as a reason to delay the introduction of cost-effective measures intended to prevent such effects.

(d) Any information provided by a transnational corporation or other business enterprise with regard to the purchase, use, content, maintenance, storage and disposal of its products and services shall be provided in a clear, comprehensible and prominently visible manner and in the language officially recognized by the country in which such products or services are provided. Transnational corporations and other business enterprises, when appropriate, shall also provide information regarding the appropriate recycling, reusability and disposal of its products and services.

(e) Consistent with paragraph 15 (e), where a product is potentially harmful to the consumer, transnational corporations and other business enterprises shall disclose all appropriate information on the contents and possible hazardous effects of the products they produce through proper labelling, informative and accurate advertising and other appropriate methods. In particular, they shall warn if death or serious injury is probable from a defect, use, or misuse. Transnational corporations and other business enterprises shall supply appropriate information of potentially harmful products to the relevant authorities. This information shall include the characteristics of products or services that may cause injury to the health and safety of consumers, workers, or others, and information regarding restrictions, warnings and other regulatory measures imposed by several countries as to these products or services on the grounds of health and safety protection.

G. Obligations with regard to environmental protection

14. Transnational corporations and other business enterprises shall carry out their activities in accordance with national laws, regulations, administrative practices and policies relating to the preservation of the environment of the countries in which they operate, as well as in accordance with relevant international agreements, principles, objectives, responsibilities and standards with regard to the environment as well as human rights, public health and safety, bioethics and the precautionary principle, and shall generally conduct their activities in a manner contributing to the wider goal of sustainable development.

Commentary

(a) Transnational corporations and other business enterprises shall respect the right to a clean and healthy environment in the light of the relationship between the environment and human rights; concerns for intergenerational equity; internationally recognized environmental standards, for example with regard to air pollution, water pollution, land use, biodiversity and hazardous wastes; and the wider goal of sustainable development, that is, development that meets the needs of the present without compromising the ability of future generations to meet their own needs.

(b) Transnational corporations and other business enterprises shall be responsible for the environmental and human health impact of all of their activities, including any products or services they introduce into commerce, such as packaging, transportation and by-products of the manufacturing process.

(c) Consistent with paragraph 16 (i), in decision-making processes and on a periodic basis (preferably annually or biannually), transnational corporations and other business enterprises shall assess the impact of their activities on the environment and human health including impacts from siting decisions, natural resource extraction activities, the production and sale of products or services, and the generation, storage, transport and disposal of hazardous and toxic substances. Transnational corporations and other business enterprises shall ensure that the burden of negative environmental consequences shall not fall on vulnerable racial, ethnic and socio-economic groups.

(d) Assessments shall, inter alia, address particularly the impact of proposed activities on certain groups, such as children, older persons, indigenous peoples and communities (particularly in regard to their land and natural resources), and/or women. Transnational corporations and other business enterprises shall distribute such reports in a timely manner and in a manner that is accessible to the United Nations Environmental Programme, the ILO, other interested international bodies, the national Government hosting each company, the national Government where the business maintains its principal office and other affected groups. The reports shall be accessible to the general public.

(e) Transnational corporations and other business enterprises shall respect the prevention principle, for example by preventing and/or mitigating deleterious impacts identified in any assessment. They shall also respect the precautionary principle when dealing, for example, with preliminary risk assessments that may indicate unacceptable effects on health or the environment. Further, they shall not use the lack of full scientific certainty as a reason to delay the introduction of cost-effective measures intended to prevent such effects.

(f) Upon the expiration of the useful life of their products or services, transnational corporations and other business enterprises shall ensure effective means of collecting or arranging for the collection of the remains of the product or services for recycling, reuse and/or environmentally responsible disposal.

(g) Transnational corporations and other business enterprises shall take appropriate measures in their activities to reduce the risk of accidents and damage to the environment by adopting best management practices and technologies. In particular, they shall use best management practices and appropriate technologies and enable their component entities to meet these environmental objectives through the sharing of technology, knowledge and assistance, as well as through environmental management systems, sustainability reporting, and reporting of anticipated or actual releases of hazardous and toxic substances. In addition, they shall educate and train workers to ensure their compliance with these objectives.

H. General provisions of implementation

15. As an initial step towards implementing these Norms, each transnational corporation or other business enterprise shall adopt, disseminate and implement internal rules of operation in compliance with the Norms. Further, they shall periodically report on and take other measures fully to implement the Norms and to provide at least for the prompt implementation of the protections set forth in the Norms. Each transnational corporation or other business enterprise shall apply and incorporate these Norms in their contracts or other arrangements and dealings with contractors, subcontractors, suppliers, licensees, distributors, or natural or other legal persons that enter into any agreement with the transnational corporation or business enterprise in order to ensure respect for and implementation of the Norms.

Commentary

(a) Each transnational corporation or other business enterprise shall disseminate its internal rules of operation or similar measures, as well as implementation procedures, and make them available to all relevant stakeholders. The internal rules of operation or similar measures shall be communicated in oral and written form in the language of workers, trade unions, contractors, subcontractors, suppliers, licensees, distributors, natural or other legal persons that enter into contracts with the transnational corporation or other business enterprise, customers and other stakeholders in the transnational corporation or other business enterprise.

(b) Once internal rules of operation or similar measures have been adopted and disseminated, transnational corporations and other business enterprises shall – to the extent of their resources and capabilities – provide effective training for their managers as well as workers and their representatives in practices relevant to the Norms.

(c) Transnational corporations and other business enterprises shall ensure that they only do business with (including purchasing from and selling to) contractors, subcontractors, suppliers, licensees, distributors, and natural or other legal persons that follow these or substantially similar Norms. Transnational corporations and other business enterprises using or considering entering into business relationships with contractors, subcontractors, suppliers, licensees, distributors, or natural or other legal persons that do not comply with the Norms shall initially work with them to reform or decrease violations, but if they will not change, the enterprise shall cease doing business with them.

(d) Transnational corporations and other business enterprises shall enhance the transparency of their activities by disclosing timely, relevant, regular and reliable information regarding their activities, structure, financial situation and performance. They shall also make known the location of their offices, subsidiaries and factories, so as to facilitate measures to ensure that the enterprises, products and services are being produced under conditions that respect these Norms.

(e) Transnational corporations and other business enterprises shall inform in a timely manner everyone who may be affected by conditions caused by the enterprises that might endanger health, safety, or the environment.

(f) Each transnational corporation or other business shall endeavour to improve continually its further implementation of these Norms.

16. Transnational corporations and other business enterprises shall be subject to periodic monitoring and verification by United Nations, other international and national mechanisms already in existence or yet to be created, regarding application of the Norms. This monitoring shall be transparent and independent and take into account input from stakeholders (including nongovernmental organizations) and as a result of complaints of violations of these Norms. Further, transnational corporations and other business enterprises shall conduct periodic evaluations concerning the impact of their own activities on human rights under these Norms.

Commentary

(a) These Norms shall be monitored and implemented through amplification and interpretation of intergovernmental, regional, national and local standards with regard to the conduct of transnational corporations and other business enterprises.

(b) United Nations human rights treaty bodies should monitor implementation of these Norms through the creation of additional reporting requirements for States and the adoption of general comments and recommendations interpreting treaty obligations. The United Nations and its specialized agencies should also monitor implementation by using the Norms as the basis for procurement determinations concerning products and services to be purchased and with which transnational corporations and other business enterprises develop partnerships in the field. Country rapporteurs and thematic procedures of the United Nations Commission on Human Rights should monitor implementation by using the Norms and other relevant international standards for raising concerns about actions by transnational corporations and other business enterprises within their respective mandates. The Commission on Human Rights should consider establishing a group of experts, a special rapporteur, or working group of the Commission to receive information and take effective action when enterprises fail to comply with the Norms. The Sub-Commission on the Promotion and Protection of Human Rights and its relevant working group should also monitor compliance with the Norms and developing best practices by receiving information from non governmental organizations, unions, individuals and others, and then by allowing transnational corporations or other business enterprises an opportunity to respond. Further, the Sub-Commission, its working group and other United Nations bodies are invited to develop additional techniques for implementing and monitoring these Norms and other effective mechanisms and to ensure access is given to NGOs, unions, individuals and others.

(c) Trade unions are encouraged to use the Norms as a basis for negotiating agreements with transnational corporations and other business enterprises and monitoring compliance of these entities. NGOs are also encouraged to use the Norms as the basis for their expectations of the conduct of the transnational corporation or other business enterprise and monitoring compliance. Further, monitoring could take place by using the Norms as the basis for benchmarks of ethical investment initiatives and for other benchmarks of compliance. The Norms shall also be monitored through industry groups.

(d) Transnational corporations and other business enterprises shall ensure that the monitoring process is transparent, for example by making available to relevant stakeholders the workplaces observed, remediation efforts undertaken and other results of monitoring. They shall further ensure that any monitoring seeks to obtain and incorporate input from relevant stakeholders. Further, they shall ensure such monitoring by their contractors, subcontractors, suppliers, licensees, distributors, and any other natural or legal persons with whom they have entered into any agreement, to the extent possible.

(e) Transnational corporations and other business enterprises shall provide legitimate and confidential avenues through which workers can file complaints with regard to violations of these Norms. To the extent possible, they shall make known to the complainant any actions taken as a result of the investigation. Further, they shall not discipline or take other action against workers or others who submit complaints or who assert that any company has failed to comply with these Norms.

(f) Transnational corporations and other business enterprises receiving claims of violations of these Norms shall make a record of each claim and obtain an independent investigation of the claim or call upon other proper authorities. They shall actively monitor the status of investigations, press for their full resolution and take action to prevent recurrences.

(g) Each transnational corporation or other business enterprise shall engage in an annual or other periodic assessment of its compliance with the Norms, taking into account comments from and encourage the participation of indigenous peoples and communities to determine how best to respect their rights. The results of the assessment shall be made available to stakeholders to the same extent as the annual report of the transnational corporation or other business enterprise.

(h) Assessments revealing inadequate compliance with the Norms shall also include plans of action or methods of reparation and redress that the transnational corporation or other business enterprise will pursue in order to fulfil the Norms. See also paragraph 18.

(i) Before a transnational corporation or other business enterprise pursues a major initiative or project, it shall, to the extent of its resources and capabilities, study the human rights impact of that project in the light of these Norms. The impact statement shall include a description of the action, its need, anticipated benefits, an analysis of any human rights impact related to the action, an analysis of reasonable alternatives to the action, and identification of ways to reduce any negative human rights consequences. A transnational corporation or other business enterprise shall make available the results of that study to relevant stakeholders and shall consider any reactions from stakeholders.

17. States should establish and reinforce the necessary legal and administrative framework for ensuring that the Norms and other relevant national and international laws are implemented by transnational corporations and other business enterprises.

Commentary

(a) Governments should implement and monitor the use of the Norms, for example, by making them widely available and using them as a model for legislation or administrative provisions with regard to the activities of each enterprise doing business in their country, including through the use of labour inspections, ombudspersons, national human rights commissions, or other national human rights mechanisms.

18. Transnational corporations and other business enterprises shall provide prompt, effective and adequate reparation to those persons, entities and communities that have been adversely affected by failures to comply with these Norms through, inter alia, reparations, restitution, compensation and rehabilitation for any damage done or property taken. In connection with determining damages, in regard to criminal

sanctions, and in all other respects, these Norms shall be applied by national courts and/or international tribunals, pursuant to national and international law.

19. Nothing in these Norms shall be construed as diminishing, restricting, or adversely affecting the human rights obligations of States under national and international law, nor shall they be construed as diminishing, restricting, or adversely affecting more protective human rights norms, nor shall they be construed as diminishing, restricting, or adversely affecting other obligations or responsibilities of transnational corporations and other business enterprises in fields other than human rights.

Commentary

(a) This savings clause is intended to ensure that transnational corporations and other business enterprises will pursue the course of conduct that is the most protective of human rights – whether found in these Norms or in other relevant sources. If more protective standards are recognized or emerge in international or State law or in industry or business practices, those more protective standards shall be pursued. This savings clause is styled after similar savings clauses found in such instruments as the Convention on the Rights of the Child (art. 41). This provision and similar references in the Norms to national and international law are also based upon the Vienna Convention on the Law of Treaties (art. 27), in that a State may not invoke the provisions of its internal law as justification for its failure to comply with a treaty, the Norms, or other international law norms.

(b) Transnational corporations and other business enterprises are encouraged to express their own commitment to respecting, ensuring respect for, preventing abuses of, and promoting internationally recognized human rights by adopting their own internal human rights rules of operation which are even more conducive to the promotion and protection of human rights than those contained in these Norms.

I. Definitions

20. The term 'transnational corporation' refers to an economic entity operating in more than one country or a cluster of economic entities operating in two or more countries – whatever their legal form, whether in their home country or country of activity, and whether taken individually or collectively.

21. The phrase 'other business enterprise' includes any business entity, regardless of the international or domestic nature of its activities, including a transnational corporation,

contractor, subcontractor, supplier, licensee or distributor; the corporate, partnership, or other legal form used to establish the business entity; and the nature of the ownership of the entity. These Norms shall be presumed to apply, as a matter of practice, if the business enterprise has any relation with a transnational corporation, the impact of its activities is not entirely local, or the activities involve violations of the right to security as indicated in paragraphs 3 and 4.

22. The term 'stakeholder' includes stockholders, other owners, workers and their representatives, as well as any other individual or group that is affected by the activities of transnational corporations or other business enterprises. The term 'stakeholder' shall be interpreted functionally in the light of the objectives of these Norms and include indirect stakeholders when their interests are or will be substantially affected by the activities of the transnational corporation or business enterprise. In addition to parties directly affected by the activities of business enterprises, stakeholders can include parties which are indirectly affected by the activities of transnational corporations and other business enterprises such as consumer groups, customers, Governments, neighbouring communities, indigenous peoples and communities, nongovernmental organizations, public and private lending institutions, suppliers, trade associations and others.

23. The phrases 'human rights' and 'international human rights' include civil, cultural, economic, political and social rights, as set forth in the International Bill of Human Rights and other human rights treaties, as well as the right to development and rights recognized by international humanitarian law, international refugee law, international labour law, and other relevant instruments adopted within the United Nations system.

Index